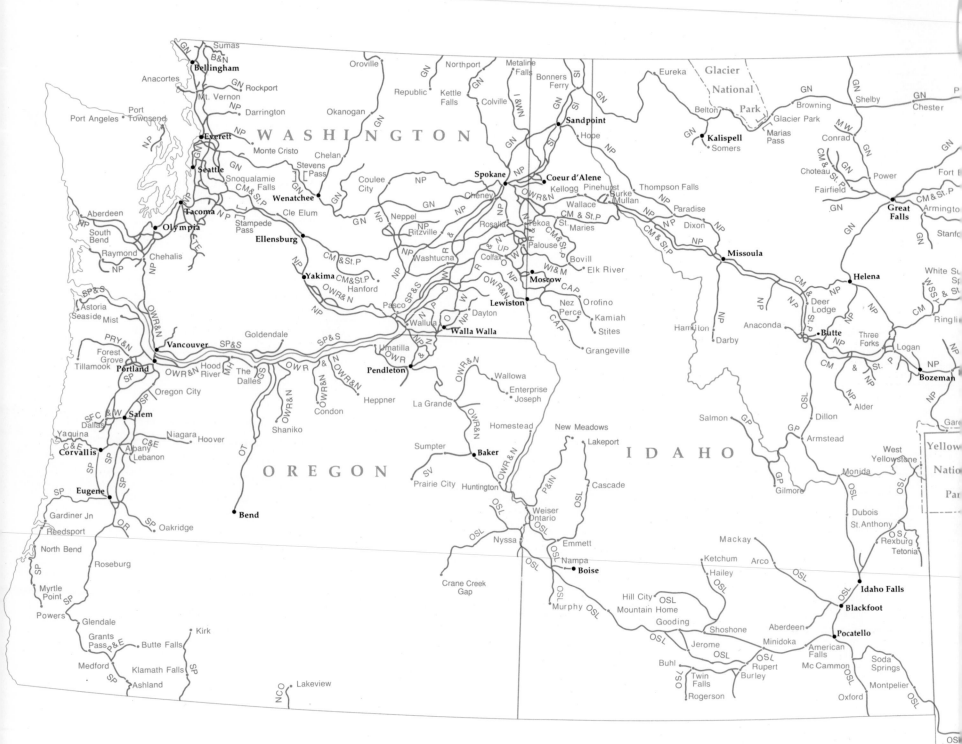

# Railroad Signatures
## Across the Pacific Northwest: ca. 1916
### (Exclusive of Logging and Electric Interurban Railroads)

| | |
|---|---|
| **Bellingham and Northern** | B&N |
| **Camas Prairie** | CAP |
| **Chicago and North Western** | C&NW |
| **Chicago, Burlington and Quincy** | CB&Q |
| **Chicago, Milwaukee and St. Paul** | CM&St.P |
| **Colorado, Wyoming and Eastern** | CW&E |
| **Corvallis and Eastern** | C&E |
| **Gilmore and Pittsburgh** | GP |
| **Great Northern** | GN |
| **Great Southern** | GS |
| **Idaho and Washington Northern** | I & WN |
| **Mount Hood** | MH |
| **Nevada-California-Oregon** | NCO |
| **Northern Pacific** | NP |
| **Oregon Short Line** | OSL |
| **Oregon Trunk** | OT |
| **Oregon-Washington Railroad and Navigation Company** | OWR & N |
| **Pacific and Eastern** | P&E |
| **Pacific and Idaho Northern** | P&IN |
| **Pacific Railway and Navigation Company** | PRY&N |
| **Salem, Falls City and Western** | SFC&W |
| **Saratoga and Encampment** | SE |
| **Southern Pacific** | SP |
| **Spokane International** | SI |
| **Spokane, Portland and Seattle** | SP&S |
| **Sumpter Valley** | SV |
| **Tacoma Eastern** | TE |
| **Union Pacific** | UP |
| **Washington, Idaho and Montana** | WI&M |
| **White Sulphur Springs and Yellowstone Park** | WSSY |

▲
**N**

0 ——————————— 100 miles

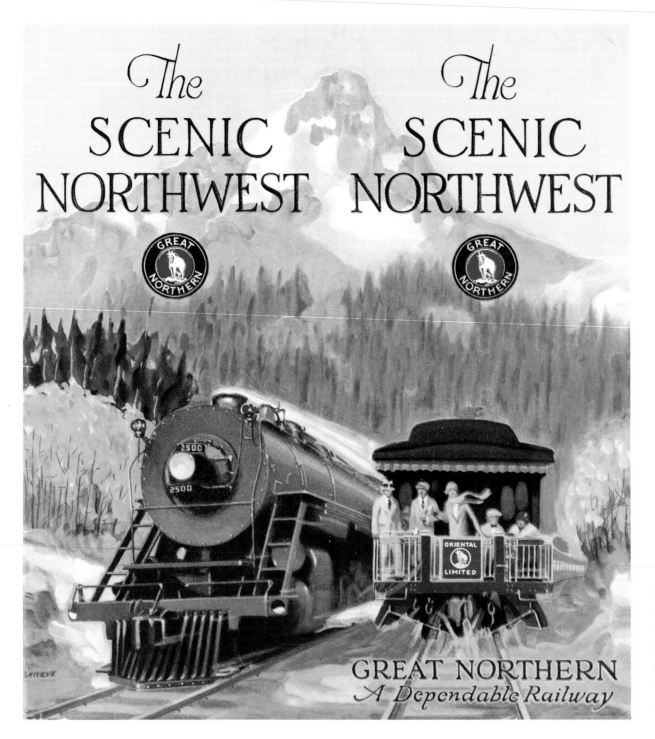

*A* *vivid illustration typical of railroad art during the 1920s depicts the Great Northern corridor through the Cascade Range. Mount Index is prominent in the background. Courtesy Richard Piper.*

To four friends
who have influenced
my interest in
transportation history:

Richard L. Day
William S. Greever
Alfred Runte
W. Thomas White

*M*ost railroad publications
emphasized national parks, but
this brochure promotes national
forest vacations. Note the bear
motif that was popular in tourist
promotions of the 1920s and 1930s.
Minnesota Historical Society.

This popular Milwaukee Road brochure shows a settler plowing gold coins from the fertile Montana soil. University of Montana.

The colorful cover of a Southern Pacific brochure advertised tourism at Crater Lake National Park in 1916. California State Railroad Museum.

# Contents

"One of America's Fine Trains"

NORTHERN PACIFIC
YELLOWSTONE PARK LINE

The North Coast Limited
Silver Anniversary Year

*The Northern Pacific issued an elaborate brochure to celebrate the silver anniversary of its North Coast Limited in the mid-1920s. Minnesota Historical Society.*

*In crowded St. Louis I had never felt so close to America as I did now on this pathless plain. I knew that as I touched the steel linking one rail to another, I was linking myself to the new country and building my own solid road to a new life.*
—*Stoyan Christowe,* My American Pilgrimage *(1947)*

# Preface

MANY BOOKS ABOUT RAILROADS concentrate on locomotives. What follows is not a book about railroad engines but about railroads *as engines* of regional development and social change. I approach the subject from the perspective of a student of the Pacific Northwest rather than that of a specialist in railroad or business history. Train buffs will look in vain for extended discussions of equipment and technology, yet I do hope that *Railroad Signatures across the Pacific Northwest* captures for all readers the human drama of a complex subject.

My approach probably reflects the way I was introduced to railroad history some forty summers ago in Wilmington, North Carolina. After dinner at my grandparents' home we often adjourned to the front porch in search of ways to make a muggy evening tolerable. Mostly we spent our time talking and swinging and waiting for a breeze, or perhaps for one of the thunderstorms that brought to the region of the lower Cape Fear River spectacular displays of lightning, torrential rains, and a measure of relief from the heat. My grandfather was a source of knowledge about many things that interested small boys. Together with his father and brother he had once worked for the Atlantic Coast Line Railroad. Years before I was born, my grand-

father had been a member of a "wrecking crew" whose job it was to reopen the tracks following a derailment. When the great shopmen's strike of 1922 prematurely ended his railroading career, he became a policeman, detective, and finally chief of police in Wilmington. I remember Granddaddy Casteen as a gifted checkers player and storyteller; I could never beat him at either one.

Wilmington in the 1950s was still a railroad town, home of the Atlantic Coast Line until the company did an unthinkable thing and moved its headquarters to Jacksonville, Florida, in 1961. Neighbors on both sides of my grandparents had worked for the Coast Line, and much of our evening's conversation naturally turned to railroading or detective work. If there was some sort of connection between my grandfather's elaborate, often humorous accounts of police work and my career as historian, I could never prove it, although I am still partial to history as a well-crafted piece of detection.

My early interest in railroads lingered and grew. It could not have been otherwise. The backyard of my parents' home in Greenfield, Indiana, abutted the main line of the Pennsylvania Railroad between New York City and St. Louis. Every morning a parade of streamlined passenger trains sped west to St. Louis, and every afternoon the parade headed in the opposite direction. Never could I have imagined then that those tracks would be ripped up in the 1980s, leaving only a weed-covered embankment to remind me that the all-Pullman Spirit of St. Louis once sped the Who's Who of America past my backyard. Over breakfast in the dining car such folk may have discussed the war in Korea, debated whether President Truman was right to fire General MacArthur, and speculated on Henry J. Kaiser's latest automobile venture. Or, when conversation flagged, they may have casually wondered what kind of people lived in the cities and towns bisected by Pennsylvania Railroad tracks across central Indiana.

Never once did it occur to me to ponder whether we lived on the right or wrong side of the tracks. I only felt fortunate to have a front-row seat from which to view all the drama of what John Stilgoe would later call the Metropolitan Corridor.[1] From that vantage point I witnessed the railroad industry's historic transition from steam to diesel motive power and the slow decline of its passenger service.

In October 1957 I made a trip to Block's department store in Indianapolis and acquired book number one for my personal library: Lucius Beebe and Charles Clegg's *Age of Steam*.[2] Fifteen dollars for a single book seemed like a staggering sum to a twelve year old. During the intervening years I have continued to add transportation books to my library—often wishing that they still sold for as little as fifteen dollars—as well as an eclectic and seemingly unending stream of notes to my file cabinets. Here I must pause to emphasize the encompassing term *transportation* as distinct from *railroad*. I have always enjoyed traveling by passenger train, but a flight from Miami to Rio de Janeiro in 1952 to visit my paternal grandparents introduced me to the romance of winging over Amazon jungles on Aerovias Brasil's DC-4 at a time when air travel was still a luxury and an adventure. Because no one then was worried about air piracy, pilots still invited children into the cockpit to help "fly" the plane.

This delightful experience, like others I have mentioned, invariably influenced my thinking.

Quite simply, *Railroad Signatures across the Pacific Northwest* seeks to capture the impact of railroads on everyday life in one region of the United States within the context of competing modes of transportation. At one time I thought I wanted to write a social history of the American passenger train during the early automobile age, but with some encouragement from Julidta Tarver of the University of Washington Press, my research finally yielded a more encompassing study that combined my love of Pacific Northwest history with that of railroads and other forms of transportation. In later chapters I do devote more attention to passenger than to freight service, but that is because after 1920 most citizens evaluated the impact of railroads on their lives mainly in terms of passenger trains.

*Railroad Signatures* is not meant to be a definitive history of Pacific Northwest transportation but rather a work of interpretation and synthesis. It could not have been anything else and remained readable. According to one survey more than five hundred railroad companies were incorporated in Washington alone between 1860 and 1948.[3] I would not propose to provide detailed histories for even a fraction of these carriers; I do, however, take full responsibility for my interpretations and for any errors or omissions that may appear in this book.

The curiosity first aroused in that porch swing in North Carolina has taken me to many places and caused me to pile up a mountain of intellectual debts that now need to be acknowledged. Thanks go first to students in my history classes. For a variety of reasons I am also indebted to Judith Austin, Elizabeth Jacox, and Merle Wells of the Idaho State Historical Society; Lawrence Dodd, Marilyn Sparks, and G. Thomas Edwards of Whitman College; James P. Ronda of the University of Tulsa; Lory Morrow, Rebecca Kohl, and Dave Walter of the Montana Historical Society; Dale L.

# Railroad Signatures across the Pacific Northwest

**CARLOS A. SCHWANTES**

University of Washington Press   *Seattle & London*

*Railroad Signatures across the Pacific Northwest* is published with the assistance of a generous grant from Burlington Northern.

Copyright © 1993 by the University of Washington Press
Second printing (pbk.), 1996
Designed by Audrey Meyer
Endpaper maps by Allan Jokisaari
Printed in Hong Kong by C & C Offset Printing Co., Ltd.

Library of Congress Cataloging-in-Publication Data
Schwantes, Carlos A., 1945–
Railroad signatures across the Pacific Northwest /
Carlos A. Schwantes
    p.  cm.
Includes bibliographical references and index.
ISBN 0–295–97535–0 (alk. paper)
1. Railroads—Pacific, Northwest.  I. Title
TF23.7.S39    1993          93–6505
385'.09795—dc20        CIP

The paper used in this publication meets the minimum requirements of American National Standard for Information Sciences—Permanence of Paper for Printed Library Materials, ANSI Z39.48–1984. ∞

*This Union Pacific pamphlet urging tourists to explore unknown corners of Idaho is typical of the attractive travel brochures of the 1920s and 1930s. Union Pacific Museum.*

Johnson of the University of Montana; Susan Seyl and Elizabeth Winroth of the Oregon Historical Society; Earl Pomeroy, Fraser J. Cocks III, and James D. Fox of the University of Oregon; William G. Robbins and Thomas C. McClintock of Oregon State University; Robert E. Burke and Richard Engeman of the University of Washington; David Nicandri and Edward Nolan of the Washington State Historical Society; W. Thomas White of the James Jerome Hill Reference Library; and Terry Abraham of the University of Idaho.

I further appreciate the help of David Farmer and Dawn Letson of the DeGolyer Library of Southern Methodist University; Kathey Swan of the Denver Public Library; Ruth Ellen Bauer, Dallas R. Lindgren, and Ruby Shields of the Minnesota Historical Society; Mark J. Cedeck of the St. Louis Mercantile Library Association; Paul Woehrmann, Thomas Altmann, Sandy Broder, and Jim Scribbins of the Milwaukee Public Library; Ellen Schwartz and Blaine P. Lamb of the California State Railroad Museum; Christine Droll of the Oakland Museum's Art Department; Don Snoddy of the Union Pacific Museum; Don Hofsommer of St. Cloud State University; Jonathan Dembo of the Cincinnati Historical Society; Terrence M. Cole of the University of Alaska, Fairbanks; Richard Orsi of California State University, Hayward; Leonard Arrington of Salt Lake City; and two aviation professionals, Ray Arnold and Christian Zimmermann, met through the Depot Institute of Cascade, Idaho.

Working with yet another book with my many friends at the University of Washington Press has been a genuine pleasure. In particular, I want to thank Don Ellegood, director; Naomi Pascal, editor-in-chief; Julidta Tarver, managing editor, who patiently oversaw this project from beginning to end; and Audrey Meyer, art director, who did a splendid job of combining prose and illustrations into a truly beautiful book. In addition, Carol Zabilski, associate editor of the University of Wash-

ington's *Pacific Northwest Quarterly*, deserves praise for sculpting my often unruly prose into final form.

Richard Maxwell Brown of the University of Oregon history department made it possible for me to spend the summer of 1981 in Eugene teaching a class and going through the university's large collection of railroad materials. A research grant from the Idaho Humanities Council initiated the writing of *Railroad Signatures* and enabled me to share early findings with audiences in Cascade, Boise, and Pocatello. The Idaho State Board of Education generously provided funds for a reduced teaching load during the spring semester of 1991 and for research travel. Once again the University of Idaho's John Calhoun Smith Memorial Fund provided the money necessary to finish the project.

As the book was ready to go to the printer, I was surprised and gratified when Burlington Northern provided a generous grant to the University of Washington Press to help with the publication of *Railroad Signatures across the Pacific Northwest*. Their interest in the region's variegated railroad heritage, not just in the history of Burlington Northern and its predecessor companies, is both commendable and magnanimous.

Michael Walsh, former chairman of the Union Pacific Railroad, gave generously of his time during a visit to the University of Idaho and later arranged for me to visit the Harriman Dispatching Center in Omaha. Over the years I have also developed an enormous debt of gratitude to numerous unsung railroaders, from ticket agents and telegraphers to car inspectors and locomotive engineers, who shared with me stories from their daily work lives. They helped to strengthen my determination to keep focused on the social history of railroading.

I thank the University of Idaho administration for continuing to provide me a congenial atmosphere in which to teach and write. Without support from Kent Hackmann, chair of the history department; Doyle E. Anderegg, associate dean of the College of Letters and Science; Kurt Olsson, dean of the College of Letters and Science; Thomas O. Bell, provost; and Elisabeth Zinser, president, this book would not have been possible. *Railroad Signatures across the Pacific Northwest* is one of four book projects sponsored by the University of Idaho's Institute for Pacific Northwest Studies.

Allan Jokisaari of the University of Idaho's Cart-O-Graphics Lab prepared the two large maps that appear as endpapers, and Nancy Dafoe of the History Department helped me in an incredible variety of ways. Finally, I want to thank my colleagues Lawrence Merk and James Toomey for inviting me to test my ideas in their "World of Corporate Business" class.

I am especially indebted to four scholars who have in a variety of ways encouraged my study of transportation history. Richard L. Day is a retired professor of geography at the University of Idaho; W. Thomas White, curator at the James Jerome Hill Reference Library, helped make it possible for me to travel to St. Paul for research in the papers of James J. Hill and his son Louis Hill; Alfred Runte broadened my horizons by helping me see the relationship between railroads and the national parks. My predecessor in the University of Idaho history department, William S. Greever, has been an unfailing source of professional support. He kindly shared his large private library of railroadiana with me. It is to these four friends that *Railroad Signatures across the Pacific Northwest* is dedicated.

*The Milwaukee Road often paused to salute its technological prowess. This brochure featuring a bipolar electric locomotive appeared in 1936. Only one of the massive engines survived: it is preserved in the National Museum of Transport near St. Louis. Denver Public Library, Western History Department.*

# Railroad Signatures across the Pacific Northwest

*The pioneer railroads had to bring the people who furnished the traffic; had to open up the state's first coal mines; set the pace in lumber operations, point out the way to apply irrigation principles, donate manufacturing sites to encourage the building of coast seaports, build and maintain the first line of grain warehouses, exploit the possibilities of foreign trade and give financial encouragement to the first struggling shippers. Then, in order that nothing in the way of paternalism might be overlooked, the earlier railroads took complete charge of the state's legislative efforts and even indicated where the streets in the larger cities should run so as not to interfere with railroad terminals.*
—M. M. Mattison, "Rail Transportation in Washington,"
Pacific Monthly *(April 1908)*

*See all the Northern Pacific mountains you can on your journey, for they are unsurpassed anywhere in the world! Twenty-eight ranges are visible from your train window—the same vast mountains that Lewis and Clark overcame, rich now in the lore of pioneer days in the Northwest, wearing the mantle of glamor that gold prospector, railroad builder, and "dude" rancher have put upon their mighty shoulders!*
—Northern Pacific: 2000 *Miles of Scenic Beauty ([1931])*

*This is what the railroad has done. It has lengthened life and shortened space.*
*Space has been cut down by steam and our lives have been relatively lengthened.*
—*James J. Hill in* Pacific Monthly *(January 1909)*

# Introduction: Railroad Time and Space in the New Northwest

*This classic photograph of the Northern Pacific's luxurious North Coast Limited dates from the early twentieth century: the train was hurrying west from Portland to the ferry connection at Goble, where it would cross the Columbia River and continue north to Tacoma and Seattle. University of Oregon, Angelus 1761.*

ANYONE WHO HAS TRAVELED east along the Columbia River from Portland will recall a mountain-and-water landscape so awe-inspiring that Congress in 1986 designated it the Columbia River Gorge Scenic Area. Rand McNally's *Road Atlas* for 1991 named the portion of Interstate 84 through the gorge one of America's eight Top Scenic Routes. No other stretch of superhighway was included in this most select list. Occasional low clouds and mist that shroud distant promontories only heighten the gorge's appeal for romantics inclined to use words like *brooding* and *mysterious* to describe the landscape.

The ninety-mile-long stretch of river is equally rich in history: rocky palisades that drop abruptly four hundred feet or more to the water's edge presented one final obstacle to pioneers who first headed their covered wagons west along the Oregon Trail in the 1840s. With the long-sought promised land of the Willamette Valley lying just beyond the Cascade Range, would-be settlers who had already endured nearly two thousand miles of challenges were forced to confront the treacherous Columbia. Waters that drained from an area larger than France squeezed between the confining walls of the gorge, and the resulting maelstrom forced immigrants either to risk their lives in makeshift rafts or to

detour south of Mount Hood along a primitive toll road. Even experienced rivermen hired by early-day fur companies sometimes miscalculated and drowned in the Columbia's massive falls, chutes, and whirlpools. The challenge was no less great for railroad builders in the early 1880s, who used ropes to lower Chinese laborers down towering rock walls to drill and blast a narrow ledge for tracks of the Oregon Railway & Navigation Company.

The Columbia Gorge probably witnessed more key events in the region's transportation history than any comparable site. Not many of the "first" or "most significant" developments are today obvious from Interstate 84; some are not even commemorated with roadside markers. Yet it was in the Columbia Gorge that workmen hammered into place the wooden tracks of a crude portage line in 1851. That first railway ran a short distance along the Washington bank of the river and was designed to carry passengers and freight around a dangerous stretch of white water known as the Cascades. Only gradually did a network of tracks emerge that was independent of portage lines and the large fleet of steamboats that once plied the Columbia and other major waterways.

Railroad tracks, whether fashioned from wood, iron, or steel, remained an inconspicuous addition

*T*rains of the Spokane, Portland & Seattle Railway followed the north bank through the Columbia Gorge. The photographer took this picture near Cascades, Washington, where a portage railroad once linked steamboats on two separate segments of the river. Tracks of the rival Oregon Railroad & Navigation Company, a Union Pacific subsidiary, extend along the opposite bank. Oregon Historical Society, 67347, File 891-C-1.

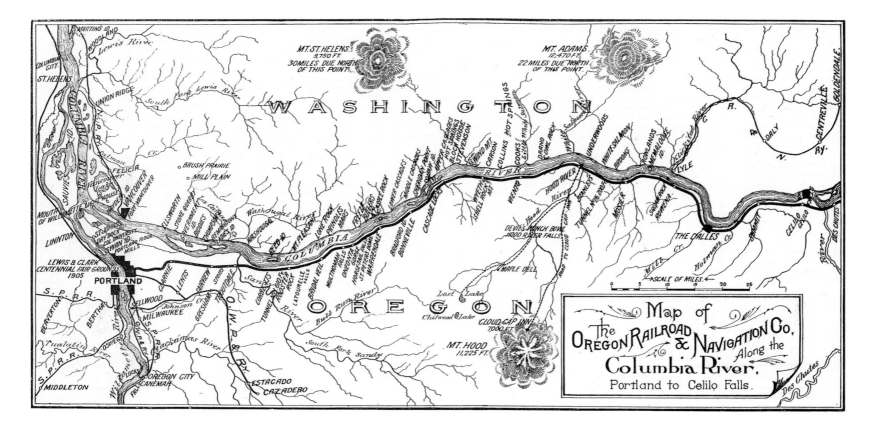

The following labels appear on the map:

MT. ST. HELENS. 9,750 FT. 30 MILES DUE NORTH OF THIS POINT.

MT. ADAMS. 12,470 FT. 22 MILES DUE NORTH OF THIS POINT.

W A S H I N G T O N

O R E G O N

MT. HOOD 11,225 FT.

CLOUD CAP INN. 7000 FT.

PORTLAND

THE DALLES

Map of The Oregon Railroad & Navigation Co, Along the Columbia River, Portland to Celilo Falls.

*A turn-of-the-century map shows the route of the Oregon Railroad & Navigation Company through the Columbia River Gorge. The company succeeded the venerable Oregon Railway & Navigation Company in the late 1890s. Oregon Historical Society, 086217.*

to the regional landscape until the late 1870s. Not until a frenzy of tracklaying gripped the region between 1880 and 1893 did railroads write clearly legible signatures across the Pacific Northwest. When a nationwide depression temporarily halted construction in mid-1893 and ended the first railway age, an 8,000-mile network of tracks stretched across Oregon, Washington, Idaho, and Montana. The Pacific Northwest's second railway age lasted from the return of prosperity in 1897 until America entered World War I in early 1917. During those two decades workmen spiked another 8,000 miles of new line into place and upgraded numerous older sections. The region's first railway age emphasized construction of new lines and spurred the rise of whole new cities and industries. The second emphasized improved plants and equipment and was a time of growing, and ultimately suffocating, public

regulation of railroads. During both ages, railroads publicized the Pacific Northwest as a promising field for investment, settlement, and tourism, and in that way they functioned as engines of empire.

The pattern of railroad signatures was never random. Where practicable, builders followed the banks of rivers and lakes. The region's five historic trunk lines were all synonymous with waterways: the Southern Pacific with the Willamette River; the Northern Pacific with the Yellowstone, Clark Fork, and Yakima rivers; the Union Pacific with the Umatilla and Columbia rivers and the vast Snake River plain of southern Idaho; the Great Northern with the Flathead, Kootenai, Wenatchee, and Snohomish rivers and with Puget Sound; and the Chicago, Milwaukee, St. Paul & Pacific with the Musselshell, St. Joe, and Yakima rivers. The main body of water to figure in the strategies of all transcontinental railroad builders was the Pacific Ocean. Its name appeared in the corporate titles of all but one northern trunk line as well as in that of the Canadian Pacific Railway, which extended from Montreal to Vancouver.

To railroad builders, some rivers of the Pacific Northwest appeared totally uncooperative: waters of the Salmon or River of No Return rushed through the mountains of central Idaho with such force that they turned back the explorers Lewis and Clark in the early 1800s as well as every railroad builder who later contemplated a line through the river's narrow confines. The Snake did likewise as it churned through Hells Canyon, and that formidable barrier was a primary reason why no railroad line ever ran the length of the Gem State. Waterways played a key role in track location, but more than topography alone determined the shape of railroad signatures. They reflected the aspirations of metropolitan centers like Portland, Seattle, and Spokane; they were sensitive to the location of valuable mineral deposits, such as copper in Butte, Montana, silver in the Coeur d'Alene Valley of northern Idaho, and coal in the Cascade foothills east of Seattle and Tacoma; and they defined areas of large-scale agricultural production.

Finally, the signatures reflected the egos of a handful of powerful railroad builders. Historians in recent years have become reluctant to attribute too much influence to a few "great men," yet it was undeniable that three men above all others—Henry Villard, James J. Hill, and Edward H. Harriman— shaped the modern Pacific Northwest by the way they wrote their corporate signatures in steel. The fact that Burlington Northern freight trains thunder through the Columbia Gorge along the north bank of the river while Union Pacific freights follow the south bank reveals as much about individual egos as about geography and geology. In the early twentieth century, Hill supported construction of an expensive new railroad between Portland and Spokane in an

effort to wrest a portion of Oregon's growing commerce from his arch-rival, Harriman, who dominated the state's transportation at that time by controlling both the Union Pacific and Southern Pacific systems. When Harriman used his ownership of the little-used and largely forgotten portage line at the Cascades to block Hill, lawyers for the rail titans waged a vigorous battle that ended in Hill's favor.

Railroad construction slowed noticeably by the eve of World War I. With the onset of a new age of competition, highway engineers used tax money from an increasingly automobile-minded public to write bold new signatures in concrete and asphalt. Once again the Columbia River Gorge was the setting for momentous developments: the first section of the Columbia River Highway opened in 1915, and seven years later the engineering marvel connected Portland and The Dalles. Construction of the present superhighway through the gorge in the 1960s destroyed portions of the early road. Significant sections nonetheless remain intact and usable by any motorist willing to slow down and seek out the Historic Columbia River Highway that parallels parts of Interstate 84 and provides entrance to a series of moss-and-fern grottos and waterfalls that delight hikers and landscape photographers. Along one twelve-mile stretch of the old route, eleven waterfalls are either visible or readily accessible to motorists. In some places the sound of rushing water competes with that of Union Pacific freights rumbling along nearby tracks.

## Time: Starvation Creek and Days of Two Noons

CONSIDER THE LITTLE STREAM that flows unnoticed beneath Interstate 84 and the Union Pacific tracks about ten miles east of the town of Cascade Locks.

**M**ultnomah Falls is a veil of water and mist that drops 620 feet, more than three times the height of Niagara Falls. For years Union Pacific passenger trains paused or slowed at the base of the scenic wonder to afford travelers a better look. Union Pacific Museum, *700036*.

The name Starvation Creek gives only a hint of the drama that took place there in the winter of 1884, an event that demonstrated how railroads redefined something so basic as the meaning of time in a pioneer society. In their passenger service, railroads brought to everyday life in the Pacific Northwest a degree of discipline previously unknown. Where stagecoach lines had shut down with winter snows and waited for spring thaws to reopen roads and trails, railways sought to master nature by using armies of men and a variety of special equipment to battle ice and snow. Sometimes, however, they lost the struggle, as they did in the Columbia River gorge in 1884.

On December 19 a blizzard piled up massive snowdrifts across the newly completed tracks of the Oregon Railway & Navigation Company and trapped the Pacific Express, the overland limited

that ran daily between St. Paul and Portland. The train was due to arrive in the Oregon metropolis by midmorning, but instead it braked to an unscheduled stop in the Columbia Gorge. Seemingly within seconds, blowing snow buried both engines and partially covered the rest of the train. It was impossible to return to Hood River, only ten miles back, much less continue fifty miles ahead to Portland, where many of the 148 passengers expected to spend their Christmas holidays. They might just as well have been stranded on the remote plains of eastern Montana. At least the abrupt stop injured no one, and there was food enough aboard for the day's meals. The conductor Edward Lyons rummaged through the baggage car, where he located three cases of oysters, two quarters of beef, some mutton, and about seventy-five jackrabbits.

Initial efforts to dig out the train failed, but

during a lull in the storm, crewmen succeeded in backing the cars a few hundred feet onto a small wooden trestle where they hoped passengers were out of danger from avalanches. As the fury of the storm increased again, blowing and drifting snow prevented plows from reaching the stranded train from either Portland or The Dalles. On December 22, a dwindling food supply forced Lyons to send nearly every able-bodied man out into the blizzard, each to seek his own safety. All survived the arduous trek to Troutdale, where rescuers from nearby Portland met them. Men on skis managed to pull heavy sleds of food to feed the remaining passengers.

Christmas came and went. Holiday dinner consisted of bacon, beans, canned fruit, pickles, and coffee. Rescue efforts continued around the clock, but progress was agonizingly slow. Drifts topped fifty feet in places, and snow mixed with ice formed a solid wall across the tracks between Multnomah Falls and Oneonta Gorge. Plows derailed and a locomotive tipped over, fatally crushing an engineer. An army of a thousand men recruited in Portland used picks and shovels to hack and dig away at snow and ice walls. New Year's Day passed, but the train remained snowbound until the weather abruptly warmed a few days later. Shortly after midnight on the morning of January 8, the remaining passengers finally steamed into Portland. They arrived almost three weeks late.

At the time of the 1884 blizzard, through train service between the Pacific Northwest and the East had been in operation slightly longer than a year. Before that, winter had simply brought normal life to a halt in much of the nation's Far Corner. Miners endured a bleak life in isolated camps and occasionally suffered from scurvy as a result of diets lacking in fresh fruits and vegetables. There was joyful weeping in the streets of Virginia City, Montana, in May 1864 when the first wagonload of flour arrived after a five-month hiatus caused by snow blocking

Rocky Mountain passes.[1] Even in Portland, the region's commercial metropolis, the pace of life slowed noticeably during winter months.

Northwesterners had once reckoned travel mainly in terms of seasons: in the 1840s and 1850s emigrants headed their covered wagons west from the valley of the Missouri River in spring when grasses of the Great Plains were lush and green. They fattened their draft animals in anticipation of the mountains and deserts ahead. They hoped to reach the Continental Divide at South Pass by midsummer and the Willamette Valley by early fall. The region's rural residents continued to measure time by the larger rhythms of life, by seasonal changes, sunrise and sunset, and Sunday as the start of a new week. Preindustrial societies did not ordinarily require more precise measurements. Although Pacific Northwest residents eventually refined their concept of time to include hours, railroads demanded even

*Two locomotives of the Oregon Short Line struggle through winter snows of eastern Idaho near Monida Pass to haul a Union Pacific passenger train north to Butte from Pocatello. Idaho State Historical Society, 74-78.41K.*

shorter intervals. They required people to think in terms of minutes, a measure that clearly defined the pace of life in industrial America.

In the Pacific Northwest, and elsewhere in the United States during the 1880s, the typical railroad consisted of a single track with sidings (or turnouts) spaced every few miles to permit trains to pass one another. Safe operations demanded that conductors and engineers follow thick books of rules, employee timetables, and special orders; the meeting places of trains had to be designated precisely in hours and minutes to prevent collisions. By the early 1920s an army of approximately four thousand inspectors and assistants regularly checked the watches of a million railroaders a year in the United States and Canada to maintain the margin of safety.[2]

Accident-free operation further demanded that crews synchronize their watches at the beginning of each run. For that reason the boundaries between standard time zones invariably coincided with places where train crews changed. In the Pacific Northwest, railroad towns like Troy, Montana; Hope, Idaho; and Huntington, Oregon, marked the boundaries between Mountain and Pacific time. Huntington still does today. Railroads also standardized to the minute the distance between such metropolitan centers as Portland and San Francisco. In 1905, for instance, the Southern Pacific's Shasta Express required exactly seventeen hours and five minutes to cover the 772 miles that separated the two cities. After standardizing distance in terms of hours and minutes, carriers took all steps necessary to maintain their schedules even in the face of unpredictable winter storms.

Time zones themselves were a railroad invention. They did not exist prior to November 18, 1883, the "day of two noons," when many influential railroads of the United States arbitrarily resolved fifty-six

standards of time into just four standard zones without any authorization from either state or federal governments. Railroads centering on Portland waited until Sunday, December 16, to adopt the new Pacific time. In either case, until late 1883 no meaningful time standard prevailed in America. A traveler going from Eastport, Maine, to San Francisco had to change his watch twenty times during the trip. At least twenty-seven local times existed in Michigan and twenty-three in Indiana.

As long as individual railroad companies operated their trains only short distances, time differences were of little consequence. But as railroads grew longer and more complex and their trains passed through major cities observing different standards of time, confusion resulted. Especially was that true for passengers trying to make connections between railroads that used time standards based on different cities. Trains running between Omaha and Chicago in 1870 used Chicago time, which was twenty-three minutes later than Omaha. Those between Omaha and Cheyenne operated by Union Pacific time, which was eleven minutes later than Omaha time. Trains south to Kansas City followed yet a third standard. When an employee asked about the difference between Union Pacific time and that of its headquarters city, he was told that the railroad followed the clock in its telegraph office in Omaha, which was originally on local time. However, "the clock has not been set for three years and during that time it has gained 11 minutes."[3]

After railroads adopted standard time, there were inevitable holdouts. Some ministers objected to railroads taking unto themselves a power reserved only to God. An Indianapolis newspaper complained, "The sun is no longer boss of the job. People, 55,000,000 of them, must eat, sleep and work as well as travel by railroad time."[4] The railroads' reordering of time perhaps symbolized better than anything else the far-reaching changes they were capable of promoting.

# What Time Do You Have?

If you ask that question of Conductor Thomas or Engineer Sullivan, of the Rock Island "Midcontinent Special," they will both answer: "Hamilton time." These veterans in railroad service know that Hamilton time means accurate time; Hamilton, to them, is just another word for accuracy.

And that's the way most railroad men feel about it. They know that Hamilton is all that a railroad watch should be—a timepiece of accuracy, sturdiness and dependability. They know that Hamilton embodies every worthwhile feature known to watchmaking science, even though its makers never boastfully "blow smoke" about it.

When you need a watch—and perhaps during 1928 you will want to make a change—insist on owning a Hamilton. That is the best way of insuring yourself watch satisfaction. Write for a copy of the new Hamilton Time Book and folder dealing with the various railroad models. You will find them both mighty useful.

HAMILTON WATCH COMPANY
999 WHEATLAND AVENUE, LANCASTER, PENNA., U. S. A.

Hamilton railroad models are now available fitted with either the famous Hamilton 992 movement, 21 jewels, adjusted to five positions, or the Hamilton 950 movement, 23 jewels, adjusted to five positions. Your jeweler will be glad to show you any of these models—in filled white, green or yellow gold.

"The Railroad Timekeeper of America"

Our Advertisers are Patronizing Your Magazine

*An advertisement for Hamilton watches in the mid-1920s emphasized the importance of accurate timekeeping. Minnesota Historical Society, Great Northern Railway Company Records, 19.A.10.3B.*

*The introduction of stock- and refrigerated cars during the last years of the nineteenth century opened up markets as distant as Chicago for Northwest beef. Pictured here, in what was once a common scene along the railroad corridor, is the Armour Packing Plant in Spokane in 1942. Eastern Washington State Historical Society, L85-143.66.*

Without question, until the dawn of highway competition and the rise of big oil companies, no form of corporate enterprise exercised more power in a greater variety of ways in the Pacific Northwest than railroads did during their heyday from the 1880s through the 1920s. Apart from requiring a pioneer generation to perceive time in a new way, they fostered numerous other changes.

Consider something so basic as food and drink: apples, pears, and other fruits formerly regarded as luxuries could be rushed from Pacific Northwest orchards to dinner tables across the continent, while oranges fresh from California traveled north to consumers in Oregon and Washington. The first refrigerator cars of the Northern Pacific Railroad brought ten tons of Chesapeake Bay oysters to Tacoma from Baltimore, Maryland, in October 1883. From the other direction, boatloads of tea sailed from China to Tacoma, where special trains rushed the cargo on to New York. Refrigerator cars and the new technique of pasteurization of beer spelled doom for many a small-town brewery within the

region. It is this type of railroad-induced change in everyday life that is the subject of *Railroad Signatures across the Pacific Northwest*.[5]

## Space: The Book
## That Gathered No Dust

BECAUSE OF THE APPARENT SIMplicity of its design, it is easy to overlook the revolutionary implications of a highway composed of twin ribbons of iron or steel spiked to wooden ties. It was revolutionary not just in terms of length, but even more so for width: the standard distance between the rails in the United States was four feet, eight and one-half inches. Because most tracks in North America, unlike those in Europe and Australia, conformed to a single gauge after the mid-1880s, the thousands of different railroad companies that served the United States, Canada, and Mexico could readily interchange freight and passenger cars to create a continent-wide market.

Perhaps nothing better recalls the physical dimensions of the region's once extensive railway network than a single bulky periodical, *The Official Guide of the Railways and Steam Navigation Lines of the United States, Porto Rico, Canada, Mexico and Cuba*. At one time it was the world's biggest monthly publication: more than sixteen hundred pages listing passenger-train schedules and related information. The first issue appeared in June 1868 in New York City, and today the *Official Guide* is still published regularly in an updated format. It has been described as a book that gathers no dust because for years it enjoyed heavy use in every railroad station across the United States. It is not coincidental that the widely acclaimed "inventor" of standard time was William F. Allen, who became editor of the *Official Guide* in 1873.[6]

Month after month for more than a century, the publication's pages faithfully chronicled the expansion, consolidation, and contraction of the North American railway network. Only rarely did even the smallest, most insignificant steam-powered railroad fail to list a timetable for its passenger trains. For any given minute the *Official Guide* told where all regularly scheduled passenger trains in North America were supposed to be. Not since the heyday of the railroads has it been possible to time the intercity travels of so many Americans with such accuracy.

The sixteen hundred pages of the *Official Guide* for June 1916, for instance, offer a window on a long lost world of transportation at a critical time. According to statistics compiled annually by the Interstate Commerce Commission, on June 30, 1916, the railroad network of the United States climbed to a total of 254,251 miles, up 462 miles from the previous year.[7] Until then, each year since the federal regulatory agency issued its first statistical report in 1888 the nation's rail mileage had increased. What no one could know in mid-1916 was that the network had reached its all-time high. Before the end of another year, the United States would be at war, and rails from lightly used or redundant lines would be removed to make armaments.

In the four Pacific Northwest states of Oregon, Washington, Idaho, and Montana, a 16,494-mile-long network of steel rails defined major aspects of daily life in 1916. Although the railroad network in that still developing part of the United States would continue to expand by another 722 miles to reach an all-time high in 1933, the year 1916 could still be taken as the high-water mark of the region's railway era, especially if measured in terms of not just mileage but also influence.

The most important trunk lines of the Pacific Northwest were oriented along an east-to-west axis, from St. Paul, Omaha, and Kansas City to Puget Sound and Portland. The main exception extended north from San Francisco to Portland, with connections to Seattle and Vancouver. North-to-south lines of lesser importance also ran from Umatilla in eastern Oregon to Spokane, from Salt Lake City to Butte, and from Denver to Billings and Great Falls. From this latticework of track, branch lines extended to any place of consequence.

The names of major railway companies, like Ford and IBM today, were household words in 1916. The Southern Pacific, which dominated transportation in western Oregon, extended from Portland to New Orleans. Its passenger-train schedules occupied thirty pages in the *Official Guide*. The Northern Pacific running from St. Paul to Puget Sound required sixteen pages to list its timetables, most of which were for branch-line trains that served sparsely populated towns and villages of the northern tier

states. The Great Northern, paralleling the Northern Pacific at a more northerly location, required seventeen pages. The Union Pacific needed twenty-five pages to provide schedules for the sprawling system that linked Omaha and Kansas City with Portland and Seattle. A latecomer among the big five carriers of the Pacific Northwest was the Chicago, Milwaukee & St. Paul Railway, completed between Chicago and Puget Sound in 1909. Its schedules occupied twenty-seven pages of the *Official Guide*, and its system map alone—like those of most trunk lines— spread across two pages.[8]

A few companies indulged in wishful thinking and took up far more of the printed pages than

their modest length warranted: the Central Railroad of Oregon, all thirty miles of it, boldly projected a ninety-one-mile line extending from Sparta, Oregon, across the Blue Mountains to Walla Walla, Washington. It also bragged that the Hot Lake Hotel and Sanitarium was "Equal to the Hot Springs of Arkansas" and that its line passed through "the finest" fruit, grain, and timber lands of the West. Boasting was what the Central Railroad of Oregon apparently did best, for its tracks barely reached the base of the Blue Mountains, much less crossed them. Its exaggerated claims harked back to another time, when seemingly anything was possible in the world of railroad construction.

In the Pacific Northwest in the summer of 1916, thoughts turned to vacations, trips to Pacific coast resorts, to mountain lakes in northern Idaho, or to one of the region's national parks—Yellowstone, Glacier, Crater Lake, or Mount Rainier—each with a major railroad to promote it as a tourist destination. The Great Northern Railway ran nearly a full-page advertisement in the *Official Guide* proclaiming that all three of its transcontinental trains operated via Glacier Park, "America's foremost summer playground."

That summer Mexico was in its sixth year of revolutionary violence, and the timetable published in the *Official Guide* for the Southern Pacific Railroad

*Railway yards in Spokane were alive with activity when this photograph was taken about 1908. Eastern Washington State Historical Society, L86-625.*

life. Many industry executives in 1916 found it difficult to anticipate the competitive impact of an expanding network of highways and an increasing number of people traveling by automobile. Yet portents of change and trouble ahead were all too obvious to those who had eyes to see: during the previous year, 42,000 miles of railroad were in receivership, an amount greater than ever before. That was one-sixth of the entire rail mileage in the United States.

By the dawn of 1916, for the first time since the automobile industry attained national stature, the average price of a new car had fallen below two thousand dollars. It was "the most radical downward revision in annual automobile prices on record."[9] Some models now sold for less than four hundred dollars. Also for the first time in modern history, Congress provided grants-in-aid to states to build better highways to accommodate the growing number of automobiles. At that time there were 132,755 motor vehicles registered in the four Pacific Northwest states; by 1920 the total had swelled to 389,221.

The *Official Guide* for June 1916 also recalls the extensive network of coastal steamers that had operated between Pacific Northwest ports and California since the 1850s. Names like the Pacific Coast Steamship Company and the Oregon Steamship Company were even more venerable than those of the Great Northern and Milwaukee Road. As recently as 1914, eleven companies competed for coastal passenger and freight traffic, although Pacific Coast Steamship did more business than all the rest combined. Its spacious and luxurious fleet of coastal liners operated from 1876 until September 1916, when Captain H. F. Alexander bought the company and reorganized it as the Admiral Line.

For all its bulk and wealth of details, there was still transportation that the *Official Guide* overlooked. The book clearly favored steam-powered common carriers. Some electric interurban lines—

*A scene on one of Oregon's many logging railroads in 1905. Eventually thousands of miles of such lines snaked through the woods of the Pacific Northwest. Many of them were less than twenty miles long, but some totaled a hundred or more miles of main line and spurs. Library of Congress, 11601-262-56636.*

Company of Mexico tersely advised travelers, "Service temporarily interrupted" south of Mazatlan. Canada was already at war in Europe, but for the United States it was one last summer of peace before it too joined the Allied effort to make the world safe for democracy. Changes as cataclysmic as the Great War were coming to American railroads, but like many things, they were nearly unimaginable before they actually happened. For two generations, railroads had defined major aspects of American

notably the Oregon Electric Railway, linking Portland and Eugene, and the Spokane & Inland Empire Railroad, extending from Spokane to Coeur d'Alene and Moscow, Idaho—listed their schedules, but timetables for most of the nation's several hundred electric interurban lines never appeared on its pages.

Missing too were listings for hundreds of stagecoach routes that once supplemented railway lines. In several locales in 1916, operators offered motorized stages, but there were remote parts of the Pacific Northwest where horses still prevailed. Nor is there mention of the numerous logging railroads that snaked through the region's extensive forests. Development of special logging railroads in the 1880s opened up hitherto inaccessible stands of timber at a time when trees near tidewater had already been harvested. The number of such carriers once totaled approximately nine hundred for Washington, five

hundred for Oregon, fifty for Idaho, and thirty for Montana. Most of them would be gone by the end of World War II, victims of a technological revolution brought about by heavy duty diesel-powered log trucks.[10]

The *Official Guide* also contained a "Personal" section for officials of the railroad industry. That for June 1916 recorded the retirement from active service of David E. Burley, general passenger agent for the Union Pacific's subsidiary Oregon Short Line Railroad and a prime mover in development of irrigated lands across southern Idaho. The *Guide* noted, too, that on May 29, 1916, death had claimed James J. Hill, a key builder of the New Northwest. These departures, as much as new highway construction and rising competition from automobiles, signified the passing of an era for Pacific Northwest railroads.

*P*hotographer Henry R. Griffiths captured Craig Mountain Lumber Company activity near the sawmill town of Winchester, Idaho, on August 28, 1946. The railroad not only hauled logs but also maintained a regular passenger train between Winchester and the Camas Prairie line at Craig Junction. Idaho State Historical Society, 72-139.4.

*I*n "Big Sky country" near Homestead, Montana, the Farm Security Administration photographer Marion Post Wolcott recorded this timeless scene along the Great Northern Railway in August 1941. Library of Congress, 15761 LC-USF34 57949.

# I / *Signatures in Steel*
## *The First Railway Age, 1868–1893*

*Ties, rails, spikes, and muscle power were fundamental to creating a railroad's signature in steel. These workers are laying track at Arrowrock, Idaho, August 31, 1911. The United States Reclamation Service operated a seventeen-mile railroad from Barber to Arrowrock Dam. National Archives, 115-JC-458.*

*The track ahead was but a thin stripe upon the earth's white expanse. And upon this band of steel the hundred men, like animated tumbleweeds, bent and twisted, bored and scratched. Upon the white bosom of American earth we engraved a necklace of steel—set in tie plates, clasped with bolts and angle bars, brocaded with spikes. And there it lay secure to the earth, immovable.*
—*Stoyan Christowe,* My American Pilgrimage *(1947)*

*A good railroad should be complete in all respects; track should be full bolted, full spiked, well ballasted, surfaced, lined, and gaged, and nothing omitted in its construction that would contribute toward making it a perfect and safe track. A poor track no more deserves to be called a railroad than a shanty does to be called a house, and trackmen who are in the habit of doing poor work with the means at hand to do better, never learn how to do good work.*
—*J. Kindelan,* The Trackman's Helper *(1900)*

*Before the construction of railroads to the Pacific, the States of California and Oregon were, owing to the difficulty of reaching them, practically as remote from the Atlantic and [Mid]Western States as though they formed part of another continent.*—Oregon . . . for the Use of Immigrants (1876)

# Portages by Rail

**B**EGINNING IN THE LATE 1860S A swelling volume of wheat poured from the Walla Walla Valley, some of it destined for ports as distant as Liverpool. Dozens of British and American sailing ships carried it from Portland around South America through the storm-swept Strait of Magellan to markets in England. The 16,000-mile ocean voyage may have been the easy part of the journey, however. Perhaps even more challenging was the 330-mile stretch of sagebrush plain and untamed river that separated Walla Walla from Portland. Here the grain trade confronted a bewildering variety of natural and man-made obstacles.[1]

It particularly irked the pioneer Walla Walla merchant Dorsey Syng Baker that teamsters who hauled wheat by wagon thirty miles to the nearest steamboat landing charged twelve dollars a ton, a fee equal to that for the much longer journey down the Columbia River to Portland. Baker believed that transportation costs could be reduced significantly if only a railroad could be built from Walla Walla to Wallula, the ramshackle collection of buildings on a sandy stretch of beach where wheat was loaded aboard steamboats.

On paper the task appeared simple enough. The proposed Walla Walla & Columbia River Railroad had only to follow the general course of the Walla Walla River to its confluence with the Columbia. There were neither mountains nor major rivers to cross, and only thirty-two miles of track had to be spiked into place. If the line was narrow gauge and built mostly from local materials, the cost of construction could be kept low.

Funds to build even a three-foot-gauge line would have to be raised mainly from local sources, and finding investment capital in a frontier community as small and new as Walla Walla was at best a slow and time-consuming process. The community in 1870 had only sixteen hundred inhabitants, and many of them were openly skeptical of Baker's project. Although Walla Walla had become the transportation hub of the inland Northwest—a supply center for mining camps scattered through eastern Washington, Idaho, Montana, and southern British Columbia—a railroad, even a short one, was a complex and expensive undertaking; successful operation of a packtrain or freight wagon line, by contrast, required only modest investment and limited technological expertise. And even if money were forthcoming, the nearest source of iron rails and locomotives was Pittsburgh, more than half a continent away.

An established physician, merchant, and banker

in his late forties when he took up the new career of railroad builder, Baker was undaunted by naysayers and finally obtained some local backing. Construction began in 1871 with several gangs of Chinese laborers grading the line. Other workmen floated logs down the Yakima River to a small sawmill at "Slabtown," an eddy on the Columbia River just north of Wallula, which was capable of turning out a mile of track material a week.

The sawmill provided not only ties but also rails. As a cost-saving measure, regular T-shaped iron rails were to be used only on the curves; on straight sections Baker substituted wooden rails topped with lengths of strap three-eighths of an inch thick and two inches wide. While track work moved ahead more or less successfully, Baker had two small saddle-tank locomotives shipped from Porter, Bell & Company in Pittsburgh around Cape Horn to Portland. Called the Walla Walla and Wallula, they were the first of six locomotives used on the Walla Walla & Columbia River Railroad. In all, the line cost approximately a third of a million dollars to build and equip.

Finally, on October 23, 1875, Walla Walla celebrated the realization of Dr. Baker's dream. The passenger train to Wallula crept along at not quite six miles an hour, but even a five-hour journey was significantly faster than the two-day trip previously required. On later runs, pieces of strap iron occasionally worked loose and sprang violently upward to knock holes in the floors of passenger cars. These so-called snake heads frightened travelers but never caused any serious injuries.

*F*ort Walla Walla in 1862. Washington's modern city of Walla Walla arose at this site. Library of Congress, 11604 2-62 7287.

Because of the peculiarities of the homegrown enterprise, it was variously called Dr. Baker's Road, the strap iron road, and the rawhide road, the last a derisive name arising from a confused and erroneous notion that the cost-conscious Baker had used strap leather instead of iron. Many a Walla Walla joke centered on this railroad, and one national journal even claimed that during a particularly hard winter wolves desperate for food ate the rawhide and temporarily severed Walla Walla's link to the outside world. In fact, wooden rails were not unusual in the far Northwest. Before Baker launched his road, he had seen them used successfully on portage lines in the Columbia Gorge.

The truth is that, by charging only half of what teamsters formerly received, the Walla Walla & Columbia River Railroad reaped staggering profits that helped to make Baker a very rich man. The line hauled 4,021 tons of flour and grain in 1874 even before it was completed. Four years later the amount increased to 27,366 tons of flour in addition to a variety of other agricultural commodities. In 1879 Baker sold six-sevenths of his railroad to the Oregon Railway & Navigation Company, and the new owners immediately removed the strap iron to upgrade the track. They widened the line from three feet to standard gauge in 1881 in preparation for a through route to Portland. Baker, meanwhile, invested his growing fortune in other frontier enterprises. In the end, the real joke was on those who had declined to invest in Dr. Baker's "rawhide" money-making machine.[2]

The Walla Walla & Columbia River line was not the first railroad in the Pacific Northwest, and like other frontier carriers its economies included light rails and sharp curves, bridges built of wood, not masonry, and locomotives that burned wood, not coal, for fuel. Also like most of the region's early railroads, Baker's line functioned as a supplement to already established water routes. When Baker completed his wheat carrier in 1875, there were two portage lines in the Columbia River Gorge and another farther upriver at The Dalles.

There was also the Northern Pacific, or at least the western segment of what some hoped would become the first northern transcontinental line. In 1875 its tracks ran from Kalama, a steamboat landing on the Columbia, north a hundred miles to Tacoma and formed a land bridge between Puget Sound and the Columbia Valley. South of the Columbia, two modest railway lines extended from Portland up the Willamette Valley. One of these, the Oregon & California Railroad, reached as far south as Roseburg before it ran out of money.

The only other part of the entire Pacific Northwest to hear the sound of a locomotive whistle regularly in 1875 was Franklin, a Mormon village in remote southeastern Idaho. A year earlier the Utah Northern Railroad hesitatingly extended a narrow-gauge line eighty-five miles north from Ogden across the Idaho boundary into Franklin before work stopped. This little line had at least one advantage none of the other railroads of the far Northwest did: at Ogden its tracks met those of the Union Pacific and the Central Pacific roads, which had already joined at nearby Promontory Summit in 1869 to form the nation's first transcontinental line. Thus, in all the Pacific Northwest only Franklin could boast of national railroad connections in 1875.

Nearly five hundred miles of sagebrush country separated the tracks of the Utah Northern from those of the Walla Walla & Columbia River Railroad, the closest rail line farther west. Only an optimist could have imagined in 1875 that the region's scattered lines of different gauges and parentage would somehow come together to form a legible signature in steel. The one thing that seemed certain was that most early railroads only reinforced established patterns of trade along the Pacific Northwest's major waterways. There was no railway system, and no one was in a position to predict how and when one might take shape.

## Waters of Empire

INLAND RIVERS AND LAKES TOGETHER with the Pacific Ocean and its many tidal estuaries formed the earliest and easiest avenues of communication and transportation in a region fractured by numerous mountain ranges and possessing only widely scattered centers of population. Puget Sound was a marvelous water highway that linked settlements in western Washington Territory and permitted large sailing ships to load lumber at sawmill towns for distant markets.

Rivers of the inland Northwest, by contrast, had a certain perversity about them. Except for the Missouri, Willamette, Columbia, and lower Snake rivers, most were navigable by steamboat only for relatively short distances. Even transportation up the Columbia and Willamette rivers from Portland was no simple matter. The falls at Oregon City required passengers and freight traveling to and from Eugene City and other upper Willamette landings to portage at that point. Even more formi-

dable obstacles interrupted navigation on the Columbia. Blocking passage through the Columbia Gorge was a stretch of white water known as the Cascades. Farther up were two more obstacles to navigation known as the Grand Dalles and Celilo Falls. Portaging around them was tedious business, but attempting to run through them was dangerous if not suicidal, depending on the season and the volume of water pouring down the great River of the West.

Until 1896 it required three separate steamboats to travel four hundred miles up the Columbia and

Snake rivers from Portland to Lewiston, gateway to the mines and forests of northern Idaho. A wooden tram was built along the north bank of the Columbia River at Cascades Rapids in 1851. Called the Cascade Railroad, it used mules to pull flatcars along six-inch-square wooden rails topped with strap iron. For seventy-five cents, one hundred pounds of "emigrant effects" could be portaged the six miles around the rapids.[3]

A competing line, the Oregon Portage Railroad, was completed along the opposite bank in late 1858. Workmen laid 4½ miles of wooden track

*Carleton E. Watkins captured this image of the Cascade Railroad on the Washington side of the Columbia River in 1867. The Oregon Steam Navigation line maintained its transportation monopoly through ownership of key portage railways along the Columbia River. Oregon Historical Society, 13577, no. 891-A-7.*

between the site of what is now Bonneville Dam and Cascade Locks. Over its tracks rumbled trains of four or five cars pulled by horses and mules. A few months later workmen affixed to the wooden tracks a bearing surface of sheet iron. The Oregon Pony, the first steam locomotive in the Pacific Northwest, began portaging passengers and freight in 1862. Farther upriver, near Dalles City (now The Dalles), a longer portage line replaced a crude wagon road in 1863. Its tracks climbed eleven miles past the Grand Dalles to slack water above Celilo Falls.[4]

Even before the portage railroads joined together separate stretches of the Columbia River, a system of steamboat transportation had already begun to take shape. The sidewheeler *Columbia* initiated regular service between Astoria and Portland in

1850, becoming the first steamship to ply the Columbia as a common carrier. Steamboat service to the interior Northwest above Celilo Falls commenced in late 1858 with the stern-wheeler *Colonel Wright*. This became the first steamboat on Idaho waters when it brought a load of gold seekers to Lewiston in 1861. Steamboats carried miners, merchants, soldiers, and settlers up the river and returned with cargoes of grain, cattle, and gold.

Monopolizing Columbia River traffic in the early years and reaping a fortune during the gold rush to Idaho was a group of Portland capitalists who organized the Oregon Steam Navigation Company in 1860. The three who dominated the "financial wonder of its day" were J. C. Ainsworth, R. R. Thompson, and Simeon G. Reed. They and other

investors grew rich when the rush to Idaho mines filled company coffers to overflowing. After only six months in operation, the company declared a 20 percent dividend, and that was only a promising beginning. The line of freight wagons at its Portland docks appeared to be unbroken day and night, seven days a week.[5]

By 1865 the Oregon Steam Navigation Company operated a fleet of nearly thirty passenger and freight steamboats, thirteen schooners, and four barges on the Columbia River alone. One Oregon Steam Navigation boat on the middle river was the new side-wheeler *Idaho*. It dominated the 38-mile run between the Cascades and The Dalles and is probably the source of the name of the modern state of Idaho.[6]

The reach of the Oregon Steam Navigation Company extended south along the Willamette River and east as far as the middle Snake River in southern Idaho and the Clark Fork River in western Montana. By 1867 it was possible to ship goods from Portland to Helena, Montana, in only seven days. The company competed for the trade of the inland Northwest with merchants from California and Missouri. In the eyes of many Northwesterners, however, the combination of high profits and monopoly power on the Columbia and Willamette rivers made the Oregon Steam Navigation Company an object of envy and hatred for two decades after 1860.

Although the water that raged through Hells Canyon prevented steamboats from traveling very far up the Snake River beyond Lewiston, other stretches of inland water proved receptive to steamboat traffic.[7] A large fleet once operated in the Idaho panhandle along the St. Joe River and across Lake Coeur d'Alene. These vessels appeared on the lake with the 1884 mining boom and regularly hauled passengers and freight up the Coeur d'Alene River as far as the landing at the old Indian mission at Cataldo. From there, freight destined for silver

and gold mines continued upriver in dugouts and bateaux. Steamboat whistles also echoed from the banks of the Clearwater and Pend Oreille rivers; the Columbia River above Wenatchee and Lake Chelan in Washington; and the Kootenai, Clark Fork, Missouri, and Yellowstone rivers and Flathead Lake in Montana.

East of the Continental Divide, steamboat connections between St. Louis and Fort Union, near the confluence of the Missouri and Yellowstone rivers, were established as early as 1832 with the voyage of the side-wheeler *Yellow Stone*. By 1860 steamboats had probed as far up the Missouri as Fort Benton, where traffic headed overland along the Mullan Road through a series of mountain ranges to reach Walla Walla and finally the Columbia River. The special "mountain steamboats" that navigated the upper Missouri were characterized by broad bottoms and shallow hulls. Legend held that they drew so little water that they could navigate on a heavy dew. Cargoes of the Missouri River steamboat fleet were associated mainly with the fur trade until the mining boom of the northern Rocky Mountains in the 1860s. The peak year of traffic was probably 1867 when some forty steamboats were in the trade. The coming of the Northern Pacific Railroad in the early 1880s left only local service along the river between Bismarck and Fort Benton, and even that was gone by the end of the decade.[8]

On the Columbia River and its main tributaries, the heyday of steamboat transportation lasted from the 1860s until the late 1920s, when traffic declined as a result of rail and highway competition. River transportation remained in the shadow of the railroads until the federal government completed a series of dams and locks on the Columbia and Snake rivers in the 1960s and 1970s that rejuvenated the water highway from Lewiston to the sea.

## Golden Harvests and Transportation Innovation

**D**URING THE GREAT ERA OF RIVER transportation, nothing seemed to call forth more technological ingenuity than the lucrative grain trade from eastern Washington and Oregon. In the interior Northwest, where it could cost as much to haul a crop to market as to raise it, cheap and efficient transportation was vital. This consideration not only spurred Dorsey Baker to build his Walla Walla & Columbia River Railroad but also gave rise to other forms of transportation innovation.

Until development of an extensive network of railroads during the 1880s made it relatively easy to ship carloads of wheat from the inland Northwest to the ports of Seattle and Portland, moving grain to overseas markets presented a formidable challenge. Most grain from the Columbia plateau, unlike other wheat-producing regions of the United States, traveled to market in sacks. One reason for that was the number of times it had to be handled between Walla Walla and Portland. An equally compelling

reason was fear that bulk cargoes were liable to shift dangerously in rough seas or spoil as a result of exposure to the prolonged warmth of the tropics. For several decades marine underwriters simply would not insure bulk cargoes of Northwest grain.

Dr. Baker's railroad addressed part of the problem facing grain growers when it provided a cheap and efficient way to haul their crop out of the Walla Walla Valley, but the topography of the Palouse country farther north presented growers there with even more formidable challenges. Once their grain was harvested in July or August, it had to be transported to the rim of the Snake River canyon and then down to steamboat landings two thousand feet below. Because hauling heavy wagonloads of wheat along steep and winding roads was laborious and dangerous work, various tramways and chutes were developed. One of Baker's associates, Major Sewell Truax of Walla Walla, devised a wooden chute four inches square and thirty-two hundred feet long.

But the speed of the drop partially milled the grain and wore holes in the chute. Attempts were made to line the chute with glass and, alternatively, to build diversion chambers to slow the descent and protect the grain. After growers solved their initial technical problems, they built additional chutes, although by 1892 the future belonged to tramways that used pulleys and platform cars to lower sacks of wheat to the river's edge. This system eliminated the need to dump and resack the grain.

Growers also developed bucket or cable tramways.

One of these, the Mayview tram, remained in operation until the eve of World War II and lowered hundreds of thousands of sacks of grain, mostly wheat and some barley. After the 1880s when numerous railroad lines were completed through the agricultural regions of eastern Washington and Oregon, boxcars increasingly replaced steamboats and, together with good roads in the 1920s and the switch to bulk shipment of grain in the 1930s, doomed the trams.[9]

## Wheat Sacks to Sea

One contemporary observer counted the
amount of handling necessary to transport
a single load of wheat from Walla Walla to Portland:

1. Wagon to warehouse in Walla Walla
2. Warehouse to railway cars in Walla Walla
3. Railway cars to wharf-boat in Wallula
4. Wharf-boat to steamer at Wallula
5. Steamer to warehouse at Celilo
6. Warehouse to railway cars at Celilo
7. Cars to warehouse in The Dalles

8. Warehouse to steamboat at The Dalles
9. Steamer to wharf-boat at Upper Cascade
10. Wharf-boat to cars at Upper Cascade
11. Cars to wharf-boat at Lower Cascade
12. Wharf-boat to steamer at Lower Cascade
13. Steamer to wharf in Portland
14. Wharf to truck in Portland
15. Truck to wharf in Portland
16. Wharf to barge, steamer, or ship in Portland.

—*Idaho Tri-Weekly Statesman* (Boise), Nov. 20, 1879

*The Lewiston loads wheat at Illion, Washington, in the early twentieth century. This was one of several steamboat landings along the lower Snake River. Similar boats also operated along the Willamette River from Portland to Eugene and along the Columbia and Snake rivers to The Dalles and Lewiston, Idaho. Steamboats plied Puget Sound to connect Seattle to Port Orchard, Port Gamble, Port Blakely, and Victoria, as well as to lesser points like Dog Fish Bay. Moorhouse collection, 261, Special Collections, Knight Library, University of Oregon.*

## Foot and Walker's Transportation Line

GRAIN WAS NOT THE ONLY commodity to foster improved transportation links between the interior Northwest and the coast. During the mining rush to Idaho in the 1860s, steamboats carried gold seekers up the Columbia River as far as Umatilla and Wallula, jumping-off points for interior camps, and, if the Snake River was running high enough, all the way through to Lewiston, trail head for the northern mines. From steamboat landings on the Columbia River, pack- and saddle trains hauled passengers and freight overland to Boise Basin mining towns.

A single train might include as many as one hundred animals, each carrying 250 to 400 pounds of freight. It took thirteen days to cover the three hundred miles from Umatilla to Boise City, which soon became the transportation hub of southern Idaho. Some gold seekers simply strapped packs to their backs and hit the trail for the long hike overland. This most elementary form of transportation was jokingly referred to as Foot and Walker's Transportation Line. Eventually freight wagons and stagecoaches dominated the route as roads improved. It was a succession common in other parts of the Pacific Northwest as well.

Of all forms of early transportation, none seemed more ubiquitous than the stagecoach. How much it once meant to hear the cry, "Stage!" In isolated camps and villages the one great event of the day

was the arrival of the stage with its load of mail and passengers. Like the locomotive engineeer of a later era, the stage driver was a popular and respected man.

Because isolation was a chief drawback of pioneer life, inauguration of regular mail, passenger, and freight service, however crude and inefficient, was welcomed as a sign of liberation and progress. Probably the first common carrier in the Oregon Country was an ox-powered stage that began twice-weekly service between Oregon City and the Tualatin plain in 1846. It promised to operate "rain or no rain—mud or no mud—load or no load—*but not without pay*." Other primitive stagecoach lines soon followed. By 1857 a Concord coach was able to complete the fifty-mile run from Portland to Salem

in a single day. Three years later the California Stage Company established direct and regular service between Portland and Sacramento, a distance of seven hundred miles. The journey required six days.

Travelers by stagecoach had convenient connections from Sacramento southwest to the growing metropolis of San Francisco and east as far as St. Louis. Stages continued to haul passengers and mail between Portland and Sacramento until the Oregon & California Railroad completed a through line in 1887. Another notable carrier was Wells, Fargo & Company of San Francisco, which established a far-flung network of stagecoach and freight lines in the 1860s and 1870s to serve mining regions in the interior Northwest.

Travel by stage was never without its trials. Early

*A stagecoach pauses at Branco station, about five miles south of Silver City, Idaho, in this undated photograph. Hundreds of small stage lines ran from railheads to places like Yellow Jacket and Bayhorse, Idaho; Eagle Point, Oregon; Crab Tree, Washington; and Lump City, Montana. Idaho State Historical Society, 541-E.*

*Various forms of horse-drawn transportation filled the main street of Ruby, Washington, when this photograph was taken in the late 1880s. Eastern Washington State Historical Society, 8178.*

roads were often little more than dirt paths, and rain could turn stretches into knee-deep quagmires. One traveler remembered a driver ordering, "First class passengers, keep your seats. Second class passengers, get out and walk. Third class passengers, get behind and push."[10] In dry weather the dust spread over passengers like the waves of the sea. The alkali made their skin sore and rough and burned their eyes and noses. Still more alarming were the roads that wound down steep hillsides. But even after a network of railway lines extended into many parts of the Pacific Northwest, stagecoaches and pack animals did not disappear. And despite the advent of motor-

ized vehicles in the early twentieth century, horse-drawn stages continued to supplement rail service in several remote areas until the 1930s, when motorized transportation became common.

Carriers employing a variety of conveyances—packtrains, stagecoaches, freight wagons, steamboats, sailing ships, and railroad trains—tied the region together and integrated it with the larger world. Yet without the construction of a railway network, it would be impossible to account for the rapid commercial and urban growth that the Northwest experienced after the mid-1880s.

## Envisioning a Northern Transcontinental Railroad

EVEN AS PACIFIC NORTHWEST entrepreneurs improved intraregional transportation, one scheme clearly stood apart from all others during the 1860s and 1870s. That was the proposed Northern Pacific Railroad, a transcontinental line that would connect Lake Superior and Puget Sound. Because of America's expanding trade with China during the 1840s, Asa Whitney, a New York merchant who had spent several years in the Far East, suggested a transcontinental railroad to Congress in late 1845. His motives were not entirely economic; he wanted also to promote settlement and believed that "Nature's God had made this for the grand highway to Civilize and Christianize all mankind."[11] Although Whitney was an eloquent speaker well armed with statistics and a variety of arguments, his dream evoked only sneers and ridicule.

While federal lawmakers remained unmoved, Whitney generated popular enthusiasm for his proposal in mass public meetings. He obtained resolutions of endorsement from several state legislatures. Like earlier dreams of a Northwest Passage by sea or an easy portage across the Rockies, the idea gradually won influential backers. More than any other person, Whitney added serious discussion of a transcontinental railroad to the public agenda at a time when even conceptualizing such a link represented a bold feat of imagination. American railroads had barely advanced beyond the experimental stage by 1850, and only a handful were longer than 150 miles.

Formidable as technological problems might be for an industry still in its infancy, there were also matters of finance. Who should pay for so massive an undertaking? A railroad to the Pacific dwarfed anything attempted in the East, where railroad building had begun with local capital and on a small scale. Eastern railroads generated freight and passenger business by serving already established population centers and markets. Western lines, by contrast, had to build across hundreds, even thousands of miles of rugged and lightly populated country. They would have to generate passenger and freight revenue by running from nowhere in particular to nowhere at all. In other words, the railroads of the West would have to create new towns and markets and foster settlement of vast expanses—by promising investors a share of future wealth, a task that sobered even the most optimistic westerner. In the West, moreover, the labor needed for construction was high priced and difficult to obtain.

The West was a debtor region; its residents lacked capital sufficient to build local railroads, much less national ones. The region was unlikely to attract necessary funds from hardheaded eastern financiers. Few individuals wanted to risk their private fortunes on such dubious enterprises. Clearly, only the federal government had the resources to support a transcontinental railroad.

The imaginative Whitney petitioned Congress to grant him a sixty-mile-wide strip of land along the right-of-way of a proposed railway line from the Great Lakes to the lower Columbia River. He would sell the land—an area larger than the state of Illinois—to finance construction. Congress refused, but Whitney's northern transcontinental scheme elicited proposals from other regions, each with its special plan and route for reaching the Pacific. One congressman in 1852 ridiculed Whitney's plan to "build a railroad through a barren, uninhabited, frozen region," urging instead a southern route.[12]

In the early 1850s, Congress finally authorized the United States Army to conduct five transcontinenal railway surveys to find a feasible route to the Pacific. The northern survey, under the direction of Isaac I. Stevens, also first governor of the new Washington Territory, worked its way west from St. Paul; Ste-

*The end of Northern Pacific track near Brainerd, Minnesota, about 1870. At the time of its financial collapse in 1875, the railroad consisted of two poorly built lines separated by more than 1,500 miles of mountain and prairie: the eastern section extended 450 miles from Lake Superior to the Missouri River, the western section a little more than 100 miles from Tacoma south to Kalama on the Columbia River. Minnesota Historical Society, HE6.2N.*

vens's subordinate, Lieutenant George B. McClellan, explored the Cascade Range for suitable passes. The government published the survey reports between 1856 and 1861, and they provided a comprehensive picture of what lay ahead for dreamers of a Northwest land passage. Only in 1862—after the Civil War broke the regional deadlock over the best route—did Congress authorize loans and grants of land to subsidize construction of a railway along a central route. Sixty-one separate railroads received federal land grants totaling 131,350,534 acres before Congress terminated the program in 1871.

Congress chartered the Northern Pacific Railroad in mid-1864. The staggering cost of the Civil War prevented it from providing a cash subsidy for each mile of track laid, as it did for the central route, but it authorized instead the largest land grant in American history, a sixty-million-acre swath of land the size of the six New England states. On a map the Northern Pacific grant resembled an elongated checkerboard of alternating one-mile squares of government and railroad land extending from Lake Superior to the Pacific Ocean. It varied in width from forty miles in Minnesota and Oregon to eighty miles in the territories. The government deeded the odd sections to the railroad upon completion of each twenty-five miles of line.

This land grant, it must be noted, came with certain strings attached. The grant obligated the railroad to provide reduced rates on federal shipments such as mail until 1946. It further bound the company to finish its entire transcontinental line by July 4, 1876, an impossible task. Ultimately the Northern Pacific forfeited some of the land for noncompliance. Even so, the company still gained more than thirty-nine million acres, an area twice as large as any other railroad received. As a result, the Northern Pacific's successor (in 1970), the Burlington Northern Railroad, became one of the largest nongovernment landholders in the United States.

As generous as the original Northern Pacific land grant was, the lack of a cash subsidy created severe financial difficulties and hampered construction. The company further labored under the twin burdens of having no sizable population centers to serve and having to convince investors that the north country was not too cold to permit successful railroading and settlement. From February 1868 until February 1870, the demoralized company failed to hold even a single board meeting.

One key person who did come to believe in the Northern Pacific project was the noted Civil War financier Jay Cooke of Philadelphia. But before he undertook to raise money for construction, Cooke collected all available information on the subject. To be certain of the value of the land grant, he carefully studied a mountain of books, maps, and letters on his desk. He also equipped two expeditions at his own expense in 1869 to confirm the wisdom of building a line at so northerly a location. One led by Governor William R. Marshall of Minnesota probed from Lake Superior across the Dakota plains to the Missouri River; the other led by the engineer W. Milnor Roberts ranged more widely, coming up the Columbia River, the Clark Fork, and across central Montana to Fort Benton on the Missouri. Their reports confirmed Cooke's hopes, and he enthusiastically threw his influence behind the project in early 1870.[13]

With the prestigious firm of Jay Cooke and Company acting as the Northern Pacific's financial agent, money at last flowed in. Cooke proposed to sell $100 million in bonds, for which his firm would receive $12 on each $100 sold. By 1871 bonds totaling $30 million had been sold, mainly to investors in the United States. Promoters hired to create public enthusiasm for the project so insistently proclaimed that the Northern Pacific country possessed a mild climate like that in tidewater Virginia and other agreeable features that the region came to be popularly caricatured as "Jay Cooke's Banana Belt."[14]

Groundbreaking took place near Duluth in July 1870. There were no towns worthy of the name west of there for a thousand miles. Two years later the Northern Pacific line had opened for business as far west as the Red River valley separating Minnesota and Dakota Territory. Work began also at Kalama, Washington Territory, in 1870. Northern Pacific directors soon selected Tacoma as their Pacific terminus and the Clark Fork route through the Rocky Mountains for their right-of-way.

To solidify its position in the far Northwest, the railroad purchased three-quarters of Oregon Steam Navigation Company stock. As strategically sound as the move was, it obligated Cook to find $500,000 in gold to cover part of the $1.5 million purchase price. This placed a heavy burden on the financier just as the nation's economy unexpectedly slumped. Northern Pacific tracks had only reached Bismarck, Dakota Territory, when on September 18, 1873, Jay Cooke and Company closed its doors. Failure of the respected firm precipitated the financial panic of 1873 that spread through Wall Street and ultimately down the main streets of would-be cities in the Pacific Northwest. During the hard times that lasted most of the decade, construction halted; in January 1875 the Northern Pacific defaulted on interest on its bonds.

Many Pacific Northwesterners must have wondered if they would live long enough to see the bankrupt Northern Pacific completed. Lack of construction in the mid-1870s caused frustrated citizens of Seattle and eastern Washington to propose building their own Seattle & Walla Walla Railroad across the Cascade Range through Snoqualmie Pass. As for Asa Whitney, the man who spent his personal fortune trying to promote the idea of a transcontinental railroad west from Lake Superior, he died in poverty in 1872, well before his vision became reality.

## From Stagecoach King to Railroad Baron

SOUTH OF THE COLUMBIA RIVER in the Willamette Valley lay evidence of yet another railroad dream waiting to be realized. Here two rival groups proposed to build a line linking Portland with San Francisco Bay. Congress in 1866 provided incentive in the form of a 3.7-million-acre land grant that included some of the world's richest stands of Douglas fir timber. Federal lawmakers provided that Oregon legislators should choose a recipient, and they in turn awarded the land and timber bonanza to backers of the Oregon Central Railroad, or West Side line. But that did not end the rivalry between West Siders and East Siders. After groundbreaking in 1868, the two companies competed on opposite sides of the Willamette River to develop the valley's vast resources. The Willamette Valley, an area the size of Massachusetts, was the first part of the Pacific Northwest extensively settled by a non-Indian population. By the mid-1860s it had become an agricultural cornucopia and an attractive prospect for local railroad builders.[15]

Joining the fight to dominate Willamette Valley commerce was Ben Holladay, a handsome, energetic, and unscrupulous financial adventurer. He treated Oregonians to a spectacle the likes of which old-timers had never seen before. Holladay's was the classic rags-to-riches story: born in a log cabin in Kentucky in 1819, he made his fortune in transportation and kept mansions in Washington, D.C., New York City and White Plains, New York, and Portland and Seaside, Oregon. Disdained by many as a semiliterate boor, he entertained lavishly and vulgarly.

Before coming to Oregon, Holladay had already organized a far-flung network of stagecoach and freight wagon lines, riverboats, and coastal steamers and won for himself the popular titles of Stagecoach King and Napoleon of the West. His stagecoach empire reached its greatest extent in early 1866 when the Holladay Overland Mail & Express Company stretched west along five thousand miles of roads between Atchison, Kansas, and the Pacific Slope.

In August 1868 Holladay traveled from California to Oregon, where he used the financial muscle created by selling his staging business to Wells, Fargo & Company to wrest control of Willamette Valley railroads from local businessmen. He perceived an opportunity to increase his already considerable fortune by gaining control of the vast land grant awarded by Congress. To that end he distributed money and favors lavishly, subsidized newspapers, hired lawyers, and purchased politicians. Holladay, who bragged openly of his control of the press and his influence over Oregon politics, introduced the Pacific Northwest to an era of corruption aptly described as a great barbecue.

Holladay sided with backers of the Oregon & California Railroad, which operated east of the Willamette River, against supporters of the Oregon Central Railroad. During the 1868 legislative session in Salem, he unblushingly wooed and corrupted the Oregon legislature: for $35,000 he purchased legislation enabling him to wrest the federal grant originally awarded to the West Siders. Not only did he win the prized land, but the Oregon & California soon acquired its erstwhile rival, the Oregon Central, which he operated as a subsidiary company.[16]

Holladay recklessly sold bonds at 60 to 75 percent of par value to raise money for further railway construction. English and German capitalists acquired some eleven million dollars' worth by 1873. With money thus raised at ruinous discount rates, Holladay stepped up construction and spent extravagantly until 240 miles of track were built and a portion of the land grant was secured. The Oregon & California completed a line south from Portland to Roseburg in 1873 and, together with the Oregon

*Ben Holladay (1819–77). When Holladay was forced to retire in the mid-1870s, his transportation empire collapsed. More than one hundred lawsuits punctuated his final years. Holladay died in Portland in his sixty-eighth year, having lost fame and good health along with his fortune. Oregon Historical Society, 49501, no. 516-A.*

Central, opened new country by promoting immigration to Oregon.

Possessed by the need to dominate whatever field of transportation he entered, Holladay sought to eliminate the threat of steamboat competition on the Willamette River, which paralleled his railroads. He purchased the People's Transportation Company in 1871 and thus brought nine more steamships into the fold of his North Pacific Transportation Company, which he reorganized the following year as the Oregon Steamship Company. The bold plan gave him a monopoly on transportation in the Willamette Valley. Meanwhile, he engaged in a myriad of dealings throughout the West that included land and mining speculations and the first street railway line in Portland.

Holladay dominated Oregon politics and transportation for nearly a decade, yet his great business

*Oregon City as it appeared in a Carleton E. Watkins photograph taken in 1867. The locks opened in 1873 to permit steamboats to navigate the length of the Willamette Valley from Portland to Eugene. Oregon Historical Society, 21591, no. 823.*

enterprise rested upon a surprisingly shaky foundation. He was forever rearranging his holdings by creating or merging subsidiaries. His steamship and railroad interests were interlocked in a bewildering arrangement of double pledging their securities to creditors. The result, observed Henry Villard, the man who finally beat him at this game, was that Holladay's creditors, though among the shrewdest and most experienced bankers in Europe, allowed themselves to be caught in his financial machinations. Holladay eventually overreached himself. The panic of 1873 left his companies destitute and unable to pay interest to bondholders. To untangle the snarl, German bondholders dispatched Villard to Oregon in 1874 as their agent to see what might be salvaged from their American misadventure. Villard and his backers gradually tightened the financial noose until on April 18, 1876, he acquired complete control of the Holladay properties and vanquished the erstwhile transportation king.

Villard entered the Pacific Northwest as a troubleshooter for German investors. More than anyone else he combined widely scattered pieces of railroad track—the portage lines along the Columbia River, Dr. Baker's "rawhide road" in the Walla Walla Valley, Holladay's Willamette Valley lines, and even the Northern Pacific—into a true railroad system. For the Pacific Northwest, the decade after 1875 could accurately be described as the age of Henry Villard.

*It can truly be said that besides financing and building most of the Northern Pacific main line, Henry Villard laid the foundations broad and deep for the Union Pacific, Southern Pacific, Great Northern, and Northern Pacific in the Pacific Northwest.—Robert Strahorn, "Ninety Years of Boyhood" (1942)*

# Henry Villard and the Empire of the Columbia

*Japanese tracklayers mingle with corporate executives during the final spike ceremony held by the Chicago, Milwaukee & St. Paul Railway four miles west of Garrison, Montana, on May 19, 1909, to mark completion of its Pacific Coast extension. Montana Historical Society.*

FINAL SPIKE CEREMONIES PERIODically celebrated the achievements of railroad builders. The one at Promontory, Utah, on May 10, 1869, signified completion of the nation's first transcontinental railroad. Immortalized by photographs, paintings, and postage stamps, it was by far the most famous of these events. Sometimes the driving of the last spike was a strictly local affair, as when the Gilmore & Pittsburgh Railroad reached the tiny community of Salmon, Idaho, in 1910 and townspeople turned out in their Sunday best to celebrate. These occasions were much like

the lift-off that once riveted America's attention to its manned space program. Each in its own way was a popular event that attracted considerable media coverage. As time went on, such public affirmations of technological prowess tended to become almost commonplace. Officials of the Milwaukee Road, last of America's northern transcontinentals, held only a small ceremony when its lines met east of Missoula, Montana, in May 1909.[1]

Never in Pacific Northwest history was there a more lavish final spike ceremony than the one that took place in September 1883 at a site approximately

sixty miles west of Helena, Montana Territory, near the confluence of the Clark Fork River and Gold Creek. Alongside newly laid Northern Pacific track stood a sign that read, "Lake Superior 1,198 miles / Puget Sound 847 miles." Close by and decorated with pine boughs, bunting, and the flags of Germany, Great Britain, and the United States was a wooden pavilion. It was capable of seating nearly a thousand people, including five trainloads of special guests from both coasts. Festivities at Gold Creek captured in microcosm the significance of railroads in a hitherto remote part of the United States.

## Gold Creek and a New Northwest

HENRY VILLARD, A HANDSOME, genial man in his mid-fifties, hosted the festivities. As president of the Northern Pacific, Villard believed that his company's triumph over nature and economic adversity merited international attention. To the last spike ceremony he invited hundreds of politicians, bankers, railroad officials, investors, and journalists—not only from the United States but also from Great Britain and Germany, two countries that had given him substantial financial support. He personally orchestrated the symbolism of the occasion by displaying the flags of the three nations.

Morning festivities finally got underway at 3 p.m. on Saturday, September 8, when Villard gave the signal to begin. A brass band opened with "The Star-Spangled Banner" and other popular selections. Villard then summarized the twenty-year saga of the Northern Pacific. He later wrote that he felt "indescribably elated at this consummation of his peaceful conquest of the West."[2] Here was the realization of a long-standing quest for a cheap and easy land route to the far Northwest.

The day's featured speaker was the former secretary of state William Evarts. A local paper observed that his oration was "impressive" but its weightier passages bored the restless Montanans in his audience. Numerous other dignitaries, including the former president Ulysses S. Grant and governors of the states and territories through which the railroad passed, dutifully trooped to the podium to extoll the glory and importance of the Northern Pacific's achievement. They speechified so long that the sun had dropped behind the hills before it was time to drive the final spike.

Everyone adjourned to the right-of-way to watch rival construction teams lay the remaining twelve hundred feet of track. Although the two ends of the line had already met a few days earlier, this section was taken up to be spiked down again in a public display of joining East and West. After about twelve minutes of furious work, only one spike remained to complete the job. Guests crowded around. A variety of people took turns hammering it home, including Grant and Villard's wife, Fanny, after her infant son, four-month-old Hilgard, "had touched the spike with his little hands."[3]

The final spike and sledgehammer were specially wired so as to telegraph each blow to company officials waiting in Portland, St. Paul, and New York. Their receivers recorded a last click at 5:18 p.m., signaling that the northern transcontinental railroad was at last a reality. Because standard time had not yet been adopted, the final spike was driven home at 6:00 p.m. in Gold Creek and 5:30 in Portland, Oregon, where one newspaper described the day's festivities as an "iron wedding."[4] In Gold Creek, cannons boomed, bands played, locomotives whistled. Musicians concluded the ceremony with "God Save the Queen" and "Wacht am Rhein." Following a lavish banquet, many of Villard's guests accompanied him to the West Coast where still more celebrations and welcomes awaited them.

The festivities at Gold Creek proved a great promotional success for the Northern Pacific and signified the dawn of a new era for Pacific North-

*Photographer F. Jay Haynes immortalized completion of the Northern Pacific's transcontinental line at Gold Creek, Montana, on September 8, 1883. Haynes Foundation Collection, Montana Historical Society, H-999.*

westerners. The newness lay not in the railroad itself—local lines had existed in the region since the 1850s—but in the direct and convenient connection it provided to the East. Fourteen years after Promontory, Gold Creek opened the first railroad route to the far Northwest. Daily passenger trains now linked St. Paul and Portland, with connecting service north to Tacoma.

The new line reduced to five or six days a tiresome journey that once had required several months. For investors and homeseekers from distant regions as well as residents of the Pacific Northwest, an era of isolation had ended. Newcomers traveling by rail poured into the region, especially into Washington Territory, at a rate unimaginable only a decade earlier. Cities and farms transformed the landscape, and large-scale corporate enterprises and organized workers attained a prominence and power in the far Northwest that they had never possessed there before. The Oregon of the pioneer "is a thing of the past," observed the Portland *Oregonian*. "The transcontinental railroad has annihilated time and space, and at our door stands a train that is composed of cars loaded through from ocean to ocean. A new Oregon springs up to-day."[5]

Everything about Gold Creek was symbolic. That was Villard's intent. Yet some of the day's symbolism was subtle and ironic, and none more so than the various forms of juxtaposition so clearly visible to invited guests. Milling about the platform and reviewing stand were the financial barons of three nations dressed in the accoutrements that bespoke power in America's Gilded Age, while huddled nearby in a small and somewhat sullen group were Crow Indians, citizens of a shrinking hinterland already doomed to suffer great and lasting changes. During the previous summer on the plains of eastern Montana, hunters had waited in vain for the great herds of buffalo that annually ranged south from Canada in search of food. Out of the millions of shaggy beasts that roamed the Great Plains only a

decade earlier, fewer than two hundred remained in the entire American West by 1883. Only a year before, the Northern Pacific had hauled two hundred thousand hides out of Montana and Dakota.

Villard's "iron wedding" also represented the juxtaposition of city and country. Remote Gold Creek, like every other western settlement along the railway corridor, found itself enmeshed in a vast new market created by the nation's expanding network of railway lines. Westerners would supply raw materials needed to fuel America's industrial expansion, while manufactured goods from the East and Midwest would flow west to stock the shelves of general stores and lumberyards. Many would call this a colonial relationship. Here too were the men who supplied muscle power to build the new railway line. They worked for wages despite the popular impression that people went west to achieve personal freedom.

For one moment the old West of Indians, trappers, and pioneers stood face to face with the new West of high finance, nationwide markets, and rapid advances in communication and transportation. Wherever railroad tracks went, the old West confronted the new, but seldom so graphically as at Gold Creek. During the next quarter century, several more transcontinental lines were completed, each extending numerous branches into Northwest mining, timber, and agricultural country. But no decade would rival the 1880s for miles of track laid across the region, and the person doing most to create a coherent railway system amidst all the building was Henry Villard.

## Villard Takes Charge

LIKE THE EARLY HISTORY OF THE Northern Pacific Railroad, Villard's life was a chronicle of triumphs and bitter disappointments. Born Henrich Hilgard

*Crow Indians at the Northern Pacific's last spike ceremony at Gold Creek. Haynes Foundation Collection, Montana Historical Society, H-996.*

in German Palatine in 1835, he immigrated to the United States eighteen years later after a disagreement with his tyrannical father. He adopted the name Villard to prevent his father from learning of his whereabouts and forcing him back to Germany and service in the army. Penniless and an academic failure, he struggled to support himself as a common laborer.

Young Henry only gradually emerged from the German community, breaking free from a succession of menial jobs around the Midwest by working first as a reporter for German-American newspapers and then for the English-language press. He covered the Lincoln-Douglas debates of 1858, the presidential election two years later, and the Civil War. His Americanization continued when he married Fannie Garrison, only daughter of the well-known abolitionist, William Lloyd Garrison, in 1866. The ambitious young journalist also found time to study the rudiments of law, railroad promotion, and finance.

Villard pushed himself so hard that he suffered a physical breakdown and was forced to seek relief in the spas of Europe. It was there in 1872-73 that a group of worried German bondholders who had invested in Ben Holladay's Oregon railroad schemes asked Villard to become their overseas agent. This arrangement soon made him a rich man.

When Villard gained full control of the Oregon & California Railroad, the Oregon Central, the Oregon Steamship Company, and other Holladay properties in early 1876, his primary concern was to remedy the financial mess in the Willamette Valley. He soon found himself expanding upon and perfecting his predecessor's dreams of a transportation empire. Using Holladay's rail and river monopoly in the Willamette Valley as his financial base, Villard maneuvered to secure a similar position in the Columbia Valley by acquiring the venerable Oregon Steam Navigation Company for five million dollars in mid-1879. He reorganized the enterprise as the Oregon Railway & Navigation Company.

From the Oregon Steam Navigation Company, Villard acquired a Columbia River fleet of fourteen vessels, all but four of which were less than three years old, three portage railways, the Walla Walla & Columbia River Railroad, a telegraph line from Walla Walla to Portland, and various docks, wharves, and parcels of commercial real estate. The three portage lines consisted of the Cascades Railroad on the north bank of the Columbia, with six miles of roadbed and track, three locomotives, three passenger cars, and thirty-five boxcars; the largely abandoned Oregon Portage Railroad, with five miles of grading and trestles; and The Dalles & Celilo Railroad.

As its name implied, the Oregon Railway & Navigation Company operated a network of steamboats and railway lines spreading east from Portland to tap the agricultural riches of the Walla Walla Valley and other interior points. Originally, steamboats formed the backbone of the system and railroads functioned only as portage or feeder lines, but construction of hundreds of miles of railroad tracks during the first half of the 1880s reversed the roles.

In the spring of 1881 an army of two thousand laborers, most of them Chinese, began the tedious work of blasting and hacking a right-of-way through the Columbia River Gorge from The Dalles to Portland. Meanwhile, rails were in place, and a line opened from The Dalles east to Walla Walla by midsummer. Later, in 1882, the Oregon Railway & Navigation Company extended north from Walla Walla across sixty miles of rolling wheat country to the Snake River at Texas Ferry (Riparia), where steamboats carried passengers to Lewiston.

Even before tracks were in place, railroad officials prepared to inaugurate a luxury class of passenger service. They shipped parts for two sleeping cars from East Coast suppliers and had them assembled at shops in The Dalles. When displayed in Portland in 1882, the Wallula and Walla Walla attracted thousands of curious sightseers. Here was something new and even a bit bewildering to pioneer settlers. When one old frontiersman made his first trip by

*Henry Villard (1835–1900) combined the talents of a journalist, financier, railroad builder, and promoter to write an impressive signature across the landscape of the New Northwest. Oregon Historical Society, 555645, no. 1080.*

sleeping car, he brought along an ample supply of bedding, not realizing that such amenities were provided.

To develop the region's natural resources, Villard organized the Oregon Improvement Company in late 1880. Carried along by a boom psychology, he moved quickly to secure at almost any price choice coal and timber lands in the Cascade Range and agricultural lands in the Palouse country. He acquired the twenty-one-mile-long Seattle & Walla Walla Railroad, a coal hauler in the western foothills of the Cascades, and through this enterprise gained a large interest in the Pacific Coast Steamship Company, which dominated traffic along the western seaboard from Alaska south to Mexico.[6] Villard had already acquired the Oregon Steamship Company to serve primarily as an oceangoing counterpart to his Oregon Railway & Navigation Company monopoly. Controlling rail, river, and ocean traffic in the far Northwest proved exceedingly profitable. The Oregon Railway & Navigation Company quickly became one of the wealthiest transportation systems in the United States.

Like Holladay, Villard centered his financial interests on Portland, which in the 1860s and 1870s was the one true city in the Pacific Northwest. A visitor in the early 1870s observed,

Being the first city of importance north of San Francisco and the brains of our northwest coast, Portland was full of energy and vigor, and believed thoroughly in her future. The great Oregon Steam Navigation Company had their headquarters here, and poured into her lap all the right trade of the Columbia and its far reaching tributaries. . . . Back of her lay the valley of the Willamette, and the rich heart of Oregon; and her wharfs, indeed, were the gateways to thousands of miles of territory and trade, in all directions.[7]

Villard realized that to protect Portland's hegemony and prevent a Puget Sound community from becoming a dangerous rival, he had to consider the Northern Pacific Railroad a threat. It had previously selected Tacoma as its western terminus, although for much of the latter part of the 1870s the Northern Pacific seemed moribund. Yet if someone did succeed in reviving it, the northern transcontinental could jeopardize Villard's Portland-based transportation monopoly and real estate investments and create financial nightmares for him and his backers.

## Triumph and Crack-up

WHEN PROSPERITY RETURNED toward the end of the 1870s, the reorganized Northern Pacific Railroad under the leadership of Frederick Billings again pushed construction slowly forward. Villard attempted to limit its competitive impact by proposing the lower Snake River as a dividing line between Northern Pacific interests and his own. But when negotiations failed, Villard concluded that somehow he had to gain control of the Northern Pacific.

In an act of financial daring unprecedented in American history, Villard raised eight million dollars in the famous "Blind Pool" of 1881 to buy control of the Northern Pacific. Otherwise cautious investors whose respect for Villard verged on childlike faith (to this time he had exhibited a golden touch) put their money into a project about which they knew nothing. Villard took the equally bold step of forming a holding company, the Oregon & Transcontinental, in June 1881 to "protect" and harmonize his interests in the Northern Pacific, Oregon Railway & Navigation, Oregon & California, and Pacific Coast Steamship companies. It was one of the earliest uses of this form of corporate organization in the United States.

After Villard gained control of the Northern Pacific, the railroad at last seemed poised to fulfill its transcontinental destiny. Construction gangs began work at Ainsworth, a camp at the confluence of the Snake and Columbia rivers near where Pasco now stands, and pushed tracks northeast toward Montana. They reached Spokane in 1881, then only a village but soon to overtake Walla Walla as the main population center and transportation hub of the inland Northwest. Because of complex geology along the Clark Fork River, the 130 miles of track east from Lake Pend Oreille proved some of the most difficult to construct on the entire Northern Pacific Railroad. When outside contractors demanded exorbitant rates, the railroad undertook the job itself, using Chinese laborers and a variety of hand tools. Work continued through the winter with one crew shoveling snow so that another could lay track. The unexpectedly high cost of construction along the Clark Fork caused Villard serious financial trouble.

Rail service between Bonneville and eastern Washington commenced on May 20, 1882, and six months later the long anticipated day arrived when the first through passenger train left Portland for eastern Washington points. In charge was the conductor Edward Lyons, who a year later had responsibility for keeping passengers alive on the snowbound Pacific Express in the Columbia Gorge.

Attention now centered on completing the Northern Pacific line. In mid-1883 Villard became so obsessed that he abandoned all restraint as he raised money to pay for one final burst of construction. He became careless of financial details. One of his backers, William Endicott, grew disillusioned and even quipped to Villard that he had not yet made up his mind "whether it is you or Barnum . . . that has the greatest show on earth."[8]

When Northern Pacific rails finally met at Gold Creek in September 1883, Villard controlled a vast transportation empire and stood at the peak of his railroading career. The festivities represented a personal triumph, giving him a chance to demon-

strate to the world his passage from rags to riches. But what few onlookers realized at the time was that the real show at Gold Creek was Villard's walking along the edge of a financial precipice as storms gathered rapidly on all sides. A primary purpose of that last spike extravaganza was to commit the railroad's financial backers, especially the Germans, emotionally to the project before details of an embarrassing $14 million cost overrun became public knowledge a few weeks later.

Looking back, an observer could easily conclude that Villard's improbable career ended in one final blaze of glory. Within weeks of Gold Creek, a money crisis caused by his haste to complete the transcontinental tested the limits of Villard's financial genius. Disaster rained down on him from all sides. His physician warned him that stress could cause his physical collapse at any time. On January 4, 1884, Villard resigned from the Northern Pacific, citing nervous prostration as the primary reason. Only days earlier he had surrendered control of the Oregon Railroad & Navigation Company.

Villard left the United States the following June for Germany, where he spent the next two years seeking relief from his second physical breakdown. Many believed he was an utterly shattered man who would never regain health or power. Yet in 1887 he confounded all detractors by rising like a phoenix to take a seat on the Northern Pacific's board of directors and serve as head of the holding company he had created, the Oregon & Transcontinental. Backing him were German investors who had grown alarmed at the apparently senseless duplication of railways lines in the Pacific Northwest. Villard served as chairman of the Northern Pacific from 1889 until the railroad went bankrupt following the panic of 1893. During his second tenure, he tried unsuccessfully to mediate differences between Portland and Puget Sound–oriented carriers.

*Chinese and other workers prepare a roadbed for the Northern Pacific along the Clark Fork River at Big Bluff, Montana. At one time in 1882, Henry Villard's Oregon & Transcontinental holding company employed an army of 25,000 laborers, including 15,000 Chinese, all working furiously to complete both the Oregon Railway & Navigation Company line through the Columbia Gorge and the Northern Pacific through northern Idaho and western Montana. Oregon Historical Society, CN 002822, LOC/ORIG 0301-P-83.*

## Short Line to Oregon

**T**HE OREGON RAILWAY & NAVIGA-
tion Company tracks ran east from
Portland in the early 1880s to realize two
objectives: to tap the rich wheat country
of eastern Oregon and Washington and to form
a single connection into Portland for both the
Northern Pacific and Union Pacific roads. On the
map the tracks of the Oregon Railway & Navigation
Company somewhat resembled a funnel with its
base emptying at Portland. The mouth widened at
Umatilla: one side bent north along the Columbia

River to Wallula and a connection with the Northern
Pacific, while the other extended east over the Blue
Mountains toward Idaho where a potential rival had
emerged in the Union Pacific.

Villard's tracklaying frenzy in the early 1880s had
not been favorably regarded by Jay Gould, who
wanted the Union Pacific to have a West Coast
outlet of its own. Gould, like Villard, had risen from
rags to riches, but their business styles differed
greatly. Villard enjoyed putting his power on public
display, while Gould had such a penchant for secrecy
that newspaper cartoonists sometimes caricatured
him as a predatory spider lurking quietly in the

shadows. At the Union Pacific he held no office except as a member of the executive committee; the venerable Sidney Dillon served as president. Yet it was clear that the real power behind Dillon was Gould. During the years that Gould dominated the carrier (1874-84, 1890-92), he *was* the Union Pacific Railway Company. "His will was just as much law in it as the will of the captain of a frigate on board his ship."[9]

In March 1874 when Gould gained control of the Union Pacific, the railroad was complacent, tainted with scandal, and riddled with inefficiency. For several years after the final spike at Promontory, the Union Pacific seemed content to confine its activities to the Great Plains and central Rocky Mountains and let the Central Pacific line from Ogden to San Francisco Bay provide it access to the Pacific Coast. Gould developed an encyclopedic understanding of Union Pacific affairs in hopes of turning the company around. He also decided that the railroad would profit from a line to the Pacific Northwest, where a wealth of natural resources awaited development. In this way the Union Pacific emerged as the Northern Pacific's major competitor.

In the fall of 1877, when he was forty-one years old, Gould took over another moribund property, the Utah Northern Railroad, and pushed its narrow-gauge tracks across eastern Idaho toward the booming mines of Butte, Montana. In March 1880 the line crossed the Montana border at Monida Pass to become the first railroad in that territory; the following year it reached Butte. Gould considered building west from there to Oregon but decided instead to follow a route across southern Idaho

1615. MARUET GULCH TRESTLE

toward a connection with Villard's Oregon Railway and Navigation Company.[10]

With that goal in mind, a Union Pacific subsidiary company, the Oregon Short Line, was formed in April 1881. It commenced building west from Granger, Wyoming, on the main trunk of the Union Pacific and completed fifty miles of track that first year. Three years later, Oregon Short Line tracks stretched across the Snake River plain of southern Idaho and over the Snake River into Huntington, Oregon, where they met those of the Oregon Railway & Navigation Company.

In a very low-key ceremony on November 25, 1884, officials from both companies drove the final spike and had their locomotives touch pilots to signify the completion of a second transcontinental railroad to the Pacific Northwest. Six days later, through passenger trains began traveling the 1,820 miles that separated Omaha and Portland. A journey that once required six tiresome months on the Oregon Trail, the historic road that roughly paralleled the Union Pacific route much of the way to Portland, could now commence on Monday and be completed by Friday. A passenger with money could even enjoy the luxury of a through sleeping car.

Until this time, travelers and merchandise crossed the southern part of Idaho Territory by stagecoach or freight wagon from Central Pacific Railroad stations at Kelton, Utah, or Winnemucca, Nevada. In the early 1880s the first-class fare from Omaha to Kelton by train and on to Boise by stage was $96.75. A traveler could continue to Walla Walla by stage for a total of $106.75. An alternative was to take the train all the way to San Francisco and from there board a ship for Portland. Supporters of the latter route boasted that it offered no "disagreeable staging" over dusty roads.

When the Oregon Short Line was completed, it added several hundred more miles to the Union Pacific system. Unlike the railroad's other extensions at the time—which typically ended in some boom-and-bust Rocky Mountain mining camp—the Oregon Short Line actually went someplace. True to its name, its provided a shortcut from Omaha and Kansas City to Portland by eliminating the need to go by way of San Francisco. Within a year of its completion, the Oregon Short Line shipped millions of dollars' worth of gold bullion, livestock, and wool. Cattle traveled from Walla Walla to stockyards in Chicago, and wool went from Oregon and Idaho sheep ranches to mills as distant as Omaha, Philadelphia, and Boston.

A seventy-mile-long branch extended north from the main line at Shoshone into Idaho's Wood River valley, where important new discoveries of gold and silver had been made in the early 1880s. With the coming of railroads, managers brought in heavy machinery to tackle ever bigger mining jobs and transport low-grade ores profitably to distant smelters and markets. The Wood River branch not only tapped a new source of revenue but also enabled Gould and other affluent Americans to spend summer holidays with their families in the Wood River valley. The trains that hauled tourists brought settlers and helped stimulate economic development and population growth.

In 1885 the Oregon Short Line across southern Idaho served only one community of more than five hundred people. That was Weiser with seven hundred residents.[11] Pocatello, where the Oregon Short Line crossed the Utah & Northern, emerged as one of the Pacific Northwest's leading railroad centers. In 1881 the site was little more than a sagebrush-covered plain, but the Oregon Short Line reached Pocatello the next year and built the Pacific Hotel to accommodate its passengers. Pocatello by 1900 had become a transportation center—the Gate City, as it liked to style itself—and contained within its boundaries an industrial complex of railroad shops and yards.

*The heart of Oregon Short Line operations was Pocatello, Idaho, pictured here in 1914. Idaho State Historical Society, 2170-A.*

## Railroad Rivalry

WHEN VILLARD'S OVEREX-tended transportation empire collapsed in early 1884, the Oregon & Transcontinental lost control over the Northern Pacific but retained the Oregon Railway & Navigation Company, which for a brief time continued to provide a single link to the West Coast for both northern transcontinentals. In time the Oregon Railway & Navigation Company gravitated to the Union Pacific and became one of its subsidiaries. The Villard failure thus dashed any hope of creating a coherent railroad system in the Pacific Northwest. It left the Northern Pacific dependent on a rival to bridge the gap between Wallula and Portland, and it left an Oregon Railway & Navigation Company branch in the Palouse country north of the Snake River dependent on a Northern Pacific connection. The result was that by the late 1880s the Northern Pacific and Union Pacific were locked in a wild contest not only to rationalize their separate systems but also to build a latticework of competing lines across eastern Washington.

As for Portland's dream of serving as the hub of railroad service in the Pacific Northwest, in the summer of 1883 the Northern Pacific reluctantly decided to build its own main line west from Pasco, on the Columbia River, up the Yakima Valley and over the Cascade mountains to Tacoma. Although the 240-mile-long Cascade Branch would give the railroad access to Puget Sound entirely over its own tracks, its primary purpose was to forestall renewed efforts by Seattle citizens to build their own line to the Walla Walla Valley.

Mud, snow, and landslides plagued the builders of the Cascade Branch. They also experienced labor troubles. In the army of workers in 1886 were a thousand Chinese, but popular hostility to Asian labor was so great that the Chinese had to live under the protection of armed guards hired from the Thiel Detective Agency of Portland.

The biggest challenge was to bore a 1.8-mile-long tunnel under the crest of the Cascade mountains at Stampede Pass. Only one railroad tunnel in the United States was longer at the time. On February 13, 1886, drillers commenced work at the east portal using crude hand tools and blasting powder; later they used modern and more efficient pneumatic drills. After twenty-eight months of intense labor, workmen completed the tunnel. Surmounting the pass, 3,725 feet high, had formerly involved a complicated system of switchbacks—a series of zig-zag ascending and descending tracks; now Northern Pacific trains could cross the mountains with relative ease.[12]

On May 27, 1888, the first train rolled through Stampede Pass tunnel and opened a new gateway from Tacoma and Seattle to the East. As Portland backers feared, Northern Pacific trains over Stampede Pass redirected a substantial portion of the inland grain trade to Puget Sound ports. For the first time the metropolis on the Willamette River faced a serious challenger for economic dominance of the Pacific Northwest.[13]

Even as the Cascade Branch neared completion, intense competition between the Northern Pacific and Union Pacific led to massive overbuilding of the railroad lines across the Palouse country of eastern Washington and northern Idaho. As unbelievably productive as its seemingly endless wheatfields were, the Palouse had only widely scattered settlements and a minuscule population that could not possibly keep all the new miles of track profitable. It was just the sort of ruinous situation that Villard had returned to America in 1887 to prevent. But neither Villard nor anyone else could stop the madness.

The Columbia & Palouse Railroad, a subsidiary of the Oregon Railway & Navigation Company, tapped the Palouse country from the west by extending its tracks from the Northern Pacific main line at Connell to Colfax in 1883. This arrangement worked well enough when the three companies were allied

*A Northern Pacific train pauses near Stampede Pass in the late 1880s. White flags indicate that it was an extra or unscheduled train. Minnesota Historical Society, s4224.*

under Oregon & Transcontinental control, but Villard's collapse left the Columbia & Palouse an orphan, miles from the nearest Oregon Railway & Navigation tracks. Even so, several hundred Chinese laborers continued with hand tools and horse-drawn scrapers to prepare roadbed for tracks that finally reached Pullman and Moscow in mid-1885.

The Northern Pacific decided to run its own tracks into the Palouse from the north. A subsidiary, the Spokane & Palouse Railway, extended from the main line at Marshall Junction (near Spokane) as far south as Genesee, Idaho. There the company paused and seemed to have second thoughts about building a railway down the face of a two-thousand-foot escarpment to reach Lewiston and the Snake River. Tracklayers began instead at Pullman and built east through Moscow and down another canyon. They got as far as tiny Juliaetta in October 1891, when work ceased. Seven years later the Northern Pacific finally reached Lewiston.

A SNOW SHED.

The story was much the same south of the Snake River in the Walla Walla Valley, where the Union Pacific's successor to Dr. Baker's Road had long enjoyed a monopoly. Trouble erupted in 1888-89 when a little-known entrepreneur, George W. Hunt, built a second railroad from the Columbia River to Walla Walla with a branch south to Pendleton, Oregon. At one point Hunt's 161-mile-long Oregon & Washington Territory Railroad boldly talked of

striking out for southern Oregon and California's Sacramento Valley. Portland backers raised a subsidy of $500,000 to encourage Hunt to build down the Columbia River to their city, but the depression of 1893 prevented this. It was not clear who was behind Hunt, but the Union Pacific detected the hand of an old nemesis, the Northern Pacific.[14]

Viewing the Hunt system as an invasion of its territory south of the Snake River, the Union

Pacific's Oregon Railway & Navigation Company retaliated with a construction war, the last in the nineteenth century in the United States. Its tracks bridged the Snake at Riparia in 1888 and plunged boldly through the heart of the Palouse country to reach Spokane in 1889. South of Spokane, the railway also thrust a line east from the farming center of Tekoa into the booming Coeur d'Alene mining district and offered competitive rates to Portland for smelting and refining ores.[15]

On at least one occasion the railroad contest in eastern Washington turned violent: on September 16, 1887, a gang of men tore up Oregon Railway & Navigation tracks at Garfield. In the end, senseless duplication cost both railroads money. Yet the network of tracks also created a new "Inland Empire" of agriculture, mining, and logging all linked to the rapidly growing city of Spokane.

## Making Connections

RAILROAD CONSTRUCTION DURing the 1880s was not limited to eastern Washington, although its pace in the Palouse and in the Walla Walla Valley was far more accelerated than in any other part of the Pacific Northwest. The region's other great farming area in the 1880s was the Willamette Valley, but there the spur of competition was lacking. After a hiatus of almost ten years, construction resumed in 1883 on a line south from Roseburg toward the California border, to connect with Collis P. Huntington's Southern Pacific. At that time the Oregon & California Railroad consisted of two standard-gauge divisions, the East Side extending 262 miles south from Portland to Glendale, through Salem, Albany, Eugene, and Roseburg, and the West Side through Sheridan and Monmouth for 28 miles. A narrow-gauge division spanned the 90 miles from St. Paul to Coburg, Oregon.

Oregon & California tracks had only reached Ashland, 140 miles south of Roseburg, by the winter of 1884 when Villard's empire collapsed. The Oregon & California went into receivership and passed into Southern Pacific hands in 1887. The San Francisco–based railroad wasted little time completing a through line to Oregon, including a 3,700-foot tunnel under the Siskiyou Mountains in southern Oregon. Finally the line that had helped ruin both Ben Holladay and Henry Villard was a reality.

At a formal ceremony held in Ashland on December 17, 1887, Charles Crocker, one of California's original "Big Four" who built the Central Pacific line, drove the final spike. He reminded observers that Portland and New Orleans were now linked together by the tracks of the Southern Pacific Railroad Company, the longest railway system in the world with a network of approximately five thousand miles of line. For years the Southern Pacific remained the largest nongovernment employer west of the Mississippi River, and as a result of land acquired through the Oregon & California Railroad, it became one of America's largest private landholders.[16]

In the United States, the term *transcontinental railroad* was generously applied to any line that joined the Midwest with the Pacific coast. In fact, during the 1880s only the Southern Pacific extended from sea to sea, or at least from the Gulf of Mexico to the Pacific Ocean. North of the border, however, the Canadian Pacific forged a true transcontinental line extending from Montreal to the Pacific port of Vancouver. On November 7, 1885, Donald Alexander Smith drove home a final spike at Craigellachie, in the Rocky Mountains west of Revelstoke, British Columbia. His first attempt was a glancing blow that bent the plain iron spike. Smith's second try was more successful. With a connecting line south to Seattle opened in 1891, it offered residents of western Washington easy access to the vast dominion served by the Canadian Pacific.

*One of the Oregon Railway & Navigation Company's mixed freight-and-passenger trains paused atop the 900-foot-long Alto trestle in western Columbia County in this undated photograph. Located ten miles north of Waitsburg and forming a vital link in the line between Pendleton and Spokane, the structure collapsed without warning on August 5, 1894. A train of sixteen cars loaded with wheat, flour, and ore plunged into the ravine. None of the five crew members was killed, although two suffered broken arms, bruises, and cuts. The engine had just made it across when the engineer felt the bridge start to sway. Angelus collection, 650, Special Collections, Knight Library, University of Oregon.*

One more northern transcontinental line, James J. Hill's Great Northern Railway, was completed before the financial panic of 1893 abruptly ended the Pacific Northwest's first railway age. Hill, working almost entirely without benefit of land grants and having to pay market prices for a right-of-way, carefully reached west from St. Paul to Seattle by building or acquiring track in a variety of ways. In 1887 his St. Paul, Minneapolis & Manitoba Railway headed west to serve the rapidly growing Red River valley that separated Minnesota and Dakota Territory and eventually reached Minot. From there an army of ten thousand graders and bridge builders pushed

onward six hundred miles to Great Falls, Montana, a city recently platted on the banks of the upper Missouri River. Laying an average of 3½ miles of track a day, Hill's men meet the Montana Central Railway building northeast from Helena. Tracks of the expanding system continued south to the mining city of Butte, where they connected with those of the Northern Pacific and Union Pacific roads.

It soon became clear that Hill did not intend to stop in central Montana. Early in 1889 he acquired the Fairhaven & Southern Railroad in Washington Territory and extended it from the Canadian border south to the town of Burlington. The line would

*This is part of the army of construction workers that built the St. Paul, Minneapolis & Manitoba Railway across Montana in 1887. Between April 2 and November 19 the men finished grading and tracklaying across 642 miles of the territory. When rails reached the Rocky Mountains, the "skyscraper" dormitory cars had to be cut down to fit through tunnels. Minnesota Historical Society, HE6.41G/P12.*

play a key role in facilitating Hill's entry into western Washington and the rich farmlands of British Columbia's lower Fraser River. In late December, John F. Stevens, a widely respected civil engineer, located Marias Pass in western Montana, where a railroad could cross the summit of the Rocky Mountains at an elevation of only 5,214 feet. This discovery, which was contrary to popular expectations that Hill could not find a low-cost route through the Rocky Mountains, opened the way for him to build west to the Pacific Coast. In August 1890 work began on a Puget Sound extension from a point four miles west of Havre, Montana. At about the same time, Hill was elected president of the recently incorporated Great Northern Railway, which absorbed the Manitoba Road. The new name

reflected not only the territory it served but also the high opinion Hill and his associates had of the Great Northern Railway in England.

Hill considered Bellingham Bay for his Pacific terminus, but Judge Thomas A. Burke persuaded him to choose Seattle instead. The Northern Pacific, which had a vested interest in promoting Tacoma as the metropolis of Puget Sound, originally relegated upstart Seattle to a branch line. A bitter rivalry pitted the two communities against one another. It was in the context of their battle that Burke organized the Seattle & Montana Railway to bring Great Northern tracks into Seattle. He also acquired sixty acres at Smith Cove, on the north edge of town, to provide space for the Great Northern's shops and docks. But not until 1900 did Hill's

selection of Seattle seem irrevocable. By that date, however, Seattle had surpassed Tacoma in population and during the next decade would pull ahead of Portland.

The driving of a final spike in late 1891 completed a railway line between Seattle and the Fraser River towns of New Westminister and Vancouver. East of the Cascade Range, the tracks of the Pacific extension reached Spokane on June 1, 1892. Hill persuaded city fathers to grant the Great Northern a right-of-way through the heart of town lest he bypass Spokane altogether. Working in various locations, Hill's Swedish and Italian tracklayers forged ahead with remarkable speed. On August 13, 1892, they set the daily record for the Pacific extension by spiking down slightly more than four miles of track near Harrington, Washington.

Workmen narrowed the gap between east and west and finally closed it on January 7, 1893, at Madison (later Scenic), 13 miles west of the summit of the Cascade Range and 1,727 miles from St. Paul. Starting work at 6:00 a.m., tracklayers completed the last nine thousand feet of track at 8:00 that evening. Illuminated only by lanterns and locomotive headlights, the superintendents Cornelius Shields and J. D. Farrell took turns driving home the final iron spike. So unpretentiously was the deed done that laborers standing only a few years away were not aware of what happened until the little group on the spot cheered. Two hundred jubilant workers commenced to yell as the two superintendents fired their revolvers into the night air. Hill was ill in St. Paul and could not attend, but the Twin Cities celebrated completion of his Pacific extension on June 7, 1893. Seattle held its own celebration on July 4, two weeks after the Great Northern's first regularly scheduled passenger train arrived from St. Paul.

After the tracks were joined in January, Hill was impatient to launch through passenger service to tap the market created by the Chicago world's fair in

1893, but the Northern Pacific thwarted his plans by reducing the time for its premier train from Puget Sound to St. Paul to seventy hours, a schedule the Great Northern could not hope to match on its newly laid and not yet settled track. On June 18, however, the Great Northern established a seventy-two-hour schedule for its fastest passenger train from St. Paul to Seattle, and that included crossing the Cascade Range by means of a slow and cumbersome system of switchbacks. Work began on a 2.6-mile-long tunnel in 1897. When it opened in 1900, it reduced the elevation of the Great Northern's Cascade crossing from 4,059 to 3,375 feet. But as the worst railroad accident in Pacific Northwest history later demonstrated, even that elevation was not low enough to avoid destructive avalanches.

## End of an Era

THE FIRST RAILWAY AGE ENDED not with a natural disaster but with a financial one. Panic on Wall Street in mid-1893 whipped up a storm of economic troubles across America. For nearly half a decade, until 1897, the Pacific Northwest suffered through the worst depression in its history apart from the hard times of the 1930s. Within the first six months nearly five hundred banks and sixteen thousand businesses failed in the United States. Of the five transcontinental railroads only the Great Northern and Southern Pacific remained solvent.

For the Union Pacific the financial collapse of the 1890s marked the end of a long struggle. When Jay Gould lost control of the Union Pacific in 1884, it passed into the hands of New England investors. Charles Francis Adams, Jr., a Bostonian, served as president from 1884 to 1890. He sought to reduce expenses and rebuild the property, but he was not a good administrator. Adams later admitted that he was over his head and never could master the complex

*Madison Street ended at the station and yards of the Seattle, Lake Shore & Eastern Railway. This Seattle location was also the western end of James J. Hill's Great Northern Railway. City residents were in the process of rebuilding from the disastrous fire of 1889 when F. Jay Haynes took this picture. Haynes Foundation Collection, Montana Historical Society, H-2258.*

financial structure of the badly overextended Union Pacific system.

After Gould and Sidney Dillon regained direct control in November 1890, they broke off the costly construction war in the Pacific Northwest. But neither draconian measures nor the wealth of its Oregon Railway & Navigation subsidiary could save the Union Pacific after 1893. Gould, however, was not around to see the crash. He died on December 2, 1892. At the age of fifty-six, he was a man worn out by a long struggle to build a railroad empire and amass a fortune of $72 million. Before prosperity returned in 1897, the railroad had been shorn of both the Oregon Short Line and the Oregon Railway & Navigation Company. Only after the financier Edward H. Harriman acquired and reorganized the Union Pacific did the carrier become what it remains today, one of the most financially secure railroads in the United States.

The collapse of the Northern Pacific in 1893 for the second time in a decade ended Henry Villard's extraordinary railroad career. The one-time financial baron—who had also served as president of the Edison General Electric Company from 1889 to 1892—died in 1900, though not without leaving behind an impressive signature in the Pacific Northwest. It was a signature written not just in iron and steel rails but also in the form of books, laboratory equipment, and other aid he gave the University of Oregon and the University of Washington during their years of financial struggle.

If the hard times of the 1890s produced a clear winner it was the Great Northern Railway and James J. Hill, who saw his cautious approach to empire building vindicated. Unlike the Union Pacific or Northern Pacific, two companies that suffered from a heavy burden of debt, the Great Northern—Hill's Folly, the critics had called it—worked its way west almost entirely on a pay-as-you-go basis, constructing branch lines and encouraging agricultural settlement along the right-of-way rather than depending on government land grants. So soundly was the Great Northern financed that it survived the depression of the 1890s in good financial health while scores of other lines across the United States went bankrupt. By "close economy we were able to weather the storm," Hill later bragged to an associate.[17] Hill and Harriman would emerge as the dominant figures in the new railway age that dawned with the return of prosperity in 1897.

*Built upon faith in a virgin country, with a restless, expansive, ambitious people,*
*the road is ever solicitous for development, being wholly unable to look upon its*
*plains and mountains except with the eye of the prophetic imagination.*
—Ray Stannard Baker, "Destiny and the Western Railroad," Century Magazine
*(April 1908)*

# Shapers of a New Northwest

EARLY IN THE FALL OF 1877, JAY Gould invited the Union Pacific's general passenger agent, Thomas L. Kimball, to join him on a fishing trip to Lake Gogebic in a remote corner of Michigan's upper peninsula. Those who knew Gould guessed correctly that he had something more important than bass and pickerel on his mind. He was a man of such intense seriousness that he seemed unable to relax even on family outings. In fact, Gould had been giving a great deal of thought to expansion of the Union Pacific, which in 1877 consisted primarily of a trunk line from Omaha, Nebraska, to Ogden, Utah. With competitors, real and imagined, threatening to invade Union Pacific territory from the north and south, Gould prepared to fight back with a new line to the Pacific Northwest. He wanted to make certain that homeseekers and investors followed on the heels of his tracklayers into the undeveloped country.

When discussion on Lake Gogebic turned to matters of advertising, Kimball handed Gould a copy of a recent publication he had hastily thrown into his suitcase before leaving Omaha. It was called *The Hand-Book of Wyoming and Guide to the Black Hills and Big Horn Regions for Citizen, Emigrant and Tourist*. Its author was Robert Strahorn, a relatively unknown journalist based in Denver. Gould thumbed through the book and was sufficiently impressed to ask Kimball, "Might not this fellow Strahorn be a good man to put over our publicity?"[1]

Gould wanted Strahorn to form a "literary" department for the railroad and prepare a book of several hundred pages setting forth the resources and attractions of the country west of the Missouri River. He was to follow this with a flood of leaflets, maps, folders, and special newspaper inserts. Strahorn's assignment would be nothing less than to create a New Northwest of the imagination. Only recently he had reported on the aftermath of the Custer massacre at Little Big Horn; now he could become a key player in a process that railroad publicists would later describe as the second winning of the West.

## Robert Strahorn's Second Winning of the West

ROBERT EDMUND STRAHORN WAS a tall, angular man with piercing black eyes and a distinctive black mustache that curled up at the ends. His face would never be as familiar as that of James J. Hill or Edward Harriman, but he might well have been involved in more phases of empire building than many better-known figures were. During the Pacific Northwest's first railway age, he was primarily a publicist. From 1877 to 1885, when he had charge of the Union Pacific's Literary Bureau, he wrote seven different guidebooks. He prepared another five on his own during the latter half of the 1880s. Of the first set, the legislatures of Idaho, Wyoming, and Montana purchased and distributed copies by the thousands. Strahorn was also involved in town-building projects, notably Caldwell, Idaho. During the region's second railway age, "Uncle Bob" emerged as a builder of electric power systems and railroad lines. Ironically, he died insolvent in 1944 at the age of 92, and for a man who was so successful a publicist, he never succeeded in getting his own autobiography into print.

In his lengthy manuscript (written in 1942) Strahorn records that he was born in Pennsylvania in 1852 of Scots-Irish ancestry. As a teenager he spent five years in Missouri learning the printing trade. But that state's numerous problems after the Civil War caused him to wonder, "Why struggle with the wreckage, with the poignant memories of defeat, when a virgin land in the West opened wide its arms to welcome new effort at victory?"[2] The call of the West took Strahorn to Denver, Colorado, in 1870, where he worked as editor, correspondent, and reporter for seven years. In 1877 he wrote his first publication devoted to the West, the one about Wyoming that fell into the hands of Jay Gould. The book represented a turning point in his life.

Strahorn, however, almost dropped out of Gould's Literary Bureau before it got properly launched when J. T. Clark, general superintendent of the Union Pacific, refused to allow Strahorn's bride of a few weeks to accompany him on fact-gathering trips through the West. The angry husband blurted out, "Very well, then, here is where the Union Pacific and the Strahorns part company." As Strahorn made his way to the door, Clark bellowed back to

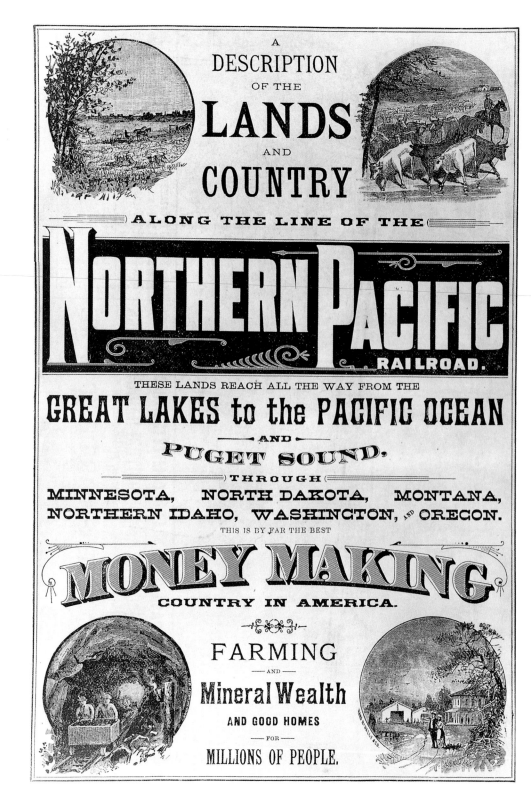

his secretary, "Oh, well, Jack, if this damned funny youngster can't travel without his wife, I guess we'd better make an exception, so fix her up with a pass."[3]

It is fortunate that Clark relented: Carrie Adell Strahorn recalled five strenuous years of travel from her own perspective in a delightful book, *Fifteen Thousand Miles by Stage* (1911). After accompanying her husband on many fact-gathering trips, she described his work: "We spent some weeks on Wood River gathering statistics which Pard [her husband] wove into entertaining narrative, clothing it in attractive garb that it might coquette with restless spirits in the far East who were waiting for an enchantress to lure them to the great mysterious West."[4]

With her at his side during most of his adventures, Strahorn recalled, "There were the hundreds of mines to burrow into, the hundreds of businessmen, farmers, stock raisers, and public authorities to interview, all in three short months, for the book must be written, printed, and in circulation in four. I soon learned to make notes and even roughly write under every imaginable condition, except when asleep."[5]

Strahorn had a passion for collecting accurate facts and figures and for reprinting human-interest stories. He also became involved in promoting tourism as well as settlement. In various editions of *To the Rockies and Beyond* published in 1878 and 1881, he was one of the first persons to trumpet Shoshone Falls, Payette Lake, the mineral waters of Soda Springs, and other natural wonders of southern Idaho, an area formerly regarded as a desert. During his years with the Union Pacific, Strahorn prepared and launched "carloads" of promotional literature upon a public "that was eagerly receptive," but he later lamented that compared to Henry Villard's massive publicity campaigns his own looked puny. In 1882 alone, Villard's Northern Pacific Railroad contracted with hundreds of agencies in Europe to distribute thousands of pamphlets in several languages to extol the virtues of the Pacific Northwest.[6]

## Promotion of Settlement and Investment

GOVERNOR EDWARD S. SALOMON of Washington complained in 1871 that "numerous reports have been written and published on the resources of this Territory, many of which have been too highly colored. People, misled by the representations, have come here with great expectations and found themselves sadly disappointed. Our Territory offers inducements enough to settlers, and it is entirely unnecessary to state anything but the truth."[7]

Salomon was wrong: truth was not enough. The Pacific Northwest did not sell itself. Of four million people who immigrated to the West Coast between 1850 and 1910, the vast majority went to California. Boosters needed to sell the Great Northwest to people who might otherwise easily gravitate to the Golden State. Salesmanship was especially vital before completion of the Northern Pacific Railroad in 1883 made overland travel to the nation's Far Corner easy.

Promotion of the Oregon Country dated back to 1817 and the fanaticism of Hall Jackson Kelley. A little more than a decade after Lewis and Clark returned from their three-year trek to the North Pacific coast, and well before anyone could imagine a railroad line across the continent, the Boston schoolmaster became obsessed with the idea of planting a colony of American settlers in Oregon. His proposal was clearly designed to bolster America's tenuous claims to the distant region.

Kelley and other early boosters of the Pacific Northwest, like Senator Thomas Hart Benton of Missouri, were most effective in drawing public attention to the Willamette Valley and the fertile agricultural land that was free for the taking. That was a powerful enough attraction to lure thousands of settlers in the 1840s and 1850s despite an arduous journey by land or sea. Other parts of the region, however, were still depicted in negative terms: explorers and Oregon-bound settlers alike had little good to say about the seemingly endless sagebrush plains of southern Idaho and eastern Oregon. As late as the 1860s and 1870s, only gold and silver could draw a significant number of non-Indians there, and then most newcomers were only temporary residents.

Over the years the work of selling the Great Northwest proceeded in haphazard fashion. A common pattern was for state or territorial governments to establish immigration or promotion bureaus but fail to fund their work. Oregon formed a State Board of Immigration as early as 1874, but because a penurious legislature failed to appropriate any money, the board remained little more than a private outlet for Portland businessmen.

Unlike the Midwest, the Pacific Northwest was less a product of systematic state-backed promotions than of individual boosters, real estate agents, newspaper editors, private immigration societies, chambers of commerce (often called commercial clubs), various "improvement companies," and especially railroads. All had a common desire to attract settlers and investors in order to promote economic growth and guarantee a prosperous future. "Real Estate is the foundation of all wealth, as well as the backbone of the universe. The golden opportunity of becoming the Rothschild of Seattle is now within your grasp. Why delay?" asked one promoter of land near suburban Green Lake in 1888.[8]

In a later era, primarily in the early twentieth century, timber companies became promoters in order to sell their logged-off lands to agriculturalists. Thousands of acres of "virgin logged-off land" of proven fertility awaited development, claimed one

Potlatch Lumber Company brochure, *Fertile Logged-off Lands of Latah County, Idaho*. This was only one of hundreds, perhaps even thousands, of *different* promotional pamphlets designed to sell the New Northwest. "One is simply amazed at the vast amount of money, energy, patience, and persistence there is devoted to setting forth the resources, advantages, capabilities, and wonders of this part of the continent," observed one visitor in 1888.[9]

Advertising was not limited to printed materials. It also took the form of oratory and elaborate displays at fairs and expositions, including the great national ones held in Philadelphia in 1876 and Chicago in 1893. The Union Pacific in the mid-1880s hired a special agent to distribute samples of potatoes and apples from the Pacific Northwest to prospective settlers.[10]

In all forms of promotion, it was clear by the 1870s that railroads had taken the lead. When the pioneer settler Ezra Meeker wrote and published a book in 1870 called *Washington Territory West of the Cascade Mountains*, the financier Jay Cooke bought every copy. Joking that he would not tolerate competitors in the far Northwest, he proceeded to distribute Meeker's book as part of his own effort to promote the Northern Pacific. At one time Cooke ran advertisements for the railroad in eleven hundred different newspapers. One popular publication was the *Northern Pacific Settler's Guide*, which first appeared in 1872.

The Northern Pacific, needing to convert its immense landholdings into cash to finance construction, became for a time the region's most important promoter and colonizing agent. Under the energetic leadership of James B. Power, the company's land department scattered agents throughout the United States and Europe. After Villard gained control of the Northern Pacific in 1881, the promotional efforts further accelerated. The apparent payoff was the flood of new settlers into areas tributary to the Northern Pacific in the 1880s.

Villard's involvement in merchandising the Northwest dates from 1874, when he urged the Oregon & California Railroad to establish a land office in Portland to expedite sale of its holdings. The company also opened an office in Boston, which Villard contrived to have designated the Eastern Bureau of the Oregon State Board of Immigration. From there he hoped to encourage migration of farm families from rural New England to Oregon. Both offices displayed samples of Pacific Northwest products and issued brochures that reached even northern and western Europe, where inquiries encouraged publication of additional brochures in languages other than English. The Boston bureau issued twenty thousand special immigrant brochures in English and another five thousand in German. Villard himself wrote several circulars and pamphlets. The railroad soon opened agencies in England and Scotland as well as additional ones closer to home, in Omaha and Topeka, where agriculturalists from the Great Plains might be enticed to the Pacific Northwest.

In 1875 the Oregon & California Railroad undertook an even more extensive promotional campaign, spending $24,000 on its Portland and Boston agencies that year alone. The following year the railroad's land department also had an exhibit at the Centennial Exposition in Philadelphia, but by that time it was also clear that rival agents boosting California diverted many would-be immigrants to the Pacific Northwest. The Oregon & California sent a special representative to San Francisco to challenge local boosters, while another Villard enterprise, the Oregon Steamship Company, sought ways to speed transfer of Oregon-bound settlers from trains to ships in San Francisco before the Golden State could seduce them.

T. R. Tannatt, who became head of promotional activities for the various Villard companies, traveled through the East in 1878 to distribute samples of Pacific Northwest products and arrange for ticket sales to the region. Following formation of the Oregon Railway & Navigation Company in 1879, extensive efforts were also made to boost eastern

portions of Oregon and Washington as well as Idaho, areas hitherto largely ignored by promoters except for Robert Strahorn. Pamphlets issued by various organizations emphasized the legendary fertility of the soil and the mild climate in order to lure midwestern farmers. Also helping to focus public attention on lands east of the Cascade Range was Villard's Oregon Improvement Company, which purchased 150,000 acres of Palouse land from the Northern Pacific for $2.60 per acre and established a special department to colonize them.

After the Northern Pacific came under Villard's control, both it and the Oregon railroads devoted special attention to European immigration to the Pacific Northwest, especially from Germany and the United Kingdom, the two countries that provided Villard so much financial support. In 1883 the Northern Pacific had 831 active local agents in the United Kingdom alone. They distributed Pacific Northwest brochures to agricultural shows, fairs, and weekly stock and grain markets. Another 124 agents were busy on the continent recruiting immigrants from Norway, Sweden, Denmark, Holland, Switzerland, and Germany. More than six hundred thousand copies of Northern Pacific publications were distributed in English, Norwegian, Swedish, Dutch, Danish, German, and Finnish.[11]

The publicist who came closest to being Robert Strahorn's counterpart on the Northern Pacific was Eugene V. Smalley. To each of the several

*Displays inside the Northern Pacific's exhibition car allowed visitors to view for themselves the wonders of the New Northwest. Haynes Foundation Collection, Montana Historical Society, H-3311.*

hundred special guests gathered at Gold Creek in September 1883, Villard proudly presented copies of Smalley's 437-page *History of the Northern Pacific Railroad*. A former correspondent for the New York *Tribune* and an old friend of Villard's, who was also once an employee of the *Tribune*, Smalley contracted with the Northern Pacific to produce a series of guidebooks and pamphlets. In 1885 he lived in a caboose for eight weeks traveling between St. Paul and Tacoma to gather statistics for a new guidebook, *The Great Northwest* (1888). He also edited the *Northwest Magazine*, a promotional journal first published in Minnesota in 1883 and subsidized by Villard and the Northern Pacific. Articles were often reprinted as special flyers, and copies of the magazine were sometimes reissued in German, Swedish, and Norwegian.[12]

Strahorn was correct when he observed that his promotional efforts for the Union Pacific paled in comparison to those of the Villard companies. But Villard had the added incentive of converting land grants into money: his Oregon & California and Northern Pacific lines had land grants; Union Pacific subsidiaries in the Pacific Northwest did not. North of the border the Canadian Pacific also had vast landholdings at its disposal, but the Great Northern had only about a million acres, remnants of grants made to predecessor lines. That did not discourage the ever-resourceful Hill, whose agents lured farmers to settle along the Great Northern by a variety of methods, including distribution of eight hundred purebred bulls to improve their stock.

## Reshaping the Pacific Northwest through Promotion

UNLIKE RAILROAD LINES IN Great Britain or the eastern half of the United States, which slipped easily into the existing landscape, those in the West played a major role in reshaping the countryside through promotional activity. A good example was the Great Northern's extension from mid-Montana to Seattle. When the railroad company completed the line in 1893, the *Northwest Magazine* observed that only three important freight-producing centers—Kalispell, Bonners Ferry, and Spokane—lay along the entire fifteen hundred miles of track. Yet within a decade, the Great Northern had made possible the rise of numerous farms, orchards, cattle ranches, and sawmills that forever changed the landscape.[13]

Perhaps nowhere was the process of transformation better illustrated than in Idaho. The first book with a reference to future Idaho was Sergeant Patrick Gass's journal, initially published in 1807. As a member of the Lewis and Clark expedition, he saw with his own eyes the "horrible mountainous desert" about which he wrote. In another place he described the Bitterroot Range as "the most terrible mountains I ever beheld."[14]

In 1836 when the noted author Washington Irving published his history of the 1810-12 overland journey of fur traders known as the Astorians, he portrayed the Snake River plain in equally unflattering terms. It was a barren and desiccated place where the would-be fur traders meandered needlessly and suffered hunger, sickness, and death. So great was the thirst of the Astorians that they were, in Irving's delicate language, driven "to the most revolting means of allaying it"—by drinking their own urine.[15]

The explorer John C. Fremont commented in a government report widely disseminated by his father-in-law, Senator Thomas Hart Benton, that at Fort Hall (near present-day Pocatello) "there does not occur, for a distance of nearly three hundred miles to the westward, a fertile spot of ground sufficiently large enough to produce the necessary quantity of grain, or pasturage enough to allow even temporary repose to the emigrants."[16] Here was where Oregon-bound immigrants most feared

Indian attack and where the heat of summer and the lack of water withered their once high spirits.

The most that could be said for the Snake River country was that it contained fascinating geological features like Shoshone Falls, Thousand Springs, and Soda Springs. The missionary Narcissa Whitman and other early travelers commented on these natural phenomena.[17] Discovery of precious metals in the Clearwater country and Boise Basin in the early 1860s attracted gold seekers to Idaho, and also merchants, stock raisers, and farmers. Mormon agrarians established a series of settlements in the extreme southeastern corner of Idaho.

Even so, Idaho was not widely promoted as a desirable place for home, health, or recreation until the advent of transcontinental railroads during the 1860s and 1870s. None of the northern transcontinentals had touted Idaho as a final destination, but all had an interest in developing the land through which they passed. Their promotional activities sought to create new and desirable landscapes to lure investors and tourists and, most especially, settlers. When the Oregon Short Line issued a pamphlet for agriculturalists called *Man with the Hoe in Idaho*, it was a reflection of how railroads, combined with irrigation, had transformed an area once considered only a desert.

## The Right People:
## Patterns of Settlement

TO POPULATE THE AREA ALONG their tracks, railroads of the Pacific Northwest regularly ran homeseekers' specials and carried immigrant families and their belongings at reduced rates. Railroad land sold for prices that ranged from $1.25 to $20.00 an acre, depending on its perceived value, but the companies frequently gave discounts for cash. They also instituted a variety of low down-payment plans to speed

settlement and generate much-needed traffic. Agents met immigrants at dockside in New York and other East Coast ports and helped them travel west to settle on lands the company had reserved for specific nationalities. This arrangement was one reason why Germans, Scandinavians, and Russian settlers tended to cluster in distinct rural communities along railroad corridors from the Dakotas through Washington. Though some observers claimed that railroads could not afford to be choosy about the immigrants needed to populate their land, the focus of promotional activity made it plain that railroads sought only the "right sort" of people. In this they mirrored the widely held belief that some immigrant groups were undesirable.[18]

Oregon's new governor Sylvester Pennoyer spelled out this notion clearly in his 1887 inaugural address when he urged legislators to remove "the curse of Chinese labor." Once they had done so, "the hardy immigrants of our own race will flock here without invitation and help build up our free institutions and enlarge the glories of our State."[19]

Hostility to the Chinese was widespread, but they were not the only victims of popular prejudice. Henry Villard in 1874 had personally selected Boston over New York City for the Oregon & California's East Coast bureau because he "believed New England immigrants were the most desirable ones for the state, and certainly more so than the motley crowds of foreigners landing in the other city." An 1884 editorial in the *West Shore*, a prominent literary and promotional journal published in Portland, distinguished between "intelligent foreigners" and all others. The magazine made it clear that "honest peasant farmers and laborers" came from England, Ireland, and Germany; Italians and Hungarians were willing "to live like beasts." The editor of the *West Shore* was Samuel Leopold, who, like Villard, was originally from Germany.[20]

The Northern Pacific Railroad emphasized in its 1882 report to stockholders that through its agents in

*The Northern Pacific advertised for Scandinavian laborers to help construct its Cascade line. The company hoped that once the tracks were in place, workers who built the line would take up farms along the right-of-way. Minnesota Historical Society, 54215.*

**200 Skandinaviske Arbeidere Önskes**

i

**Washington Territory.**

**Daglönnen: $2.00.**

**200** Skandinaver kan finde Arbeide ved begyndelsen paa

**Cascade Linien av NORTHERN PACIFIC Jernbanen.**

i Washington Territory for **$2.00** om Dagen; kan man endog faa erholde Kontrakt paa

**"Station"-Arbeide.**

Reisen for halv Pris til Washington Territory for Skandinaviske Familier. Denne Pris gjälder kun for gifte Mänd med Familier. Arangemang er bleven treffet med Northern Pacific Jernbanen for at transportere 200 Skandinaviske Familier til

**NORTH YAKIMA, Washington Territory**

**För $25.** Börn emellen 5 og 12 Aar halv Pris og under 5 Aar frit. Husholdnings gjendstande $100.00 per Car Läs.

Dette er en udmarket anledning for 200 Skandinaviske Familier i ansögning maa ske strax at forskaffe sig billig Reise til Washington Territory hvor Arbeide kan umiddelbartigen erholdes med god Daglön eller Station Arbeide ved Jernbanen, som gaar igjennem et rigt Jordbrugs- og Havuland, hvilket Land ogaa er rigt paa Miniraler. Arbeidet vil vare de 12 följende Maaneder, maaske meget lengere. Arbeiderne kan om dem önsker blive Settlere paa Gouvernement- eller Jernbane-Land, tage sig Farm og erholde sig gode Hjem.

Der findes millioner Acres av frugtbart og smukt Land i disse Regioner, nu aabnet for Settlere under "homestead", "pre emption", og "timber culture" Loavene og billigt Jernbane Land paa tem og ti Aars betalningstid.

Ansögning maa gjöres strax, kun 200 Familier modtages paa disse Villkaar her nämt.

Ansögning gjöres hos

**S. D. Mason,**

Principal Assistant Engineer,

**Northern Pacific Jernbane.**

**Principal Office:**

**ST. PAUL, MINN.**

Europe the company engaged in a systematic and successful effort "to secure a good class of settlers for the country tributary to the Northern Pacific Road." The report specifically mentions promotional activity in the United Kingdom, Sweden, Norway, Denmark, Switzerland, and northern German ports:

These efforts have resulted in sending large numbers of industrious and thrifty people from foreign countries to the Northern Pacific territory. In this connection the fact is worthy of mention that a large portion of the laborers employed in the construction work on the Yellowstone Division are intelligent Scandinavians and Germans, who will settle on the line of the road as soon as it is completed, and aid in developing the country tributary to it.[21]

Villard's own northern European heritage clearly influenced railroad thinking on immigration.

As for the first inhabitants of the Pacific Northwest, railroad builders considered Indian reservations to be nonproductive land. The Northern Pacific informed stockholders in 1884, "The Coeur d'Alene, the Yakima and the Puyallup Indian reservations continue to embarrass the Company, prevent the settlement of the lands, and deprive the Company to that extent of the benefits that would otherwise be had."[22]

As late as 1907 a Milwaukee Road pamphlet boasted that "one by one the Indian reservations are being turned over to the settlers who can till the ground intelligently." An especially desirable tract was the Flathead reservation of western Montana: "This has not yet been opened up, but the would-be settlers are watching eagerly for chances to make entries there." It took a year or two, added a commentator in the *Outlook*, "'to get the Indian out of the soil,' as the phrase goes; and very often within the year the land begins to show in tilled fields and the homes of men."[23]

The "ideal settler for Montana and the one we are trying to reach," emphasized the Milwaukee Road,

"is the man who has made a moderate success in the East, but who is too ambitious to be satisfied with slow progress and too wise to overlook great opportunities in the West." This comment was made in 1910 and illustrates how trunk-line railroads of the Pacific Northwest and their boosters maintained their selective approach to European and Asian immigration in the early twentieth century. "The average colonist today is not the 'undesirable,' but the best type, middle class sturdy American," insisted one *Pacific Monthly* author in 1910. "There is still foreign blood, but it has been Americanized, the broad 3,000 mile stretch between the Atlantic and the Pacific acting as a sieve that drops out the first generation from the Old Country, and leaves behind the less hardy, resourceful, and ambitious."[24]

The Oregon Railroad & Navigation Company issued a promotional brochure in 1904 that claimed, "The Pacific Northwest has for citizens the best class of settlers from the oldest sections of the East and Middle West. The foreign immigrant received is of the highest standard." At the same time it assured readers that "Oregon, Washington, and Idaho are all well protected from any large movement of Orientals."[25]

The Northwest Development League, which formed in 1911 to unite the promotional efforts of various northern tier state and local organizations, planned to send lecturers to the *northern* countries of Europe. Louis W. Hill, James J. Hill's son and successor as president of the Great Northern Railway, told members of the league that immigrants

## Opening of Indian Reservations

### Registration, July 15 to August 5, 1909.     Drawing, August 9, 1909

### REGISTRATION

#### FOR 160-ACRE FARMS IN THE

**Flathead Reservation (450,000 acres)** - - - - - **Missoula, Mont.**
**Coeur d'Alene Reservation (200,000 acres)** - - **Coeur d'Alene, Ida.**
**Spokane Reservation (50,000 acres)** - - - - - **Spokane, Wash.**

Any qualified applicant can register for a 160-acre farm **on all three** of these reservations. But if he is successful in the drawing of a farm on one reservation, he cannot file an application for land on the other reservations.

THE CHICAGO MILWAUKEE AND ST. PAUL RAILWAY

### HOMESEEKERS' ROUND-TRIP FARE—JULY 20, 1909

| FROM | To Missoula and Return | To Kalispell and Return | To Coeur d'Alene and Return | To Spokane and Return | FROM | To Missoula and Return | To Kalispell and Return | To Coeur d'Alene and Return | To Spokane and Return |
|---|---|---|---|---|---|---|---|---|---|
| Beloit . . . . . . . . . . Wis | $39.00 | $39.00 | $55.10 | $57.50 | Milwaukee . . . . . . . Wis. | $39.00 | $39.00 | $55.10 | $57.50 |
| Cedar Rapids . . . . Iowa | 36.50 | 36.50 | 52.60 | 55.00 | Mineral Point . . . . " | 39.00 | 39.00 | 55.10 | 57.50 |
| Chicago . . . . . . . . . Ill. | 39.00 | 39.00 | 55.10 | 57.50 | Minneapolis . . . . . Minn. | 34.00 | 34.00 | 50.10 | 52.50 |
| Council Bluffs . . . . Iowa | 36.50 | 36.50 | 50.10 | 52.50 | Omaha . . . . . . . . . Neb. | 36.50 | 36.50 | 50.10 | 52.50 |
| Davenport . . . . . . . " | 36.50 | 36.50 | 52.60 | 55.00 | Oshkosh . . . . . . . . Wis. | 39.00 | 39.00 | 55.10 | 57.50 |
| Decorah . . . . . . . . " | 36.50 | 36.50 | 52.60 | 55.00 | Ottumwa . . . . . . . Iowa | 36.50 | 36.50 | 52.60 | 55.00 |
| Des Moines . . . . . . " | 36.50 | 36.50 | 52.60 | 55.00 | Racine . . . . . . . . . Wis. | 39.00 | 39.00 | 55.10 | 57.50 |
| Dubuque . . . . . . . . " | 36.50 | 36.50 | 52.60 | 55.00 | Rockford . . . . . . . . Ill. | 39.00 | 39.00 | 55.10 | 57.50 |
| Freeport . . . . . . . . Ill. | 37.75 | 37.75 | 53.85 | 56.25 | Rock Island . . . . . . " | 36.50 | 36.50 | 52.60 | 55.00 |
| Green Bay . . . . . . Wis. | 39.00 | 39.00 | 56.20 | 58.60 | Rockwell City . . . . Iowa | 36.50 | 36.50 | 52.60 | 55.00 |
| Janesville . . . . . . . " | 39.00 | 39.00 | 55.10 | 57.50 | St. Paul . . . . . . . . Minn. | 34.00 | 34.00 | 50.10 | 52.50 |
| Kansas City . . . . . Mo. | 36.50 | 36.50 | 52.60 | 55.00 | Sioux City . . . . . . Iowa | 36.50 | 36.50 | 50.10 | 52.50 |
| La Crosse . . . . . . Wis. | 36.50 | 36.50 | 52.60 | 55.00 | Spencer . . . . . . . . " | 36.50 | 36.50 | 52.60 | 55.00 |
| Madison . . . . . . . . " | 39.00 | 39.00 | 55.10 | 57.50 | Wausau . . . . . . . . Wis. | 39.00 | 39.00 | 55.10 | 57.50 |
| Mason City . . . . Iowa | 36.50 | 36.50 | 52.60 | 55.00 | Winona . . . . . . . . Minn. | 36.50 | 36.50 | 52.60 | 55.00 |
| Mendota . . . . . . . . Ill. | 39.00 | 39.00 | 55.10 | 57.50 | | | | | |

Low rates from other points and on other dates.  Low excursion rates to North Pacific Coast points, with stop-over privileges, available for trips to above registration points.

Additional information and descriptive folder free.

**F. A. MILLER, General Passenger Agent, CHICAGO**

*The Chicago, Milwaukee & St. Paul Railway used its public timetables in 1909 to advertise land on Indian reservations. Milwaukee Road Collection, Milwaukee Public Library.*

from northern Europe were the best kind of settlers. "It is largely people from the northern part of Europe that settled the middle west and they are among the best and most prosperous citizens in the country." Hill emphasized that "we want only the very best class of immigrants. We don't want to go all over Europe."[26] Such ethnic and racial selectivity may be a principal reason why the great majority of Pacific Northwesterners today trace their ancestry to northern and western Europe.

### Tons of Lying Pamphlets?

IF PACIFIC NORTHWESTERNERS WERE publicly critical of regional boosters it was not because the promotional pamphlets encouraged racial or ethnic discrimination, but because they aroused unrealistic expectations. Labor leaders in Oregon in the mid-1880s worried that "tons of lying pamphlets" only served to lure thousands of people west to flood local job markets and depress wages. Organized labor worked hard in the 1886 gubernatorial race to elect Sylvester Pennoyer, who had as one of his top priorities the abolition of the State Board of Immigration. Pennoyer wondered aloud in his inaugural address (in appalling ignorance of the Oregon Trail), "If the early pioneers of forty or fifty years ago could find Oregon without a trail through the forests or over the deserts, immigrants that desire to come here now can undoubtedly find their way."[27] When legislators agreed and denied the Immigration Board further funding, a group of Portland entrepreneurs took over its functions, thereby probably confirming labor's suspicions that publicity benefited businessmen more than workers.

Exaggeration and outright deception inevitably appeared in pamphlets. One Union Pacific brochure issued in 1889 claimed that Oregon and Washington "entreat the laborer to accept a pleasant home where ample reward for industry surely awaits him; where opportunities for work are so extensive that the wage-earner has never been driven to seek relief or protection in the 'strike' nor the capitalist, to preserve or augment his power, ever resorted to the 'lock-out.'"[28] The author neglected to mention that only a few months earlier there had been a bitter strike in the coal mines of Washington.

Other claims, if not actually dishonest, struck some observers as outlandish and worthy of ridicule. Frances Fuller Victor, riding on a train through eastern Washington in the early 1890s, was fascinated by a promoter's injunction to "Keep Your Eye on Pasco!" "When you arrive," she wrote, "you look about for anything on which to keep your eye, which being blown full of sand refuses to risk more than the briefest glimpse afterwards." She noted that promoters claimed that irrigation would redeem the sandy sagebrush waste around the hamlet, "but in the interim, keeping one's eyes on Pasco is a painful experience."[29]

In his unpublished autobiography, Robert Strahorn offered anecdotal evidence of how exaggerated prose won converts, among them his own father in Missouri, who getting hold of "some of my effusions" had sacrificed his productive farm in the Ozarks for the New Northwest his son had described in such glowing terms. The father was disappointed and finally relocated to a comfortable life in southern California. Another Strahorn, Robert's brother John, got hold of some of "my extravagant word paintings" describing the climatic glories of Union Pacific territory, and moved from Escanaba, Michigan, to North Platte, Nebraska (which Robert privately called a cheerless, blizzard-swept place).[30]

Once when traveling through a lonely mountain pass between Idaho and Montana, Strahorn came upon a woman sitting on a wagon tongue holding a crying baby while men were trying desperately to raise a tent in the face of a blizzard. He wondered why they did not continue into the valley below where they would be protected from the weather. "Because," responded the woman, "I'm not going another foot and want to go straight back to Missouri, where we came from, and if this is Strahorn's paradise, all I've got to say is I wish he had to live in it."[31]

Strahorn could wink at excesses seemingly inherent in the frenzied promotional activity that typified the Pacific Northwest's first railway age. But during the early twentieth century, exaggerated claims made in the era of Strahorn and Smalley sometimes caused people to discount boosterism in general. Such skepticism forced a new generation of promoters to be more careful what they asserted, and as a result promotional activity during the second railway age became more sophisticated than it had been before. Moreover, recent advances in color printing technology helped to make many turn-of-the-century brochures true works of art.

Just how many settlers the various promotional pamphlets and exhibits attracted to the Pacific Northwest will never be known. Contemporaries, like Oregon's labor leaders in the mid-1880s, certainly believed that brochures and booklets found a large and receptive audience. Villard noted that records kept by the steerage department of the Oregon Steamship Company showed that between 1874 and 1877 alone no fewer than thirty thousand persons migrated to Oregon.[32]

It was hardly coincidental that the massive railroad promotional campaigns conducted during the 1880s and again during the first two decades of the twentieth century were each accompanied by unprecedented numbers of newcomers to the Pacific Northwest. "Ask any settler in some part of the West why he immigrated," observed the well-known journalist Ray Stannard Baker in 1908, "and he will invariably point you back to the beguiling road, a pamphlet, a fevered folder, an enthusiastic agent."[33]

*Monida, Montana, on the Oregon Short Line, in 1898. It was near here that the promoter Robert Strahorn encountered a Missouri woman who bitterly denounced the area as "Strahorn's paradise." Haynes Foundation Collection, Montana Historical Society, H3778.*

*The West is impregnated with the idea that it has not received fair treatment at the hands of the railroad.*—United States Investor *(April 28, 1894)*

# Traveling Too Fast: Adjustments to Railroad Power

RAILROAD POWER REQUIRED RESidents of Washington's Yakima Valley to make a series of abrupt and traumatic adjustments. When the Northern Pacific Railroad first proposed to route its Cascade Branch through the area in the mid-1880s, the five hundred residents of Yakima City were confident that their community would prosper. Yakima City's growing population and its location at a constricted part of the valley, where tracklayers had no choice but to pass through the town, seemingly guaranteed that the Northern Pacific would select the site for its station and yards. But the railroad ran its tracks straight through Yakima City without erecting so much as a tool shed and chose instead to build an entirely new town on railroad land a few miles away. On a sagebrush plain the Northern Pacific laid out a settlement called North Yakima.

A wail of protest went up from residents of Yakima City, but to no avail. Northern Pacific officials dismissed the proposed station site in Yakima City as marshy and unsuited for building, although some people claimed that the railroad had earlier failed to extort free land for its right-of-way and station and was now exacting its revenge. Regardless of the circumstances, Yakima City residents looked on helplessly as Northern Pacific trains steamed through their town without stopping.

North Yakima dated from February 4, 1885. Its city plan reserved space for the new capitol of Washington, which many observers expected to be moved soon from Olympia to a more central location. The Northern Pacific also provided that any businessman who wanted to relocate from Yakima City could have a new building site free. As a result many stores and business structures were moved intact on rollers to North Yakima. The local bank continued to operate as usual as it crept along to the new location.

Some residents of Yakima City stubbornly fought back, however, and one of them threatened to use a few cans of nitroglycerine to destroy the railroad facilities. That was perhaps not an idle threat, for someone did bomb the office of the Yakima *Signal* as the newspaper inched its way to the new town. Finally, in order to defuse the threat of violence, the railroad agreed to pay transportation costs for anyone who wished to relocate, not just for merchants, but hostility to what many people perceived as an unprecedented display of railroad power lingered. An editorial cartoon in the Seattle *Press* on October 17, 1887, showed a Northern Pacific official riding a train through tumbledown Yakima City and thumbing his nose, while just ahead lay a prosperous

*Busy Yakima Avenue as Asahel Curtis recorded it in October 1908. North Yakima was the largest city in central Washington at the time. Washington State Historical Society, Curtis 11302.*

Traveling Too Fast: Adjustments to Railroad Power

North Yakima. Antirailroad agitation formed the basis of several political protest movements in the Yakima Valley during the next two decades.

By early 1918 when North Yakima officially shortened its name to Yakima and became the metropolis of a prosperous agricultural valley, the original Yakima City was long gone. But what happened there thirty years earlier illustrated how westerners not yet a generation removed from pioneer life were forced to make rapid and often painful adjustments to the new America created by transcontinental railroads. The Yakima episode was one vivid example of the type of transformation that the region's first railway age demanded.[1]

## The New Equation

IN 1880 THE FOUR PACIFIC NORTH-west states and territories contained only 1,124 miles of railway line out of a nationwide total of 44,016 miles, and none of this trackage was linked together in any meaningful way. By the end of the decade, however, the figure had climbed to 6,090 miles out of the nation's total of 87,117 miles, and all of the tracks were part of a network of rails that spanned the continent. These signatures in steel represented first and foremost a cluster of powerful relationships. The railroad industry was America's first big business, and at the turn of the century it still comprised most of the firms listed on the New York Stock Exchange. Railroads of the Pacific Northwest were influential not only because of their monopolistic powers and political clout in state and territorial legislatures but also because of their vast landholdings, which in many cases included extensive federal grants of timber, agriculture, and mineral properties that ranked them second only to the national government as agencies of settlement and development.

The size of its domain gave the Northern Pacific

intimidating power, especially in eastern Washington, where the slow rate at which the railroad organized its land grant caused early settlers to fear that they might be evicted or forced to pay exorbitant fees to gain legal title to farms and ranches they already occupied. The railroads' methods of winning friends and influencing people by distribution of free passes and other favors also angered many in the industrializing West, where railroads represented new forms of massed capital that threatened to overwhelm the simple economic and political structures that had served pioneer society so well. Even if railroads had been less blatant about their displays of power, their monopolistic position in many localities would still have generated resentment.

Something so fundamental as the right-of-way itself represented the power of human knowledge to transform landscapes into standard measures of curvature and elevation and to shrink the vast distances of the West. *Magic* was a word often used to describe the complex feats of engineering that enabled railroads of the Pacific Northwest to bridge once impassable canyons and bore through mountain barriers that nature seemed to place in the way of development. Where the land was high and windswept, the winters were cold and harsh, and the summers were hot and arid, the twin ribbons of iron or steel converted inhospitable terrain into friendly space, at least for people traveling by train. A trip on business or to visit friends and relatives became easy, and if a person went first class in one of the era's ornate sleeping cars, the journey might actually be pleasurable. So luxurious were accommodations that some people who had struggled west in covered wagons in the recent past must have regarded the new mode of travel as almost sinful. Certainly the sense of isolation of pioneer days was gone.

Nowhere was the ease of travel by train more obvious than in the arid lands of the West. Wagons

*Asian laborers align Oregon Railroad & Navigation track in the Columbia River gorge in 1910. To keep their trains running safely and efficiently, railroads required an army of well-disciplined maintenance-of-way workers. At this time every hundred miles of track required an average of 156 laborers to maintain it, and Japanese workers had largely replaced the Chinese of earlier years. An assistant superintendent of the Union Pacific observed in the* Railway Age Gazette *in 1912 that Japanese track foremen "exhibit a desire to master details, are apt scholars, are always alert to duty, have a facility of imparting their knowledge to their laborers, and seldom, if ever, repeat an error which has once been brought to their attention correctively. These characteristics do not develop in foremen of other nationalities." Oregon Historical Society, 01548s, LOC/ORIG: 0311-Z-74.*

They opened the door to distant markets for local products—especially for bulky items produced by the region's fields, forests, and mines—and created new jobs and fortunes, but they also increased competition for local merchants. If prices on main street were too high, the twin ribbons of steel made it possible for citizens of once isolated communities like Klamath Falls and Coeur d'Alene to thumb through catalogs from Sears Roebuck or Montgomery Ward and order a watch made in Connecticut, a hat from Pennsylvania, or a dress from New Hampshire and have it shipped west from Chicago by mail.

Except for residents of Pacific Coast settlements accessible by water transportation, westerners were much more dependent upon railroads than most people living east of the Mississippi River. Many a western community was a child of the steel rail, and especially in the interior Northwest, vital timber, mineral, and agricultural industries relied heavily on rail transportation for survival. Not surprisingly, the paradox of a new freedom coupled with new dependency caused Pacific Northwesterners to develop a love-hate relationship with their railroads.

on the Oregon Trail followed waterways to surmount the Continental Divide at South Pass; Union Pacific tracks, by contrast, took a more direct route across Wyoming, plunging across waterless stretches of land that would have been the ruin of the pioneers. Even coastlines were not barriers: during the heyday of railway power in America, the tracks of the Florida East Coast went to sea, skimming from island to island to reach Key West. Here was a standard-gauge highway that extended as far as engineering prowess, finances, and political will permitted.

Nationwide railroad connections gave everyday life in the Pacific Northwest a whole new contour.

## A Love-Hate Relationship

WHEN TRACKS FIRST REACHED a community, it was invariably time for a celebration. People welcomed new lines to their settlements, believing that rail connections guaranteed permanence, growth, and prosperity; and they sulked when railroads passed them by. They came to realize all too well that any community without the steel rails faced a bleak future. For this reason, would-be cities on Puget Sound fought bitterly with one another in the early 1870s to be designated terminus of the Northern Pacific. Even when the new town of

Finck's OVERALLS
"Wear like a pig's nose"

"Your **Nose** was made before my **Overalls**, but my **Overalls** wear like your **Nose**. They are the most comfortable and roomy garments I have ever had for the money and it is economy for me to pay a little more for

FINCK'S
"Detroit-Special"
OVERALLS

Railroad Men can purchase "Detroit Specials" at all leading dealers who realize what a good work garment means to them and to you.

W. M. Finck & Co.
Detroit, Michigan

Remember the *Maine*
To Hell with Spain,
And don't forget
To pull the chain—
Tacoma needs the water!

When the Northern Pacific upgraded its line to Seattle, it reluctantly acknowledged the city's hegemony in western Washington.

The fate of the two Yakimas illustrated how railroads might bless one community and blight another, yet even when a settlement secured rail connections, its citizens still had to make sudden and unexpected adjustments to railroad power. Residents of Eagle Rock (now Idaho Falls) believed that their town's future was assured when it became a division point and site of the Utah & Northern's repair shops in 1880. Seven years later when the railroad moved its shops south to the budding community of Pocatello, Eagle Rock's population

*"**W**ear like a pig's nose" was one slogan used in 1916 to sell long-lasting overalls to the army of railroad men who faced a tough and dirty day's work. Milwaukee Road Collection, Milwaukee Public Library.*

*__O__pponents of the Northern Pacific's massive land grant denounced it as a "black cloud" blighting settlement of Washington. Their map failed to show what was in reality an immense checkerboard of alternating sections of railroad and government land. Oregon Historical Society, 836116.*

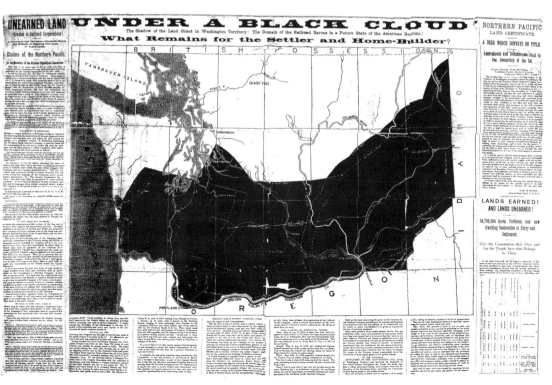

Tacoma won the prize, its rival, Seattle, refused to concede, although the Northern Pacific initially relegated it to the end of an unimportant branch extending north from Auburn. The future of Seattle looked considerably brighter after Hill selected it as the Pacific terminus for his Great Northern Railway.

For years Seattle and Tacoma remained locked in a bitter contest for supremacy. In 1898 a Seattle partisan gave the rivalry an international twist when, after the battleship *Maine* exploded and sank and the United States subsequently declared war on Spain, he scrawled on the men's room wall in the Great Northern station:

dropped precipitously from 1,400 to 250 and the town had to battle to survive without the benefits that a railroad payroll conferred on workers and merchants. In Pocatello, by contrast, Union Pacific operations in 1896 employed 300 conductors, brakemen, engineers, and firemen. The largest railroad shops between Omaha and the Pacific Coast provided jobs for 200 to 350, and offices and a railroad-operated hotel employed another 100.

Yet another variation of this theme occurred at Fort Benton, Montana, once the beneficiary of considerable steamboat traffic along the Missouri River. When James J. Hill's St. Paul, Minneapolis & Manitoba Railway built through Fort Benton on its way to Great Falls in the late 1880s, it doomed any remaining river commerce. The number of steamboats that docked annually at Fort Benton dwindled to zero, and the community became simply another of the small central Montana towns strung like beads along a railroad line. Fort Benton, though, was more fortunate than old Yakima City: it survived, and today its historic waterfront is a magnet for tourists.

Rail connections guaranteed neither metropolitan status nor future prosperity, but by the eve of World War I it was axiomatic that no place of consequence could hope to exist beyond the sound of a locomotive whistle. Apart from traveling on coastal liners that linked Pacific Northwest ports with Alaska and California or on Puget Sound steamboats, a person journeyed by water mainly to reach a backwater settlement where the population was small and future prospects were limited to production of a natural resource, like lumber or seafood. For the same reason, interior stagecoach lines extended to settlements too small to attract railway lines.

Given their power to reshape the urban Pacific Northwest, railroads seemed to some observers to be potential agents of social regeneration. The historian Frederick Jackson Turner, traveling west by train to give the commencement address at the University of Washington in 1914, overheard a man telling how if he were a multimillionaire he would use railroads to solve the problem of slums in eastern cities. He would haul the indigents west "and let them loose in our vast forests and ore-laden mountains to learn what life really is!"[2]

Even more impressive than any physical or economic changes wrought by railroads in the Pacific Northwest was the speed of the transition. Within the span of a single generation, orchards and grainfields replaced sagebrush and bunchgrass across vast stretches of the region. In the early 1880s herds of cattle still roamed eastern Washington at will, undisturbed by barbed wire fences. But only ten years later, continuous blocks of cultivated fields and neat and substantial clusters of farm dwellings, barns, and grain bins had vividly transformed the

*Shipping fruit from Washington's Yakima Valley in September 1910. National Archives, 115-JAI-638.*

rural landscape. Everywhere villages became cities with the modern accoutrements of electric lights, telephones, municipal waterworks, streetcars, cement sidewalks, brick and stone business blocks, and up-to-date schoolhouses. The region experienced temporary setbacks—such as the fires that ravaged Seattle, Spokane, and Ellensburg in 1889—but during the thirteen years from 1880 to 1893, the Pacific Northwest still experienced a rate of growth seldom equaled in any section of the United States. Growth was even more impressive in individual communities like Tacoma and Spokane.

In 1880 Spokane was but a village of approximately 350 residents. Nationwide rail connections after 1883 helped to spur such unprecedented growth that by the end of the decade Spokane had 19,222 inhabitants, nearly four times as many as Walla Walla, which began the decade as Washington's largest city. During the 1880s Spokane became the primary distribution point for eastern Washington and northern Idaho.[3]

The coming of railroads to Spokane, however, was no more an unmixed blessing than it had been for Eagle Rock or Fort Benton. Trouble arose when railroads granted lower rates from eastern points to West Coast ports like Portland and Seattle than they did to Spokane and other inland towns. In fact, Spokane residents paid freight charges equal to those for hauling the goods to tidewater then back again to Spokane. "We in the East live in peaceful ignorance of freight rates," Ray Stannard Baker once noted, "but if you talk any length of time with any western business man, you will find him veering around sooner or later to freight rates."[4] That was because, for residents of inland communities like Spokane, railroad freight rates were a bread-and-butter issue, not an arcane or abstract matter.

Suppose, for example, a Spokane resident ordered something from Sears Roebuck in Chicago in 1897. The cost to ship a hundred pounds of freight first class from Chicago to Seattle or Portland was $2.40, but from Chicago to Spokane the rate was $3.60, or 50 percent more, although Spokane was closer to Chicago than was Seattle. The reason for this difference, claimed the railroads, was competition from waterborne carriers, which landlocked Spokane lacked. The rate difference translated into a higher price in Spokane for everything from seeds and soap to bicycles and underwear. Factories on the coast could also ship merchandise to towns in the inland Northwest cheaper than nearby Spokane could.

Spokane in 1892 appealed to the newly created Interstate Commerce Commission, and that agency ordered railroads to reduce their rates. Railroads simply ignored the mandate, and in 1897 the United

States Supreme Court ruled that the Interstate Commerce Commission had no power to prescribe freight rates anyway. After this the railroads raised their rates until it became possible to ship goods more cheaply from the East Coast to Asia than to Spokane. James J. Hill observed that, while the Interstate Commerce Commission ruled that Spokane should have a rate from the East pegged at 82 percent of the coast rate, "The present rate is 120%, and the people are in a very ugly mood."[5]

After several more years of battle, Spokane finally got terminal rates in 1911 on orders from an Interstate Commerce Commission reinvigorated by congressional mandate. On July 26, citizens of Spokane celebrated with bells, whistles, horns, a parade, rallies, and street dances. But their celebration proved premature, for once again railroads appealed to the Supreme Court and a long legal contest followed. Not until 1918 did Spokane win terminal rates.[6]

During numerous court and commission hearings, the extent to which railroad rates arbitrarily blessed or blighted cities became clear. Spokane, in fact, while not enjoying terminal rates, was nonetheless granted special rates that enabled it to establish dominance over other communities in the inland Northwest. Jobbers and wholesale houses found it cheaper to do business from Spokane than from elsewhere in eastern Washington or northern Idaho. When asked why their rates favored Spokane over Walla Walla or Pendleton, railroad spokesmen replied only that it was an arbitrary arrangement.

Railroad rates could also hurt or help entire industries. Until the early 1880s, logging was largely confined to the water's edge, where "cargo mills" along Puget Sound, Grays Harbor, the lower Columbia River, and Coos Bay served far-flung markets. The orientation of the industry was toward San Francisco, largest consumer of timber products on the West Coast and home to several businessmen who reaped fortunes from cheap and easily acquired timberlands of the Pacific Northwest.[7]

Completion of the Northern Pacific line offered access to markets east of the Rocky Mountains, but the key to success remained railroad rates low enough to allow Pacific Northwest lumber to compete with that from the Great Lakes and the South. That did not happen until after the turn of the century. Until then, the chief impact of railroads on the Northwest timber industry was to create a local market for ties, bridge timbers, and building materials needed for stations and other trackside structures.

Railroads made commercial agriculture the lifeblood of the Palouse country. By the mid-1880s farmers there enjoyed rail access to world markets and a robust cash economy. Every year, hundreds and then thousands of carloads of wheat were shipped from the Palouse over tracks of the Northern Pacific and Oregon Railway & Navigation Company. Almota, a port on the Snake River, had for several years served as a principal shipping point for wheat country to the north, but with the advent of railroad connections, trade down the river fell off. However, when farmers were unable to secure enough boxcars to haul an unusually heavy harvest of grain, 1890 became known as the year of the "wheat blockade." When prices dropped before growers could get their wheat to market, farmers angrily charged that railroad and elevator companies had combined against them.[8]

Frustrated Palouse agriculturalists agitated for a railroad line to Puget Sound independent of the big transcontinental carriers. They also sought relief through politics. Serious legislative challenges to railroad power began as early as the 1870s in the midwestern states and led to enactment of restrictive granger laws, almost all of which were later voided by federal courts. Congress responded in 1887 with the first of the great federal regulatory agencies, the Interstate Commerce Commission, but the federal judiciary soon stripped it of power.

that became especially prominent in mid-decade. Populists advocated a variety of measures including government ownership. Railroad leaders feared that public clamor for lower railway rates would influence the major political parties.

It was concern over Populist agitation that caused James J. Hill to warn an associate in England not to publish accounts of the Great Northern's finances unless he could avoid "their coming back to the Populistic West." With the Great Northern doing far better than its competitors during the depression of the 1890s, Hill emphasized, "We do not feel it at all wise to invite attack on our revenues by showing too large a surplus." At that time, railroad finances were pretty much a private matter, and Supreme Court decisions had reduced the fledgling Interstate Commerce Commission to little more than a statistics-gathering agency. Federal regulators could condemn rates as unjust and unreasonable but not reduce them.[9]

Following on the heels of Populists in the early twentieth century were progressive reformers in both the Democratic and Republican parties. They persisted in efforts to rein in railroad power through state and federal regulation, and Hill was no less afraid of their attacks than he had been of the Populists'. He confided to the New York financier Jacob Schiff in 1901,

At the present time there is a widespread and general feeling of dissatisfaction which will I think increase as we go on and will by say 1903 be in full blast. The pulpit and the press are doing their full share to draw intelligent people into the fold of agitation; college professors who as a rule are not well qualified to speak, are active, all inciting the public mind.

*A*n artist's view of the "wheat blockade" in St. John, Washington, in 1890. Special Collections Division, University of Washington Libraries, 6322.

Further attempts to control the carriers occurred during the 1890s, when additional displays of power in public life made railroads high-profile targets for reform candidates. Chief among the protesters were the Populists, members of a third-party movement

Hill's low opinion of reformers notwithstanding, Congress passed the Hepburn Act in 1906 to give the Interstate Commerce Commission a variety of new powers, including authority to fix maximum rates.[10]

## Commonwealth of Toil

THE HEPBURN ACT AND OTHER regulatory measures forced railroads to adapt to changes demanded by an increasingly complex social and economic system that the carriers themselves had helped create. Regulation was only one of numerous unintended results of railroad building. Another was the redefinition of both the physical and the economic landscapes of the Pacific Northwest. A widening gap between rich and poor, for example, was visible on nearly every passenger train during the depression years: paying customers rode inside in comfort, while outside, an army of freeloaders clung to every imaginable perch and handhold, from car roof above to brake beams and bolstering rods below.

The popular mind usually lumped nonpaying passengers together indiscriminately as hoboes, tramps, and bums, but for the most part they were itinerant laborers who risked considerable danger traveling from job to job. From the grainfields of Montana's high plains and the orchards of Oregon's Rogue River valley to the tall timber country of western Washington, a veritable army of nomadic laborers supplied the muscle needed to harvest products of the Pacific Northwest's forests, fields, and coastal waters, mine precious and base metals, drill for oil, and load ships. They were indispensable in construction of the region's railroads, dams, irrigation canals, and many other building projects. Before the advent of railroads made such projects possible, the large army of casual laborers had not existed in most of the Pacific Northwest.[11]

Even in the best of times an unusually high percentage of workers in the Pacific Northwest

*Hundreds of laborers still followed the harvest across the Great Plains of South Dakota and eastern Montana in the early 1920s. Railroads spurred growth of the Northwest's several natural resource–based industries, and their trains facilitated movement of itinerant laborers from job to job. Minnesota Historical Society, SA4.52/P40.*

depended on jobs in natural resource–based industries that were infamous for recurrent bouts of cyclical and seasonal unemployment. Boom-and-bust cycles made it necessary to move frequently to find work. Depending on the season a dock worker from Seattle might be found in eastern Washington sacking the annual harvest of wheat. A metal miner might travel from Bisbee, Arizona, north to Idaho's Coeur d'Alene district, and even to Alaska mines during the course of a single year. In extreme cases an itinerant laborer might remain on the job for as few as three hours before walking off in search of something else. So high was the turnover in the typical railroad construction camp that a common saying was that three crews were always present: "one coming, one going, one on the job."[12]

From the employers' perspective, payday was often the itinerant worker's undoing. An officer of the Chicago, Burlington & Quincy Railroad complained that "too often the hard earned monthly wage, minus the board and van [room] account, is spent in one glorious week-end spree, while the foreman waits or struggles on with a few weaklings or new men, but without the hands whom he has worked so carefully or organized into a quickly responding human machine."[13]

No paying passenger, not even those who endured the hardest and most uncomfortable seats, faced the same hazards as itinerants traveling from job to job. Fatal accidents reportedly claimed nearly twenty-five thousand trespassers from 1901 to 1905 alone. The Great Northern and other railroads usually looked the other way when hauling the laborers so vital to the region's extractive economy, but Hill lamented that his company could not separate legitimate itinerant workers from bums

who are not willing to work but rather congregate together and intimidate or rob those who do work. . . . Until the different county officers, judges, and sheriffs are more in earnest in enforcing the law and protecting

**Justice Douglas on "Riding the Rods"**

*Long before he became a justice of the United States Supreme Court, William O. Douglas worked as an itinerant laborer in the grainfields of eastern Washington. He likened traveling on freight cars in the days of his youth to hitchhiking at the present time. One popular technique was called "riding the rods":*

*"Though freight cars have changed over the years, in the days when I was a boy, there were two rods under most of these cars. They were two or three feet apart, about eighteen inches beneath the car and about ten inches from the ground, running under the car for almost its entire length.*

*"The trick was to get a couple of boards and lay them across the rods to form a small platform. We'd lie on the boards, on our stomachs, our heads on our arms and our eyes tightly closed. It was a miserable place to ride because the suction of the train kept dust and cinders constantly swirling. Unless you fell asleep, it wasn't particularly dangerous, although you did come out pretty grimy."*

*—William O. Douglas, Go East, Young Man, The Early Years: The Autobiography of William O. Douglas (1974)*

those poor men who are willing to work from being maltreated by the floating population whose presence is dangerous, I see no relief for the situation. Last year we had a great many cars burned by these people building fires in them or under them and going away leaving them to burn.[14]

Hard times not only called widespread attention to the phenomenon of transient labor but also gave rise to the some of the region's most visible and troubling labor disputes, notably the Great Northern and Pullman strikes of 1894, the latter of which disrupted rail service throughout the West during much of May and June. These dramatic episodes focused public attention as never before on the fact that railroading was a way of life as well as an occupation.[15]

The industry was in many ways a business pioneer, especially when growing size and complexity forced American railroads to devise new ways to govern numerous employees scattered across a large area. Problems of scheduling and safety demanded more supervision and employee accountability than could be expected from the traditional factory system of owner, foreman, and worker. To address that problem, railroads established an elaborate new type of managerial hierarchy adapted at least indirectly from the military. Instead of generals and colonels, railroads had vice-presidents and superintendents. In the operating department, for instance, were the locomotive engineers, popularly regarded as holding the most glamorous of all railroad jobs. Though celebrated in ballad and popular fiction, engineers actually endured long and irregular hours, grime and heat in cramped locomotive cabs, and unexpected danger along the road. A person typically became an engineer only after he had spent time firing a switch engine, then advanced to firing in freight and finally passenger service. In this way the engineer acquired a thorough knowledge of technology and operating rules.

Aboard a train, however, engineers actually ranked second in command to conductors, who together with brakemen and flagmen filled the ranks of trainmen. Like engineers they advanced by reason of ability and seniority. The hierarchy of the typical operating department also included many other positions, from division superintendents and trainmasters to dispatchers and switch tenders. In the maintenance-of-way department, section foremen and trackwalkers inspected each foot of main line, sometimes twice or more a day.

Not only were railroaders subject to close supervision and irregular hours, but their jobs were often as dangerous as any found off a battlefield. The Interstate Commerce Commission found that during the year that ended on June 30, 1893, 2,727 railway employees were killed and another 31,729 injured in the line of duty. One of every 320 employees was killed that year, with the greatest number of deaths occurring while the workers coupled or uncoupled cars. Before widespread adoption of automatic couplers in the late nineteenth century, brakemen risked injury and death dozens of times daily as they stepped between moving cars to guide a coupling link into a slot and drop a pin into place. Until air brakes became common on freight trains in the early twentieth century, brakemen scurried along the tops of swaying boxcars in all kinds of weather to set or release brakes manually according to signals whistled from the locomotive. The all-time high

*Montana photographer L. A. Huffman found this contingent of Coxey's Army of the unemployed in Forsyth in the spring of 1894. Several hundred Coxeyites stole a Northern Pacific freight train in Butte and set out for Washington, D.C. There they planned to join thousands of like-minded protesters in a living petition to Congress to provide them work. After a lengthy chase by federal marshals, United States Army troops from Fort Keogh finally captured the group in eastern Montana. Montana Historical Society, Huffman 981802.*

accident rate among railroad workers occurred in 1907, when one of every eight engineers, firemen, conductors, and brakemen was injured on the job. The response of railroad employees to management as well as to long hours and dangers in the workplace was organization: locomotive engineers were among the first workers to form craft unions in the Pacific Northwest, in some cases as early as the 1860s. Typically, however, in recognition of their special status as railroad workers, they called their organizations brotherhoods and held aloof from close association with other trade unions.

Until hard times ended the Pacific Northwest's first railway age, the work of laying tracks across the region had gone forward at a furious pace, and a growing number of workers took pride in their status as railroad men. By the time construction slowed almost to a halt in the mid-1890s, both a way

of life and a pattern of railway lines had been established. Across the four-state region a network of steel rails linked together every major population center. When the pace of construction picked up again with the return of prosperity in 1897, track-laying was confined mainly to completing the last northern transcontinental railroad and the feeder lines into still undeveloped corners.

The speed and magnitude of change in the Pacific Northwest during the two railway ages can best be observed by using the Northern Pacific's final spike ceremony at Gold Creek in 1883 as a reference point. Just forty years earlier the first mass migration of non-Indian settlers to the region had taken place when wagon trains creaked west along the route destined to be immortalized as the Oregon Trail; and just forty years later, in 1923, it was already certain that automobiles would figure prominently in meeting the region's transportation needs. A harbinger of even more wondrous developments occurred in 1916 in the Seattle workshop where William Boeing and his employees first assembled the spindly wood-and-wire airplanes of the era. During a span of eighty years—one long lifetime— the Pacific Northwest had undergone a transformation from packtrains and oxcarts to automobiles and airplanes, from wilderness to an urban-industrial way of life.

Perhaps no one understood better than Ezra Meeker, a pioneer settler of western Washington who emerged as popular symbol of the changes that had occurred in a single lifetime. Meeker first traveled to the Pacific Northwest by covered wagon in 1852; in the early twentieth century he repeated his journey, this time returning from west to east. When he drove his covered wagon replica to the White House and then up Wall Street, he generated the type of popular curiosity accorded a ghost from a bygone era. Meeker also took several trips by air, on one occasion winging over the Palouse country from Clarkston to Spokane at more than.

O. R. & N. Co.

**More Deadly Than War**

"Railroading is more nearly akin to warfare than any other humane profession. The number of casualties to persons on our railways for the year ending June 30, 1907, was 122,855, of which 11,839 represented the number of persons killed and 111,016 the number injured. . . . the passengers killed were 610 and those injured 13,041. The personal injuries, fatal and non-fatal, assume much the same aspect to the general officers in charge of a railway as to the general officers in command of an army. The responsibility of the railway officer, however, is greater, for he has not the excuse of war."

—W. L. Park, in *Railroad Age Gazette* (Feb. 19, 1909)

*The Pullman strike of 1894 as recorded in Billings, Montana. Federal and state troops were dispatched to several locations around the Northwest. During this time of widespread labor unrest, courts and the military functioned almost as adjuncts of the railroads and in time symbolized their widespread corporate power. Montana Historical Society.*

sixty miles per hour. The flight prompted him to recall that he had originally crossed the continent at a speed of approximately two miles per hour. Reflecting on transportation developments he had seen in his lifetime, Meeker wondered, "In fifty years or less may not railroads and steamers be replaced almost entirely by the safer and far swifter flying machine? Who can tell?"[16]

**EMPIRE BUILDER**

*The Great Northern used unusual perspective to promote sightseeing on its Empire Builder in the early 1960s. Author's collection.*

# The Railway Landscape

WHAT MOST IMPRESSED THE novelist Hamlin Garland about the shadowy landscape of the Pacific Northwest was its dominant color: green—and nothing but shades of green—seemed to define western Washington. In prose that was positively chartreuse, he described the scene for readers of the November 1893 *Atlantic Monthly*, referring to the "bronze-green of firs, gray-green and emerald-green of the mosses, the yellow-green of the fern, the blue-green of the pines, the pea-green of the little firs, and the tender timid grass blades."[1]

Garland most likely observed the landscape from the windows of a Northern Pacific passenger train as it climbed the western flank of the Cascade Range. A businessman surveying the same landscape may well have calculated the number of board feet of lumber the trees contained, and a civil engineer might have described the challenge of constructing a railway line through so rugged a country. After all, only a short distance ahead lay the Stampede Pass Tunnel, nearly two miles long. Garland and anyone else who traveled by train likely emphasized different aspects of the passing landscape, yet theirs was still the common vantage point afforded by a railway passenger car.

ACROSS THE CONTINENT

CHICAGO, MILWAUKEE AND PUGET SOUND RAILWAY

"*A*cross the Continent": The front and back cover of a sixty-page promotional brochure issued by the Chicago, Milwaukee, and Puget Sound Railway in 1911. Written by Isabelle Carpenter Kendall, and lavishly illustrated throughout with color images evocative of the New Northwest, it signified the new railroad's confidence in the region it served. Author's collection.

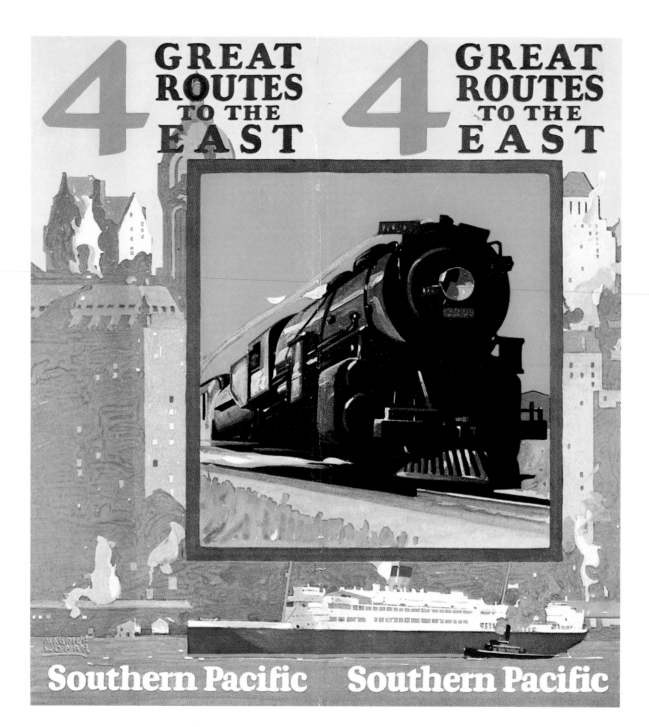

The Southern Pacific employed the well-known California artist Maurice Logan to create a dramatic image equating speed and power with travel comfort. Logan's stylized landscapes appeared on several Southern Pacific tourist brochures during the 1920s. California State Railroad Museum.

The cover of Railroad Stories depicted a once common scene along American railroads. Other illustrators often portrayed the hobo as a sinister figure. DeGolyer Library.

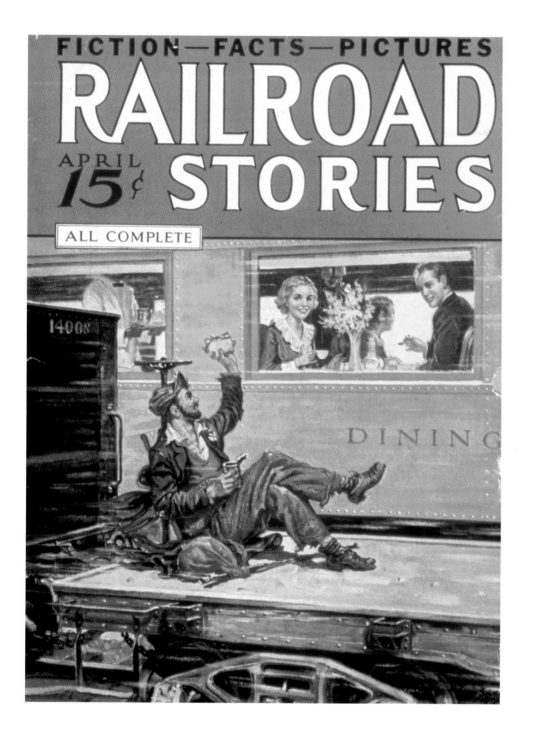

Passenger trains represented a way of shaping popular impressions of the West. For travelers the swaths of the Pacific Northwest framed by car windows formed the railway landscape. Across the plains of Montana and southern Idaho it was broad, extending from trackside to mountain ranges often fifty or more miles away. But threading the canyons of the Bitterroot and Cascade ranges, the railway landscape was scarcely wider than the tracks themselves. In either case, it was the location engineers who determined what passengers saw.

As if to emphasize their power to package the landscape, railroad companies provided guidebooks to identify sites along the way. These were variously titled *From the Car Windows* on the Great Northern, *Wayside Notes* on the Southern Pacific, and *Sights and Scenes from the Car Windows of the World's Pictorial Line* on the Union Pacific. What passengers came to know of the countryside, emphasized a Northern Pacific pamphlet published in 1893 and called 6,000 *Miles through Wonderland*, "must be learned from what they see from car windows as they roll onward at thirty or forty miles an hour."[2]

"The scenery combines all that is picturesque and beautiful in mountain, stream, forest, cataract and cascade," claimed a 1904 guidebook issued by the Oregon Railroad & Navigation Company to describe its route through the Columbia Gorge. It asserted that nothing in the United States, if in the world, surpassed the eighty-eight miles from Portland to The Dalles for scenic beauty, "the train for the greater part of the distance running so close to the Columbia River that the traveler can look from the car window into the water below."[3]

The appeal of the Columbia Gorge was obvious, but in other areas the location engineers found the best route for efficient operation only to create special problems for scenery-conscious travelers and railroad promoters. Much of the Northern Pacific main line across the Pacific Northwest passed either through dense forests or along narrow valleys or coulees bordered by arid hills. The location of Northern Pacific tracks across eastern Washington made it especially difficult for travelers to believe the railroad's glowing accounts of the rich, rolling prairies that supposedly lay just beyond the horizon: "Seeing is believing, says the old proverb, and as the traveler cannot look upon this land of plenty, he half suspects that its existence is a fiction of railroad literature."[4] That would not have been a problem had the Northern Pacific run its main line across the Palouse country instead of through a stark landscape that geologists would later label the channeled scablands.

A Northern Pacific brochure from 1890 offered one easy solution to the dilemma: "The traveler who desires to form anything like an adequate conception of the agricultural wealth of Washington Territory should not fail to leave the main line of the Northern Pacific at Spokane Falls and make a journey over this branch [the Spokane & Palouse Railway] through the wonderfully fertile Palouse Country."[5]

Beyond the railway landscape lay a largely unknown West. To travel there meant leaving the train and hiring a horse or carriage or changing to a stagecoach. For all practical purposes, that West did not exist for most turn-of-the-century travelers. By that date they found it simply inconceivable that any place of consequence existed apart from the twin ribbons of steel.

Railroads not only decided what travelers saw of the Pacific Northwest by where they located their tracks and stations but also determined when they saw it. They usually arranged the schedules of premier passenger trains to cross flatlands by night and mountains by day, thereby reinforcing a common prejudice that plains were boring and mountains picturesque. This arrangement was so important that the Great Northern Railway emphasized in its 1928 annual report that the new Empire Builder would "traverse the most scenic region in the north-

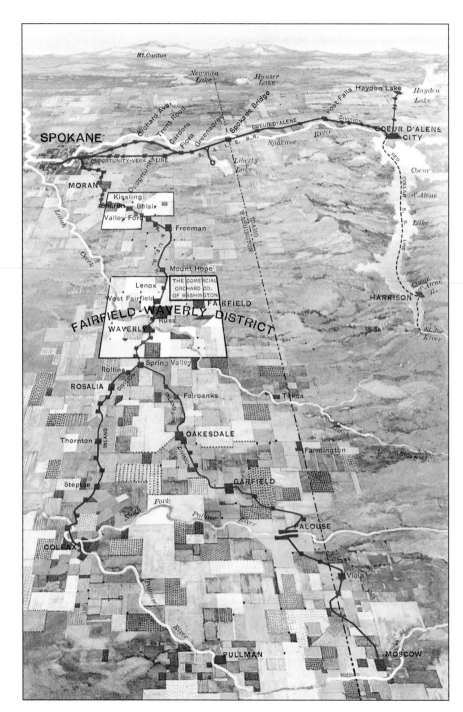

*T*he Spokane & Inland Empire Railroad used elevated perspective to emphasize the agricultural potential of the area adjacent to its tracks across eastern Washington. *Special Collections Division, University of Washington Libraries.*

*"See America First" from the perspective of a railway passenger car was the theme of a Great Northern annotated timetable in 1916. California State Railroad Museum.*

western United States in daylight."[6]

When the Milwaukee Road changed the schedule of its Olympian in 1929 to cross scenic parts of the Bitterroot Mountains by day, it had to consider how best to present the railroad corridor in its brochures. The company official who asked the commercial photographer Asahel Curtis whether he had any pictures of the area explained, "We have been criticized heretofore for the reason that most of our photographs contain no life, and we would like to have included in them, so far as possible, persons and animals, or both."[7]

A skilled publicist could even make sightseeing after dark exciting. For instance, the Oregon Railroad & Navigation Company in 1900 called travelers' attention to its locomotive headlights of the latest design:

And besides all this, it heightens incalculably the picturesqueness of night travel. The train looks like a huge battleship flying through the vast forests, amid mountains and canyons, over wide-stretching plains, and along wild lake and river sides, with its mighty searchlights in full play. In the swiftly moving light, lonely farm houses flash by like gilded palaces or fabrics of fairyland. Columbia River fishwheels gleam for an instant, fit homes for the water-nymphs and deities of the floods and streams, instead of death-traps for the royal chinook."[8]

The railway landscape also included the tracks themselves, and the stations, roundhouses, bridges, section houses, and other assorted structures that formed a railroad's own built environment. A well-maintained right-of-way might become an asset in its own fashion, as it did when the Northern Pacific's passenger traffic manager, A. B. Smith, emphasized that his company was "not 'just a railroad.' It is a railroad of character, of high ideals, of superior operating efficiency. I invite your most critical inspection of our trains—our roadbed—all of our property. From the trim, precise electric block

412   O.S.L. ROUNDHOUSE, POCATELLO, IDAHO                    92449

*The Oregon Short Line's roundhouse in Pocatello, Idaho, was once a smoky hive of activity. Courtesy Washington State Historical Society.*

447  ELECTRIC LOCOMOTIVE PULLING THE ORIENTAL LIMITED EMERGING FROM CASCADE TUNNEL ON GREAT NORTHERN RAILWAY

*The Great Northern's Oriental Limited emerges from the old Cascade Tunnel. Washington State Historical Society.*

*The Spokane, Portland & Seattle Railway's new bridge across the Columbia River at Vancouver, Washington. Hand-tinted postcards depicting such feats of railroad engineering were popular among tourists. Washington State Historical Society.*

190. COLUMBIA RIVER BRIDGE, 2 MILES LONG, SPANNING COLUMBIA RIVER.

*A color postcard shows Tacoma's Beaux Arts–style station, used by both the Union Pacific and Northern Pacific, not long after it opened on May 1, 1911. It was based on plans drawn up by the architectural firm of Reed and Stem of St. Paul. Among its most prominent features was the massive copper-covered dome. Tacoma's press in 1911 touted the station as the third largest in the United States, after New York's Pennsylvania Station and Washington's Union Station. The last Amtrak train departed on June 14, 1984. Special Collections Division, University of Washington Libraries.*

Northern Pacific Depot from Tracks, Tacoma, Wash.

signals to the washed gravel ballast beneath the ties—everything on the right of way is of high standard. Even the section markers seem to have just been painted. . . . No detail of perfection is overlooked."[9]

All changes in the landscape were important to railroads serving the Pacific Northwest, even if they were unintended. During the first railway age the trunk-line carriers not only promoted a New Northwest but also dramatically transformed corridors of land where they chose to locate their tracks and related structures.

*In an elaborate brochure issued in the mid-1920s, the Northern Pacific juxtaposed luxury accommodations with a rugged mountain landscape. That contrast, after all, was a major appeal of travel aboard the North Coast Limited. Minnesota Historical Society.*

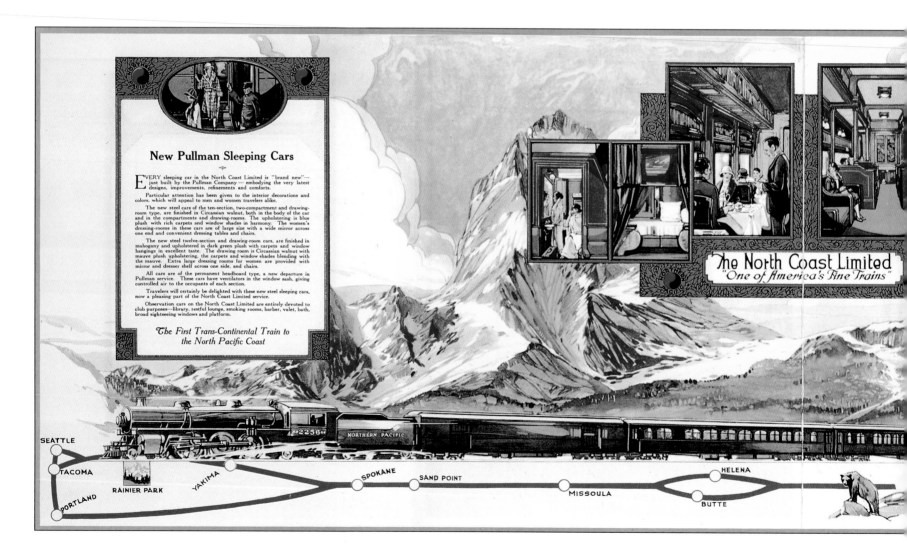

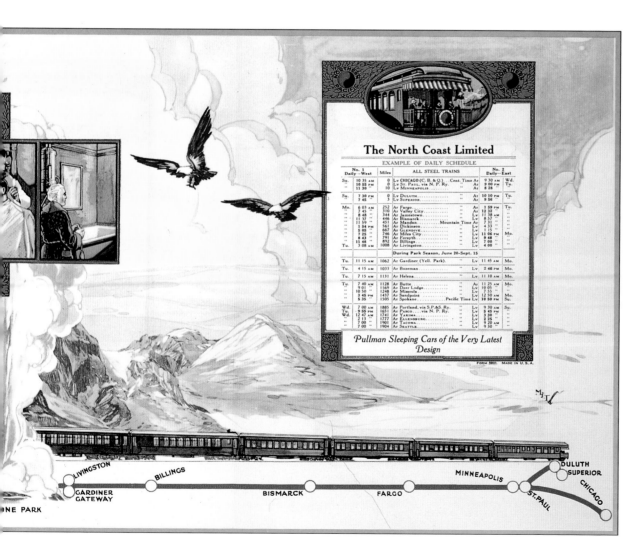

## The North Coast Limited

### EXAMPLE OF DAILY SCHEDULE

| No. 1 Daily—West | | Miles | ALL STEEL TRAINS | | No. 2 Daily—East | |
|---|---|---|---|---|---|---|
| Su. | 10 35 AM | 0 | Lv CHICAGO (C. B. & Q.) . . . .Cent. Time Ar | | 9 30 AM | Wd. |
| " | 10 55 PM | 0 | Lv ST. PAUL, via N. P. Ry. | Ar | 9 00 PM | Tu. |
| " | 11 30 " | 10 | Lv MINNEAPOLIS | Ar | 8 28 " | |
| Su. | 7 30 PM | 0 | Lv DULUTH . . . . . . . . . . . . . . | Ar | 10 10 PM | Tu. |
| " | 7 45 " | 3 | Lv SUPERIOR | Ar | 9 56 " | |
| Mo. | 6 03 AM | 252 | Ar Fargo . . . . . . . . . . . . . . | Ar | 1 59 PM | Tu. |
| " | 7 45 " | 310 | Ar Valley City . . . . . . . . . . . | Ar | 12 32 " | " |
| " | 8 48 " | 344 | Ar Jamestown . . . . . . . . . . | Lv | 11 38 AM | " |
| " | 11 37 " | 446 | Ar Bismarck . . . . . . . . . . . | Lv | 8 57 " | " |
| " | 11 59 " | 451 | Ar Mandan . . . . . . . . Mountain Time Ar | | 7 31 " | " |
| " | 1 54 PM | 561 | Ar Dickinson . . . . . . . . . . | Lv | 4 33 " | " |
| " | 5 05 " | 667 | Ar Glendive . . . . . . . . . . . | Lv | 1 15 " | " |
| " | 7 25 " | 746 | Ar Miles City . . . . . . . . . . | Lv | 11 06 PM | Mo. |
| " | 8 43 " | 791 | Ar Forsyth . . . . . . . . . . . . | Lv | 9 48 " | " |
| " | 11 48 " | 892 | Ar Billings . . . . . . . . . . . . | Lv | 7 00 " | " |
| Tu. | 3 08 AM | 1008 | Ar Livingston . . . . . . . . . . | Lv | 4 00 " | " |
| **During Park Season, June 20-Sept. 15** | | | | | | |
| Tu. | 11 15 AM | 1062 | Ar Gardiner (Yell. Park) . . . . | Lv | 11 45 AM | Mo. |
| Tu. | 4 15 AM | 1033 | Ar Bozeman . . . . . . . . . . . | Lv | 2 46 PM | Mo. |
| Tu. | 7 15 AM | 1131 | Ar Helena . . . . . . . . . . . . | Lv | 11 10 AM | Mo. |
| Tu. | 7 40 AM | 1128 | Ar Butte . . . . . . . . . . . . . | Ar | 11 25 AM | Mo. |
| " | 9 01 " | 1169 | Ar Deer Lodge . . . . . . . . . | Lv | 10 05 " | " |
| " | 10 50 " | 1248 | Ar Missoula . . . . . . . . . . . | Lv | 7 55 " | " |
| " | 3 45 PM | 1437 | Ar Sandpoint . . . . . . . . . . | Lv | 12 50 AM | Mo. |
| " | 5 35 " | 1505 | Ar Spokane . . . . . . . Pacific Time Lv | | 10 50 PM | Su. |
| Wd. | 7 00 AM | 1885 | Ar Portland, via S.P.&S. Ry. . | Lv | 9 30 AM | Su. |
| Tu. | 9 55 PM | 1651 | Ar Pasco, . . . via N. P. Ry. | Lv | 5 45 PM | " |
| Wd. | 12 47 AM | 1741 | Ar Yakima . . . . . . . . . . . | Lv | 3 30 " | " |
| " | 2 13 " | 1777 | Ar Ellensburg . . . . . . . . . | Lv | 2 25 " | " |
| " | 7 00 " | 1901 | Ar Tacoma . . . . . . . . . . . | Lv | 9 20 AM | " |
| " | 7 00 " | 1904 | Ar Seattle . . . . . . . . . . . | Lv | 9 30 " | " |

*Pullman Sleeping Cars of the Very Latest Design*

FORM 5801.   MADE IN U.S.A.

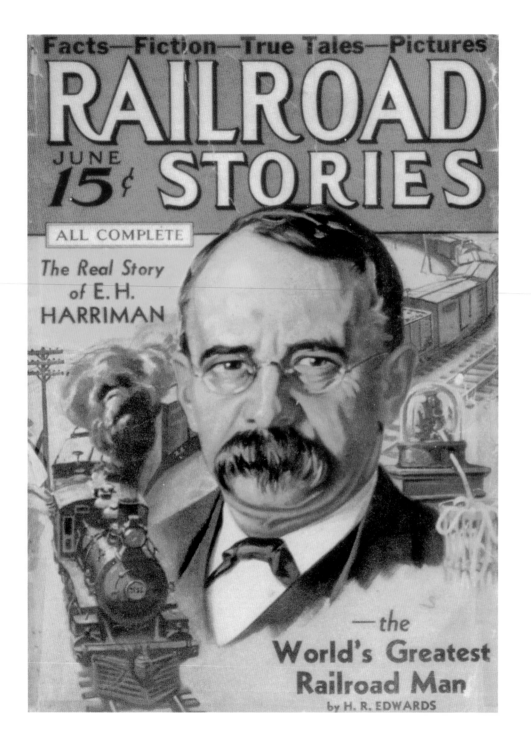

Edward H. Harriman, depicted on the cover of Railroad Stories, energetically reshaped the landscape of the Union Pacific Railroad in the early twentieth century. Union Pacific Museum.

# II / *Northwest Passages*
## *The Second Railway Age, 1897–1917*

*To the California visitor in search of a new variety of scenery and a more interesting and diversified route for the return trip from the land of sunshine and flowers, we offer the "Great Northern Way," through America's real Adventure Land—on the world-famed highway of steel which James J. Hill constructed in regions where the bold Verendryes, the fearless David Thompson and our own Immortals, Lewis and Clark, had explored but a few generations before.*
—California through Adventure Land *([1926?])*

*The world that caught its breath as it read of the engineering master strokes by which the early empire builders hewed a new country out of the great West, would be breathless indeed should it travel through the Pacific Northwest today.*

—The Land of Opportunity Now *(1923)*

# New Beginnings for a New Century

**W**HEREVER PACIFIC NORTH-west railroads ran their tracks, they left names on the land. "Some official put an inky finger on the map. 'There,' he said, 'is a good place for a city. Call it Smith's Coulee, after our master-mechanic.'" In his account of the naming of Smith's Coulee, the popular journalist Ray Stannard Baker sought to explain to easterners the encompassing role that railroads played in western life. Although Smith's Coulee existed only in his imagination, Baker accurately described a process repeated countless times across the New Northwest.[1]

In eastern Washington are the towns of Oakes-dale, named for Thomas F. Oakes, general manager of the Northern Pacific Railroad; Prescott and Endicott, for C. H. Prescott and William Endicott, Jr., two directors of Henry Villard's Oregon & Transcontinental holding company; and Starbuck, for General W. H. Starbuck, a "Nantucket Yankee" associated with the Oregon Railway & Navigation Company, who gave the town its first church bell. In Idaho, the town of Burley recalls a longtime official of the Oregon Short Line, and Avery was named for the son of William Rockefeller, a director of the Chicago, Milwaukee & St. Paul Railway.

When tracks of the Washington, Idaho & Mon-tana Railway headed east from Palouse, Washington, into the white pine country of the Idaho panhandle, they came first to the new mill town of Potlatch (meaning "great feast") and then to Princeton. The next town was called Harvard. This set a pattern for naming the rest of the townsites: Yale, Stanford, Vassar, Cornell, Purdue, and Wellesley. Most were chosen by young college men who surveyed the right-of-way and supervised construction. Despite the impressive appellations, few of the places ever amounted to more than lonely railroad sidings.

Virgil Bogue, a Northern Pacific engineer, recalled how his reconnaissance party affixed a name to the Stampede Pass area east of Tacoma: "Just at this moment we caught sight of a lone eagle, flying about in widening circles, directly above our heads. This appearance, which seemed to all a good omen, furnished a timely suggestion as to a name for the canyon we were leaving; and ever since it has been known as Eagle Gorge."[2]

Louis W. Hill was aboard a Southern Pacific train in 1923 when a sudden inspiration regarding tourism and the Great Northern Railway caused him to send instructions to an associate: "We want to tie up the two—Spokane and Glacier Park." Hill suggested having pictures of Glacier Park inserted into menus at Spokane's posh Davenport Hotel. "I would

suggest that you select a fine photograph of Glacier Park, of some unknown mountain, and we will name it 'Mount Davenport,' and if we can find another, we will name it 'Mount Spokane.' This will get you across."[3]

It was about this time that Hill had the Great Northern rechristen many of its stations east of Glacier Park with romantic-sounding names better suited to a western locale—thus Kilroy became Spotted Robe, Lubec became Rising Sun, Cadmus became Gunsight, and Egan changed to Grizzly. For similar reasons the Commercial Club of Sandpoint, Idaho, suggested renaming the town Grandpoint, but nothing came of the idea. H. R. Williams, vice-

president of the Milwaukee Road, named thirty-two stations across the state of Washington according to a predetermined formula that required each place-name to be reasonably short, easily spelled, pleasant sounding, and unlikely to cause confusion when telegraphed in Morse code or written in train orders. Among his choices were Othello, after the Shakespeare play; Horlick, after a brand of malted milk; Warden, after a major stockholder; and Vassar, after the women's college (and obviously a popular name among males of the time).[4]

Curiously, no city or even whistle-stop recalls the name of Henry Villard. Nor were two of the region's most notable personalities in the early twentieth century—James J. Hill and his rival Edward H. Harriman—so commemorated. Hill had been building a railroad empire between the Great Lakes and Puget Sound since the late 1880s; Harriman was the newcomer. To a remarkable extent the Pacific Northwest's second railway age became a personal contest between these two individuals.[5]

## Newfound Prosperity and the Second Railway Age

I F THE FIRST RAILWAY AGE ENDED abruptly with the panic of 1893, the second railway age began in much the same way. Four years of depression were seemingly forgotten in a single day, July 17, 1897, when the Alaskan steamer *Portland* nosed into Seattle's Elliott Bay and brought news of an incredible gold discovery in the Yukon Territory. Passengers held up sacks stuffed tight with thousands of dollars' worth of the yellow metal to disarm even the most stubborn skeptics. Within days, parlors and pool halls from Puget Sound to Massachusetts Bay buzzed with talk of finding fortunes in Canada's fabulous Klondike. Merely thinking about the precious metal revived hopes and dreams battered by years of monetary crises, widespread unemployment, and popular unrest. The trains that brought thousands of gold seekers to the Pacific Northwest also brought uncounted numbers of land speculators, industrialists, financiers, railroad barons, and others who realized that economic revival made the vast natural resources of Oregon, Washington, Idaho, and Montana every bit as attractive as those of the remote Klondike.[6]

The Pacific Northwest's second and final great era of railroad building took place from 1897 to 1917, a time of unprecedented growth and prosperity. Ray Stannard Baker observed in 1903 that within the region "everything seems to have happened within the last ten years."[7] And in many ways it had.

Boosters pointed with pride to the growing number of acres under irrigation—the number in Idaho doubled from 1.2 million in 1900 to 2.2 million in 1910—and to completion of the world's tallest dam on the Boise River in 1916. Half the counties in Idaho date from the first two decades of the twentieth century, when water and railway lines transformed the parched Snake River plain into new gardens of Eden, attracted thousands of settlers, and gave rise to entirely new communities like Twin Falls. Much the same thing happened in Montana, where waves of new settlers rolled across the eastern plains.

There was also the promise offered by hydroelectric power, or "white coal." Some regional enthusiasts claimed that the Pacific Northwest possessed one-third of all hydroelectric power likely to be generated in the United States. Spokane boosters predicted that white coal and the city's extensive railroad connections would make it a great national manufacturing center. Developers of even greater vision talked of prosperity that growing trans-Pacific commerce would bring to the region. That was not entirely wishful thinking, because a variety of statistical indicators offered reason to view the future with confidence. During the decade from 1900 to 1910, the population of Oregon increased by two-thirds and that of Montana by half; Idaho and Washington populations more than doubled. A total of 2.5 million people lived in the four Pacific Northwest states in 1910.

The region's manufacturing output and payrolls doubled between 1900 and 1914, the year the Panama Canal opened, and gave boosters an additional reason to think that an era of growth was only beginning. The great age of Pacific Northwest timber production dawned when at the turn of the century lumbermen from the Great Lakes states looked west to replace their dwindling sources of supply, and when construction of dozens of new mills made the region truly a "sawdust kingdom."

During the first decade of the twentieth century, Portland and Seattle hosted world's fairs. Portland's Lewis and Clark Exposition of 1905 drew about three million visitors and Seattle's Alaska-Yukon-Pacific Exposition of 1909 almost four million. Each extravaganza represented a coming-of-age party for a city and a region, a time to reflect on the past and wax eloquent about the future.

*Supplies needed for the Klondike rush line the streets of Seattle outside the Northern Pacific's downtown ticket office in 1898. Special Collections Division, University of Washington Libraries, A. Curtis 345a.*

During these years every major city acquired a new skyline. Stimulated by the Lewis and Clark Exposition, Portland embarked on a building boom that gave it a vertical dimension for the first time. In Boise, completion of the Idanha Hotel in 1901, an elegant French chateau structure six stories high, initiated a building trend that created the appearance of a modern metropolis. The population of every city pushed out to the suburbs and beyond. For railroads, the region's building boom and new prosperity translated into traffic and profits.[8]

James J. Hill observed in 1906 that just a decade earlier the Great Northern Railway had moved an average of fewer than 100 carloads of freight a day east over the Cascade mountains. Now it handled 150 to 250 carloads a day; for the Northern Pacific the toal was 350 to 400 carloads a day. "The business of our Northern lines is increasing so fast that we shall have to begin double-tracking," Hill predicted.[9] It was this sort of phenomenal growth and prosperity that revived railroad construction on the Pacific Slope. At least one-third of all railroad mileage there was built during the twentieth century, and almost all of it before 1914. Much of the increase came from the opening of three additional transcontinental lines. New rails joined Salt Lake City and Los Angeles in 1905, St. Paul and Seattle in 1909, and Salt Lake City and Oakland in 1910.

*T*he camera of Asahel Curtis recorded Seattle life at the intersection of First Avenue and Yesler Way in August 1911. According to the recent federal census, Seattle had surpassed Portland to become the most populous city in the Pacific Northwest. Washington State Historical Society.

*R*ailroad Avenue was a center of activity in early
twentieth-century Seattle. *Special Collections Division,
University of Washington Libraries, 1675.*

## Enter Edward H. Harriman

ON NOVEMBER 1, 1897, THE Union Pacific Railway was sold at auction in an Omaha freight house. About five hundred people gathered to watch the proceedings. They did not see much, however, because the sale was over in less than a minute. A syndicate of New York bankers headed by Kuhn, Loeb and Company, with Edward H. Harriman as a participant, purchased the main line from Omaha to Ogden for $58.5 million.

What they had bought, some cynics observed, was little more than an apple tree with no branches. During the hard times of the 1890s, the Union Pacific had shrunk from a system almost eight thousand miles long to one only forty-four hundred miles long by 1895, and then as various subsidiaries were stripped away, its trackage decreased to only two thousand miles. To some observers the position of the Union Pacific was hopeless, but receivership in 1893 had forced a settlement with the federal government and freed the railroad from Uncle Sam's domination and a crushing load of debt. This resolution of long-standing difficulties made the Union Pacific competitive once more, something the canny Harriman must certainly have realized.

At the time of the purchase Harriman was still very much an unknown to most Americans, a stockbroker of increasing but not yet spectacular wealth whose experience in railroading was limited mainly to serving as a director of the Illinois Central. But after he became chairman of the Union Pacific's executive committee in May 1898, he launched a whirlwind tour of the railroad to see firsthand what needed to be done to rehabilitate it. Accompanied by his two older daughters, Mary and Cornelia, and various railroad officials, Harriman toured 6,236 miles of line in twenty-three days. From the vantage point of an observation car pushed by a locomotive, he carefully noted grades, curves, ballast, rails, and

virtually every other physical aspect of the railroad from the Missouri River to the Pacific Ocean. His energy and curiosity seemed boundless as he immersed himself in the smallest details, on one occasion wondering why long bolts were used to fasten rails together when shorter ones would work just as well. He refused to accept the explanation that that was the way it had always been done. His mind quickly calculated how much money the Union Pacific could save by using shorter bolts.[10]

Even as Harriman learned about the Union Pacific, people around the Pacific Northwest learned more about this newcomer to the West's complicated railroad scene. He was a small, swarthy man with thick glasses and a walrus mustache. An intense person possessed of immense energy and few words, he was not good at public relations. His brusqueness, in fact, was legendary.

Edward Henry Harriman was born in 1848, the son of an Episcopal minister. His life resembled that of Jay Gould. Both left school at an early age to go to work, and both ended up on Wall Street. Harriman started on Wall Street at the age of fourteen as an office boy and only eight years later had saved enough money to purchase a seat for himself on the New York Stock Exchange. His marriage opened the way to greater involvement in the railroad world. But whereas Gould became nationally known while still in his thirties, Harriman dwelled in obscurity until his fifties. Gould had pushed the Union Pacific through undeveloped country; Harriman would rebuild it to serve modern needs. When he received authorization to spend $20 million on improvements, he and his capable lieutenants immediately launched an energetic reconstruction program. Although the Union Pacific was hardly the two streaks of rust some Harriman admirers have claimed, it certainly was not in good physical shape.

During the reconstruction process, an army of workmen used tens of thousands of tons of iron, steel, and stone to rebuild roadbed and tracks. They

*This map shows the extent of the Harriman lines in 1909. The 15,000-mile-long aggregation of track included both the Union Pacific and Southern Pacific roads and such subsidiaries as the Oregon Short Line and the Oregon Railroad & Navigation Company. It was the longest such system in the United States. Union Pacific Museum.*

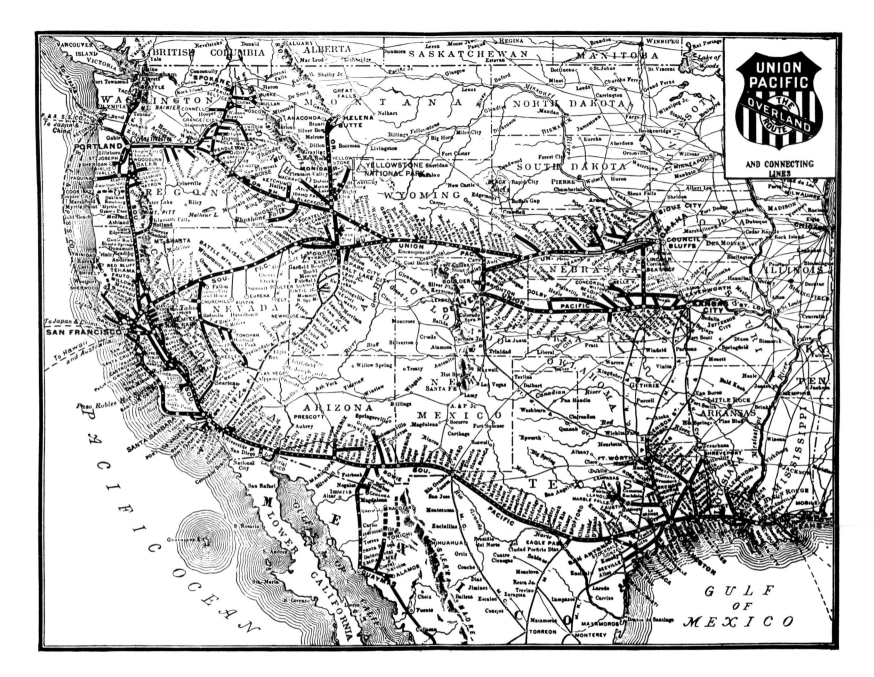

reduced steep grades, bored tunnels, strengthened bridges, and straightened difficult curves. They also double-tracked much of the main line and installed new block signals for greater safety and speed. The railroad acquired larger and more powerful locomotives. Reconstruction was not limited to upgrading the trunk line from Omaha to Ogden. Harriman hastened to reacquire many of the subsidiary companies shorn away during the depression. By 1900 both the Oregon Short Line and the Oregon Railroad & Navigation Company were again part of the Union Pacific system.

When Harriman realized that the Southern Pacific, the Union Pacific's connector to California, did not measure up to the standards of his new Union Pacific and that its line west of Ogden created a traffic bottleneck, he quickly moved to acquire the carrier. When Collis P. Huntington, one of the Southern Pacific's original Big Four, died on August 13, 1900, Harriman seized the opportunity to enlarge his holdings by acquiring Huntington's interest for $75 million. On the Southern Pacific the reconstruction process proceeded with no less vigor than it had on the Union Pacific. Harriman's lieutenant on the Southern Pacific was Julius Krutschnitt, who oversaw the task of bringing the road up to Union Pacific standards. When Krutschnitt asked how soon he was to spend reconstruction money, Harriman snapped that he should do so in a week if possible.

Most reconstruction work on the two great railroads was completed by 1902, although it never really stopped during Harriman's lifetime. Workers continued to replace telegraph lines with telephones and dilapidated stations with new ones. The increased efficiency and a dramatic surge in traffic were reflected in the price of a share of Union Pacific common stock, which climbed from a low of 16⅛ in 1898 to a high of 195⅜ in 1906. Observers could accurately describe the Union Pacific under Harriman as a brand-new railroad. It had been rebuilt into one of the nation's finest rail systems.

The tracks of the Union Pacific and Southern Pacific systems created an empire that dominated transportation in many parts of the American West. Especially was that true in southern Idaho and eastern Oregon, where few miles of line existed apart from Harriman's Oregon Short Line and Oregon Railroad & Navigation Company. In other parts of the Pacific Northwest, Harriman confronted Hill, each man relentlessly determined to extend his reach. It was inevitable that they should clash.

## The Hill Lines

OF THE ENTREPRENEURS ASSOCIated with the Northwest's great era of railway building, no one, not even Edward H. Harriman, better merited the title Empire Builder than James J. Hill, a businessman with diverse interests across the northern tier states. Born in Canada, near present-day Guelph, Ontario, in 1838, he planted himself in Minnesota in 1856, where he began his business career modestly enough as a shipping clerk in St. Paul. While still in his twenties, Hill started his own warehouse and express business. In 1878, shortly before he turned forty, he and a group of eastern associates acquired the bankrupt St. Paul & Pacific Railroad, predecessor of the St. Paul, Minneapolis & Manitoba. From that modest acorn grew a mighty oak, the Great Northern Railway, financially the strongest of all northern transcontinentals.

During the hard times of the 1890s, when other transcontinental railroads slid into receivership, the Great Northern continued to earn and pay a 5 percent dividend. Even in fiscal 1894, the worst year of the depression, net income of the Great Northern jumped 33 percent; the following year it leaped another 66 percent. This was in contrast to the troubles that beset the Northern Pacific. Hill, who gloated that his was the only Pacific line paying a dividend on its shares, was now in an enviable position to build a railroad empire at the expense of erstwhile competitors.

Although Hill was obligated to numerous allies and supporters who provided much of the financial support for the Great Northern, he still took intense personal pride in everything about the railroad. More than any other major railroad in the United States, the Great Northern was the personal creation of one man. "The Great Northern comes very near to being Mr. Hill's private possession, if not in point of actual ownership, at least as regards its

*James J. Hill (1838–1916) of St. Paul, Minnesota, assembled a railroad empire that stretched across the northern tier states from Chicago to Seattle and Portland. In that area he was known as the Empire Builder because of the many development activities of his Great Northern and affiliated railroads. James Jerome Hill Reference Library.*

actual management," observed one financial analyst.[11]

Unlike Villard and Gould, who were essentially financiers, Hill immersed himself in the day-to-day operation of his road. But his vision encompassed far more than simply running a successful railroad. He knew that profits depended on development of the land through which the Great Northern passed. Hill believed that if settlers along the right-of-way were prosperous, the railroad would be too. He also understood that the Great Northern had to develop Pacific Rim markets to balance the traffic flow between East and West.

To that end Hill looked to Asia to generate part of the revenue he needed to make his line to Puget Sound a success. In 1900 he formed the Great Northern Steamship Company with capital of $6 million and had two mammoth ships built. The *Minnesota* entered service in 1903, and the *Dakota* followed a year later. They were combination passenger and freight vessels (floating hotels, some

said) designed to run from the end of Great Northern tracks in Seattle's Smith Cove to Philippine, Japanese, and Chinese ports.

Hill's dreams, many of which he was able to implement successfully during his lifetime, made him the subject of many popular legends and anecdotes: "Give me enough Swedes and whiskey and I'll build a railroad to Hell," he is reputed to have said. When the engineer John F. Stevens located the route for the Great Northern switchback over the Cascade Range in the early 1890s, he sent the information to Hill, who responded that he did not like one aspect of the plan and was "coming out to see about it." He directed that no work be done at that particular place, but Stevens went ahead anyway. When Hill arrived, some associates expected him to fire Stevens, but Hill strode to the point in question, looked it over, and responded, "That is all right, you could have done nothing else." He personally ordered a substantial raise in Stevens's salary.[12]

The story is also told that on one occasion an angry Hill threw a telephone through a window. On another he summarily fired an inoffensive Great Northern clerk named Spittles, saying he did not like his surname. Whether nor not the latter tale is apocryphal, it could well have happened in an age innocent of the large body of labor and regulatory law on the books today.[13]

The prevailing economic and social philosophy in Hill's day was laissez-faire, which, despite an occasional flare-up of anticorporation protest like populism, discouraged state and federal interference with business activity. Thus, Hill's generation of corporate leaders had nearly a free hand in running their businesses, restrained only by conscience, common sense, and such power as an extremely weak labor movement might occasionally muster.

Hill hid Great Northern profits not only from a suspicious public but also from stockholders who might have demanded larger dividends instead

*A*sahel Curtis recorded this view of Smith Cove in Seattle in 1905 as the Oriental Limited rolled past Hill's two great steamships Minnesota *and* Dakota. *The wharf, warehouse, and elevator complex embodied Hill's dream of a steady flow of traffic between North America and Asia to keep the freight cars of the Great Northern Railway full beyond whatever freight the Pacific Northwest could generate. Special Collections Division, University of Washington Libraries, A. Curtis 6577.*

The image contains the following labels: VANCOUVER, SEATTLE, EVERT, NEW TRANSCONTINENTAL, WINNIPEG LINE, DULUTH, FARGO, MINOT NEW COAST LINE, BISMARK, MINNEAPOLIS, ST PAUL, SIOUX CITY, DENVER, PLANS FOR 3000 MILES OF NEW LINES IN U.S.

**A** *newspaper caricature of Hill's plan for 3,000 miles of new railway lines in the western United States. Minnesota Historical Society, C.N.34.*

penetrating brown eyes to bear upon you he looks larger and larger as the minutes lapse." Capable of blunt speech and withering sarcasm, he was widely reputed to be emotionally cold, but a St. Paul newspaper reporter noted on one occasion that when his son and designated successor, Louis, started to board a special train of boosters bound for the Pacific Coast from Minnesota, "the railroad magnate impulsively threw his arms about the younger man's neck, gave him a big fatherly hug and kissed his son goodbye."[15] The fact that Hill's display of affection was newsworthy may reveal something about press perception of the man.

Hill kept a railroad map of the Northwest close at hand as he plotted his strategy. But he hardly needed a map to know that when the Northern Pacific fell into the hands of receivers in 1893 it created a golden opportunity for him. Working closely with the New York banker J. P. Morgan in 1896, he launched a successful drive to gain control of his onetime rival. He entered the directorship of the Northern Pacific in 1901.[16]

Like Harriman on the Union Pacific, Hill undertook to upgrade the Northern Pacific. Its main line in the late 1890s was laid primarily with fifty-six-pound rail, which was far too light to bear the weight of modern locomotives and cars. Northern Pacific motive power was also out of date and needed to be replaced.

Hill sought to strengthen his growing system's eastern connections by acquiring the Chicago, Burlington & Quincy Railroad. The carrier not only linked St. Paul and Chicago but also gave Hill access to extensive coalfields in southern Illinois. It had its most extensive network of track in midwestern states that were timber consumers, and it thus made a perfect match for railroads serving the forests of the Pacific Northwest. The Burlington, moreover, was an immensely profitable company in its own right.[17]

It was Hill's drive to control the Burlington that

of allowing him to reinvest them to upgrade the railroad. "We have tried to keep all of our published statements of earnings and income as low as possible," he confided to J. P. Morgan. "Had our accounts been kept on the same basis as those of most of the other roads, including the Northern Pacific, our net income would have shown nearly $15,000,000 as against the $13,075,000 reported.[14]

Hill was a small man, stockily built, who appeared to some observers to be far bigger than he actually was. "When he begins to talk and to bring these formally touched off a lengthy battle with Harriman. The Burlington posed a competitive threat to Harriman because some of its lines ran west from Chicago to Omaha and on through Union Pacific country to Denver, as well as north to Billings, Montana, which it reached in 1894. Conversely, Hill's biggest concern became Harriman, who seemed determined to intrude into his affairs. When Hill quietly increased his holdings of the Northern Pacific, Harriman nearly thwarted him by making extensive purchases of his own. He did the same thing when Hill sought control of the Burlington.

On November 12, 1901, after Hill had battled Harriman to a draw for control of the Northern Pacific and the Chicago, Burlington & Quincy, he formed the Northern Securities Company, a giant holding company capitalized at $400 million, to coordinate the interests of the Hill Lines and

protect them from further Harriman raids. In the end his nemesis became the United States Supreme Court, which by a 5–4 vote in 1904 ordered the Northern Securities Company dissolved as a violation of the Sherman Anti-Trust Act. The setback did not prevent Hill from maintaining control over his empire in other ways, by purchasing or building new lines to link Spokane and Portland, or from battling Harriman for access to central Oregon. In fact, the railroad combination ostensibly torn asunder in 1904 was put together in 1970 as the Burlington Northern Railroad.

As for Harriman, Hill growled, "His vanity has no bounds." About 1905 when someone asked Harriman whether he had a plan to get even with Hill for some perceived mistreatment, his response was an ominous, "Not yet."[18]

*A work train of the Burlington & Missouri River Railroad was photographed in eastern Montana at the turn of the century. The woman standing in the doorway was a cook. Montana Historical Society.*

## Local Pride

THE CONTRAST BETWEEN HARRIman and Hill was not limited simply to building competing lines; each man also acquired railroads built by others. The Pacific Northwest was full of short lines, but by one accounting, there was only a handful of independents left by 1908. Like giant magnets drawing metal filings, the two empire builders collected local railroads. No one knew when a remote feeder line might become a useful pawn in someone's imperial scheme.

The process of fashioning larger and more complex railroad systems probably began in the late 1870s when Oregon Railway & Navigation absorbed Dr. Baker's Walla Walla & Columbia River and Jay Gould acquired the Utah Northern for the Union Pacific. In 1892 the Northern Pacific gained the Seattle, Lake Shore, & Eastern Railway, which gave it a line to Sumas on the Canadian border and a branch to timber country at North Bend, Washington. At about the same time, it acquired the Spokane & Palouse Railway south from Spokane and the Central Washington Railroad west from Spokane to Coulee City. The Washington & Columbia River Railway in the Walla Walla Valley became Northern Pacific property in 1892, although the smaller company did not lose its separate identity until more than a decade later.

Some independent lines had grandiose names that belied their modest size. The Great Southern Railroad completed a thirty-mile line from The Dalles to Dufur, Oregon, in 1905. The Washington, Idaho & Montana Railway extended from Palouse, Washington, to Bovill, Idaho, a distance of fifty miles and well short of the Montana border. It still served its purpose by hauling logs and lumber for the Potlatch Lumber Company, and it also carried mail and passengers from 1905 until 1955.

The Columbia Southern commenced running from Biggs Junction to Shaniko, the heart of Oregon's sheep country, in May 1900. It eventually became the Union Pacific's Shaniko branch and was later abandoned. Another short line reaching south from the Columbia River valley was the Mount Hood Railroad that in 1905 was completed from Hood River to Parkdale, a distance of about twenty-five miles. It was built by the Utah lumberman David Eccles. Another Eccles carrier was the Sumpter Valley Railway, a three-foot-gauge line that traced a roundabout course through the mountains west of Baker, Oregon, to tap local timber resources. Construction started in 1891 and went forward by fits and starts to reach Prairie City, a cattle-raising center eighty miles distant, in 1910. There was some speculation that Eccles really wanted to extend the railroad as far as Lakeview in southern Oregon, where its tracks would connect with another narrow-gauge line running north from Reno. Nothing came of the idea, however. For much of its life, the Sumpter Valley used largely hand-me-down equipment made available when the Union Pacific converted the Utah & Northern to standard gauge.[19] Passenger service on the Sumpter Valley ended in 1937, and the railroad itself ceased running in 1947. A short stretch of track was relaid in the 1970s to carry tourists. The other Eccles line, the Mount Hood Railroad, was for a time part of the Union Pacific before becoming independent again. Like many other short lines in the Northwest today, it operates tourist trains to supplement its freight revenues.

It is impossible to generalize about all the small railroad companies that once linked the region's interior mining and sawmill towns and farm centers to metropolitan corridors formed by the main lines, but many of them were synonymous with one individual. Hill and Harriman had their regional counterparts in men like David Eccles, his fellow timber baron F. A. Blackwell, who was the power behind the Idaho & Washington Northern Railroad,

and Daniel Chase Corbin. Although Hill and Harriman attracted the most attention during the turn-of-the-century years, local empire builders like Corbin continued to add to the Pacific Northwest's expanding network of tracks.

During the course of two decades, Corbin helped to launch a series of railroads to funnel the wealth of an expanding hinterland into Spokane. His first venture was the Coeur d'Alene Railway & Navigation Company, started in 1886. It headed east into Idaho using trains and a steamboat link across Lake Coeur d'Alene to tap the riches of the silver valley. Corbin's second scheme was the Spokane Falls & Northern Railway, which in 1889 began building northwest from Spokane toward the Columbia River. Through a series of subsidiaries it reached Rossland and Nelson, British Columbia, in the mid-1890s to channel mineral wealth south to Spokane. Yet a third venture was the Spokane International Railway,

which headed northeast from Spokane to reach the international boundary and a Canadian Pacific connection at Eastport, Idaho, in 1906.[20]

Corbin's Coeur d'Alene Railway & Navigation Company eventually passed into the hands of the Northern Pacific, his Spokane Falls & Northern went to the Great Northern in 1898, and his Spokane International went first to the Canadian Pacific in 1917 and then to the Union Pacific in 1958. During the first decade of the twentieth century, no matter how small and seemingly insignificant a local railroad was, it might still serve as a pawn in the regionwide chess game waged between Hill and Harriman, as was the case, for instance, with the Corvallis & Eastern Railroad.

In the late 1860s, Colonel T. E. Hogg, a former Confederate officer, hatched a plan to build a line from Yaquina Bay (now Newport) on the Oregon coast east to Corvallis and from there to a transcontinental connection near the Oregon-Idaho border. The Oregon Pacific Railroad never got any farther east than Idanha at the crest of the Cascade Range, where its tracks dead-ended in the 1880s. Its successor company was the Corvallis & Eastern Railroad, a pitiful remnant of Hogg's once grand scheme, which the Southern Pacific acquired in 1907. The purchase gave the Harriman system a feeder line, but even more important, it kept the Corvallis & Eastern out of the hands of Harriman's arch-rival, Hill.

Even in southern Idaho and eastern Oregon where Harriman's control was nearly complete, he could never be certain that a new railroad might not serve Hill's purposes. One rumor had Hill acquiring two small Idaho railroads, the Pacific & Idaho Northern Railway and the Gilmore & Pittsburgh Railroad; connecting them via a new line down the Salmon River; and having them form the basis for a new line extending from Twin Bridges, on a Northern Pacific branch in central Montana, to Boise, to Lakeview in southern Oregon, and finally to a connection with the Western Pacific to California.[21]

Anything seemed possible during the battle of the two railroad barons.

Most people would have had a hard time even locating the Gilmore & Pittsburgh on a railroad map of the Pacific Northwest, much less envisioning it as part of a new Hill line to California. Yet there was no denying that the Hill-allied Northern Pacific had put up $4.8 million to help finance its construction in 1909. Although the Gilmore & Pittsburgh totaled 120 miles, ran from Armstead, Montana, to Salmon, Idaho, through some of the most isolated parts of the entire Pacific Northwest, and lacked a physical connection to Northern Pacific track, it was popularly perceived to represent a Hill invasion of Harriman territory.

Equally ominous from Harriman's point of view would be Hill's acquiring the Pacific & Idaho Northern Railway. This line began building north from Weiser in 1899 as a way to open up the mountainous Seven Devils country—rich in copper, lead, gold, and silver—and to funnel the mineral wealth to the Union Pacific. After the first spike was driven on May 16, 1899, the line reached Cambridge by December 31 and Council a few months later. A steady stream of settlers followed the tracks

as they inched their way north into the "Golden Heart" of Idaho.

In 1911 the railroad reached New Meadows where its president, Colonel Edgar M. Heighho, erected a $40,000 hotel and a railroad station that would "surpass anything of its kind in Idaho." These were built in anticipation that additional tracks would branch north and east from there. A handsome observation car called Coeur d'Or carried tourists north to New Meadows during the summer months where auto-stages were planned to take them on a twenty-mile drive to Payette Lake at McCall for vacations.[22]

Hill also considered invading Harriman territory by extending a line down the Oregon coast to Tillamook, and from there using a fleet of steamships to reach San Francisco. With that goal in mind, his location engineers were active in western Oregon from the Columbia River to the Siskyou Mountains. Nothing could strike a more telling blow than the Great Northern reaching San Francisco, "which is the very center of their stronghold," observed Hill of the Harriman competition. It was this kind of bitter rivalry that threatened to redraw the railroad map of the Pacific Northwest.[23]

*A train of the Union Pacific's Idaho Northern subsidiary steams through the snows of Payette River canyon on the last day of 1947. The branch reached McCall in 1914 but extended no farther north. As a result of abandonments, the line now extends only as far north as Cascade, where the refurbished station functions as a community center called the Depot Institute. Henry R. Griffiths and the Barriger Railroad Collection, St. Louis Mercantile Library.*

*On the whole, I see no reason why the Darwinian theory does not apply to railways, and the survival of the fittest ought to leave us comfortable.*

—*James J. Hill to Henry L. Higginson (Sept. 30, 1899)*

# Fiefdoms and Baronies: Harriman and Hill Redraw the Railroad Map

ROBERT STRAHORN, THE ONETIME promoter of Union Pacific country, became a familiar figure around Yakima, Washington, after 1903 when he arrived from Spokane and bought a local water and power franchise. Three years later he announced formation of the North Coast Railroad, which proposed to build a line from the Columbia River up the Yakima Valley and across the Cascade Range through Cowlitz Pass to reach the tracks of the Tacoma Eastern Railroad. This connection would provide access to Puget Sound. Strahorn's North Coast Railroad scheme would make Yakima the hub of a 750-mile system that extended west to Seattle, Tacoma, and Portland and east to Spokane and Walla Walla. In addition, he proposed to organize the Spokane Terminal Project to bring together five railways in one grand union station.

For Yakimans, Strahorn's new railway was a dream come true. It promised to free them at last from Northern Pacific monopoly. Yet, when they wondered aloud who was behind the North Coast venture, Strahorn refused to say. The question puzzled Pacific Northwesterners for several years. Was it the Milwaukee, the Burlington, the Canadian Pacific, the Harriman system, the Chicago & North Western, or perhaps the Soo Line? Could it be the

Northern Pacific itself? Detectives shadowed Strahorn's movements and tried to trace his checks. Only in late 1910, when tracks through the Yakima Valley were spiked firmly into place and his position in Spokane was seemingly secure, did Strahorn announce his alliance with Harriman.[1]

In his unpublished autobiography, Strahorn revealed how Harriman became involved in the mystery project. In late 1905 the Yakima Valley promoter traveled to New York City to interest Harriman in the North Coast Railroad. Harriman's lieutenant, Julius Krutschnitt, met Strahorn and took him to Harriman's Madison Avenue mansion. There he found the financial wizard of the age brusque and absorbed in a stream of long-distance phone calls.

In response to Strahorn's North Coast proposal, Harriman snapped, "I'm not interested. We can duplicate anything you have more economically, and avoid the disagreeable results of publicity which would almost inevitably result from such an arrangement." Strahorn recorded that he felt like sliding under the table to dodge Harriman's withering gaze.

As he hastily gathered up his maps and papers, however, Strahorn remarked that Hill would look with favor on what he proposed to build in Washington.

*Robert Strahorn became known as the Sphinx because he raised millions for his North Coast Railroad project without identifying his backers. For five years he refused to reveal the source of the money. He was also involved with the Yakima Valley Transportation Company, an electric interurban line. Spokane Public Library.*

Harriman, who was crocheting and struck Strahorn as "the very picture of a serene, frugal, and practical housewife," Harriman became a man transformed. He would be glad to meet Strahorn alone in his office in the Equitable Building, he said. But "don't let a soul know of your coming."

On his second visit with Harriman, Strahorn spoke enthusiastically of the merits of the North Coast project, but Harriman again cut him short. "Oh, you western promoters make me so tired." Yet out of the meeting came an agreement by which Harriman worked behind the scenes to finance Strahorn, but only on condition of absolute secrecy. Harriman made it clear that the two were never to be seen together in public.[2]

## Harriman versus Hill

THE NORTH COAST RAILROAD WAS Harriman's way of thrusting a dagger deep into the heart of Hill's domain in central Washington in retaliation for what the Empire Builder threatened to do to him in Oregon. It was one more case of each man struggling for advantage over the other. Techniques of railroad empire builders were much like those of imperial nations seeking to colonize adjacent territories, fill their treasuries, and secure future prosperity while impoverishing their neighbors. Each wanted an entrenched position. To that end they made diplomatic alliances, waged rate wars, and engaged in flanking maneuvers.[3]

James J. Hill used the occasion of his visit to the Lewis and Clark Exposition in Portland in 1905 to remark that Oregon was a great state and he intended to aid its development. When he publicly confirmed that he planned to build a railroad to Portland, he electrified his listeners and caused the *Oregonian* to exult that with the new line "Oregon is at last free from the Harriman thraldom."[4]

"Well," retorted a visibly irritated Harriman, "I am not interested." As the three men walked down the hall toward the front entrance, Harriman quietly suggested to Strahorn that the two of them step back into the parlor. There in the company of Mrs.

At this time Hill's only access to the Oregon metropolis was via a ferry and the single-track Northern Pacific line that extended south from Seattle to the Columbia River. Hill had once considered making an agreement with Harriman to use Oregon Railroad & Navigation Company tracks into Portland and to limit "territorial contests" by reviving the proposal for the Snake River as dividing line between their expanding empires, but nothing came of this.[5]

Hill's expansive rhetoric at the Lewis and Clark Exposition alarmed Harriman and provoked a response. Out of their mutual hostility and fear came the greatest burst of railroad building the Pacific Northwest had seen since the Great Northern was completed to Seattle in 1893. The Harriman-Hill duel began in earnest on August 23, 1905, when the Great Northern and Northern Pacific announced joint incorporation of the Portland & Seattle Railway Company to link Spokane and Portland via the north bank of the Columbia River. This arrangement would provide the Hill lines their first water-level route through the Cascade Range and pry the area bordering the great river from the grip of Harriman's Union Pacific. The Portland & Seattle Railway also acquired the Astoria & Columbia River Railroad in 1907 and in that way extended Hill's reach beyond Portland to the mouth of the Columbia and down the Oregon coast another eighteen miles to the resort community of Seaside.

The new carrier changed its name to the Spokane, Portland & Seattle Railway on February 1, 1908. On March 11, company officials ran the Golden Spike Special to carry four hundred excursionists from Portland and Vancouver to Lyle, Washington, to celebrate completion of construction. By the end of the year the entire line was open from Portland to Spokane.

The Spokane, Portland & Seattle Railway, or North Bank Road, was probably the finest piece of railroad ever constructed in the Pacific Northwest.

One commentator labeled it the "billiard table line" because of its amazingly level profile from Pasco to Portland. The ruling grade along the Columbia River did not exceed ten feet in a mile. But such technological virtuosity commanded a steep price: construction costs averaged an astounding $100,000 per mile.[6]

When the price of building the North Bank Road ballooned to ten million dollars over the original estimate, Hill grew increasingly worried. He fretted that he had lost control of the project and came to regard construction of the Spokane, Portland & Seattle as the most unsatisfactory thing that had ever occurred during his long career in railroading. "As you know," he grumbled to George F. Baker, "I have always felt that the whole North Bank enterprise cost much more than it should have, measured by any standard of reasonable economy." He complained that rock cuts, for instance, were made wider than necessary, and this should not have been allowed.[7]

Irritated by the affair, he asked a trusted associate, John F. Stevens, the engineer who two decades earlier had located Marias Pass, to get him the facts. After considering all evidence, Hill forced President G. B. French of the North Bank Road to step down in mid-1910 and replaced him with Stevens. Hill also implemented plans to increase traffic beyond what Portland and Columbia River localities would likely generate. One obvious way to make the railroad pay was to run feeder lines south into Oregon. A particularly attractive prospect was the central part of the state, an area roughly the size of Ohio without any rail service. Because local people blamed Harriman's monopoly for their isolation, Hill could portray himself as a public benefactor and strike a telling blow against his competitor.

In 1909 the North Bank Road acquired the Oregon Trunk Line, a Nevada company chartered in 1906 but still trackless. John Stevens recalled that, in order to keep the transaction secret from Harri-

# OREGON-WASHINGTON RAILROAD & NAVIGATION COMPANY

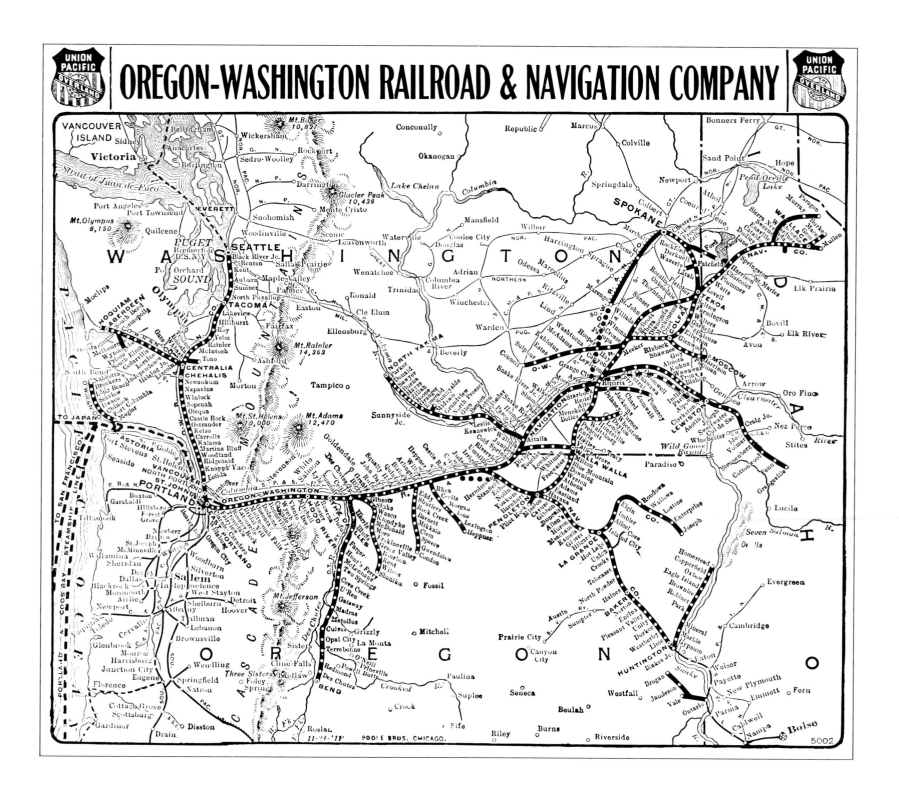

First Train To Cross
Crooked River Bridge
Oregon Trunk. R.Y.
Central Oregon.
Length 340 FT. Height 320 FT.

man, he met a representative of the Oregon Trunk in mid-1909 "about midnight in the rain under a tree in a public park in Portland and verbally closed its transfer, passing a large-sized check the next day, not to be cashed for several days." In late July, construction crews started building south from Fallbridge (later renamed Wishram), Washington, toward Bend, 156 miles away. Stevens served as president of the new line.[8]

Harriman interests tried to block or counter Hill's incursion into central Oregon every step of the way. When the Spokane to Portland line was first proposed down the north bank of the Columbia River, its projected right-of-way had to cross the old Cascade Railroad in four places. Harriman used his ownership of the property to block Hill's access to a strategic section of riverbank. The legal battle, however, ended in victory for Hill.

Next both Hill and Harriman decided to build lines south from the Columbia Valley up the rugged Deschutes River canyon to exploit the potential agricultural wealth of the high plateau country around Bend. After being shunned by railroad builders for the better part of three decades, central Oregon awoke to find herself the object of the affections of two intensely jealous suitors. It was in the Deschutes Canyon that the two railroad barons' war of words and legal contests turned violent.

Hill hired the construction company Porter Brothers to help grade a right-of-way for the Oregon Trunk; Harriman used the Twohy Brothers to do likewise for his Des Chutes Railroad. There was little brotherly love on either side. At one point, the Porter Brothers bought land across which the Twohy Brothers had built a wagon road to haul supplies from Grass Valley. A sign now warned, "No Trespassing. Porter Brothers." The Porter Brothers also brought a spring from which teamsters for the Twohy Brothers took water and put up a sign, "No water to spare. Porter Brothers." Harriman tried to checkmate Hill by preventing him from securing a vital right-of-way through the Warm

Springs Indian Reservation located midway up the valley, but federal officials in Washington, D.C., came to Hill's rescue.

Two rival armies of laborers recruited mainly from Portland and Spokane commenced grading along opposite sides of the Deschutes River. They worked primarily with black powder and hand tools. Occasionally they hurled curses and homemade bombs at their counterparts. Almost every train back to the Columbia carried one or more battered laborers, or so claimed the Sunday supplement writers who enjoyed dramatizing the duel up the Deschutes. In fact, probably more ink than blood was spilled during the contest. President Stevens did not recall any fatalities.

On the opposite side of the Cascade Range, Hill interests acquired the Oregon Electric Railway, which had been completed from Portland to Salem in 1907, and they finished it to Eugene in 1912. Southern Pacific fears of the Sherman Anti-Trust Act had made the railroad giant hesitant to acquire the parallel interurban tracks. In this way Hill gained access to the rich Willamette Valley and prompted Harriman's Southern Pacific to electrify several of its own lines in the area to compete more effectively.

The game of thrust and counterthrust was played out at yet another location, in the Yakima Valley. South of Yakima at Union Gap, roughly the location of old Yakima City, Hill forces tried to block Strahorn's North Coast Railroad from gaining access to Yakima and the numerous orchards of the upper valley. An expensive court fight ensured, delaying Harriman interests for a year. Legal fees totaled $40,000, but when the court finally awarded the North Coast Railroad access to the vital passage, the jury appraised the value of the conquered territory at a mere twenty dollars. Hill forces also tried unsuccessfully to block Harriman and the North Coast Railroad from gaining entrance to Spokane via Marshall Canyon, the most logical route into the city from the west.

*A Spokane, Portland & Seattle train in Devils Canyon near Kahlotus, Washington, before World War I. When, in early 1991, workers began removing tracks from the now abandoned line, this remote corner of eastern Washington probably had a smaller population than when the railroad arrived eighty years earlier. Oregon Historical Society, 73641.*

Among Union Pacific countermeasures was the Yellowstone Park Railroad Company, a subsidiary that completed a branch from St. Anthony, Idaho, to West Yellowstone, Montana, in 1908 to tap growing tourist traffic long monopolized by Hill railroads. The Union Pacific also extended a line east along the Snake River from Riparia, Washington, to Lewiston, Idaho, and publicly wondered whether it should continue along the Snake to join Lewiston with southern Idaho. In 1910 the Union Pacific was rumored to be constructing a branch north through Hells Canyon to Lewiston from Huntington and Homestead on the Oregon Short Line. Harriman was also supposed to be placing large gangs of surveyors along the Snake River between Lewiston and its confluence with the Salmon River to block Hill, should he try to extend Gilmore & Pittsburgh tracks across central Idaho.[9]

The contest between Harriman and Hill in western Oregon helped motivate the Southern Pacific to complete a branch west from Hillsboro (near Portland) to Tillamook in January 1912. This line was designed to block Hill, who seriously contemplated running tracks south along the coast from Seaside to Tillamook. When the route proved too rugged to be practicable, Hill established the Great Northern Pacific Steamship Company in 1915 to operate the luxury steamships *Northern Pacific* and *Great Northern* in service between Astoria (Flavel) and San Francisco. Not to be outclassed, Harriman's San Francisco & Portland Steamship Company offered competition in the form of the liners *Bear, Beaver,* and *Rose City.*

## Enter Rockefeller and Standard Oil

EVEN AS THE HILL AND HARRIMAN interests battled one another, two additional railroads seemed likely to reach the far Northwest from Chicago. In 1906

the Chicago & North Western Line, the Midwest's wealthiest carrier, extended as far west as Lander, Wyoming. It now contemplated running tracks from there to the Pacific Slope, possibly down central Idaho's Salmon River canyon and on to Coos Bay, a port on the central Oregon coast that some boosters claimed would one day rival Portland or San Francisco. The company actually surveyed a line from Lander to St. Anthony, Idaho, and did reconnaissance down the Salmon River to Lewiston. Nothing came of the North Western's rumored Pacific extension (a fortunate break for the company), but another long-established midwestern carrier, the Chicago, Milwaukee & St. Paul Railway, did complete a line to Seattle and Tacoma in May 1909.[10]

The Milwaukee Road had considered building to the Pacific Coast as early as 1901. At that time it had 6,596 miles of primary track, with its westernmost point being Evarts, South Dakota. The company was widely respected for its sound finances and capable management. But developments in the Pacific Northwest in the early twentieth century seemed to threaten. Its chairman, Roswell Miller, was alarmed by the growth of Hill's empire, particularly its acquisition of the Burlington, which would give Hill a line from Chicago to Puget Sound. Miller was also irritated that Harriman was not directing more traffic to the Milwaukee Road at their interchange near Omaha. Feeling bottled up in South Dakota with Hill to the north and Harriman to the south, the Milwaukee Road dispatched an engineer to study the cost of duplicating the Northern Pacific line to the Pacific. His report confirmed preliminary estimates of $45 million.

Even with Hill and Harriman empires to contend with, boom times in the far Northwest seemed to guarantee enough traffic to support yet another northern transcontinental line. Hill, when asked about the possibility of the Milwaukee Road building west, responded in a public speech in Seattle: "By all means build to the Coast; extend your

*R*obert Strahorn was the inspiration behind the Joso Trestle, the high bridge across the Snake River. When the Oregon-Washington Railroad & Navigation Company built its new line from Ayer Junction to Spokane, it shortened the distance from Spokane to Portland by forty-three miles (bypassing Tekoa and the stretch along the Idaho border) and eliminated problems caused by a hill out of Starbuck in the Snake River valley. Union Pacific Museum.

*T*he Oregon-Washington Railroad & Navigation Company controlled the Ilwaco Railway & Navigation Company, a narrow-gauge line *seen here about 1920, which served Washington coastal points north of the mouth of the Columbia. Summer was a busy time when steamboats brought vacationers from Astoria and Portland to Megler, where they boarded trains for ocean resorts. The diminutive line, known locally as the Irregular Rambling and Never-Get-There Railroad, operated from 1889 to 1930, then became a victim of increased automobile traffic. Union Pacific Museum.*

road—if you do not, somebody who has more enterprise than you will take the business and will keep it on their rails and you will have to fight to get a share of it."[11] Equally encouraging were newspaper reports that traffic from the Pacific Northwest had filled Northern Pacific, Great Northern, and Union Pacific lines nearly to capacity.

As important as economic considerations were in the Milwaukee Road's decision to build to the Pacific Coast, contemporary observers believed that the contest between Hill and Harriman also figured somehow in that decision. Persistent rumors held that Harriman was linked to the plan. Certainly the Union Pacific and the Milwaukee Road did later

work together closely in the Spokane area. It also seems probable that if Harriman had been able to wrest control of the Northern Pacific from Hill that railroad might well have served as the northwestern connection for the Milwaukee Road.

By 1905 it appeared that practical control of the Milwaukee Road rested firmly in Standard Oil hands. At one time Standard Oil heirs William Rockefeller and Percy A. Rockefeller constituted two of the six members of the railroad's executive committee, but a noticeable connection also existed between the Milwaukee and the Union Pacific, on the board of which sat Rockefeller representatives as well as Albert J. Earling of the Milwaukee.[12]

Another subject of speculation was where the actual line should be built. One reconnaissance party examined the country west from Chamberlain, South Dakota, to Eureka, California; another studied the Snake and Clearwater valleys across Idaho; a third followed the Columbia River and probed through the Cascade Range over Naches Pass. One after another the parties returned with discouraging news, except for the surveyors who examined St. Paul Pass and found a promising route through the Bitterroot Mountains of northern Idaho.

Their reports went to the chief engineer for a decision. It was upon his recommendation that the railroad's board of directors on November 28, 1905, authorized building a line west from Mobridge, South Dakota, through St. Paul Pass to Puget Sound, a distance of 1,489 miles. Work crews began construction four months later. Their standing orders were to build the Pacific Coast extension to top-quality standards only.

Across central Montana the company fashioned a main line from existing track of the Montana Railroad Company as well as from new track being extended from three separate locations. Farther west it launched a new subsidiary, the Chicago, Milwaukee & St. Paul Railway Company of Washington, which together with other companies became the Chicago, Milwaukee & Puget Sound on December 31, 1908. From Maple Valley to Seattle, its trains used the track of the Pacific Coast Railway.

The president of the Milwaukee Road during its evolution from a prosperous granger line serving the states of the upper Midwest into a transcontinental giant was Albert J. Earling. Between groundbreaking at Mobridge, in 1906, until the driving of the final spike near Garrison, Montana, on May 19, 1909, he was in constant contact with the project, making frequent inspection trips. When he visited Spokane and the Pacific Northwest in early 1906, he was greeted with enthusiasm and feted by chambers of

Along the New Line to the Pacific Coast

Opportunities on the
CHICAGO
MILWAUKEE & ST. PAUL
RAILWAY

*Engineering a new railroad landscape synonymous with opportunity was a motif used on the front cover of a Milwaukee Road promotional brochure issued about 1907. Montana Historical Society.*

commerce, businessmen's associations, and municipal officials. But all was not well with the project.

Construction moved along at a rapid pace, although Earling now reported that the cost of the Pacific Coast extension would be closer to $60 million, some $15 million higher than the original estimate. That extension was being pushed west at the same time as the Western Pacific and two new Canadian lines. The stepped-up pace of construction on the Pacific Slope drove up the cost of labor and building materials. As a result, though the line was completed exactly one day short of three years, the actual cost was a staggering $250 million. That princely sum purchased a well-engineered right-of-way that crossed five mountain ranges and served

*Steam shovels sped construction of the Milwaukee Road near Missoula. The Pacific Coast extension went forward under the guise of various company names and from several locations where supplies could be brought in by existing carriers. Montana Historical Society.*

a country as rich in scenery as it was devoid of population centers. This forced the Milwaukee Road to become deeply involved in promotion and settlement. In 1913 the Milwaukee Land Company boosted twenty new towns in Montana alone.

The railroad began the work of selling Montana in late 1906. Perhaps its most famous advertisement appeared as a black and white centerfold in its system timetable in 1908 and showed a plowman turning up gold dollars from the Montana soil, symbolism no agrarian could misunderstand. This illustration also appeared in various popular magazines and again in color on the cover of a Milwaukee Road promotional booklet issued in 1910 (see p. 6).

The Pacific Coast extension opened for through freight traffic on July 4, 1909, and for local passenger trains a few days later. For the next two years it provided service during daylight hours only. The carrier feared that it was not safe to operate passenger trains at express speeds or at night because of the newness of the roadbed and the volume of construction still in progress.

The posh Olympian and Columbian passenger trains began their first trips between Chicago and

the North Pacific coast on May 28, 1911. Travel time was shortened when the Snoqualmie Tunnel opened through the Cascade Range on January 17, 1915, and eliminated 6.4 miles of tortuous line over the mountains and much of the threat of snowslides. The railroad originally bypassed Spokane because of the high cost of surmounting the irregular terrain west of the city. But in 1913, after obtaining trackage rights from the Oregon-Washington Railroad & Navigation Company, the Milwaukee Road rerouted its long-distance passenger trains through the eastern Washington metropolis.[13]

Given the enormous cost of its Pacific extension, the railroad needed not only Spokane traffic but also whatever other revenues it could generate by construction or acquisition of branch lines. During the decade after its through trains first reached the eastern edge of Puget Sound, the Milwaukee Road built or acquired lines that took it still farther west to the edge of the Pacific Ocean and deep into the timber country surrounding Puget Sound.

Among the local lines the Milwaukee Road absorbed were the Idaho & Washington Northern Railroad in January 1916, which reached north from Spokane to Metaline Falls, Washington; the Tacoma Eastern Railroad in December 1918, which carried wood and logs in the western shadow of Mount Rainier; and the Bellingham & Northern Railway, which ran north to the Canadian border at Sumas. A branch in central Montana connected the Milwaukee Road main line to Great Falls, where an imposing brick depot opened to passengers in 1914. The facility's massive size was a reflection of the railroad's optimism about the future of Montana and the Pacific Northwest.[14]

During the first decade of Earling's presidency, the railroad was widely praised for its sound finances and excellent management. Carl Snyder, an analyst for a publication of the Moody Corporation, observed, "It would be absurd, however, to suppose that this extension could severely cripple so rich

and prosperous a road as the St. Paul."[15] That sort of misplaced confidence within the railroad led it to spend additional millions of dollars to electrify mountainous portions of its main line from central Montana to Puget Sound to create a state-of-the-art railroad regardless of the cost. At its peak mileage in the early 1920s, the Milwaukee Road formed a 10,000-mile system extending from Chicago into the coalfields of southern Indiana, the timber and mineral country of northern Wisconsin, Minnesota, and Michigan, and the grain belt of Iowa, Minnesota, and South Dakota, and west to the coast of Washington, but size alone was a poor indicator of how the inordinately expensive Pacific Coast extension had imperiled the carrier's once robust financial health.

## Compromise?

THE SIGNATURE THAT THE MILwaukee Road wrote across the Pacific Northwest contained some unexpected turns and twists. So, too, did the ones that Harriman and Hill forces sought to scribe from the Columbia Valley into central Oregon. A compromise ending the senseless Deschute Canyon war was embodied in the name Hillman (now Terrebonne) for a station on the Oregon Trunk line north of Bend. The rivals agreed in May 1910 to construct a single, jointly used right-of-way fifty-three miles south from Metolius to Bend. Thus, in the spirit of uneasy harmony, the Oregon Trunk reached Bend in the fall of 1911. The first regular train from Fallbridge to Bend ran October 31, 1911.

An earlier cease-fire agreement hammered out on May 17, 1909, and given a duration of 999 years, had allowed Union Pacific trains to reach Seattle over Northern Pacific tracks from Vancouver, Washington. Without having to wage a wasteful and costly fight, the Union Pacific thereby achieved a

*A Milwaukee Road work train crosses the Columbia River on the newly built bridge at Beverly, Washington. Washington State Historical Society, Curtis 22006.*

ASAHEL CURTIS-SEATTLE

**155  Fiefdoms and Baronies**

goal it had pursued for years. The two great railroads nonetheless maintained separate passenger terminals in the Washington metropolis. Apparently as its part of the agreement, the Union Pacific abandoned plans for the North Coast Railroad to cross the Cascade Range from the Yakima Valley. Still another protracted war was avoided in central Idaho where

the Union Pacific and Northern Pacific agreed to joint operation of the new Camas Prairie Railroad from Lewiston to Grangeville. In a most unusual compromise, one company held the office of president and the other that of vice-president, but they rotated the two each year.

Undoubtedly, Hill must have lost some relish for

*The camera of F. Jay Haynes recorded this scene at the Oregon Railway & Navigation Company's landing on the Willamette River at Portland in 1885. Ferrying trains was a typical railroad economy at the time. The* Frederick

Billings *carried Northern Pacific trains across the Snake River at Ainsworth from November 1882 until April 1884. The ferryboat was subsequently used between Pasco and Kennewick until the railroad bridged the Columbia in 1888. The Northern Pacific sidewheel ferry* Tacoma *operated between Kalama and Goble from 1883 until 1908, when the Spokane, Portland & Seattle Railway completed its bridge over the Columbia between Portland and Vancouver. The* Tacoma *was then sold to the Milwaukee Road for use on Puget Sound. Haynes Foundation Collection, Montana Historical Society, H-1637.*

*The front cover from a brochure boosting Hillman, Oregon, portrays the two railroad barons, Hill and Harriman, in an uncharacteristic mood of cooperation. Not long after this, the dubious activities of a local real estate promoter actually named Hillman cast such a pall over the name that the town became Terrebonne. Oregon Historical Society, 86947.*

*James J. Hill and his son Louis pose at the Omaha Land Show in 1911. Except for promoting tourism, Louis was mainly a figurehead during his tenure as Great Northern president. His assistant, Ralph Budd, in effect ran the railroad. Minnesota Historical Society, CN 9.*

the fight after his own retirement as president of the Great Northern in 1907 and the death of Harriman two years later. Hill stepped aside in favor of his second oldest son, Louis W. (Louie), and five years later relinquished to him the post of chairman of the board. One journalist joked that the Empire Builder had retired to a relaxing day that involved only twelve instead of fourteen hours of work.

Highly visible in his stylish pince-nez glasses and sporting a dark red beard, Louis was obviously of a different breed than his father. A graduate of Yale and a good public speaker, the younger Hill was more comfortable handling the public relations of the Great Northern than taking on the mantle of empire builder. He also had less relish for a fight with Harriman than his father did. "There never was any Harriman-Hill feud," Louis claimed in 1909. "That was all a newspaper dream. It never existed."[16]

Robert Strahorn must have smiled when he read that. In eastern Washington his North Coast Railroad still had to fight its way past Hill roadblocks to reach Spokane. Louis Hill himself told Spokane boosters in 1912, "We are going to fortify ourselves as no railroad in the Northwest is fortified, by controlling, with north, south, east and west lines, all of the desirable territory of the great Northwest. We were the pioneers and we do not expect to lose our heritage."[17] His comment was probably a reference to both the Canadian Pacific and Harriman lines.

When tracks of the Oregon-Washington Railroad & Navigation Company finally did reach the heart of Spokane, the Harriman railroad erected a splendid

new Union Station within sight of the Great Northern depot. Strahorn wielded a silver hammer to drive home a gold spike to open the $500,000 facility on September 14, 1914.[18]

Harriman was not there to share Strahorn's triumph, however. Suffering from inoperable stomach cancer, he had collapsed on September 5, 1909, and died quietly at home four days later. All business on the Union Pacific–Southern Pacific–Illinois Central lines was suspended briefly on Sunday, September 12, at the start of his funeral service in Arden, New York.

Strahorn later recalled his last meeting with Harriman in the St. Francis Hotel in San Francisco. Their paths crossed in the lobby, and Harriman apparently failed to recognize the Washingtonian. But a few minutes later when Strahorn reached Harriman's room upstairs, Harriman opened it wide and laughingly remarked, "Well, wasn't that a narrow escape from being found in company with the young Sphinx from Spokane." Strahorn found Harriman in failing health yet still determined to girdle the globe with rail and water links though places as remote as Siberia and Manchuria.[19]

At the time of his death, Harriman's signature in steel extended from Portland, Oregon, to New Orleans, and from Oakland east to Omaha. Four years later a federal court forced the Union Pacific and Southern Pacific to separate. His son, W. Averell Harriman, would eventually become chairman of the board of the Union Pacific before launching a career as governor of New York, presidential candidate, and United States ambassador to the Soviet Union.

Edward Harriman was sixty-two when he died; James Hill died at the age of seventy-eight in 1916. Both men could accurately be described as self-made transportation geniuses, although Hill alone emerged as a genuine folk hero. A not entirely disinterested Robert Strahorn was later to describe the contest between the two as "a heavy freight pitted against

the Twentieth Century Limited, or as the dray horse against the racing thoroughbred. Ponderous and powerful physically and mentally, Hill was much slower than the more diminutive Harriman."[20]

So relentless was the rivalry between Hill and Harriman that not even their deaths ended it. In their respective railroad empires, executives who came to power under the two men continued to battle for advantage for several more years.

## Completing the Railway Network

EVEN AS THE LAST OF THE TRANScontinentals was completed, remaining gaps in the region's railway network were slowly filled in. When the Milwaukee Road reached Puget Sound in 1909, only three areas of the Pacific Northwest conspicuously lacked railway connections: the Olympic Peninsula, central Idaho, and central Oregon, where the rival empire builders prepared to launch construction up the Deschutes River. The Northern Pacific in 1908 had contemplated running track around the perimeter of the timber-rich Olympic Peninsula but never did. Neither was a hundred-mile gap in Idaho from New Meadows to Grangeville closed. The legislature of 1915 and Idaho's Public Utilities Commission recommended building a line north from New Meadows by way of the Salmon and Snake rivers to Lewiston, but this was never done.

During the early years of the twentieth century, the Union Pacific increased its domination in southern Idaho by acquiring or building a number of feeder lines. Among these were the Idaho Northern Railway begun in 1900 and completed by the Oregon Short Line from Nampa to Lakeport (McCall) in 1914. The extent of Union Pacific domination in Idaho could be measured in 1918, shortly after mileage of the nation's railway network peaked, when there were 2,841 miles of line in the Gem

*Robert E. Strahorn driving Golden Spike celebrating completion of O. C. &E. Railroad to Sprague River, Ore. Oct. 12, 1923.*

State, of which 1,658 belonged to the Oregon Short Line and 231 to the Northern Pacific, which ranked a distant second.

Among the last significant pieces of new railroad construction in the Pacific Northwest were the Union Pacific's Oregon Eastern branch to Burns, completed in 1924 to handle timber from the mountains north of town, and the Southern Pacific's Natron Cutoff, completed in August 1926 at the then enormous cost of $39 million. The latter permitted the railroad to reroute much of its traffic between the Pacific Northwest and California over the Cascade Range and through Klamath Falls. Although the new line was finished nearly seventeen years after Harriman's death, it actually dated back to 1905 when he sought to build a wall of railroads in Oregon and California to block Hill.

The Southern Pacific's new line was twenty-five miles shorter than the original Oregon & California route through Medford and over the Siskiyou Mountains, a line plagued by sharp curves and steep grades. As a rule four times as much power is needed to haul a train up a 1 percent grade (a one-foot rise in one hundred feet) than across a level surface, and eight times as much is required for a 2 percent grade. The Siskiyou line had 3.3 percent grades both north and south. The Natron Cutoff permitted the Southern Pacific to run seventeen- and eighteen-car passenger trains across the Cascade Mountains; the maximum over the Siskiyou line was thirteen cars.

Finally, in 1926 the Interstate Commerce Commission authorized the Oregon Trunk Railway to build a line south from Bend to Klamath Falls. The Great Northern took over the project and set San Francisco as its ultimate goal. The Bend–Klamath Falls line saw its first freight train in May 1928. By 1931 the tracks had extended southward to make connection with the Western Pacific Railway in northern California. At the hamlet of Bieber, ninety-seven miles south of Klamath Falls, Great Northern tracks met those of the Western Pacific, which offered access to San Francisco Bay. This linkage enabled Hill interests to tap San Francisco

*Robert Strahorn drove a final spike on October 12, 1923, to celebrate completion of the Oregon, California & Eastern Railway linking Klamath Falls and Sprague River. One of his last rail ventures, this line tapped a part of Oregon neglected by other railroads. Beginning in 1928 the Southern Pacific and Great Northern jointly operated the line for alternating periods of five years until the Weyerhaeuser Company purchased it in 1975. The line ran its final train in 1991. Oregon Historical Society, 021610, LOC/ORIG: 0346-P-158.*

*Great Northern tracks entered California on July 30, 1931. In anticipation of running a section of the Empire Builder down its "Inside Gateway" to California, the Great Northern built a modern station at Klamath Falls, but through passenger service never materialized. Oregon Historical Society CN 015415.*

markets in defiance of the Southern Pacific. Thus was the old Empire Builder's dream fulfilled. Great Northern officials even staged a golden spike ceremony at Bieber on November 10, 1931, that was a throwback to an earlier era of festivities.

Because of the Great Depression, the railroad never kept its promise to operate through-passenger service between the Pacific Northwest and California,

and not until World War II did the "Inside Gateway" generate the volume of freight traffic expected. Even so the long-sought California line gave an additional dimension to James J. Hill's quip when he retired as chairman of the Great Northern in 1912: "Most men who have really lived have had, in some shape, their great adventure. This railway is mine."[21]

39299
ASAHEL CURTIS

*The hour is coming when electrified train service will prevail everywhere on the Pacific Coast, from boundary to boundary, not only because this will be the cleanest but also because it will be the cheapest motive power.*
—Seattle Times, *March 5, 1920*

# The Promise of Electric Motive Power

*The Milwaukee Road staged this unusual tug-of-war between steam and electric locomotives on March 6, 1920, in Kent, Washington. The railroad repeated the contest three times, and the electric won each one. "Made a monkey out of your old steam wagon," joked the victorious engineer. Washington State Historical Society, Curtis 39299.*

TO CELEBRATE THE OPENING OF its electrified line across the Cascade mountains, the Chicago, Milwaukee & St. Paul Railway staged a number of publicity stunts, including a tug-of-war between electric and steam locomotives. A crowd of curious spectators gathered in Kent, Washington, on March 6, 1920, to watch the contest. The Mallet-type steam locomotive put on an awesome display of smoke and noise, but the bipolar electric quietly and firmly backed its adversary down the track.

The Seattle *Post-Intelligencer*, which headlined its story on electrification of the line "Six Rivers Speed Milwaukee Train across Cascades," played on the fascination Pacific Northwesterners had for "white coal," or hydroelectric power. The Milwaukee was not the first of the region's steam railroads to electrify part or all of its line—the Great Northern electrified a section of track through the Cascade Tunnel in 1909 and the Butte, Anaconda & Pacific Railway switched to electricity in 1913—but by 1920 it could claim the world's longest electrified system. Electricity also powered several interurban railroads scattered across the region.

In fact, the contest staged between electric and steam motive power at Kent seemed to symbolize the battle for passengers that electric interurban and steam railroads had waged with one another since the early part of the century. The main difference between the sham battle and the real one lay in the outcome: the surprise winner in the two-decade-long contest between steam and electric carriers was the automobile.

## The Age of Electricity

INTERURBAN RAILWAYS HAD THEIR origin in the electric streetcar craze that swept the United States after February 1888 when Frank Sprague's new invention went sparking down the tracks of the Union Passenger Railway in Richmond, Virginia. Only six years earlier, Thomas Edison's first power station began commercial operation in New York City and heralded the dawn of the age of electricity. By the end of the decade, America had witnessed the meteoric rise of a new industry.

On March 31, 1889, the first electric trolley appeared on the streets of Seattle and was followed only a few months later by the opening of lines in Spokane and Portland. By 1890 there were 1,260 miles of electrified track in the United States. The trolley not only served as a public conveyance

but also was a source of community pride, a symbol of modernity. Towns and villages as small as North Yakima and Lewiston could boast of streetcar systems.

Technological improvements at the turn of the century made long-distance transmission of electric power possible, and this encouraged development of interurbans, intercity streetcar lines. Within the span of a decade, interurban railroads perfected a service that occupied the middle ground between trolleys and steam railroads. The passenger cars on interurbans were both heavier and faster than ordinary trolleys; their physical plants were typically built to less costly and demanding standards than those of the steam railroads; and they paid their employees lower wages. They also charged lower fares and offered more frequent passenger service than steam railroads did. Because travelers could typically wave an interurban car to a stop at almost any road crossing, the new mode of transportation was often called "people's railways."

Most steam railroads initially dismissed the electric lines as hayseed carriers. Some were, but there is no generalization that fits them all. The nation's largest single interurban company was Henry E. Huntington's sprawling Pacific Electric

*The crew of an interurban car paused for a photographer on Caldwell's Main Street around 1906. In the early 1900s electric lines reached west from Boise to Eagle, Star, Caldwell, Nampa, and Meridian and finally formed a large loop in 1912. A popular Sunday ride was to take "the loop." Idaho State Historical Society, 62-53.2.*

*This three-car Oregon Electric train linked Portland and Eugene on the eve of World War I. University of Oregon Library, Angelus P 1966.*

Railway, which fostered the growth of greater Los Angeles and at its peak operated over a thousand miles of line and linked together more than fifty suburban communities. In some parts of the Midwest, interurban lines offered formidable competition to steam railways, although this kind of contest was less common in the Pacific Northwest.

One of the curious things about electric cars, unlike passenger trains on steam railroads, is that people often rode them purely for pleasure. The Sunday trolley ride was a precursor of the Sunday afternoon pleasure drive of the 1920s and 1930s. In Idaho, the 60-mile-long loop ride west from Boise to the communities of Caldwell and Nampa became a popular Sunday activity. The interurban could promise a clean, comfortable ride even in the heat of summer. "To ride up the beautiful Willamette Valley is no novel experience for Oregonians, but to be whirled along without noise, or dust, or smoke, or exasperating waits at some crossroads while the conductor gets out to tinker with the engine, this is decidedly novel. The coming of the Oregon Electric Railway has brought the change."[1]

A trip on the Oregon Electric brought city and country closer together. After rolling through industrial streets of Portland, Oregon Electric cars entered the countryside where stations were named Primrose Acres and Garden Home. They crossed the Willamette River several times and stopped at various places to let farmers put loads of raspberries aboard. Interurbans like the Oregon Electric also fostered a great deal of local travel, such as jaunts of only five or six miles to visit neighbors. Interurban lines not only provided cheap and convenient transportation but also raised property values for those living along the right-of-way. In rural areas they often sold surplus power to farmers who were able to use electrical equipment for the first time in their homes and barns.

For all the conveniences they provided, few forms

of public transportation rose and declined more quickly than the electric interurban railroad. Its heyday lasted less than two decades, from the opening years of the twentieth century, when interurban fever seemed to grip the country, until widespread adoption of the automobile after World War I. Thousands of miles of line were constructed mainly during two great bursts of activity, 1901–1904 and 1905–1908, each one ending during a nationwide wave of financial panic.

During early years, when building went forward in an atmosphere of unbelievable optimism, nothing seemed impossible. One proposal called for a high-speed electric line linking New York City and Chicago—the Chicago–New York Electric Air Line Railroad—that would run arrow straight and require only ten hours to speed passengers across 750 miles. The line would avoid all cities along the route and depend solely on through passenger traffic. The New York to Chicago interurban never amounted to anything beyond a 20-mile line in northern Indiana, but many others of more limited vision were completed.

By 1914 it was possible for a determined traveler to ride all the way from Utica, New York, to Indianapolis, Indiana, on different electric interurban lines. The trip required thirteen days and included overnight stops in hotels. In Indiana all but three towns of five thousand or more residents were served by a network of interurban lines, most of which radiated out of Indianapolis. Nationwide, interurban mileage peaked at 15,580 in mid-1916, the same time as for steam railroads. This was no coincidence: both forms of transportation suffered from the competitive inroads of a growing number of automobiles and trucks. The decline of the electric interurban became ever more noticeable after 1918, and during the years from 1928 to 1937, motor competition destroyed the industry.

## Interurbans of the Pacific Northwest

INTERURBAN RAILWAYS WERE NEVER as popular in the Pacific Northwest as they were in the Midwest or southern California. Nonetheless, interurban lines radiated from each of the Northwest's largest population centers, although their tracks were never joined together to form a regional signature in steel, as those of the steam railroads were by the 1890s. During the interurban era, Oregon was served by a total of 432 miles of line, ranking it fourth highest among states west of the Mississippi River (after California, Texas, and Iowa). Most electrified track radiated from Portland. Washington had 381 miles of interurban line, most of it concentrated east of Puget Sound along a corridor from Tacoma to Seattle and Everett or around Spokane. Idaho had 133 miles of interurban line, most of it located in the Boise Valley and linking Boise, Nampa, and Caldwell. Montana had only one line that might qualify as a true interurban railroad: it ran from Bozeman to Bozeman Hot Springs and south to Salesville, a distance of 16 miles. The Milwaukee Road acquired it as a feeder about the time it completed its Pacific Coast extension in 1909.

As in other parts of the nation, interurbans in the Pacific Northwest emerged from city streetcar service. A survey taken in mid-1902 revealed that there were 432 miles of electric railway tracks in the four Pacific Northwest states, most of them in the form of streetcar lines in Portland and Seattle. The next federal census five years later counted 1,132 miles in the region and noted the beginnings of two interurban systems: one linking Seattle and Tacoma and another heading out of Spokane to serve Coeur d'Alene, Idaho.

In late 1902 the Stone & Webster Engineering Company of Boston acquired the Puget Sound

*Workers used wooden platforms as they strung wire to electrify the Spokane & Inland Empire Railroad in the early 1900s. Eastern Washington State Historical Society, L85-184.3.*

Electric Railway that had opened earlier that year to join Seattle and Tacoma. Five years later Stone & Webster talked grandly of an electric thoroughfare extending from the Canadian border south to Olympia and Chehalis and possibly to Grays Harbor and Portland. The British Columbia Electric was ready to offer through service between Vancouver and Seattle if a line could be extended north to its tracks at the international boundary. Perhaps it was with that goal in mind that another Stone & Webster operation, the Seattle-Everett Traction Company, commenced service in 1910.

Yet one additional Stone & Webster line extended from Mount Vernon north twenty-five miles along the scenic edge of Puget Sound to Bellingham, just twenty miles below the Canadian border. In 1912 the two Stone & Webster interurban lines north of Seattle consolidated to form the Pacific Northwest Traction Company, although the crucial thirty-five miles between Everett and Mount Vernon remained the missing connection. Buses were added to bridge the gap in 1921, but when the Pacific Highway opened all the way from Seattle to the Canadian border, it spelled trouble for interurbans. The dream of an electric interurban line across western Washington and from British Columbia to Oregon never came close to realization.

The rest of Washington's interurban lines were even less integrated. The Yakima Valley Transportation Company was a forty-mile-long feeder system built between 1910 and 1913 primarily to haul fruit from the area's numerous orchards to a connection with the Union Pacific's Oregon-Washington Railroad & Navigation Company line in Yakima. Another electric line extended from Walla Walla fourteen miles south through numerous orchards to reach Oregon's twin communities of Milton and Freewater in 1908. There were also the two interurbans of the Spokane area: the Spokane & Inland Empire Railroad system and the Washington Water Power line that ran west to Cheney and Medical Lake.

Idaho, because of its low population density and difficult terrain, had a less extensive set of electric interurban railways than Washington. In addition to the Boise Valley loop, there was the Utah-Idaho Central Railroad, which linked Preston and Franklin to Logan and Ogden. The Sandpoint & Interurban Railway hauled passengers the five miles between Sandpoint and Kootenai for eight years beginning in 1909.

Oregon's interurban lines were concentrated in the Willamette Valley from Portland to Eugene. Between those two towns the Hill-backed Oregon

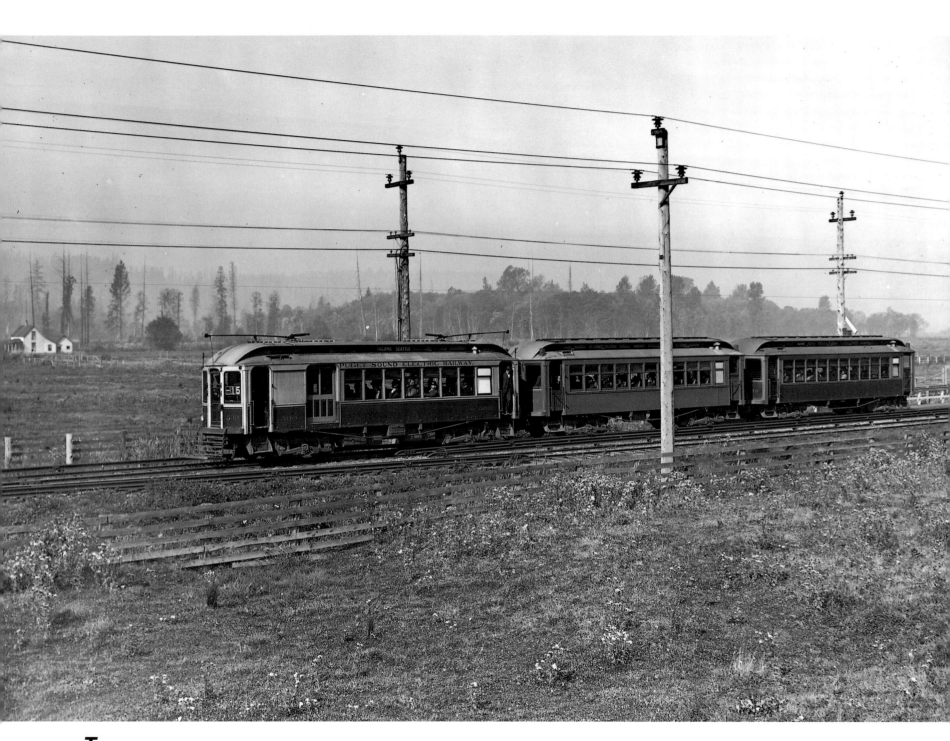

*The Puget Sound Electric Railway was originally called the Seattle-Tacoma Interurban Railway. This line was designed to unusually high standards: in many places it supplied power to its trains via a third rail that paralleled the tracks. No other interurban in the Pacific Northwest duplicated this expensive arrangement. Washington State Historical Society, Curtis 2517.*

*A car of the Seattle-Everett Traction Company paused at Beverly Park. Trains made an inaugural trip between the two cities on April 30, 1910, and thereafter offered hourly service between 6 a.m. and 8 p.m. Frequent trains were typical of interurban lines. Special Collections Division, University of Washington Libraries, Puget Power 357.*

Electric Railway constructed a line to the high standards of the Southern Pacific with which it competed. The Oregon Electric was even more unusual in that from late 1912 until 1918 it offered overnight sleeper service, making it one of only a handful of interurban companies in the United States to provide such luxury accommodations. The berths on its Santiam and Calapooya cars were similar to those on a standard Pullman, only slightly longer.

The Owl left Portland in 1916 at 11:45 p.m. and reached Eugene at 6:50 the following morning. Passengers could, however, occupy berths from 9:30 p.m. until 8:00 a.m. Ambling along at an average speed of seventeen miles an hour was one way the interurban company assured a restful night's sleep to all but the worst insomniacs.

During the day a passenger could make the same 122-mile-long journey in four hours on a limited train and enjoy a buffet meal surrounded by the stylish appointments of the parlor-observation cars Sacajawea and Champoeg. The company also did much business in milk, berries, and less-than-carload (LCL) freight. The high quality of the Oregon Electric's construction and service was a reflection of the rivalry between Hill and Harriman interests.

The Southern Pacific responded to Hill's invasion of its service territory by electrifying 133 miles of its own line serving the west side of the Willamette Valley. Its Red Electric provided through service from Portland as far south as Corvallis by mid-1917. Typically four trains a day linked the two communities. The Southern Pacific's Oregon interurban was among the nation's early users of all-steel interurban cars. After its last passenger train operated in the Portland area in 1929, the electric cars were transferred south to the Southern Pacific's subsidiary Pacific Electric, where they served the Los Angeles area until 1950.

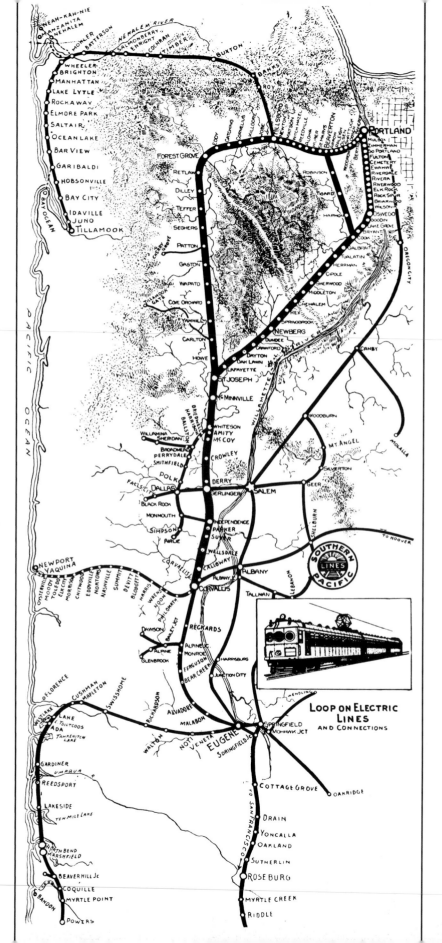

LOOP ON ELECTRIC LINES
AND CONNECTIONS

## Spokane and Inland Empire

FEW IF ANY ELECTRIC INTERURBAN projects in the Pacific Northwest were more ambitious than the Spokane & Inland Empire Railroad. Its history, in fact, well illustrates many aspects of the industry's rise and fall, and it adds a few unusual twists not duplicated by interurban companies elsewhere in the region.

The Spokane Traction Company was formed in 1903 with the mining magnate J. P. Graves as its head. Later that year, when the first train reached Coeur d'Alene from Spokane, nearly the whole population turned out to meet it. In 1906 the line was extended a dozen miles north from Coeur d'Alene to Hayden Lake. The same year the fledging interurban evolved into the Spokane & Inland Empire.

In an event marked by brass bands and numerous speeches, a final spike was driven on August 19, 1908, to complete a 90-mile-long extension south from Spokane to Moscow, Idaho. Although celebrants did not know it, the interurban at that time had reached its greatest length: 177 miles of main-line track and 36 miles of street railway. From Spokane south through the lightly populated Palouse country, the line was mostly single track; east from Spokane to Coeur d'Alene it was double. Like the Oregon Electric, the Spokane & Inland Empire was built to steam railway standards.

The interurban's best trains featured parlor-observation cars with individual wicker chairs and polished mahogany panels. But unlike typical branch-line trains on a steam railroad, electric interurbans were clean and free from the nuisance of flying cinders. They were popular with students at the University of Idaho and with farmers who lived along the right-of-way. The Spokane & Inland Empire offered special "theater trains" to take residents to Spokane for a Saturday evening's entertainment and return them home later that same night. In 1908, for instance, the Bungalow Club of Coeur d'Alene chartered two parlor cars to attend *Happy Land* at a Spokane theater. The Inland Empire system also operated the Camper's Special and Shoshone Flyer between Spokane and Coeur d'Alene.

In July 1907, 101,353 passengers traveled between the two communities, an increase of 35,000 from the previous year. Because traffic to and from the lake resort generated about half the line's revenues, the ever-growing number of suburban riders gave reason for optimism. Seemingly the only cause for concern was that in most of the area it served, Spokane & Inland Empire tracks paralleled those of the older and financially stronger steam railroads.

Like its steam competitors, the Spokane & Inland Empire Railroad carried freight and mail. Its idealistic builders even envisioned a series of model farms along the right-of-way to promote specialized agricultural colonies. The plans had to be abandoned

for lack of money, yet the interurban still hauled
many carloads of peas, lentils, wheat, milk, and
apples, which it interchanged with steam railroads in
Spokane. It provided grain-storage elevators at
some thirty locations along its tracks. These generated additional freight traffic for the railroad and
opened new markets for farmers and businessmen.[2]

Called simply the Electric or the Inland by
local residents, interurban trains through the Palouse
country stopped at stations usually named for
nearby landowners. Many a waiting area was nothing
more than a shed enclosed on three sides, with the
open end facing the platform. These places were
cold and uncomfortable, but travel by the Electric
beat spending a day fighting muddy roads in a horse

and buggy to get to town. The company also built
a handsome brick station at Palouse, Washington,
designed by Kirtland Cutter, a renowned Spokane
architect.

The years 1906 and 1907 were a time of great
optimism among electric railway enthusiasts. J. P.
Graves, president of the Spokane & Inland Empire,
predicted completion of a line to Lewiston where
he planned to make connection with electric interurbans supposedly building north from the Walla
Walla Valley and the Camas Prairie. He envisioned
that his railroad would become one of the region's
major grain carriers and Spokane the hub of an
interurban system pouring the agricultural products
of ten thousand square miles into her warehouses.

*This publicity shot was staged
near Oakesdale, Washington, to
dramatize the rich agricultural
area served by the Spokane &
Inland Empire Railroad. The
company also sold electricity to
farmers living along its right-of-
way, although when a train passed,
the resulting voltage drop was so
severe that customers experienced
momentary difficulty operating
washing machines or electric irons.
Washington State Historical
Society, A131 p. 85.*

Spokane's three-story Interurban Depot was completed in early 1906 in anticipation of a growing volume of passenger traffic. The first floor served as a passenger waiting room, and the second and third floors housed the offices of the Spokane & Inland Empire System. In 1927 the two Great Northern–affiliated interurbans serving Spokane switched their passenger operations to the parent company's station on Havermale Island, and the following year the Interurban Depot was razed. Its location at Main and Lincoln streets is now the site of the Spokane Public Library. Eastern Washington State Historical Society, 74-131.

Then disaster struck. The company bragged too soon that in three years of operation not so much as a single car had jumped the track. On July 31, 1909, as crowded special trains sped toward Coeur d'Alene from Spokane carrying excited bidders for Indian reservation land, Special No. 5 crashed head on at high speed into a regular train at Gibbs, a station a mile west of Coeur d'Alene. The impact killed seventeen passengers and injured another two hundred. Spokane residents were as shocked by the carnage as by the technological vulnerability of the interurban line: "In unusual degree the people had come to feel that the Inland Empire electric lines were peculiarly identified with their progress and prosperity."[3]

Coming on the heels of economic stresses within the company that most observers knew nothing about, the wreck publicly plunged the Spokane & Inland Empire into financial difficulty from which it never recovered. A succession of annual balance sheets told the story. The Spokane & Inland Empire's first annual report in 1907 showed net operating earnings of $219,000. This amount increased to $310,000 the following year. In 1909, the year of the Gibbs accident, net income dropped to $145,498, and the following year to only $24,892 after deducting $295,000 for the first installment of payments on the Gibbs accident. From 1909 through 1912 the interurban paid out a total of $380,000 in damage claims. For the year 1911, the Spokane & Inland

*The July 1909 collision on the Spokane & Inland Empire Railroad was among the worst to occur on an interurban in the Pacific Northwest. The company accepted full responsibility for the wreck. Idaho State Historical Society, 71-2.15.*

Empire had a deficit of $131,701, and it would never again show an annual profit.

By 1914 the problem was not so much a matter of damage claims as it was growing automobile traffic that cut into the company's revenues. Such rivalry was not confined to the Spokane area: the Oregon Electric went into the red for the first time in 1914 as a result of highway competition that only grew more intense in the coming years. By 1915, state roads paralleled the tracks of practically the whole Spokane & Inland Empire system, and local businessmen who helped bankroll the interurban soon found their investments worthless. Only Great Northern money kept the line operating. The steam railroad had acquired the company as a feeder in late 1909 and placed it under the control of the Spokane, Portland & Seattle Railway.

## Main-Line Electrification

ELECTRIFICATION ON THE COUN-try's steam railroads followed a vastly different pattern than that of interurban lines. It was mainly a matter of applying new technology to solve vexing operating problems and thus was never associated with the kind of grass-roots enthusiasm that swayed interurban builders. The Baltimore & Ohio Railroad completed the first main-line electrification through the 1.5-mile Howard Street tunnel under the city of Baltimore in 1895. Operating problems created by steam locomotives in long tunnels also encouraged the Great Northern to electrify its 2.63-mile-long bore through the Cascade Range.

A near catastrophe had occurred in the Cascade Tunnel in 1903 when nearly a hundred passengers barely escaped asphyxiation after their train broke in two and engine crews were overcome by smoke and fumes. All were saved when a fireman riding as a passenger released the engine brakes to enable the train to coast safely out of the tunnel's fetid air. Electrification came in July 1909 in the immediate vicinity of the tunnel and involved about six miles of tracks and yards.

Disaster did strike the snow-plagued portion of the Great Northern main line on March 1, 1910, when an avalanche hit two trains parked near the west portal of the Cascade Tunnel at Wellington. Snow swept them down the mountainside into the Tye Valley and killed ninety-six passengers. Only eight passengers and fourteen railway and postal employees survived the Pacific Northwest's worst railroad accident. A coroner's jury in Seattle absolved the Great Northern of any legal culpability, but after this time the railroad took numerous steps to prevent a repetition of the disaster. By 1914 newly built snowsheds covered 60 percent of the ten miles of track between Wellington and Scenic, and the railroad even changed the name of Wellington to Tye to erase memories of the disaster.[4]

Finally, in 1925 the Great Northern decided to eliminate continued operating problems and hazards by relocating 40 miles of track and constructing a new 7.7-mile-long tunnel under Stevens Pass. On January 12, 1929, the Great Northern opened what was then the longest railroad tunnel in North America with a gala celebration that included a radio hookup that reached an estimated fifteen million people. Participants included the railroad's president, Ralph Budd, and the president-elect of the United States, Herbert Hoover, himself a mining engineer.

The railroad abandoned its antiquated electrical system along with its old line and extended a state-of-the-art system from Wenatchee to Skykomish, some seventy-two miles away. The Great Northern advertised in the *Official Guide* that "the largest and most powerful" electric locomotives in the world hauled its trains across the Cascades. White coal powered Great Northern trains from 1909 until mid-1956, when diesel locomotives through the Cascade Tunnel made electrical operation obsolete.

Electricity began powering locomotives of the Butte, Anaconda & Pacific Railway in May 1913. The line had opened in 1893 to connect copper mines at Butte with a smelter complex twenty-five miles west at Anaconda. Building on its experience with electric machinery in the mines and the Great Northern's operation at the Cascade Tunnel, the Butte, Anaconda & Pacific electrified its line to take advantage of the economies that seemed certain to result. Electricity powered its trains for more than forty-three years, but changes at the Anaconda smelter decreased business for the railroad. Wires were taken down in 1967, and diesels replaced electric locomotives to haul what little traffic remained.

It was at a time when electricity clearly seemed to be the technology of the future that the Milwaukee Road built a system almost identical to that of the Butte, Anaconda & Pacific along portions of its Pacific Coast extension. The most notable difference between the two was that Milwaukee locomotives had regenerative breaking, so that during long descents their motors became generators. This not only slowed the train and saved wear on brake shoes but also fed electricity back into the system.

Hardly had the railroad been completed to the Pacific Coast in 1909 when President Albert J. Earling considered using electricity to power Milwaukee Road trains over mountainous portions of its line. The abundance of cheap hydroelectric power in the Pacific Northwest and reduced costs and greater efficiency of electrified operation on mountain grades seemed to justify the great expense involved. Moreover, John D. Ryan, the sole western member of the Milwaukee's board of directors, pushed hard for electrification, although hardly from a disinterested point of view. Ryan had organized the Montana Power Company and was also president of the Anaconda Copper Mining Company. Electrification of the Pacific extension would give him a market for both surplus power and copper, twelve thousand tons of which he ultimately sold to the railroad.

The project commenced in April 1914, and on November 30, 1915, electricity first powered a Milwaukee Road train in the Butte area. The portion from Harlowton, Montana, to Avery, Idaho, began regular operation in November 1916; from Othello, Washington, to Tacoma in March 1920; and from Black River Junction to Seattle in July 1927. The railroad electrified a total of 656 miles of its Pacific Coast extension.

That technological marvel, representing the world's most extensive railroad electrification project at the time, excited imaginations of jaded railroad travelers, science-fiction writers, and regional promoters. The latter group especially appreciated how well the innovative railroad advertised the Northwest's abundance of hydroelectric power. During the 1920s and 1930s, the Milwaukee Road published pamphlets such as *Running Trains with Water* and *How Science Aids the Traveler*, which featured one of its electrically powered passenger trains in the scenic Montana Canyon and a breathless description of how, "drawn by some invisible power, it sustains its steady flight, mile after mile, now threading the crags among those rocky sentinels that give back no echo of its passing, now holding to the canyon walls, securely, safely, as effortless as it is sure."[5] The electric line served as a prototype for similar systems around the world.

During the eight years of operation after 1916, the railroad estimated that electrification saved it more than $12 million. But tempering the good news was the fact that construction costs of both the Pacific Coast extension and subsequent electrification had increased the company's debt in public hands by some $266 million between June 30, 1909, and December 31, 1917. During the same period, earnings fell from three times its fixed costs to just one and one-quarter times. The one thing company executives had not expected when the railroad first contemplated an extension to the Pacific Coast was the competition that arose with completion of the Panama Canal and increasing motor vehicle traffic.

Until the eve of World War I and the dawn of the age of competition, railroads would continue to occupy a prominent place in public life, both as prime movers of goods and people and as the main catalyst of regional growth and development. The empire-building activities of the transcontinental lines in the early twentieth century were no less vital than they had been in preceding years.

*In its public timetable of March 1916, the Chicago, Milwaukee & St. Paul Railway dramatized electrification of the first portion of its Pacific Coast extension. Courtesy William S. Greever.*

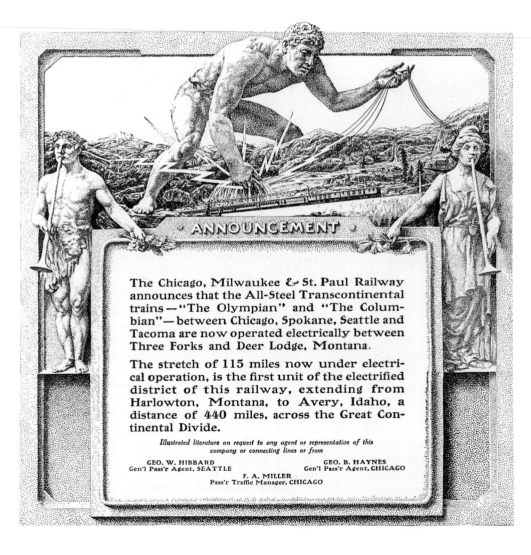

ANNOUNCEMENT

The Chicago, Milwaukee & St. Paul Railway announces that the All-Steel Transcontinental trains—"The Olympian" and "The Columbian"—between Chicago, Spokane, Seattle and Tacoma are now operated electrically between Three Forks and Deer Lodge, Montana.

The stretch of 115 miles now under electrical operation, is the first unit of the electrified district of this railway, extending from Harlowton, Montana, to Avery, Idaho, a distance of 440 miles, across the Great Continental Divide.

*Illustrated literature on request to any agent or representative of this company or connecting lines or from*

GEO. W. HIBBARD
Gen'l Pass'r Agent, SEATTLE

GEO. B. HAYNES
Gen'l Pass'r Agent, CHICAGO

F. A. MILLER
Pass'r Traffic Manager, CHICAGO

*The Milwaukee Road's Columbian paused for the camera of Asahel Curtis at Rockdale, just west of the crest of the Cascades in the early 1920s. "Cinders that blind and sparks that fall in red-hot showers, and gases that fill the tunnels and tight-sealed cars with suffocating fumes—all these are a memory of less progressive ways," bragged the Milwaukee Road in a 1924 pamphlet on electrification called* How Science Aids the Traveler. *Washington State Historical Society, Curtis 485.72.*

*But the building of a railroad is one thing, and the development of traffic is quite another. Long before our rails crossed the Dakota-Montana line we had a force of experienced immigration agents in the field prospecting, not for gold, nor silver, nor copper, but for business.*

—Milwaukee Railway System Employees' Magazine *(September 1914)*

# Twentieth-Century Empire Builders

ON THE OCCASION OF DRIVING a final spike on the railroad linking the Columbia River valley and central Oregon, Bend hosted an elaborate two-day celebration that attracted an estimated two thousand people. An uneasy mix of Hill and Harriman representatives watched bronco busting, football and boxing contests, horse and canoe races, a parade, and a baby show. On October 5, 1911, shortly after rival railway officials laid the cornerstone for Bend's new depot, James J. Hill stepped forward to drive home the golden spike.[1]

The festivities were ostensibly designed to celebrate the arrival of the railroad, although, in fact, they marked the passing of an era. For Bend, platted on the Oregon desert less than a decade earlier (1904), the opening of the Oregon Trunk Railway symbolized release from the bondage of economic isolation. For Hill, however, it meant the last stroke in carving an empire out of the wilderness. He used the occasion to savor publicly his many accomplishments and to talk to a pioneering generation about his enduring dream. Returning to the speaker's stand after the spike-driving ceremony, he addressed a large audience. They frequently applauded his words, and one listener interrupted to gush, "I have known you since 1858 and you are the best man that ever lived, Mr. Hill."[2]

The Empire Builder gave listeners the kind of advice they wanted to hear. "Go to work and build up the country, because cities would starve to death if it were not for the country, and nations that have neglected the cultivation of the soil have faded from the face of the earth. There is no reason why Central Oregon should not produce enormous

*Like an evangelist working the crowd, James J. Hill delivers a passionate speech upon completion of the Oregon Trunk Railway to Bend, October 5, 1911. Minnesota Historical Society, CN 8.*

wealth. We have a good deal of faith in it. If we did not have we could not have come here." Mindful of his company's ten-million-dollar investment in the Oregon Trunk, Hill urged listeners to "get people into this country. You could not build a prosperous community in the Garden of Eden and we could not run a railroad there if there was nobody but Adam and Eve to use it."[3]

The Oregon Trunk and its parent, the Spokane, Portland & Seattle Railway, began the task of peopling central Oregon months before the line reached Bend. The process was not as simple as railroad executives expected, for until irrigation systems were built, much of the land bore no resemblance to Eden. So many prospective settlers came, did not like what they saw, and left that Oregon Trunk officials hastily commissioned a crude survey to learn what was wrong. Each morning in May 1911, S. R. Strong, an agent aboard train 101, questioned departing homeseekers. He sent reports to Carl R. Gray, president of the Spokane, Portland & Seattle, who forwarded them to his two superiors, Louis W. Hill and Howard Elliott, presidents of the Great Northern and the Northern Pacific. After reading the first batch of reports, Elliott wrote Gray: "I believe in due time Central Oregon will be all right and that we will have a good population there, but I am afraid that the development will be slower than we all wish."[4]

Railroads were characterized by high fixed costs and a need to build traffic as rapidly as possible to pay those costs and insure profitability. The Spokane, Portland & Seattle Railway together with the Oregon Trunk represented an eighty- to ninety-million-dollar gamble that could reward backers only if they convinced an army of homeseekers to immigrate to the new empire. That proved no easy task. Throughout the West at the time, numerous other areas beckoned to new settlers, and each had a major railway company to promote it.

## Phases of Promotion and Development

DURING THE FIRST TWO DECADES of the twentieth century, railroads competed no less vigorously with one another for settlers than they had in earlier decades, although their colonization programs were much more sophisticated than they had been during the first railway age. The Northern Pacific's Immigration Department kept a close watch on its rivals by counting the number of immigrant cars passing the Minnesota Transfer in the Twin Cities in December 1911. Its tally revealed forty-five cars going west via the Northern Pacific, forty-four via the Great Northern, fourteen via the Chicago, Milwaukee & St Paul, and forty via the Soo Line (mostly to the prairie provinces of Canada).[5]

Each railroad offered special colonist fares that enabled new settlers to reach the Pacific Northwest at bargain rates. In a program called Washington Now, the Union Pacific, the Oregon Short Line, and the Oregon-Washington Railroad & Navigation Company teamed up with the newly formed Chamber of Commerce in Pullman, Washington, to offer bargain fares of thirty-three dollars to homeseekers from Chicago. This was one of dozens of similar colonization programs in the region at the time. Special rates for immigrants and their belongings were part of a larger campaign of boosterism that had for decades energized sellers of the Pacific Northwest. "On whatever part of the Pacific Coast the traveler may roam, he is sure to stumble on some publication 'devoted to the GREAT WEST,'" observed Emma Adams, a visitor in 1888. "A wild delirium 'for improvements' has settled upon papers and people."[6]

But boosterism fell into disfavor, noted Julian Ralph in the early 1890s, who saw many dead boom towns on a trip to Everett, Washington, "extinct volcanos, so to speak, and they were often wonderful to look at. They were, for the most part, mere acres of stumps, clearings hastily made in the forest, with suggestions of streets and avenues laid out at right angles among the stumps." "Something akin to nature," added Ralph, "used to build towns in the older States, wherever towns were needed, but in the new northwest the speculator is up earlier than nature. Men have to nudge the slow old dame along out there."[7]

Many of the boosters' initial advertisements amounted to little more than drab, crudely printed tracts. Their often shrill rhetoric was exemplified by an early-day promotional organization in Buhl, Idaho, that had as its motto "Pull for Buhl or Pull Out." Superlatives abounded: natural resources were portrayed as vast and inexhaustible, crop failures were unknown, and the topsoil was several feet thick.

The noted English writer Rudyard Kipling visited the Pacific Northwest during the 1880s and found men on Tacoma's still muddy streets "babbling about money, town lots, and again money." Kipling's traveling companion from California observed, "They are all mad here, all mad. A man nearly pulled a gun on me because I didn't agree with him that Tacoma was going to whip San Francisco on the strength of carrots and potatoes. I asked him to tell me what the town produced, and I couldn't get anything out of him except those two darned vegetables." Another English visitor during the late 1880s, James Bryce, found Seattle and Tacoma feverish to create instant civilizations.[8]

The *Puget Sound Catechism* published in Seattle in 1881 cited mountains of statistics and provided a series of questions and answers to bolster interest in the Pacific Northwest. A sample:

Q—How is the scenery?
A—It is the grandest in the world. One has here in combination the sublimity of Switzerland, the pictur-esqueness of the Rhine, the rugged beauty of Norway, the breezy variety of the Thousand Islands of the St.

Lawrence or the Hebrides of the North Sea, the soft, rich-toned skies of Italy, the pastoral landscape of England. . . .[9]

Another pamphlet called *Free Land and Good Wages: Information in Regard to Columbia County, Oregon* stated, "Our object in issuing this pamphlet is to secure immigration to Columbia County, but such immigrants, to be of benefit to us, must be perma-

*The Union Pacific used its passenger timetable in March 1916 to advertise special colonist fares to the Pacific Slope. Courtesy William S. Greever.*

*A publicity photograph celebrates national apple week. The first apples reached markets from Chelan, Douglas, and Okanogan counties, Washington, in 1901. Seventeen years later the railroad hauled 8,338 carloads from the district, and by the late 1920s this number had increased to 16,000 carloads annually. Minnesota Historical Society, 54223.*

nent; and therefore we propose to present the claims of our county in a manner that will bear the test of investigation. Lying statements made in the interest of real estate agents and speculators, do more harm than good to the locality they represent."[10]

In an effort to counteract popular perceptions that they stretched the truth, promoters cited an incredible variety of statistics so as to quantify virtually every imaginable appeal of the Pacific Northwest. James L. Onderdonk, territorial controller of Idaho, issued a promotional book called *Idaho: Facts and Statistics Concerning Its Mining, Farms, Stock Raising, Lumbering, and Other Resources and Industries*. In it tables using statistics compiled by the surgeon general of the United States Army showed that Idaho had the lowest mortality rate of any locality in the union. So many pamphlets brandished statistics as weapons that a promotional article in *Sunset*, a Southern Pacific journal, was forced to concede that "these figures are dry reading,

but they are authentic. They are from the year book of the Department of Agriculture, and they are quoted with malice aforethought, to silence the doubter who might question the veracity of the statements."[11]

If statistics could effectively lessen popular doubts about the honesty of regional boosters, so too could photographs. The Great Northern published a turn-of-the-century brochure called *Photographs Tell the Truth: Pictures of the Great Northwest*, which emphasized that the illustrations "are reproductions of photographs, and are therefore absolutely truthful. They give, in a very pleasing way, a perfect picture of the homes and farms of the most attractive part of Uncle Sam's big farm."[12]

Railroads in the early twentieth century continued to open booths in eastern cities and flood the country with increasingly attractive promotional literature. In 1902 alone the Great Northern had thirty-four agents at work in the country east of Chicago. They confined their activity to rural areas and typically gave illustrated lectures in country schools. They used lantern slides and samples of actual produce to excite interest in the Northwest. Agents might also visit fairs and circuses and slip bundles of Great Northern literature under the seats of farmers' wagons.

The *Pacific Monthly* illustrated the relationship among various parts of the process by following the conversion of an Illinois farmer. He learned through the local newspaper that new promotional brochures were available at the railroad station; next he noticed the booklets in the depot window and got one of each. "The family sat up an hour late that night reading the pamphlets and looking at the colored pictures." Stories that told of unprecedented opportunities on the Pacific Coast seemed too good to be true, they concluded, but lessening their doubts was a young man who gave an illustrated lecture a few nights later on "Land Opportunities in Oregon."[13]

Much of the settlement of Montana and Oregon in the two decades after 1900 was a direct result of railroad development activity that sold the country as the last, best West. The Milwaukee Road emphasized that its Pacific Coast extension "opens to settlement thousands of acres of the best farm lands. . . . The land is there. It is excellent for general or mixed farming, and Uncle Sam gives you a cordial invitation to go out and help yourself to a 160 acre farm. No drawing is necessary; first come, first serve." The Great Northern advised readers not to "spend your life renting high-priced Eastern land" when you can get free homestead land in Montana.[14]

By 1900 railroad promotional pamphlets had evolved into works of art designed to appeal to prospective settlers from a variety of backgrounds. Stewart Holbrook, a popular observer of Pacific Northwest life, said that the booster pamphlets he read as a young man in Boston "somehow left the impression that one could have a decent living in Oregon and Washington simply by eating the gorgeous scenery."[15] Indeed, the covers of many brochures featured a variety of luscious fruits in vivid color.

Railroads emerged as major publishers. The Union Pacific at the turn of the century offered the public no fewer than twenty attractive booklets, and its subsidiary companies listed still more titles. Most could be obtained for the cost of a postage stamp. Some tracts were travel guides, and some dealt with acquisition of irrigated lands. One was a guide to the Klondike goldfields. In 1914 the Northern Pacific offered twenty-five separate booklets on special topics, such *Suggestions to the Dry Farmer*, in addition to a number of tracts and leaflets on specific areas and communities. The Great Northern offered a variety of publications in 1915, including the "Glacier National Park Indian Portfolio," a portrait collection of Blackfeet Indian chiefs, for seventy-five cents. For five cents a sheet, it offered

"See America First Poster Stamps," showing scenes of Glacier National Park and other natural wonders.

Max Bass, general immigration agent for the Great Northern, urged homesteaders in the early twentieth century to "write to us for our pamphlets and books describing the West, and see what is offered you there. A postal card will bring you lots of good reading matter—free—with photographs that will show you just what the country is like. Look over our letters and descriptions, and talk it over with your family and friends.[16]

Every major Pacific Northwest railroad published a guide to sights along its right-of-way; the Milwaukee Road gave its long-distance travelers *Notes along the Olympian Trail*. Such publications typically explained to readers how to acquire land and homes in the region. Public timetables also served as instruments of advertising.[17]

*F*ood demonstrations were an integral part of the Oregon-Washington Railroad & Navigation Company's Corn Show held in Walla Walla in 1915. Union Pacific Museum.

*F*rom the perspective of Spokane boosters, all roads did lead to their city in the early 1920s. The railroad caused every small town to dream of becoming a city, and every city a metropolis. Pasco envisioned being the capital of the interior Northwest, but Spokane succeeded where Pasco failed. Special Collections Division, University of Washington Libraries, 6352.

**Why Not Go to Washington?**

*"There is no necessity for a man spending his days working on a rented farm, barely making a living, and with never a prospect of owning his own home. The* WEST *is open to you. The land of plenty, the land of unrivaled resources, the land of easy living. If you desire any information or descriptive matter upon this subject, send us your address."*

—**Great Northern Railway,** *Public Timetable* (ca. 1901)

At least one of the Northwest's electric interurban railways became involved in regional boosterism. The Spokane & Inland Empire Railroad issued a brochure called *The Truth about the Palouse Country* in 1908, an attractive publication designed to trumpet the wonders of the agricultural region south of Spokane. "The possibilities of a department of publicity are almost limitless," asserted the Spokane & Inland Empire. "The growth and development of the greater Spokane Country, in a large measure, depends on publicity."[18]

The company operated the Fruit Special that year to carry lecturers from the University of Idaho and

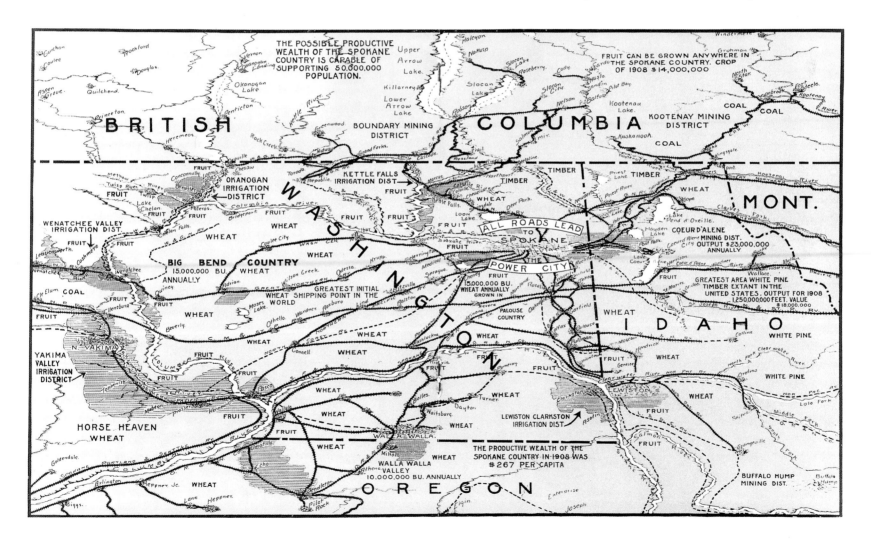

Washington State Agricultural College, two land-grant institutions, around its service territory to instruct orchardists in the best methods of raising and handling fruit. The special train stopped in small towns where the lecturers spoke to assembled listeners from atop flatcars. Demonstration trains helped to make the interurban railroad popular among farmers. Trunk-line railroads of the Pacific Northwest also used dozens of demonstration and exhibit cars to attract new settlers as well as to help established farmers become more productive. Railroads came to realize that successful colonization depended not on the number of people who came out, but on the number who remained, put down roots, and prospered.

The Great Northern in 1910 had a special advertising car that toured the country to illustrate the wonders of its territory. This mobile display was widely believed to have accelerated immigration to Montana. In the fall of 1911, the former Idaho governor James H. Brady conceived a novel twist to the railroad exhibit car by proposing to have states run a special train to exhibit their resources. Called the Western Governors' Special, it toured the Midwest and East. Crowds gathered wherever it stopped. Promoters hoped that exhibits would lure newcomers to settle the region. As easterners passed through the cars, exhibitors were pleased to overhear remarks such as, "Why, I thought the West was nothing but a desert." The turnstile on the Idaho car indicated

*The Oregon Railroad & Navigation Company's agricultural demonstration train paused in Rockford, Washington, in the early 1900s to introduce farmers to the latest equipment and techniques. Every trunk railroad serving the Pacific Northwest maintained a similar program of agricultural education. Union Pacific Museum.*

**A**n elaborate exhibit promoted the community of Opportunity, Washington, at the Spokane Interstate Fair in 1914. This was a typical forum for selling the Northwest. Eastern Washington State Historical Society, L83-181.24.

**T**he camera of Asahel Curtis recorded yet another attempt to promote Pacific Northwest agriculture—and presumably the Milwaukee Road's dining car service. Curtis Photo Company stationery in the 1920s bore the legend: "Know Your Own State; Boosters Live Better, Feel Better, Fight Harder than any other tribe on earth." Washington State Historical Society, Curtis 52644.

that ninety-two thousand people visited the touring exhibit during its trip east.[19]

The perception that easterners were ignorant of the West caused the Great Northern to confront the issue of regional peculiarity in 1900 and turn it into an asset: "There is an impression in the East that the people of the Western States are disposed to be lawless. The West is a child of the East. . . . There is as little disorder and frontier rowdiness in Montana as in any state of the Union."[20]

The Northern Pacific took a similar approach in 1910 when it reminded easterners that "the old West still lives in the mountains, but it has taken on alluring ways for Eastern folks who want to be perfectly safe, sane, comfortable and happy. Sacrifices gladly made by pioneers that they might enjoy the scenic glories and health-giving opportunities of the rugged old West are no longer required." A Milwaukee Road brochure said of Montana in 1914: "Good dwellings and well-equipped farms are a proof of refinement and prosperity and, by this test, there is nothing lacking in the social life of Western Montana."[21]

The two biggest regional promotions were the Lewis and Clark Exposition in Portland in 1905 and the Alaska-Yukon-Pacific Exposition in Seattle in 1909. Will H. Parry, chairman of the finance committee of the Seattle exposition, called it "merely a gigantic piece of advertising" for the Pacific Northwest. One correspondent who attended the Seattle fair observed, "This summer's show is essentially a bid to settlers, an invitation to home-seekers, and an advertisement for Eastern capital to come West and help develop the natural resources which offer wealth on every hand." There were dozens of promotional booths, each with its incessant chant "Boost, Boost, Boost." Massive electric letters told visitors "You'll like Tacoma," while nearby a billboard responded, "Yakima is Better."[22]

James J. Hill, who spoke at opening-day ceremonies of the Alaska-Yukon-Pacific Exposition, compared the growth of the West after completion of the transcontinental railroads to "that which follows the application of water to your soils." Members of the audience heartily applauded him at intervals, although his words could hardly be heard ten rows away. His themes had become so familiar over the years that listeners no longer needed to hear the actual words in order to commend the message.[23]

The Milwaukee Road completed its line to the Pacific Northwest only days before the Seattle exposition opened, and it immediately issued a promotional brochure extolling its accomplishments: "The wilds and wastes conquered, the business enterprise brought into being, the deserts drenched, the wilderness penetrated, and the mountains pierced—in short, the millions of homes made ready for the habitation of man by what may be called pioneer lines make up an overwhelming refutation of the new contention that the railroad is a non-producer."[24]

The Hill-allied railroads put together an elaborate joint program in the early 1920s called the Pacific Northwest Advertising Campaign. In 1923 it took the form of half a million copies of booklets with titles like *There Is a Happy Land* and *Through the American Wonderland* and *The Land of Opportunity Now*. Advertisements appeared in ten popular magazines, including the *Literary Digest* and the *Saturday Evening Post*, with a combined circulation of 9.9 million readers. Special topics emphasized the region's forests, hydroelectric power, mineral wealth, and scenic wonders.[25]

As these headings indicate, not all development activity focused on agriculture. Some was directed to mining, forestry, and manufacturing. The Northern Pacific took steps to develop Yakima Valley irrigation, and the Great Northern after 1893 took an active interest in Wenatchee Valley irrigation. Both railroads assisted with the location of factories.[26]

The intensity of railroad promotion of the Pacific Northwest peaked in the 1920s and retrenched rapidly after the onset of the Great Depression in the early 1930s. Even so, the Milwaukee Road alone in 1934 issued booklets promoting land in Washington, Idaho, central Montana, and northern Wisconsin. On some railroads, promotional programs lasted well into the century. The Union Pacific issued a revised version of its *Farm Seekers' Guide* as late as 1957, and the Northern Pacific at the same time published a development journal called *The Northwest and Its Resources*.

## Dreams of Empire

ONE MAJOR PURPOSE OF THE promotional campaign conducted by the Hill-allied railroads in 1923 was "to introduce the word 'Pacific Northwest' into the popular vocabulary—to make it convey a definite, clean-cut meaning. To make it stand for an idea." The feeling was that previous promotional efforts had been too local in orientation—directed toward individual states or communities instead of the region as a whole.[27]

Indeed, if the Pacific Northwest came to connote anything during the decades of railroad promotion it was the superlative. "The gigantic forests, tremendous logging operations, sawmills, and paper mills; the titanic hydro-electric power plants, the stupendous irrigation projects—all typical of the vast scale of things in the Pacific Northwest, are signs worth going to see," wrote one wordsmith for the Hill-affiliated carriers.[28]

All such fevered prose could be summarized with the word *empire*, probably the single favorite term of publicists of the Pacific Northwest from the 1880s through the 1920s. *Empire* was a convenient word used often to summarize aspirations for the region. Within a single year there appeared *The New Empire* (1889), a pamphlet issued by the Oregon Immigration

Board, and another called *New Empires in the Northwest* (1889), by the New York *Tribune*, and there may well have been others.

"In forty years this new American empire has been built," gushed *The Land of Opportunity Now*, a railroad pamphlet published in 1923 to extol the wonders of engineering feats. Few, if any, publications made more liberal use of the word. It was peppered with sentences like "steadily the mighty work of building an empire moved ahead." It called the Pacific Northwest "An Empire in the Making" and "An Empire of Opportunity."

Strangely, one soon becomes accustomed to the large scale operation of this large scale country. You no longer wonder at giant enterprises. You expect here to see things done on a vast, overshadowing scale. You would be surprised, you finally say to yourself, if this great empire which measures nearly everything it has— area, natural riches, created wealth—in millions and billions, did not have man-made creations in keeping with the great nature that surrounds them.[29]

A Spokane publicist popularized the term Inland Empire to describe the counties of eastern Washington, northern Idaho, and western Montana tributary to the new metropolis. "Empire of the Columbia" first appeared in a Union Pacific brochure called *The Great Pacific Northwest and Alaska*; later it became the title of a best-selling college history text on the region.[30]

Given the positive connotation of *Empire*, there could be no higher accolade for James J. Hill than to call him the Empire Builder. To honor his memory, the Great Northern bestowed that title on its premier passenger train in 1929, and even now the Empire Builder continues to be Amtrak's foremost passenger train between Chicago and Seattle. In the early years of Amtrak operation, a portrait of James J. Hill occupied its accustomed place in the dining car. The train still follows much of the old Great Northern right-of-way.

Two terms frequently used in the same breath with *empire* and intended to convey some of the same optimism about the future were "the Great Northwest" or "Great Pacific Northwest." The Northern Pacific in 1890 issued a brochure called *The Great Northwest* in an effort to make the phrase synonymous with a region of abundant resources and natural beauty. Some promoters urged people to see this fabled land for themselves; they claimed that photographs were liberally used in publicity brochures because words alone could not do justice to so great a land.

Finally, one additional word that embodied the imperial dreams of the northern transcontinental railroads was *Orient*. The Great Northern's premier passenger train from 1905 to 1929 was called the Oriental Limited, a name that aptly reflected Hill's desire to use his railroad to promote trade with Asia. For years the logo of the Northern Pacific was a monad embodying the principles of yin and yang and viewed as a symbol of good luck in Asia. The railroad's chief engineer, E. H. McHenry, claims to have seen the design first on a Korean flag in 1893 at the World's Columbian Exposition in Chicago.[31]

## Merchandising the Myth

WHEN RAILROAD EXECUTIVES talked of empire building or of developing connections to lucrative Asian markets, they combined elements of both romance and reality. James J. Hill was fully convinced after his railroad reached Montana in 1887 that the land there was fit mainly for cattle grazing, but soon a romantic vision lasting three decades inspired him to campaign to make Montana a major grain producer. The Great Northern devoted special promotional efforts to Montana portraying it as a last frontier for pioneer agrarians. In this way the railroad helped foster the spectacular

land rush that began there in 1909 and during the next eight years turned twenty-nine million acres of land into thousands of new farms. Late in his life the development of Montana seemed to delight Hill most. Giving a rundown of the prospects of western agriculture in 1913, he paused and reflected: "Then there's Montana," he told the reporter from the New York *Sun*—"That's a wonderful state."[32]

Joining him in that positive assessment was the Milwaukee Road, which published brochures containing testimonials from settlers like Samuel Smith,

a farmer living near Weede, Montana, who observed in 1911, "Now as I have been in this locality for thirty years, I find that we do not have as hard winters as we did thirty years ago, and we get more rain in the summer."[33] Employing similar promotional techniques, the Northern Pacific sold 1.3 million acres of Montana land in 1916 alone. Across the state the number of farms increased from seven thousand at the turn of the century to forty-six thousand just twenty years later.

Hill never doubted that grazing lands could

*Homeseekers arrive at Moore, a village on the Milwaukee Road west of Lewistown, during the great Montana land boom on the eve of World War I. Of the approximately 80,000 "honyockers" who flooded the state between 1909 and 1919, an estimated 60,000 were gone by 1922. Montana Historical Society, PAC 82-82.*

*In this Asahel Curtis photograph, determined but probably doomed settlers used teams of horses to clear sagebrush from would-be farmland in central Washington about 1915. Much of this land remained impossible to farm until the Columbia Basin Project supplied water beginning in the 1950s. Washington State Historical Society, Curtis 34079.*

become producers of grain, and he lived to see green fields stretch from Minnesota to the Pacific Coast, except for mountainous places. Once he enthused that "immigration and industry have wrought the transformation from barren wilderness to the home of plenty."[34] But when Hill died in 1916, his dream for Montana seemed to die with him. The next year, after a decade of extra abundant rainfall, came the longest, most brutal drought in the state's history. Following it was a succession of summers notable for hot winds, plant diseases, and a variety of insect pests. For the first sixteen years of the century, Montana farms averaged twenty-five bushels per acre; in dry 1919, the average dropped to 2½ bushels. In that year alone Montana agrarians lost an estimated fifty million dollars to drought. Add to this a worldwide decline in farm prices, and it is no wonder that more than half of Montana's commercial banks failed between 1920 and 1926. In

heavily mortgaged areas there were actually more foreclosures than farms. "Foodless, seedless, landless, and money-less," in the words of the Montana historian K. Ross Toole, many settlers simply abandoned their farms and moved away. As a result Montana lost about seventy-five thousand residents between 1919 and 1926.[35]

Invariably, there were those who came West with unrealistic expectations and were soon disenchanted when they learned that publicists occasionally merchandised more myth than reality. Other people, however, accepted the challenge of starting life afresh in the new settlements and savored their roles as twentieth-century pioneers. When, for example, the name Magic Valley came into general use in the late 1930s in south-central Idaho, it was an apt description of the transformation wrought both by irrigation and railroads functioning as engines of empire.

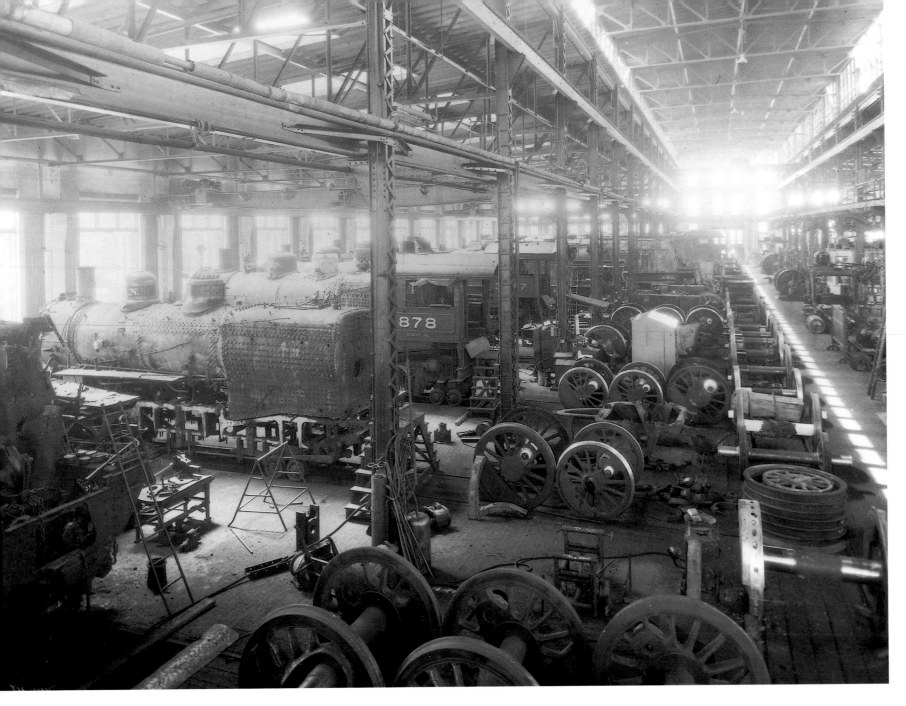

*T*he interior of Great Northern's
massive Hillyard shops in Spokane
in 1929, when steam locomotives
were still vital to railroad empire-
building in the Pacific Northwest.
*Eastern Washington State
Historical Society, L86-588.1.*

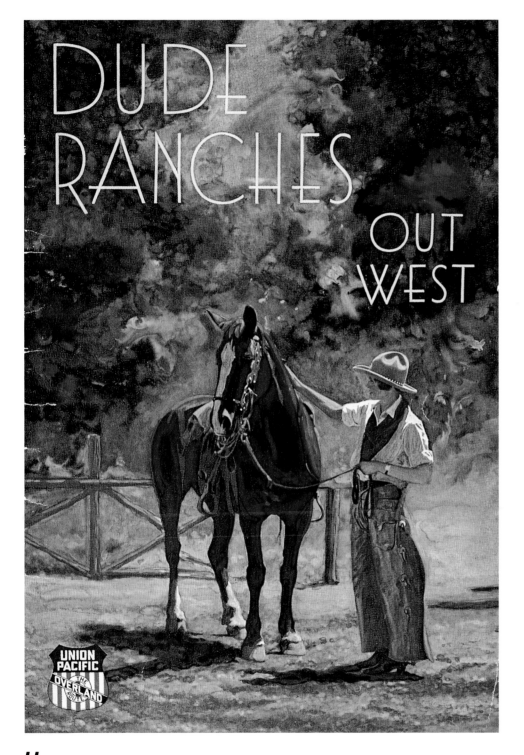

## Selling the
## Great Northwest

**O**F THE MANY DIFFERENT PAM-
phlets that railroads issued to sell the
Pacific Northwest, one group stands out
above all others. It was the remarkable
literature that poured from the union of *Sunset*
magazine's sophisticated new printing technology
and the creative talents of William Bittle Wells that
between 1907 and 1911 gave rise to what is probably
the most remarkable body of promotional literature
in Pacific Northwest history. If the region had a
golden age of railway promotion, this was it. Wells,
incidentally, would have appreciated that description
of his publications because he was by training a
classicist, a fact clearly evident in cover designs that
featured Greek and Roman figures to advertise
communities as diverse as American Falls and
Pocatello, Idaho, and Sheridan, Oregon.[1]

Wells (1872–1965) was the primary Pacific Northwest publicist for Edward H. Harriman's sprawling
railroad empire. In fact, Wells considered his promotional activity to be part of the contest between
Harriman and Hill interests. He believed that Hill
was more popular than Harriman but "into this
fascinating situation came our Community Publicity
Plan, and the Hill Lines had nothing whatsoever to
compete with it." Wells thought that this rivalry was
one reason why executives of the Harriman system

In the mid-1880s the Northern Pacific inaugurated publication of a series of "Wonderland" pamphlets to advertise Yellowstone National Park. Denver Public Library, Western History Department.

Well-clad vacationers typical of the early twentieth century enjoy the beach at Newport, Oregon. Oregon Historical Society.

*Roseburg, Oregon, was depicted in terms of luscious fruit on the cover of this William Bittle Wells brochure jointly sponsored by the local commercial club and the Sunset Magazine Homeseeker's Bureau. Oregon Historical Society.*

so readily approved the plan.[2]

The Community Publicity Plan involved having local chambers of commerce purchase one of several standard promotional packages offered by Wells. Every contract included at least one professionally designed brochure and publication of a promotional article in *Sunset* magazine, which in 1910 claimed a circulation of a hundred thousand readers. "Riches of an Inland Empire" was the title of the *Sunset* article on Idaho Falls in October 1910. "The Secret of Success in Blackfoot" followed a month later.

Beginning with a campaign to boost Medford, the Bureau of Community Publicity during its five-year existence created promotional pamphlets for a total of seventy-five communities across the Pacific Northwest, including fifteen in Idaho, seventeen in Washington, and forty-three in Oregon. Wells estimated that his bureau issued a total of twelve million pieces of promotional literature. All a community had to do was to sign a contract with the railroad, and the whole burden of community publicity shifted to the shoulders of the Harriman system. Most chambers of commerce were glad to have experts take responsibility for advertising their communities.[3]

A highly organized man, Wells provided no less than five types of literature from which a community might choose. These he labeled community, conductor, postal folders, colonist, and special brochures. Cover designs included allegorical representations, landscape paintings, and photographic reproductions. To carry out this grand scheme, he employed numerous commercial photographers, illustrators, and writers. This was to be "high-class literature" that used lavish artwork. A 1910 brochure for Hood River, which had a pressrun of thirty thousand and featured full-sized Yellow Newtowns and Red Spitzenburg apples in rich color, was the sort of publication that inspired Stewart Holbrook's quip about promotions that gave the impression that it was possible to eat the Northwest's scenery.

Wells instructed his writers to model their prose after the *Saturday Evening Post*, which was at that time the best-selling weekly magazine in the United States. The *Saturday Evening Post*, like Wells's promotional literature, sought to mirror the culture of a middle-class world that was hardworking, prudent, honest, and self-reliant. Wells essentially applied consumerism to a regional landscape.[4]

Unlike promoters of an earlier era, the writers working for Wells were instructed not to make any unsubstantiated claims. If one of them used a superlative to describe the advantage of a community, Wells later recalled, it was equivalent to "handing in his resignation." This was because so much previous publicity "indulged in the use of the superlative to such a degree that the literature lost much of its value; nobody would believe it."[5]

In his 1911 summary of bureau activities, Wells also took pride in the fact that "to date no printing in connection with our community plan has been done in the East." Wells did not identify his printers or, unfortunately, his illustrators, but most likely they were the same local artists who produced covers for *Sunset* and its Portland counterpart, the *Pacific Monthly*, or designed the era's colorful apple crate labels. He does not appear to have used well-known illustrators like Maynard Dixon, who created occasional covers for both magazines, or artists that other western railroads employed. Northern Pacific officials, for example, once hired Thomas Moran to help promote Yellowstone National Park, and the Great Northern commissioned the Austrian-born John Fery to paint more than three hundred monumental promotional images, many of them of Glacier National Park, to display in its stations and other buildings.[6]

The outpouring of Wells's highly appealing brochures prompted Judge Robert S. Lovett of New York City, president of the Union Pacific and Southern Pacific systems, to comment, "Such attractive

*A front cover from the series of promotional pamphlets issued by William Bittle Wells emphasized the beauty and economy of Kelso, Washington. Oregon Historical Society.*

*W*ells dramatized irrigated farming in Hermiston, Oregon, by depicting a Native American in classical garb in this 1910 brochure of which twelve thousand were issued. Oregon Historical Society.

publications I am afraid will make an emigrant of me." Another of Wells's superiors, E. O. McCormick, vice-president of the Southern Pacific, wrote, "I esteem it the highest plane of passenger department endeavor." Wells printed these testimonials together with numerous other supportive comments in his 1911 report. "This is the best colonization literature that I know of anywhere," added Ivy L. Lee, one of the country's foremost publicity experts. His clients included the Pennsylvania Railroad, the Guggenheim mining interests, Bethlehem Steel, and John D. Rockefeller.

In the end, Wells's promotional campaign proved much too successful. And therein lies an irony. It sparked a bureaucratic rivalry between the Harriman system's passenger and freight departments. The former received the glory, while members of the freight department, which paid most of the railroad's bills, grew ever more jealous and conspired against Wells. Anticipating trouble, he spent eight hundred dollars to prepare a report in 1911 that defended his activities. It was this document that included several pages of testimonials to the value and quality of his promotional work.[7]

For reasons that are not clear, in the late summer of 1911 Harriman officials offered Wells a salaried job at $250 a month, significantly less than he earned on the previous commission basis. He once bragged, perhaps unwisely, that as a result of his commissions for selling the Northwest he earned more than the president of the Oregon Railroad & Navigation Company, under whom he was working. Wells, who wanted at least $500 a month, appealed to those superiors who had so recently praised him, but to no avail. He quit the Harriman enterprise at the age of thirty-nine and spent the rest of his many working years as an insurance agent for New York Life. Of his years at the Harriman system, he recalled, "It was a great life while it lasted."[8]

In connection with Wells's remarkable campaign to sell the Pacific Northwest, it is appropriate to

*W*ells emphasized the rose theme on the cover of a brochure issued in March 1911 for the Portland Chamber of Commerce, the Southern Pacific, and the Oregon-Washington Railroad & Navigation Company. Oregon Historical Society.

*O*ne of several different logos that appeared in the promotional brochures prepared by Wells. Oregon Historical Society.

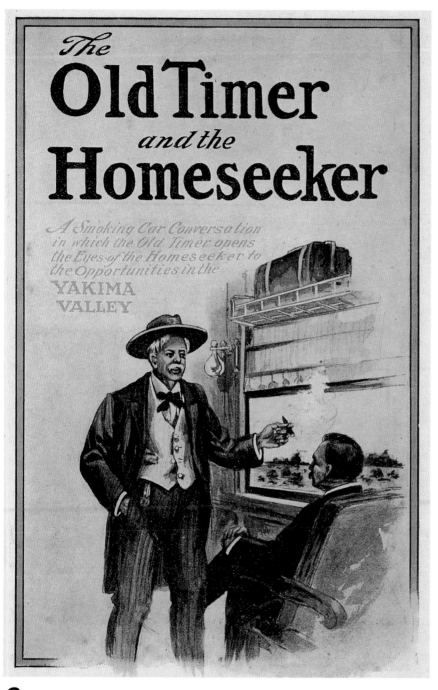

know more about the man himself and the vision he embodied in his brochures. Born in a backwoods portion of Reconstruction-era Virginia in 1872, he was one of eight children of G. M. and Lucinda Wells. After the Civil War ended, his father, a former commissary sergeant in the Confederate army, headed north to New York City, where he earned a degree at Bellevue Medical College. In 1874 he took his family west to Sonoma County, California, where he practiced medicine.[9]

From California, the family moved to Portland, Oregon, in 1881, where Wells's father and an uncle, a former officer in the Confederate navy, practiced medicine together. Young William completed the Latin course at Portland High School and then studied Greek with a private tutor. In 1897 he completed a bachelor's degree in English at the recently established Stanford University. He returned to Portland to launch a new magazine in 1898 called the *Pacific Monthly* to combine literary talents with regional promotion. He brashly chose the name to reflect the fact that he expected it to become the West Coast counterpart to the venerable *Atlantic Monthly*.

Wells was a true believer in the Pacific Northwest. Here was indeed the land of opportunity, and he was unabashed in saying so. The one theme that runs through all booklets of the Harriman system's publicity bureau is that the Pacific Northwest was synonymous with opportunity. "We believe that the West—the Pacific Coast—is the best part of the world," Wells declared. He approached his subject with religious fervor that managed to blend his own family's experience of the West as a promised land, his classical training, and his devotion to Presbyterian Protestantism. Religion, hope in the Lord, he once wrote, was "man's best possession."[10]

Although Wells did not write all his pamphlets, elements of his world view are distinct in them nonetheless. It is clear that he regarded the developing communities of the Pacific Northwest as new

THREE FORKS COUNTRY
MONTANA

CHICAGO
MILWAUKEE & ST. PAUL
RAILWAY

LEWISTON - CLARKSTON
and the Clearwater Country
Idaho - Washington

Northern Pacific Railway

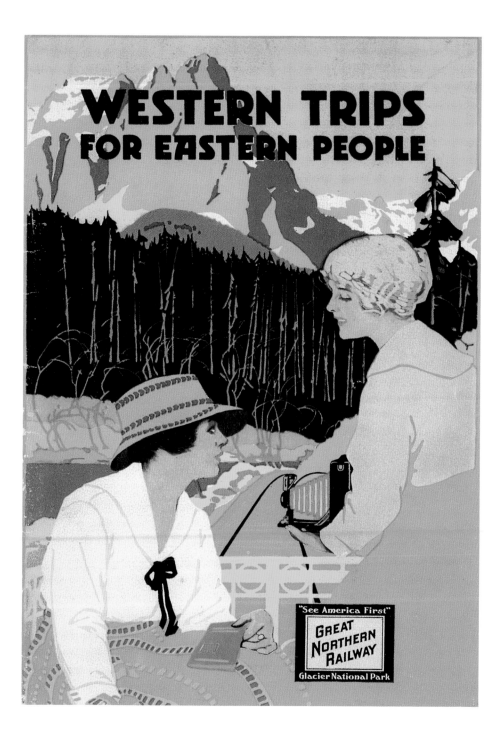

Edens and as land flowing with milk and honey. No slums, industrial ghettos, or scenes of poverty ever appeared among the numerous photographs used to illustrate his pamphlets. There is nothing to mar their consistently upbeat tone.[11]

*At about the time that William Bittle Wells boosted communities in Oregon, Washington, and Idaho, Milwaukee Road officials launched a similar campaign in Montana. This attractive brochure promoted settlement of the Three Forks country in south-central Montana. DeGolyer Library.*

*Northern Pacific publicists emphasized the potential of irrigated farmland in the Lewiston-Clarkston area in their pamphlet* Lewiston-Clarkston and the Clearwater Country, Idaho-Washington *(St. Paul Northern Pacific Railway, 1911). Special Collections and Archives, University of Idaho Library.*

*In the 1920s the Great Northern and other western railroads made special efforts to attract affluent tourists from the East. Oregon Historical Society.*

The front cover of a Northern Pacific brochure from 1915 emphasized historical aspects of "Geyserland." Montana Historical Society.

*A bear motif appeared on the cover of this whimsical pamphlet issued by the Union Pacific in 1929 to attract tourists to Yellowstone National Park. Union Pacific Museum.*

*T*he Montana State Highway
Commission responded to increased
automobile tourism with a series
of brochures as colorful as those
issued by railroads. The one
for 1937 featured a cover
illustration by Irvin Shope.
Montana Historical Society.

Headin' for the Hills

*Suffering from the hot, humid atmosphere of the Eastern and Middle States many people of delicate constitutions pass miserable summers every year of their lives. They do not know or realize that within a few days and at small expense they may be transported to a locality where nature has furnished conditions that make summer life simply ideal. . . . Nowhere in America can such a combination of climate, comfort and scenery be found as amongst the great mountains on the line of the Great Northern R'y.—Great Northern Railway,* Public Timetable *(ca. 1901)*

# Wonderlands: Railroad Tourism

IN ADDITION TO FOSTERING SETTLE-
ment of the Pacific Northwest and development of its natural resources, railroads assumed a prominent role in promoting enjoyment of the region through tourism. Few if any areas of the United States were blessed with more spectacular scenery or a greater variety of outdoor activities, but the Pacific Northwest attracted only a handful of tourists from distant locations until northern transcontinental railroads made the trip easy. After 1883, regional boosters increasingly sought to lure tourists along with homeseekers and investors.

Railroad tourism, like development activity in general, meant transforming popular perceptions, making people see landscapes once considered unappealing as veritable wonderlands. Consider how one promoter of tourism in northern Idaho conveniently ignored the perceived drawbacks of outdoor life: "To some the thought of camp life brings visions of insect pests to be endured. Not so at the majority of northern Idaho lakes, for their elevation, from two thousand to two thousand five hundred feet above sea level, is such that the nights are always too cool for insects to live or be active, thus

affording campers the most refreshing and restful sleep."[1]

Curiously, when the Jesuit missionary Nicholas Point visited the same area in the 1840s he observed, "Fish are abundant in lakes, rivers, and small streams. I will not speak here of the mosquito or of the other insects harmful to man. One is devoured by them in certain seasons. Nor will I speak of the serpents which are present in large numbers. In a single day I chased two out of my bed. Fortunately, rattlesnakes are rare there."[2] The way people described the out-of-doors obviously changed with the rise of tourism as a paying proposition.

## Capitalizing on Health and Curiosity

THE PACIFIC NORTHWEST WAS
slow to become a tourist mecca because of its remote location. Even after through passenger trains reached Portland on a daily basis, the extra time and money required to travel to the far Northwest caused most tourists

from the East to go to California and Colorado instead. Nonetheless, as early as 1886 the Union Pacific Railway issued a booklet called *Inter-Mountain Resorts* that called attention to Salt Lake City, Ogden Hot Springs, Yellowstone National Park, and three southern Idaho destinations: Soda Springs, Shoshone Falls, and Guyer Hot Springs. These places offered tourists a chance to ponder curiosities of nature or society (whether Mormons or Indians) or improve physical and mental health, two driving forces behind tourism in the late nineteenth century.[3]

Hot springs were by far the most ubiquitous of early western tourist attractions. Health considerations figured prominently in advertisements for the Northwest's many hot springs, which remained popular with tourists from the 1880s through the 1920s. When Oregon Short Line tracks reached the Wood River valley in the early 1880s, Hailey Hot Springs became Idaho's first real summer resort. Guyer Hot Springs, two miles by stage from nearby Ketchum, had waters that were "good for all nervous complaints, rheumatism, skin and blood affectations. This place is much resorted to by tourists and invalids. It is a beautiful, quiet mountain retreat."[4]

The Union Pacific also promoted Bingham Springs and Hot Lake in eastern Oregon until the popularity of hot springs waned after World War I. Of Hot Lake, one promoter claimed, "The water is delightful to taste, having something of the exhilarating effect of champagne. It has cured innumerable invalids, who had tried in vain all the noted resorts of this country and of Europe."[5]

Certainly not all geothermal attractions were located along the Union Pacific. There was Green River Hot Springs on the Northern Pacific line east of Tacoma; and in Montana were more than twenty-one hot springs, including White Sulphur Springs, that "Eldorado of Ease and Elegance, where Cool Breezes Kiss Away the Burning Rays of the Summer Sun, and a Panacea for Human Ills Gushes Forth from Mother Earth." White Sulphur Springs prom-

ised guests a variety of rustic pleasures including dancing, fishing, and ball playing, but transcontinental railroads continued to ignore the resort because of its remote location. In 1910 the White Sulphur Springs & Yellowstone Park Railway built twenty-three miles south to meet Milwaukee Road rails at Ringling, but crowds of tourists from outside Montana still failed to materialize.[6]

Health concerns also figured prominently in *Western Resorts for Health and Pleasure Reached via the Union Pacific Railway*, a booklet first published in 1888 to emphasize that the "entire Rocky Mountain region is a sanitarium. It has the sun, the mountain breeze, the crisp, mild air, which combine to invigorate and heal." Simply contemplating the gorgeous scenery might have therapeutic benefits, especially for overstressed city dwellers, and on that theme the Oregon Railroad & Navigation Company issued a brochure series in the early twentieth century called *Restful Recreation Resorts*.[7]

A Union Pacific brochure published in 1889 and called *Western Resorts for Health and Pleasure* featured Cape Horn of the Columbia River, the Idanha Hotel of Soda Springs, Idaho, and Garfield Beach near Salt Lake City, Utah. It claimed that "along the River Rhine, or Rhone, or the Hudson, there is nothing that will compare with the stately palisades of the Columbia, with their cool recesses, kept sunless by the overhanging rocks, and watered by the melting snows of their own summits."[8]

The arid Snake River plain of southern Idaho had little of the appeal of the Columbia Gorge, but it too evolved into a tourist destination in the late nineteenth century, the most notable attraction being Shoshone Falls. The site suffered from the handicap of isolation, but promoters used the anticity sentiment then common in America to transform the remoteness into an asset. "Shoshone differs from every other waterfall in this or the old country. It is its lonely grandeur that impresses one so deeply; all of the other historic places have the adjuncts of civilization, and one is almost overshadowed by a city while in their presence."[9]

The Northern Pacific responded to Union Pacific tourist promotions with a booklet called *North Pacific Coast Resorts*, which actually included attractions as far inland as the lakes of northern Idaho. One of the earliest such facilities was Highland House, located on Lake Pend Oreille next to Northern Pacific tracks and designed to accommodate tourists who wanted to take a break from long-distance train travel. Another area popular with tourists was the Washington coast north of the Columbia River. A steamboat ran from Portland to Ilwaco three times a week beginning in 1887. South of the river and down the Oregon coast was Seaside, so named by Ben Holladay, who built a resort hotel there in 1872 and called it Seaside House.[10]

In addition to being identified with good health or the beauty of nature, the Pacific Northwest emerged as a sportsman's paradise by affording tourists unusually good opportunities for hunting and fishing. "Days and weeks are passed in fishing, boating, loafing, drinking in new life and strength and hope and ambition in every breath."[11]

These activities gave "exciting and profitable employment to quite a number of persons, some of them old trappers from the Rocky Mountains, and from various other trapping grounds of the country, tough, rugged, often morose and hardened by exposure."[12] As the population in the region grew,

hunting and fishing only increased in popularity, probably because the out-of-doors remained so accessible to residents of metropolitan centers like Portland and Seattle. Beginning in the 1880s wealthy tourists might even hire a private railroad car built expressly for hunting and fishing parties. The Northern Pacific furnished the cars complete with cook and porter and would park them on sidings along its right-of-way for up to six weeks.

*Climbers on Mount Rainier posed for the camera in the early twentieth century. Then as now most tourists preferred less strenuous hikes. Library of Congress, 11601 262 48662.*

*F Jay Haynes recorded a group of tourists at Liberty Cap in Yellowstone National Park in 1888. Haynes Foundation Collection, Montana Historical Society, H-1953.*

## Railroads and the National Parks

THE NATIONAL PARKS OF THE Pacific Northwest became favorite tourist destinations after transcontinental railroads realized their potential for generating passenger revenue. The Northern Pacific was fortunate that the nation's first national park, Yellowstone (established in 1872), could easily be reached by stage from its main line at Livingston, Montana. A fifty-four-mile branch line from Livingston finally reached Gardiner on the park's northern boundary in 1903. From there it was only five miles by stage to the Mammoth Hot Springs Hotel.

The Northern Pacific could not keep so lucrative a source of passenger traffic to itself. In the early twentieth century, the contest between Harriman and Hill resulted in a Union Pacific branch line from St. Anthony, Idaho, to Yellowstone, Montana, which opened for traffic in 1908. Even before that, the Union Pacific joined with the Chicago and North Western in 1903 to organize and conduct escorted tours through Yellowstone and Rocky Mountain parks. So successful was this joint venture that the two railroads added winter tours to California. The Union Pacific considered building a grand hotel in Yellowstone Park but dropped the idea in the early 1920s when statistics showed that by then nearly two-thirds of all visitors arrived by private automobile.

Beginning in the 1880s, the Northern Pacific issued an annual Wonderland booklet to promote Yellowstone and other scenic attractions along its right-of-way. Of the national park, Olin Wheeler in *Wonderland '97* asked,

Why is it that those who can, do not use this vast, inspiring domain as a place of recreation? In all the large cities of the land—New York, Boston, Philadelphia, Chicago, Baltimore, Cincinnati, St. Louis, etc., there are men and women of wealth and leisure who are sated with the monotonous humdrum of the sea shore, of fashionable watering places and resorts. Here is a region, new, far away from artificiality, where one can drink in inspiration and life from the very clouds themselves.[13]

After Union Pacific trains reached the western gateway to Yellowstone Park, the subsidiary Oregon Short Line responded to the Wonderland booklets with a series of attractive brochures of its own, beginning with *Where Gush the Geysers*. For the Northern Pacific's *Wonderland*, the Oregon Short Line substituted *Geyserland*, and the Milwaukee Road used *Pictureland*, although it appropriated the older term for the title of its 1920s travel brochure, *Pacific Northwest: The Wonderland*.[14]

If the Northern Pacific and Union Pacific became synonymous with Yellowstone National Park, Southern Pacific advertisements sought to promote Crater Lake National Park as a tourist destination. The Southern Pacific started conducting tours to Crater Lake from Medford after the park was created in 1902. Beginning in 1906 the Tacoma Eastern Railroad promoted Mount Rainier National Park, and that relationship continued after the Milwaukee Road acquired the short line. During summers in the mid-1920s, the Milwaukee Road operated the National Park Limited between Seattle, Tacoma, and Ashford. The train, which featured coaches, parlor cars, and cafe-observation car, required three hours and fifteen minutes to complete a one-way trip.[15]

In much the same way, the Great Northern Railway became synonymous with Glacier National Park. James J. Hill's favorite form of outdoor recreation was fishing on the St. John River in New Brunswick, where Wall Street financiers often joined him for a combination of business and pleasure. His second son, Louis W. Hill, preferred to look west to the northern Rocky Mountains, which the elder Hill had regarded only as an impediment to Great Northern trains and where the younger now envisioned a magnificent national park. The elevation of the Yale-educated scion to the Great Northern presidency in 1907 at the age of thirty-five had an unmistakable effect on the railroad. Unlike his father, Louis Hill was far more interested in advertising than in day-to-day railroad operations. Some would call him a public-relations genius.

*The white man's Indian: tourists on the Great Northern Railway near Glacier National Park capture on film an enduring symbol of the American West. Louis Hill was always eager to forge links between tourism, the Blackfeet, and the Great Northern. On one occasion, the Blackfeet adopted the railroad chairman into their tribe in an initiation ceremony that lasted from 9 p.m. until 2 a.m. After addressing young Hill as Louie, they carefully daubed special red paint on his face and rechristened him Gray Horse. Barriger Railroad Collection, St. Louis Mercantile Library.*

Louis Hill was among the leaders of a campaign that culminated in 1910 when President William Howard Taft signed legislation creating Glacier National Park. The Great Northern executive saw the preserve as America's answer to the Swiss Alps and as his company's counterpart to the Northern Pacific's popular destination, Yellowstone National Park. When the railroad created the Glacier Park Hotel Company in 1914 to operate the Glacier National Park Lodge (a large hotel opened the previous year) and other tourist facilities, Louis Hill became its president. That same year the Great

*The* Georgie Oakes, *shown here on the St. Joe River about 1910, was one of several steamboats on the waters of the inland Northwest that offered Spokane residents an opportunity to escape the summer's heat. A typical excursion crossed Lake Coeur d'Alene and followed the "shadowy" St. Joe to cover a total distance of 200 miles. Occasionally a small party of campers would go ashore for an extended stay. Eastern Washington State Historical Society, L84-327.1460.*

Northern spent almost a third of a million dollars just to promote the park.[16]

Hill retained well-known artists such as John Fery to capture the grandeur of Glacier Park and the West. Their illustrations appeared on everything from Great Northern playing cards to calendars. It was in this spirit that in the early 1920s the railroad's famous Rocky Mountain goat symbol first appeared on freight cars as a way to advertise Glacier Park across the nation.

Hill was not interested in Glacier simply for the revenues it generated for the Great Northern Railway. He was a romantic who genuinely loved the Rocky Mountain West and would sometimes stay in Glacier Park for six or seven weeks at a time. He once even suggested in all seriousness that the

United States Post Office remove from its stamps the faces of obscure dead Americans and replace them with the country's famous scenic attractions. Hill wanted schoolchildren around the nation to learn the history of the New Northwest and especially the Rocky Mountain country, not just that of Europe and the East Coast.[17]

## See America First

LOUIS HILL, WHO TOOK JUSTIFIABLE pride in his role in developing Glacier Park, was a big backer of See America First, a campaign that sought to divert wealthy tourists from the traditional attractions of

*After the steamboat* Ione *was launched in 1908, it plied the waters of the Pend Oreille River in northeastern Washington for several years. During summer months the "palatial steamer" met excursion trains from Spokane at Newport and provided passengers a cool and pleasant afternoon ride. "Pure mountain air, luxury and comfort all intermingle to make this outing perfect." The cost of a round-trip ticket by train and boat in the summer of 1909 was three dollars. Eastern Washington State Historical Society, L84-327.2041.*

Europe to new ones in the American West. One promoter took precise aim at affluent vacationers when he entreated, "To the tourist who travels for pleasure, the slogan 'See America First' applies with unusual force to the whole Rocky Mountain region, and more especially to Idaho. To the invalid seeking to restore his health, the healing properties of Idaho's hot and mineral springs offer as many inducements as the famous waters of Carlsbad or Baden, to which may be added the pure, mountain air and the scent of pine forests, things not to be found in any European watering place."[18]

The See America First slogan is attributed to numerous promoters, including Louis Hill, and as early as January 1906 a See America First League was founded in Salt Lake City. American railroads spent millions of dollars annually to support the campaign. The Great Northern even added the slogan to the covers of its passenger timetables and various brochures. But nothing aided See America First more than the outbreak of war in Europe in August 1914 and the fear of trans-Atlantic travel after a German submarine sank the *Lusitania* the following year.[19]

Not all prominent promoters of western tourism were as wealthy as Louis Hill or had organizations like the Great Northern Railway or the See America First League backing them. Some were self-appointed zealots like Robert Limbert, a taxidermist and furrier in Boise, who used photo essays to publicize Idaho's diverse geography as a tourist attraction. At the Panama-Pacific International Exposition in San Francisco in 1915, he crowned a display of Idaho's increasingly famous potatoes with an eleven-foot model of the Russett Burbank variety. To the phrase See America First, he added the corollary, "Begin with Idaho." In the 1920s he came to believe that tourism would eventually supplant logging and mining as his state's leading industries. To lure sightseers, Limbert wrote and illustrated articles that appeared in mass-circulation journals, including *National Geographic*. In the process he did much to publicize the area that President Calvin Coolidge proclaimed the Craters of the Moon National Monument in 1924. Limbert also turned his attention to the Sawtooth Mountains, which resulted in a fifty-four-page promotional pamphlet for the Union Pacific in 1927. The railroad distributed one hundred thousand copies of the publication.

## Trolley Car Tourism

RAILROAD PROMOTION OF national parks was originally aimed at wealthy Americans who had both time and money for an extended stay. The word *vacation* was not part of the vocabulary of a pioneer generation of Pacific Northwesterners, and paid vacations for the masses were still largely unknown when the new century dawned. Most vacations were for the wives and children of well-to-do businessmen. But another form of tourism, railroad excursion travel, evolved to cater to a less affluent crowd.

In lieu of vacations for both workers and business executives, brief local pleasure trips by rail and boat became popular. One midwestern resident remembers railroad excursions as "those crowded, grimy, exuberant, banana-smelling affairs on which one sat up nights in a day coach, or, if a 'dude,' took a sleeper, from Saturday till Monday morning and went back to work a bit seedy." But that was not always the case, particularly as excursion travel itineraries grew longer and catered to an increasingly affluent middle class: the Oregon Railroad & Navigation Company, for example, offered personally conducted trips from Portland to the East Coast in trains that featured free reclining seats and tourist sleepers with stoves for cooking meals. "The linen is carefully laundered and it's the best. Ladies' and

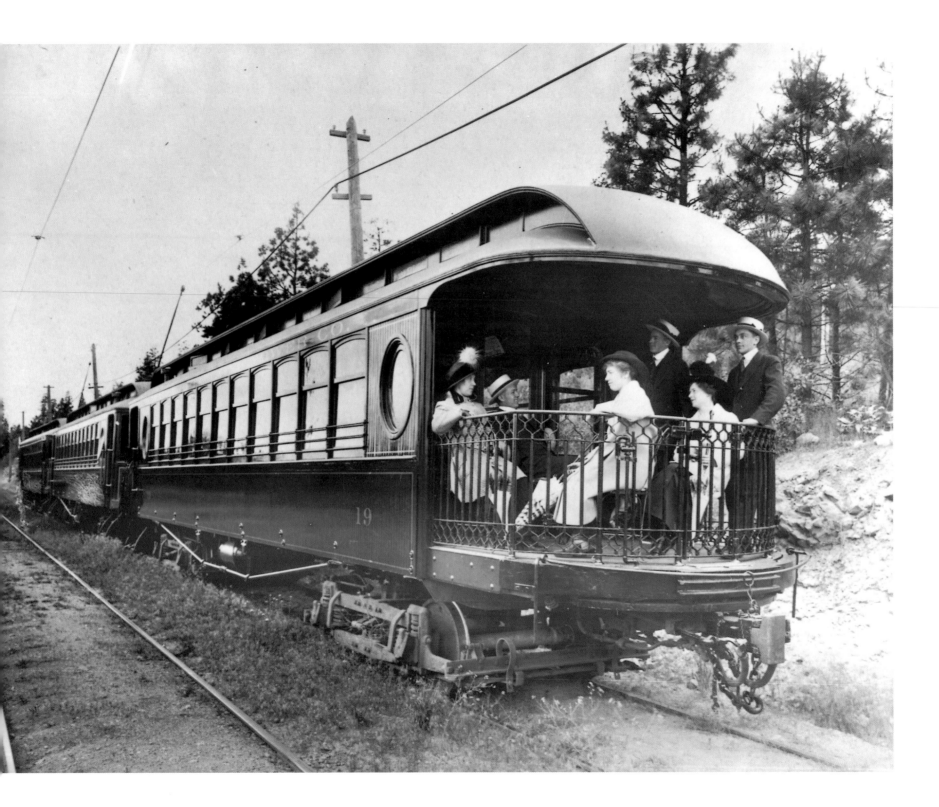

*Beginning in 1905, the Washington Water Power Company operated a seventeen-mile interurban line between Spokane and Medical Lake, a resort community long famed for the medicinal properties of its waters. Along its shores were picnic and swimming facilities and Coney Island pavilion, which hosted Saturday night dances. The Washington Water Power Company ran streetcar lines in Spokane and also operated Natatorium Park. This publicity photograph was taken at Garden Springs just west of Spokane. The line to Medical Lake (and a branch to the college town of Cheney) fell victim to the automobile in 1922 in what was the first major interurban abandonment in the Pacific Northwest. Eastern Washington Historical Society 4041.*

gentlemen's toilet and lavatories in each car."[20]

Nearer home, Seattle and Tacoma citizens could easily cruise Puget Sound in a commercial steamboat or cross over to the still pristine Olympic Peninsula. Completion of the Tacoma Eastern Railroad put the meadows of Mount Rainier within easy reach of Puget Sound residents. The railroad ran passenger trains fifty-five miles from Tacoma to Ashford, where a good wagon road and stage lines enabled tourists to reach Longmire Springs at the base of Mount Rainier. Two hotels and a mineral springs were located there.

Residents of Portland, like those of Seattle, Tacoma, and other cities of the Pacific Northwest, were well situated to take advantage of outdoor recreation made easily accessible by excursion trains and boats. Close at hand were Mount Hood and the Columbia River gorge; and it required only slightly more time and effort to reach the coast. From the railroad station at Hood River, a daily stagecoach wound along the forty-mile-long road to Cloud Cap Inn, a quaint structure built of fir logs in 1889 at the base of Eliot Glacier on the north shoulder of Mount Hood between 6,500 and 7,000 feet above sea level. "Ladies intending to go on the glacier or climb the mountain should provide stout ankle boots and short woolen skirts. Tourists cannot be too strongly urged to take this trip," the Union Pacific advised in 1892.[21]

The Spokane, Portland & Seattle Railway in mid-1916 offered numerous Sunday picnic fares from Portland to points along the Columbia River gorge. Prices for a round trip ranged from $1.25 to $1.50. For $39.10 the railroad also sold special 25-ride tickets to destinations as far inland as White Salmon, Washington, a jumping-off point for alpine tours to Mount Adams, 12,307 feet high. One option for excursionists was to go one way by train and return on the *Bailey Gatzert* or *Dalles City* of the Dalles, Portland & Astoria Navigation Company. On the opposite bank of the river, the Oregon-Washington Railroad & Navigation Company promoted "Bonneville on the Columbia River," a picnic grove that in 1911 boasted a dance pavilion, refreshment stand, baseball diamond, children's attractions, trout fishing in the nearby Columbia, and camping sites. Located only ninety minutes east of Portland by train, it was a favorite place for group picnics.[22]

The coming of electric streetcars and interurban railroads offered still other low-cost recreation alternatives for city residents. The Spokane & Inland Empire Railroad owned a minor-league baseball team in Spokane and used its games to generate passenger business. More typical was the streetcar company that for a nickel or two would whisk a patron to a bucolic setting that featured a picnic grove, small dance pavilion, and a few amusements and concession stands. "I would want my patrons to feel that they had enjoyed a trip to the country, unmarred by familiar city sights," explained one operator.[23]

Trolley-car parks were promoted as places where Sunday schools, fraternal societies, and other associations could gather. "The real excuse for the existence of any park is that it offers opportunity for out-of-door pleasures which would otherwise be denied to the vast majority of our urban population." It did not hurt that so-called electric parks and other recreation facilities boosted passenger traffic on trolleys and interurban railways, particularly on weekends when ridership might otherwise be low.[24]

Amusement parks had to a large extent superseded picnic groves and other "natural" attractions by World War I. The former dated back to the Midway at the 1893 Chicago world's fair and during the following decade evolved into the "electric park" with its brightly illuminated grounds to dazzle the eyes. Invariably, a variety of thrilling rides—among them the Helter Skelter and Shoot the Chutes—provided the main lure of such parks. "Speed is almost as important a factor in amusing the millions as is the carnival spirit," advised one park operator. "We as a nation are always moving, we are always in a hurry, we are never without momentum."[25]

In Portland the Oaks Amusement Park opened on a tree-covered sandspit in the Willamette River in 1907 and was soon billed as Oregon's Coney Island. That first season open-sided trolley cars carried three hundred thousand visitors, many of them families heavily laden with small children and bulging picnic baskets. The Seattle Electric Company owned and managed both Madrona and Leschi parks on Lake Washington. They became city property when Seattle acquired the streetcar company. Adjacent to Madrona Park was White City Amusement Park; Luna Park featured similar recreation in West Seattle near Alki Point. It was to promote such forms of entertainment nationwide that trolley executives formed the National Amusement Park Association in 1908.

Yet another popular attraction fostered by trolley companies were large and elaborate natatoriums. Ostensibly these were indoor swimming pools, but many evolved into amusement parks. The "Nat" operated by Spokane United Railways in 1924 featured an array of standard concessions: merry-go-round, Ferris wheel, electric bumper cars, penny arcade, shooting gallery, and refreshment stands.[26]

True trolley-car tourism arrived in the early twentieth century when electric interurban lines developed distant recreation getaways for city dwellers. When it came to developing the local tourist trade, as distinct from Sunday-school outings to a park, the region's most innovative interurban company was the Spokane & Inland Empire Railroad. One of its several attractions was the dance, dining, and swimming facility located at Liberty Lake, a body of water nestled in the mountains about seventeen miles east of Spokane. After the interurban opened a branch there in 1907, the Liberty Lake resort became so popular that the electric line built a hotel to accommodate visitors who wished to spend the night. Still farther out was Coeur d'Alene, another popular tourist destination, where electric cars linked up with Red Collar steamboats to offer a popular cruise on the lake.

A short distance north of Coeur d'Alene was Hayden Lake, where the Spokane & Inland Empire built one of the finest resort complexes in the entire Pacific Northwest. To implement its grand design for a "Green City in the Pines," the interurban's subsidiary Hayden Lake Improvement Company hired the noted landscape architect F. L. Olmsted, Jr., of Brookline, Massachusetts, son of the designer of New York's Central Park, to plan the 158-acre grounds. The resort centerpiece was the Bozanta Tavern, a Swiss chalet–style building designed by the Spokane architect Kirtland Cutter. The Bozanta Tavern featured a wide veranda looking over the lake that "has always been noted for its big, gamy cut-throat trout and bass." The Hayden Lake resort also featured a golf course, four tennis courts, boating and bathing facilities, and a mountain trail for climbers. When the golf course was expanded from nine to eighteen holes in 1912, it became the largest one in Idaho.[27]

The Spokane & Inland Empire was once called the most pretentious of the region's new electric interurban systems, but it did have a way of making its corporate dreams become reality. Few other interurbans in the United States developed the kind of luxury resort it built at Hayden Lake. From the time the facility opened in 1907 until the mid-1920s, Spokane & Inland Empire trains whisked excursionists between Spokane and the lakeside retreat in its elegant parlor cars in about ninety minutes. A person could leave Spokane's Interurban Depot at 1:00 p.m., arrive at the resort by 2:30, and play the nine-hole golf course twice before dinner. An early-morning train that left Hayden Lake at 7:30 allowed a businessman to reach Spokane by 9:00 and put in a full day's work. There was even a 25-ride family ticket that enabled a businessman to commute

*The Bozanta Tavern, now Hayden Lake Golf and Country Club, was a retreat for affluent Spokane residents in the early twentieth century. A visit by President William Howard Taft in 1907 confirmed the resort's upper-class status. Outdoor recreation in the Spokane area included Medical Lake west of town, and Newman and Spirit lakes—both accessible via the Idaho & Washington Northern Railroad. Eastern Washington State Historical Society, L84-207.4.65.*

to work while still spending evenings and weekends with his vacationing family. Some exceptionally affluent tourists came to the Bozanta Tavern in their private railway cars. A number of prominent Spokane families built summer homes nearby on the shore of Hayden Lake.

The Spokane & Inland Empire issued a variety of attractive folders to promote its tourist traffic. One called *Hayden Lake* was mailed out along with fresh pine needles "to carry the balsa of the forests direct to the recipient." There was nothing cheap about these brochures: "We often hear criticism about the expensive literature issued, but we insist that one folder that is artistic enough to be kept and shown or mailed to others covers more ground and makes a greater impression than twenty common, ordinary leaflets which are generally glanced over and thrown away. We have never yet seen one of our folders discarded on the floor of our cars or depots." The electric line enthusiastically employed Spokane's commercial photographers to illustrate its several brochures, because "a photograph can be read and the impression gained instantly."[28]

Unfortunately for tourism on the Spokane & Inland Empire Railroad, the brochures and advertisements that ultimately made the biggest impression on Pacific Northwest travelers during the decade after 1910 were those for new models of automobiles. Especially after the end of World War I, both steam railroad excursions and interurban resorts proved extremely vulnerable to "tin can" tourists, a new breed of cost-conscious travelers who toured the West in increasing numbers in their own automobiles. The automobile made cheap family travel possible for the masses and heralded an egalitarian era of tourism that blurred the tie between railroads and national parks and virtually erased that between trolley companies and amusement parks.

*Northern Pacific dining car service is maintained at a uniform standard of excellence throughout. The line is noted for its Great Big Baked Potatoes; eggs, milk, and cream from its own poultry and dairy farm; creamery butter put up in four separate wrappings of oiled paper; whipped cream for coffee; milk in individual bottles; bread, cakes, French pastry, pies and ice cream from its own bakeries at Seattle and St. Paul.*—Eastward through the Storied Northwest *([1913])*

# The Golden Age of Passenger-Train Travel

THE GLORY DAYS OF RAILROAD passenger service in the United States lasted from 1897 at least through 1917, from the return of prosperity to federal take-over of the railroads during World War I. Accommodations and rates were standardized; big-city stations were busy, crowded places; and names of the nation's finest trains were household words. During those two decades highway competition offered no serious threat to long-distance passenger trains, and commercial aviation was still the stuff of science fiction. "Almost every important event was once preceded and followed by a journey on a train and, like the footlights and overture in an old-fashioned theater, the trip itself became an essential part of the performance."[1]

Among railroad passengers, by far the most numerous were businessmen. That elastic category included everyone from corporate executives to traveling salesmen, or drummers, forever lugging their bulky sample cases and peddling their stock of well-worn jokes from station to station.[2]

On any given night on American railroads, several thousand travelers bedded down in the nation's largest and finest hotel chain, operated by the Pullman Company. At the turn of the century, Pullman had 3,006 cars in service (including dining

cars); individual railroads owned a mere 393 sleeping cars. Since the 1890s most railroads in the Pacific Northwest operated sleeping cars under contract with Pullman. The chief exceptions were the Great Northern, which switched to Pullman in 1924, and the Milwaukee Road, which changed only gradually after 1900. The railroads usually found it to their advantage to contract with Pullman to supply first-class accommodations because the Chicago-based company could adjust more easily than they to seasonal travel demands by shifting extra cars from its vast fleet to carry vacationers to the northern lakes and woods in summer or to Florida and California in winter.[3]

From 1900 through the 1920s, Pullman sleepers transported an increasing number of passengers to a wide variety of destinations. The number of Pullman journeys in the United States climbed from five million a year in 1900 to twenty-six million a year in 1914. By 1926 there were 8,981 Pullman cars in service, and the company employed an army of mechanics, car cleaners, clerks, and porters to keep them running. Each day in the mid-1920s, the six Pullman laundries together with fifty-nine contract laundries washed an average of a million pieces of linen. During the course of a year, Pullman went through 4.2 million cakes of soap, 126,868 gallons of liquid soap, 103 million drinking cups, 46,740 mops, and 11,701 fly killers.[4]

The Pullman sleeper during these years became an American institution. A typical car featured an aisle down the middle with open sections along each side. At night, a white-jacketed porter folded down the two facing seats in each section to form a lower berth and drew a curtain (usually red or green) to provide patrons a measure of privacy (but no protection from loud snorers). Pullman employed about twelve thousand blacks as porters in 1928 at an average salary of $72.50 a month, from which was deducted about $33 for various job-related expenses. Porters worked an average of eleven hours a day

and received an estimated $58 a month in tips from patrons who almost invariably addressed them as George.[5]

Few seasoned travelers regarded the upper berth on a Pullman car as a desirable accommodation. It folded down from the ceiling to provide only limited space for personal belongings and made undressing a difficult task at best. The proper way for a gentleman to remove his trousers in the cramped quarters, quipped one commentator, was to go to the north end of the berth, fasten the leg of the garment to a hook, and then crawl south. "By this time any fool will realize that there is so much clothing in the berth that practically no room is left for him."[6]

Another jaded traveler recalled early-morning hours in a Pullman car:

Its aisles, that are a wilderness of bulging curtains, waving trouser legs and depressing glimpses of human anatomy in the imperfection of matutinal disarray are a part of every man's experience. Its washrooms, combless, brushless—that inevitable scene and setting for wicked anecdotes where the genus traveling salesman tonsors himself, anoints his physiognomy with unguents and adjusts his galluses—is an institution of sacred and immutable permanence.[7]

No wonder vaudeville performers often featured comic routines that involved bedding down in an open-section Pullman car (sometimes with the wrong person) and critics later called them "rolling tenements." The Great Northern addressed these popular concerns in 1924 when it promoted its updated Oriental Limited by proclaiming in the daily newspapers of the Pacific Northwest: "At last! A Train for Women." Besides providing separate shower facilities for men and women in its sleeping cars, "extra large dressing-rooms with wide mirrors give women passengers opportunity for a complete and careful toilet on the new Oriental Limited."

So many aspects of railroad passenger service had become uniform by the early twentieth century that the years from 1900 to 1933 were sometimes labeled the Standard Era. The sudden, unpredictable, and ruinous rate wars of the previous century were past, and even the cars themselves had a similar appearance. Basic innovations like air brakes and interlocking or knuckle couplers were now accepted as standard safety features.

When the new century dawned, the best railway passenger cars were still built of wood, rode on six-wheel trucks, and were very heavy. Passengers and railways executives alike equated weight with strength, safety, and a smooth, comfortable ride. The typical passenger train at the beginning of the century, especially in the West, was also very slow when compared to the streamliners introduced in the 1930s. A long-distance passenger train that averaged more than sixty miles per hour in 1900 was a rarity.

Standard-era passenger cars had a distinctive clerestory roof (except those on the Harriman Lines, which were distinguished by an arch or turtle-back roofline), were not air conditioned, and featured dark wood paneling to hide the dust that blew in through open windows. For reasons of uniformity and economy, large railroads also favored red or green plush upholstery, but as one traveler recalled of coach seats, "If the plush ones didn't give you heat rash, the straw ones [rattan] tattooed you with what looked like the canals on Mars."[8]

Metal cars were a rarity during the first decade of the twentieth century. Passengers found the first ones very noisy and prone to loud drumming as they pounded across rail joints. In all but the newest passenger cars, gas and oil lamps provided illumination, which was often feeble at best. Still, many travelers found the motion of the train and the click-clack of the wheels over rail joints pleasant sensations.

## Luxury Limiteds and Plug Locals

IN THE EARLY TWENTIETH CENTURY, passenger-train service on steam railroads of the Pacific Northwest was divided between a handful of luxury limiteds and a much greater number of local trains. A third category, commuter service, was practically nonexistent in the region apart from Southern Pacific trains that linked Portland and Lake Oswego, a Willamette Valley suburb. The Butte, Anaconda & Pacific Railway also provided a form of commuter service by operating four trains a day each way between Butte and Anaconda.

Every major railroad maintained at least one premier passenger train. The company's showpiece served the largest population centers and featured its most up-to-date equipment. A journey on the Olympian, bragged the Milwaukee Road in the mid-1920s, "is accompanied by the feeling of security and the thought that vacation time dates from the moment one boards such a train."[9] Deluxe trains like the Olympian once operated along all main lines to provide through service between major cities of the Pacific Northwest and San Francisco, St. Paul, Chicago, Salt Lake City, Denver, Omaha, and Kansas City as well as to select communities along the way. There were also a few entirely regional deluxe trains that linked Portland, Spokane, and Seattle.

The North Coast Limited, inaugurated by the Northern Pacific on April 29, 1900, set a new standard for luxury travel in the Pacific Northwest. The region's first electrically lit passenger train featured wide vestibules and steam-heated cars that were richly finished inside in mahogany and leather. Its scheduled running time for the 2,056 miles from St. Paul to Seattle was sixty-two hours and thirty minutes. The Great Northern Flyer, by contrast, required six additional hours.[10]

There were actually six North Coast Limiteds, of eight or nine cars each, originally intended for

*"I was amazed to find, as late as 1926, on its branch in Oregon called the Tillamook Line, that the Southern Pacific's passenger train was composed of ancient coaches, each heated, after a fashion, by a coal-burning stove, and lighted by kerosene lamps. The seats made no concession to the human spine. The cars were filthy. The so-called right of way was such that huge fir trees were often blown down across the tracks. The baggage car always carried sufficient saws, axes, peavies, and wedges to have equipped a small logging camp. Twice, on trips to Tillamook, I took off my coat and lent a hand to the train crew engaged in bucking up and rolling a big tree from the rails. By fast work we prevented what its customers called with fine irony the Tillamook Flyer from being more than four or five hours late— on a run of eighty-odd miles. Little wonder the people served by this antiquated branch welcomed any mode of transportation that would supplant the Flyer."*

—Stewart Holbrook, *Far Corner: A Personal View of the Pacific Northwest* (1952)

The Milwaukee Road offered Pacific Northwesterners yet another option in luxury train travel from Seattle and Tacoma to St. Paul and Chicago when it inaugurated the Olympian and Columbian in 1911. Rounding out the list of railroads with luxury east-to-west passenger-train service was the Union Pacific. Its premier train to the Pacific Northwest in 1916 was the Oregon-Washington Limited.

By contrast, the Southern Pacific alone offered service between Portland and San Francisco. Until the advent of through highways and reliable automobiles, its only competitors were coastal steamships. The railroad inaugurated the Shasta Express in October 1899 as its premier passenger train on the route. A decade later it was renamed the Shasta Limited and its operation extended through to Seattle. The Shasta Limited De Luxe began service in January 1913 as an electrically lit, extra-fare train that ran from San Francisco to Seattle in thirty-six

*The North Coast Limited featured a library car with 140 volumes, a writing desk, and a brass-railed observation car. The train also had a dining car, a card-and-smoking room for men, a buffet, and a barbershop. For a reasonable charge, a first-class passenger could have a suit pressed en route. University of Oregon, Angelus 1762.*

summer service only. But the train proved so popular with passengers that it began year-round operation in 1902. The Great Northern's response to the North Coast Limited was the Oriental Limited, inaugurated between St. Paul and Seattle in December 1905. In 1909 the Soo-Spokane-Portland Train DeLuxe commenced running from St. Paul to Spokane and Portland via Canada on the tracks of the Soo Line, Canadian Pacific, Spokane International, and Oregon Railroad & Navigation Company. It featured a library-observation car, Pullman sleeper, tourist sleepers, coaches, and a dining car.

hours and forty minutes. Travel time was shortened to thirty-three hours for the Panama-Pacific Exposition in 1915. In the era of government operation, the Shasta Limited De Luxe was withdrawn from service from July 1, 1918, until November 14, 1920.

Among other named trains in the Pacific Northwest during the golden age of railroad passenger service were the North Bank Limited and the Inland Empire Express, which the Spokane, Portland & Seattle Railway operated between Portland and Spokane. The Oregon Short Line ran a summer-only train, the Yellowstone Special, between Salt

Lake City and the west entrance to the national park.

The region's most numerous passenger trains were the unnamed and generally nondescript locals that offered "daily except Sunday" service along branch lines as well as to main-line towns and villages that limited-stop luxury flyers ignored. Most local trains carried coaches only, although a few overnight ones added Pullman cars primarily for the convenience of business travelers. Sometimes local passengers were accommodated in a caboose on a mixed passenger-and-freight train, but more often

they rode on a hard-backed seat in a hand-me-down passenger car infamous for rattling noises and the drafts that blew through ancient window sashes. Employees on one railroad were instructed to couple cars in such a way that potbellied stoves were located at the forward end of the car, presumably so that drafts would carry the heat back to the passengers. When in later years seasoned travelers talked in nostalgic terms about the glory days of railroad passenger service, they usually had in mind the limited, not the local, train.

## Nothing Could Be Finer

NOTHING EPITOMIZED THE LUX-ury of train travel better than meal service. Every premier passenger train had at least one dining car, although some railroads, particularly those in the East, made the service available to first-class passengers only. Lowly coach passengers were generally expected to carry their own food or buy a sandwich or piece of fruit from a candy butcher as he passed through the car.

According to an estimate prepared for 1924, America's railway dining cars served between forty and fifty million meals in that year alone. Many different fruits appeared on the menu, but apples, oranges, and grapefruits were passenger favorites. Some twenty thousand barrels of apples, mostly from the Pacific Northwest, were baked, stewed, fried, and otherwise served to diners in 1924. The nation's railroads also served nine hundred thousand quarts of ice cream, eight million pounds of beef, and two million pounds of coffee. In the mid-1920s the Southern Pacific by itself served about six million meals annually in its dining cars, steamships, and station restaurants. The railroad operated a fleet of 125 dining cars, 26 all-day lunch cars, and 37 club cars.[11]

Although passengers occasionally complained

INTERIOR N. P. DINING CAR.

*An elaborate table setting was photographed aboard a Northern Pacific dining car, probably in the 1880s. Haynes Foundation Collection, Montana Historical Society, H-1586.*

that train meals in some parts of the country were bland and standardized, dining cars on Pacific Northwest railroads served gourmet fare at reasonable prices. Making this exceptional standard of service all the more remarkable was the fact that railroads seldom made a profit on their dining cars, and they did not expect to. The Southern Pacific estimated that in 1925 it lost approximately fifty-two cents on each meal served in its dining cars, which in most cases exceeded the cost of the meal itself. That figure was no doubt typical for railroads serving the Pacific Northwest. Union Pacific dining cars in the late 1950s recorded the highest ratio of cost to income in the United States, which was probably a measure of the still excellent quality of meal service.[12]

The Northern Pacific was among the first transcontinental railroads in the United States to offer meals aboard trains. Prior to this, most western railroads had stopped periodically to allow travelers to gulp down a meal at trackside restaurants and diners. When the Northern Pacific inaugurated through passenger trains between St. Paul and

Portland on September 12, 1883, it included dining cars in their consists.

Dining car service was an outgrowth of the Northern Pacific's hunting car of the mid-1870s. It was also one way that Henry Villard could impress European investors with the quality of the railroad and its passenger-train service. The Union Pacific followed the Northern Pacific's lead when it introduced dining cars on its trains late in the 1880s. The Great Northern put six company-owned cars into service in 1889 on the new line then being extended to the Pacific. At the turn of the century, the railroad advertised that "Great Northern dining cars are permanently attached to all transcontinental trains, and do away absolutely with all the rush and hurry that too often destroys a meal on other lines. Abundance of time, the smoothest of running and the exquisite service have made the Great Northern 'diners' famous with experienced travelers."[13]

Hazen J. Titus, who became superintendent of Northern Pacific dining cars in 1908, conceived the idea of the Great Big Baked Potato, a popular dinner item that became widely identified with the

*The Northern Pacific sought to promote its dining car's Great Big Baked Potato, but to the skeptical eye, its float seems to suggest an oversized onion. University of Oregon, Angelus P3118.*

railroad. This delicacy was popularly believed to come from Idaho but was actually from the Yakima Valley. During this time the Northern Pacific operated its own fifty-two-acre dairy and poultry farm in Washington's Kent Valley. The number of dining cars in its fleet peaked at sixty-four in 1915.

Provisioning a dining car on a long-distance train was a complex operation. On the Great Northern, for example, the dining car steward determined how much of each item to load aboard the Oriental Limited or Empire Builder in Seattle or St. Paul. Experience told him how travel and even the seasons affected passenger appetites. He had to have food enough to last the entire trip, although some items like Rocky Mountain trout might be supplied fresh along the way. His pantry was stuffed full of Wenatchee apples, Olympia oysters, Columbia River salmon, Minnesota mushrooms, and strawberries and loganberries from Oregon and Washington. The railroad's famous chicken pies, dinner rolls, and biscuits were all baked fresh for each meal.[14]

What made dining car meals even more remarkable is that everything, not just breads and rolls, was prepared from scratch aboard each train's tiny kitchen. Cooks baked, simmered, and fried their specialties using only charcoal-burning ranges and ovens, and until the 1930s they had no refrigeration other than plain ice. On all railroads the chefs, cooks, waiters, and stewards were schooled at regular intervals to learn the latest innovations in meal preparation and service.

## Down at the Depot

IF DINING CARS WERE SYNONYMOUS with the luxury of passenger-train travel, stations in the region's larger cities symbolized the power of the railroads themselves. Not without reason were some of them modeled after the great public buildings of Greece and Rome. Especially in metropolitan centers, railroad stations mirrored civic pride. They functioned as municipal showplaces as well as gateways to other destinations along the railway corridor.

The Northern Pacific Terminal Company set up by Henry Villard in the 1880s constructed the Portland Union Station in 1893–94. That facility reached maximum capacity in September 1922, when the Spokane, Portland & Seattle Railway moved the last of its trains there from the small building it had formerly shared with the Oregon Electric. Each day a total of fifty-two steam and thirty-eight electric trains arrived and departed from the Portland Union Station. The station continues to serve Amtrak, although the number of arrivals and departures has shrunk to just six a day.

Seattle's King Street Station opened for business in May 1906 to replace an antiquated depot on Railroad Avenue between Marion and Columbia streets, which was originally built for the Seattle, Lake Shore & Eastern Railway. James J. Hill initially opposed construction of a magnificent new station: "It is more important to Seattle to have goods delivered to it cheaply than to have a fancy depot, and I'm devoting my attention to more important things." But the Empire Builder relented and allowed the St. Paul architects Charles A. Reed and Allen H. Stem (who designed New York's Grand Central Station) to design a functional and relatively plain facility.[15]

The new red-and-brown brick King Street Station was typical for the era, in that it contained a coffee shop, dining room, and a capacious waiting room filled with rows of heavy oak benches. Towering above it was a 240-foot-high campanile that rang the time for Seattle's business district. The King Street Station was a monument that signified the coming of age for Seattle as well as Great Northern supremacy in the city. Great Northern and Northern Pacific passenger trains shared the station. The first Milwaukee Road passenger trains to Seattle in

*A large sign at Portland's Union Station in the early twentieth century urged travelers to go east on trains of the Oregon Railroad & Navigation Company, with "every mile protected by automatic block signals." The architects of the building were Van Brunt and Howe of Boston, who were also responsible for designing monumental Union Pacific stations in Ogden, Utah, and Cheyenne, Wyoming. Union Pacific Museum.*

1909 also stopped there but transferred across Fourth Avenue to Union Station when it opened in 1911.[16]

Portland was the only Pacific Northwest metropolis to have a single union station serving all steam railroads entering the city. Spokane, by contrast, once had four stations in operation at the same time: the Great Northern facility on Havermale Island, where the Spokane River passed through the center of town; Union Station serving Union Pacific and Milwaukee Road trains; the Northern Pacific station; and the Interurban Depot for the Spokane & Inland Empire Railroad. Except for the clock tower of the Great Northern, which was preserved as the centerpiece of Spokane's Expo '74, only the Northern Pacific station survives today. Even in smaller communities of the Pacific Northwest served by more than one railroad, separate depots were the rule. Walla Walla had separate stations for Union Pacific and Northern Pacific passenger trains, although one would have been adequate to serve the needs of both lines.

The Union Pacific opened the region's last metropolitan railroad station in Boise in 1925. In the 1880s the Oregon Short Line had routed its main tracks several miles south of the Idaho capital because Boise lay in a valley that would have created operating problems for through trains. Local trains shunted Boise passengers to and from main-line connections at Nampa. Angry Boise citizens blamed their misfortune on Robert Strahorn and hanged him in effigy. Boiseans continued to resent their secondary status until on April 16, 1925, they gained a through passenger line—and a station.

Even in the smallest village, a railroad station once functioned as a focal point for community life. Speaking of the Kaslo & Slocan Railway in southern British Columbia, an observer noted: "The one excitement in life was the arrival of the train: the whole population of Whitewater would gather at the depot when the distant whistle announced its approach. Then, after discussing the topics of the day with one another and with any passengers who happened to be on the train, one and all would adjourn to the store . . . there to await the distribution of the mail."[17]

Another person recalled with affection a similar scene in the midwestern village of 160 people where he grew up:

Going down to the depot to see the train come in was part of the regular duties of all citizens, young or old of both sexes, not otherwise engaged in tasks of an extremely confining nature. It was what was called a mixed or accommodation train. To tell the truth, the accommodations were somewhat limited. The single yellow day-coach trailing at the end of 10 or 15 box cars, preceded by a wheezy little engine, created the illusion of a giant sunflower being dragged along the countryside by an asthmatic rat terrier.

But it was all we had and who were we to carp at our sole connection with the outside world. It looked like romance indeed to a 15-year-old to see the "brakie" ride a string of empties down the lone side track. And "Dad" Ryan, the conductor—he was a personage—a widely traveled man with a voice like a foghorn and when he called "Aboard" the train moved as majestically away from the station as the Twentieth Century ever glided out of Grand Central—provided the engineer happened to be looking backward at the time to catch the signal. . . . So the arrival of the train was an event in the day's monotonous grind.[18]

This is a description that could apply to any one of thousands of small towns in the Pacific Northwest.

The typical village depot housed a telegraph operator and ticket agent, often the same person. He was responsible for processing reams of paper work from the head-end cars, so called because they were usually placed between the locomotive and passenger cars and carried mail and express. Sometimes it took an agent many minutes to load or unload a train laden with cans of milk, out-of-town newspapers, and catalog shipments. Outside the typical depot, transfer wagons and hotel carriages

***S****eattle's Union Station served both the Milwaukee Road, until it terminated passenger service to the Pacific Northwest in 1961, and the Union Pacific, until Amtrak took over America's intercity passenger trains in 1971. After that date the Union Station became a sales emporium for antiques, and the King Street Station alone served Amtrak's needs. Museum of History and Industry, Seattle, 83.10. W/S 22092.*

NO. 131 ARRIVAL OF FIRST MAIN LINE TRAIN, BOISE, IDAHO
APRIL 16, 1925.

*B*oise residents welcomed their city's first through passenger train on April 16, 1925. The Union Pacific's new Spanish Colonial–style station was located on benchland south of downtown. Beautifully landscaped grounds of the Platt Gardens afforded a sweeping view of the city. Clock chimes were added in 1927 in honor of Edward H. Harriman. Capitol Boulevard, an impressive thoroughfare through the heart of Boise, linked the station to the Idaho Capitol in 1931. Oregon Historical Society, 32439.

*This evocative image of activity at Missoula's Northern Pacific station recalls a cold, wet day in 1910. The brick structure opened in 1901. Brigham Young University, P389.*

*The ticket office in the Oregon Short Line's Boise depot was typical of facilities in all but America's largest cities in 1910. Idaho State Historical Society, 76-144.4.1/B.*

competed with one another to haul freight and passengers to their final destinations. "Right this way to the Slaughter House," was one startling invitation a passenger might have heard upon alighting from a Northern Pacific train in Slaughter, Washington. Local officials pressured the state legislature into changing the town's name to the more euphonious Auburn in 1893.[19]

As late as 1919, when commercial radio had yet to make its debut, the best way to follow world series action—other than to attend the game—was to be at the depot, where a kindly telegrapher might post each inning's score as it came over the wire. The railway station simply had no counterpart in the automobile age, which individualized most intercity travel.

## Travel by Train

WESTERN RAILROADS QUICKLY realized that their long-distance passengers enjoyed looking at scenery. Thus, every transcontinental carrier published guides, often elaborately illustrated with pictures and maps, to help passengers pass the time by identifying rivers, mountain ranges, towns, tunnels, and other features. A traveler could also while away the hours by studying various inexpensive regional handbooks like *The Pacific Northwest Official ABC Railway and Marine Guide*, published in Portland in the early twentieth century. Books of this type typically contained local timetables and bits of useful travel advice, some of it meant to entertain as well as inform. Local guides and individual railroad timetables often provided travelers with information not contained in the *Official Guide of the Railways*. That no-nonsense compendium was far too big for the average traveler to lug around, and in any case it was designed mainly for ticket agents, a humorless species in the eyes of many travelers.[20]

The Spokane, Portland & Seattle Railway passenger timetable issued on June 17, 1916, was typical in that it contained schedules not only for that company but also for subsidiaries, connecting railroads, and electric interurbans as well. It thus offers a good vantage point from which to recall travel in the Pacific Northwest near the end of the region's second railway age. The Columbia River Scenic Route, as the Spokane, Portland & Seattle Railway aptly described itself, advertised summer trips from Portland to Clatsop Beach; five round-trip commuter tickets cost fifteen dollars. An alternate destination for the summer traveler that year might be one of several Deschutes River fishing resorts. The railroad offered travelers a sixteen-page booklet called *Tips on Fishing Trips*, a map and folder called "What Central Oregon Farmers Have Done," and another publication called "Outings in the Pacific

## HINTS TO TRAVELERS

*In the early 1890s,* Koch and Oakley's Railway and Navigation Guide *of Seattle offered numerous tips to travelers. Among its words of advice:*

*"Don't pester the conductor or brakeman with trifling questions. Names of places, distances, and meal stations are all noted on the maps and time tables of the several companies.*

*"Don't disturb the sleeping car by keeping up an animated conversation all night. You have no more right to do that than you have to dance a midnight breakdown in the corridor of a crowded hotel.*

*"The company has special cars for carrying live stock. Dogs, monkeys, etc., may be carried in the baggage car, provided a satisfactory arrangement can be made with the baggage master. Fleas are an exception to this rule.*

*"Keep your temper, and don't get left at a water tank where you have alighted to enjoy the mountain scenery.*

*"See that your trunk is solid, well packed, and corded or strapped. Baggagemen haven't time to renail cracker boxes."*

Northwest." Also listed were numerous horse and auto stages that connected Oregon Trunk stations to a variety of hamlets in central Oregon. A horse-drawn stage ran from Bend to Paisley, for example, a distance of 138 miles, and charged a fare of ten dollars per person.

The Spokane, Portland & Seattle timetable offered travelers a chance to get a farm when Colville Indian Reservation lands opened in north-central Washington. It cost twenty-five cents to register for the drawing that was to be held in Spokane on July 27, 1916. Another advertisement read, "'See

America First' means see Glacier, Yellowstone, Rocky Mountain (Estes) National Parks." In yet another place the railroad called passengers' attention to the fact that "Oregon and Washington home-grown products are used and advertised in the dining cars and on the steamships *Great Northern* and *Northern Pacific*." Also, "a tempting array of French pastry is personally served by the dining car conductor."

Reading material in coaches and Pullman cars might include, besides the timetable, promotional pamphlets and a popular type of fiction called day-coach literature. One such item was Thomas W. Jackson's *On a Slow Train through Arkansaw,* a collection of sometimes humorous anecdotes the author reportedly overheard while working as a brakeman on Oregon Railroad & Navigation Company trains between Spokane and Pendleton in 1903.

*Patrons ponder the railroad landscape in this Milwaukee Road promotional brochure from the 1920s. It implied that the view aboard the Olympian was comparable to that from a fine hotel or resort. Montana Historical Society.*

THE OLYMPIAN

Chicago, Milwaukee & St. Paul Railway

The master of Seattle's King Street Station cut a suitably imposing figure in this undated photograph. Special Collections Division, University of Washington Libraries, Lee 20,011.

When *On a Slow Train through Arkansaw* was at the height of its popularity, news butchers sold a thousand copies a day. A sample of what tickled the fancy of train travelers in the early twentieth century was this:

> Are you married?
> Yes, I married a spiritualist.
> How are you getting along?
> Medium.[21]

One thing all passenger trains had in common was that they represented industrial order and discipline. Distinct sets of written rules governed every aspect of railroad operation. The rules and regulations of the Washington & Columbia River Railway prohibited gunpowder, dynamite, nitroglycerin, and similar explosives from being transported on the same train as passengers. Railroads prohibited employees from drinking intoxicating beverages, and even frequenting saloons and taverns might be sufficient cause for dismissal. Another set of rules governed relationships between employees and passengers. For instance, railroads required their conductors and trainmen to protect patrons from intoxicated or quarrelsome passengers, and women especially from rudeness, threatened violence, and abusive or obscene language.[22]

An intoxicated or disorderly passenger who used "vile or profane" language was to be expelled from the train at any usual stopping place or near a dwelling or station. Employees were themselves instructed not to use tobacco in or about passenger cars and to remove their hats when passing through a dining car. Railroads specifically urged employees to cultivate "graciousness of manner" in dealing with the public.[23]

Some travelers, however, scorned railroad discipline and order as "the tyranny of the timetable" and thought it best personified by autocratic conductors. "To many people who travel, the conductor is a high and mighty being, to be timorously

approached and gently entreated, if at all." In addition, the local station agent was a czar. "If one did not like his methods or fancies, it was 'just too bad.'" Unhappy travelers sometimes denounced them both as petty bureaucrats.[24]

There was a time, explained *Koch and Oakley's Railway and Navigation Guide* in 1891, "when railroad men had the reputation of being the most impolite of any of their sex." The guide believed that because many early-day travelers were not well informed railroaders simply grew tired of answering their numerous and often repetitious questions.[25]

Discourtesy was not the only problem travelers perceived. For all a railroad's attention to detail, in reality waiting rooms in some branch-line depots could still be a "stench in the nostrils" of the women who wished to wait there. And on many a local, passengers complained that "the drinking water was

warm and rusty—and so was the cup on the chain; using the rest room always made me think of the Gates of Hell—only it was awful cold instead of awful hot."[26]

In 1912 the secretary of the United States Treasury requested that interstate carriers, by rail or water, abolish the common drinking cup to prevent the spread of disease. State boards of health in Idaho, Montana, Oregon, and Washington already prohibited it. Railroads introduced pasteboard drinking cups instead. Health concerns also led railroads to substitute paper for the cloth towels once common in washrooms. Concerns over improved public health were closely linked to those for safe operating conditions. Because safety was so important to passengers, railroads sought to use it to competitive advantage in their advertisements.

In 1899 the Northern Pacific bragged that its best passenger limited between St. Paul and Tacoma was equipped with the "latest, improved, automatic Westinghouse brake." The Oregon Railroad & Navigation Company stated that it was a maxim of the company that nothing was or could be too good for the patrons. To that end its passenger locomotives were fitted with electric headlights of the latest design. The engineer "merely touches a button in his cab, and the marvelous mechanism of dynamos, armatures, magnets, wires, coils and carbons does the rest." Because the headlight illuminated the track for half a mile ahead, the railroad described it as "a paid-up life-and-accident insurance for every passenger."[27]

By 1906 several railroads had introduced all-metal passenger cars into service, and the following year the Pullman Company introduced the first all-metal sleeping cars. In the West the Harriman Lines led the way in the introduction of such cars, which were supposedly easier to maintain than the old ones and safer in case of an accident. Railroads and their patrons alike demanded mechanical reliability in their passenger trains. Wrecks, like blizzards and floods, represented an intolerable interruption of scheduled service. Thus new forms of technology, even items as basic as electric headlights on locomotives, represented ways to triumph over the vagaries of travel by train.

Passenger trains during the opening decades of the twentieth century were more than means of conveyance. They were the most visible manifestations of the largest and most powerful industry in the United States; and they were part of the common experience of Americans from many different geographic, ethnic, and social backgrounds. For that reason the American passenger train mirrored important social trends, from "conspicuous consumption," as exemplified in the amenities of first-class travel and sumptuous dining car meals, to rising public concern over health and safety, which was an integral part of Progressive-era reform. Trends in passenger-train travel, moreover, first introduced executives in the steam railroad industry to the growing public infatuation with automobiles and other forms of competition that became increasingly obvious after 1916.

*The motor coach, moving through the main streets of cities and towns, rather than the "backyards," and traversing generally more pleasant routes, free from smoke, cinders, and noise, adds attractiveness as well as convenience to travel, thereby enhancing the intangible, but certain, desire to "ride on rubber."*
—Railway Age *(June 25, 1927)*

# III / *The Age of Competition,*
## *1917 to 1990s*

*West of Odessa, State 7 follows a slightly winding course through sagebrush barrens broken occasionally by orchards or surprising vistas. This section of the highway is an invitation to night driving, especially during the hot weather of midsummer. As a rule, traffic is not heavy after dark, and the traveler can speed with comparative safety, for only occasionally is the straightaway broken by a sharp curve, a dip, or incline, or a winding stretch of road around the base of some cliff or coulee wall. Now and then the eyes of an approaching car appear in the distance, grow brighter and brighter, give a brief close glow, disappear. Occasionally, a truck with heavily laden trailers thunders past, or a jack rabbit, phantom-like, leaps across the road. In the spring the scent of apple blossoms reveals an orchard hidden by the darkness. Again, the headlight of a locomotive creeps across the plateau, the light growing larger as the train approaches, with seemingly accelerating speed; then with a flash the engine thunders by, and is gone, leaving only the throb of the automobile motor and the whistle of the wind.*

—Washington: A Guide to the Evergreen State *(1941)*

*This jitney served patrons along Spokane's north Monroe Street. Any contraption that ran on four wheels and gasoline and charged a nickel fare qualified as a jitney. Eastern Washington State Historical Society,* L83-113.133.

*First came the parallel electric [trolley] line, next the development of the long-distance telephone line, and now the automobile. The future will tell whether the airship is to be a fourth. But the first two of these the railroad has overcome, the third is comparatively a minor factor, the fourth a commercial nebulosity as yet.*
—Railroad Age Gazette *(Dec. 4, 1908)*

# New Competition

THE "JITNEY MOVEMENT" THAT originated in Los Angeles in the winter of 1914–15 was a transportation phenomenon with far-reaching economic consequences. Neither the bus nor the automobile was new to city streets at the time, but when some inspired individual took his private car and converted it into an unregulated common carrier by sticking a sign in the front window offering rides to and from downtown for five cents, city dwellers responded by the thousands.[1]

Many commuters who had complained for years about overcrowded streetcars during rush hour pushed eagerly into overloaded jitneys, even flirting with death by riding on the running boards. Occasionally, jitney passengers just flirted with one another, causing some commentators to worry about the vehicle's impact on morality. Jitneys were supposed to be "quite a convenience for immoral women. They find it easy to strike up an acquaintance in a crowded jitney, while the street car presents no such opportunity." One man even fantasized in verse about female passengers:

> *When they ride in a jitney bus;*
> *They do not hang onto a strap;*
> *They Ford right in and sit in your lap.*

Chauffeurs in Oakland, California, after delivering their wealthy patrons to the theater, slipped around the corner, put a jitney sign on the windshield, and reaped a financial reward before returning at the end of the show. Drivers suffered occasional setbacks, as when someone scattered carpet tacks on the streets of Seattle's University District and disabled more than fifty jitneys. Ever a resourceful lot, jitney drivers proposed to suspend magnets before their front tires to prevent future sabotage. When the phenomenon peaked in mid-1915, jitney transportation was a fact of urban life from coast to coast. An estimated sixty-two thousand jitneys competed with streetcars. Never in American history had any mode of public transportation grown so rapidly. The once struggling electric railway, now a powerful "trolley trust," was confronted with its first significant rival as well as a stunning loss of revenue.

Until the jitney, many urban dwellers had never experienced the sensation of "riding on rubber and air." Another observer remarked that "one blessed feature of the jitney is that wherever introduced it gave poor women a chance to ride in an auto for a nickel, thus affording to thousands the opportunity for the first auto ride." Once experienced, the sensation apparently became addictive.

Progressive reformers who had unsuccessfully

challenged the nation's street railway monopolies at the ballot box or in city council chambers hailed the jitney as a new emblem of personal freedom. For the Reverend Sydney Strong of Seattle, the jitney was nothing less than "a return to the old social democracy of the country store when manager and customers shook hands and swapped stories over the counter." Corporations, declared Strong, "are bound to 'walk more humbly' and 'do righteousness' more spontaneously, when they reflect that in a day their income may be cut by almost 50 percent or almost annihilated." All jitney enthusiasts shared this conviction.

The loss of revenue stunned street railway companies, but they fought back by adopting cost-saving measures and promoting municipal regulation of their new competitor. Seattle jitney drivers waged a seven-year battle against restrictive local ordinances all the way to the United States Supreme Court in what became the infant industry's classic fight for survival. Only when the nation's highest court declined to hear their appeal in 1921 did they finally abandon the struggle. Jitneys eventually disappeared from city streets. Yet even as their numbers dwindled within city limits, they asserted themselves in the promising field of intercity travel. Called super jitneys and fast-flying super stages, high-powered elongated touring cars became especially prominent in California, a state that pioneered development of a network of paved roads and was blessed by a mild climate conducive to year-round operation of automobiles.

Soon it was the Southern Pacific and the Santa Fe, not just street railways and interurbans, that lost money to jitneys. As early as 1916 an automobile could make the trip from Los Angeles to San Francisco almost as fast as an ordinary passenger train, and super jitneys soon provided such service at a fare one-third that of the railroad. Because of jitney competition, the Southern Pacific discontinued several passenger trains in southern California.

*Electric Traction* reported in July 1916 that "all sections of the country are coping with the jitney situation quite successfully, except on the Pacific Coast, where the jitneys are now affecting the interurban steam line traffic to as great an extent as they have the electric lines."

Like street railway executives, most officials of steam railroads initially viewed jitney competition as a passing fad and were certain that unpaved rural roads would confine jitneys to city streets. However, H. S. Cooper, secretary of the Southwestern Electric and Gas Association, a Texas organization, urged the transportation industry to open its eyes. He prophesied as early as January 1916 that "if the public desires and demands jitney service to the suburbs, and the lack of public roadways hinders the fulfillment of that desire or demand, the public will build the necessary roadways and laugh at the cost." And indeed they did.

The once mighty electric railway industry became the "sick man of American business." Its financial health deteriorated so alarmingly that the federal government held four months of hearings on the subject in the summer of 1919. At that time nearly fifty electric railway companies were in the hands of receivers, and many more teetered on the edge of bankruptcy. Steam railroads should have viewed the jitney phenomenon as a cautionary tale about the power of automobile competition.

## It Can't Happen Here

IN 1914 A MOTORIST BOUND FOR Portland from eastern Oregon still had to ship his car through the Columbia Gorge by boat or train. One pioneer motorist who drove an Overland automobile from Topeka, Kansas, to Portland that year left a vivid picture of the difficulties awaiting anyone who sought to duplicate his feat. At one point in Kansas he was able to cover

*An early-day automobile required on-the-spot repairs in Seattle. This all-too-common scene caused many Pacific Northwesterners initially to consider the automobile only an expensive toy. Cross-state trips were seldom attempted before 1916. Washington State Historical Society, Curtis 2411.*

Their recommendation was that anyone wishing to undertake a similar motor trip across the West should carry a shovel, several gunnysacks, a block and tackle, plenty of rope, tire chains, an extra can of gas, and extra food. "One thing I almost forgot—don't fail to have a good rifle with you, for in this sagebrush country it is very lonesome and you are liable to meet a hungry, half-starved grey wolf."[2]

Given the rigors of a cross-country trip by automobile, it is easy to see why railroad executives as late as 1914 or 1915 failed to regard long-distance highway competition as a serious threat to either passenger or freight revenues. But as the jitney phenomenon illustrated all too well, competition had a way of arising from the most unexpected quarters.

## Out of the Mud: Dawn of the Automobile Era

ELECTRIC INTERURBAN LINES AT the turn of the century gave steam railroads their first hint of the competition that awaited them in coming decades. One respected industry leader, President Samuel Morse Felton of the Chicago Great Western Railroad, estimated that interurban competition had cost steam railroads a hundred million dollars by 1916. But that sum would prove insignificant compared to revenues lost to highway competition during the following decade.[3]

When automobiles first appeared in the Pacific Northwest shortly before 1900, they were expensive and virtually inoperable in bad weather. Early models had no bumpers, no self-starters, and no doors for the driver's seat. Sputtering and unreliable headlamps that burned acetylene or kerosene made night driving a chore; and prior to 1912 or 1913, motorists could find fuel only at auto dealers or hardware stores. Because early automobiles were so

270 miles in a single day, but in Malta, Colorado, where the journey got rough, the two women accompanying him chose to go by train, and he and another man continued on alone.

Near Meeker, Colorado, their Overland became stuck in mud to the axles and required horses to free it. West of Albion, Idaho, they traveled all day across a sagebrush plain largely devoid of houses. In Buhl the travelers bought a rifle to relieve the monotony of the Snake River plain by shooting at numerous jackrabbits along the way. In central Oregon they had to back their car uphill because its gas tank was so nearly empty that it would not feed the carburetor. From The Dalles they took the steamer *Bailey Gatzert* for Portland, where they arrived three weeks later than the women who went by train.

expensive and so prone to mechanical problems, it is not surprising that many observers regarded them only as rich men's toys.

Early roads often amounted to little more than two muddy ruts across a field. Rural citizens often worked out their road tax by shoveling dirt or scraping away high spots to maintain primitive pathways near their farms and villages. A distance of seventy-five miles was a long day's drive, and such a trip included one or two delays to change a tire or to make adjustments to the engine. Idaho as late as 1918 had only five miles of oiled or semipaved highway outside urban areas. Until the early 1920s not even so much as a wagon road connected the northern and southern parts of the Gem State. There was only an Indian trail so rough that for six months of the year no one but an expert snowshoer could traverse it.

The motor vehicle law that Oregon enacted in 1905 limited top speed for each of the state's 218 registered vehicles to eight miles per hour in the country when within a hundred feet of any vehicle powered by horses. Given the lack of any direction signs, the technological limitations of early automobiles, and rough road surfaces that caused many flat tires, such low speeds were not unreasonable. A trip to Mount Hood from nearby Portland in 1908 or 1909 was an all-day adventure. Year-round motoring was not feasible until development of enclosed cars and antifreeze.

Railroads were among early supporters of the good roads movement in the mistaken belief that construction of a series of farm-to-market links would ultimately benefit them. The Spokane & Inland Empire Railroad proposed to award five hundred dollars as first prize in a 1908 contest for the best mile of highway built to serve the interurban's rural customers. "I know of no material aid to the farming population so important as the creation and maintenance of good roads," emphasized James J. Hill in 1910. Harriman likewise was an advocate of better country roads. Although a few venturesome motorists bragged about driving from coast to coast in the early twentieth century, even men as astute as Harriman and Hill failed to recognize the automobile as a serious long-distance competitor to railroads.[4]

Even now it is not easy to pinpoint the year when railroads lost the competitive advantage. It occurred in different parts of the country at different times,

---

### Columbia River Highway

**The ghost of the old Columbia River Highway lingers on in the shadows of Interstate 84 through the Columbia Gorge. The remaining sections of the historic route form a scenic byway linking together trail heads for Multnomah Falls, Oneonta Gorge, and other natural wonders east of Portland.**

**Samuel Christopher Lancaster, consulting engineer on the project, wanted a highway that was scenic as well as functional. When the first section opened to traffic in 1915, its spectacular engineering and aesthetic appeal attracted world attention. The occasion was not unlike the final spike ceremonies of railroads during the past century.**

**Mitchell Point Tunnel was probably the first important highway tunnel built in the United States. Located five miles west of Hood River and drilled through a promontory of basaltic rock, the tunnel was completed on November 10, 1915. It was 390 feet long and had five large windows cut through the rock to provide motorists a panoramic view of the Columbia River. This, the first major paved highway in the Pacific Northwest, also permitted automobile travel from Portland through the Columbia Gorge to eastern Oregon.**

**Source: Samuel Christopher Lancaster, *The Columbia: America's Great Highway through the Cascade Mountains to the Sea*, 2d ed. (1916)**

---

*A motorist pauses in the scenic Mitchell Point Tunnel on the new Columbia River Highway. The tunnel was destroyed in 1966 during construction of the present interstate highway through the gorge. Oregon Historical Society, 3587, file 266.*

and always incrementally. Only in 1913, for example, when approximately ten thousand motor vehicles were in use in Oregon, did state government enter the road-building business. Prior to this, there were only city and county roads. Oregon's newly created highway commission laid out a true system of highways for the first time. Financed by a one-quarter-mill levy on all property in the state, the measure raised $700,000 that first year and focused special attention on the three routes likely to benefit most Oregonians: the Pacific Highway from Portland through the Willamette Valley, the Coast Highway, and the Columbia River Highway.

In 1913, the same year that Oregon entered the road-building business, Henry Ford initiated assembly-line production of his Model T automo-

bile. As a result, vehicles that cost $850 in 1909 sold for a relatively affordable $440 (and even less for used ones) by 1915. That was only the beginning: a farmer needed to sell 1,412 bushels of wheat in 1913 to purchase an automobile; that figure would drop to only 506 bushels in the mid-1920s. As prices fell, auto output leaped right off the production charts.[5]

*Railway Age* estimated that in 1919 alone the American public had spent more than $5.5 billion to purchase and operate automobiles (not including the cost of highway construction and maintenance). That amount was $300 million more than it paid for railroad transportation. The magazine further estimated that by 1919 the public had invested a total of $9 billion in automobiles, and it valued at only

$19 billion all American railroads.[6]

Both electric and steam railway executives had once been certain that automobile ownership would reach the saturation point. But when sales continued to climb, the *Electric Railway Journal* sighed in 1926, "Now there seems some basis for thinking that perhaps there is no saturation point."[7] By that time the automobile was no longer popularly regarded as a toy for the idle rich—a useless "go-devil," as some farmers had called it. For the increasing number of Americans who could afford one, the automobile combined the flexibility of the horse with the speed of a trolley or steam locomotive but avoided the costs of fixed rails and attendant franchise and other legal encumbrances. Automobiles gave their owners a sense of control and power and did not require them to follow a timetable for arrivals and departures. Anyone who could scrape together a few dollars to buy a used Model T and a few gallons of gas could enter into personal competition with the most costly twelve-car luxury passenger train in the nation.

Number of Residents per Automobile

|  | 1910 | 1920 | 1930 |
|---|---|---|---|
| California | 54 | 5.9 | 2.8 |
| Idaho | 693 | 8.5 | 3.7 |
| Montana | 365 | 9.1 | 3.9 |
| Oregon | 127 | 6.8 | 3.7 |
| Washington | 156 | 7.8 | 3.5 |
| United States | 196 | 11.4 | 4.6 |

SOURCE: Peter J. Hugill, "Good Roads and the Automobile in the United States, 1880–1929," *Geographical Review* 72 (July 1982): 340.

Citizens demanded, and got, more and better roads and highways. In 1916 the federal government responded to rising clamor for "good roads" with the first of several measures that enabled it to spur highway construction. Congress placed $75

million in the hands of the secretary of agriculture to spend on rural road improvement over the next five years. Money was to be granted to states on a matching basis. Although the 1916 act did not propose to create a system of trunk highways, and its effect was largely nullified by American entrance into World War I a year later, it did lay the groundwork for a massive increase in highway construction after the war. Following the 1918 armistice, the Department of Agriculture transferred surplus war equipment worth $140 million to the states to be used in building and maintaining roads. The generous federal handout included more than twenty-seven thousand motor vehicles as well as a variety of hand tools that accelerated postwar road building.

Oregon led the nation in finding new ways to finance highway construction when in 1919 it became the first state to levy a tax on gasoline. With the new source of revenue and a rallying cry to "Lift Oregon Out of the Mud," contractors crisscrossed the state with hundreds of miles of good roads, many of them paved. Other states soon levied gasoline taxes of their own.

The federal Highway Act of 1921 broke free of the vision of farm-to-market feeder roads held by railroads. It required states to designate 7 percent of their roads as a primary highway system, and only these would be eligible for matching federal grants. Gradually a 200,000-mile system of two-lane federal highways extended across the nation, not supplementing but competing with rails. This grid was designed to interconnect every city having more than fifty thousand residents. In Oregon, the Pacific Highway was completed in 1922 and fully paved from the Columbia River to the California border by 1926. The Columbia River Highway was paved from Portland to The Dalles. The mileage of surfaced highways in the United States doubled between 1920 and 1930 and doubled again by 1940. In the Pacific Northwest, the highway construction boom resembled that in mining and timber in earlier

*When the horse was king of local transportation: the Dayton, Washington, horse show in 1907. Eastern Washington State Historical Society, 290.*

Dayton's Anual Horse Show April 20-07

*A typical farm scene in the Palouse country before the coming of good roads and the automobile. Eastern Washington State Historical Society, L84-327.1643.*

years. During the 1920s, money for streets and highways became the second largest item of government expenditure.[8]

Highway construction and technological improvement of the automobile went hand in hand, first one taking the lead, then the other. Progress in both areas made it commonplace by the late 1920s for motorists to drive 300 to 400 miles in a single day. Although the four states of the Pacific Northwest completed a basic network of roads in the 1920s, during the depression decade they continued to build and improve their roads. Highway construction was widely perceived as a way to strengthen the economy and put unemployed people to work.

Motor Vehicle Laws, July 1930

| | Max. Speed per Hour | Driver License Required? | Full Stop at RR Crossing? |
|---|---|---|---|
| Idaho | 35 | no | yes |
| Montana | Reasonable and proper | no | no |
| Oregon | 35 | yes | no |
| Washington | 40 | yes | no |

SOURCE: *Oregon Motorist* 10 (July 1930): 9.

## From Jitney to Nite Coach

AS EARLY AS 1912 AND WELL BEFORE the jitney craze, automobiles were used to carry passengers from San Diego to El Centro, California, a town in the Imperial Valley 125 miles away. Patrons waited on the curb in front of the Pickwick Theater in San Diego. This was the inauspicious beginning of the famous Pickwick Stages, which became the longest bus line in the nation by the mid-1920s. Another line that predated the jitney era used touring cars to link Oakland, San Jose, and Santa Cruz. The jitney

phenomenon gave the nascent intercity bus industry a big boost. This was most evident in California, but it also occurred in the Pacific Northwest, where during the 1920s a new intercity truck and bus industry expanded as rapidly as the region's spreading network of all-weather roads permitted.

An article by Lewis R. Freeman, who traveled by common-carrier bus from New York to Los Angeles in late 1925, may help explain why railroad executives did not initially regard long-distance bus travel as a competitive threat to transcontinental train travel. The trip, which cost Freeman $127.14 and required thirty-five different buses operated by nearly that many different companies in addition to several short rides by rail, took from the day before Thanksgiving to the week after Christmas to complete. At one location in the desert Southwest, passengers reenacted a ritual from stagecoach days when they climbed out to push the bus through a bad section of road. Near Gila Bend, Arizona, another bus broke an axle. Freeman was apparently the first person to cross the continent by bus.[9]

Like their jitney forebears, bus operators of the 1920s were members of an innovative and aggressive fraternity. Mechanics at the Pacific Northwest Traction Company of Everett developed double-decked parlor-observation coaches for service between Seattle and Vancouver, British Columbia. These buses were specially designed so that passengers could enjoy the scenery of the Pacific Northwest. Twelve passengers sat in the upper observation compartment, and thirteen in the lower compartment. "The time when passengers in motor buses were forced to huddle in their seats in a cramped position over a journey made irksome by heat or cold or dust is rapidly disappearing."[10]

By the mid-1920s, restrooms appeared on a few western buses, and some routes even offered sleeper and buffet services. The Pickwick Stages System in 1928 introduced twenty-six-passenger sleeper buses, or "Nite Coaches," between the Pacific Northwest

PHOTO OF BOTHELL ROAD
TAKEN MAY, 8, 1912
K. & S. SEATTLE, W.M.

*R*esurfacing the Bothell Road near Seattle, May 8, 1912.
*Special Collections Division, University of Washington*
*Libraries, UW 5793.*

*L*arge wooden signs provide directions on U.S. 195 near Colfax,
*Washington, in July 1941 when Russell Lee took this photograph for*
*the federal government. Library of Congress, 15761 LC-USF3439953 Q.*

*A double-decked coach of the North Coast Lines in the early 1930s. Buses of this design were popular in western Washington not only for superior sightseeing but also for dry baggage and express storage under the raised compartment. (Other vehicles placed luggage on the roof under canvas.) This type of bus antedated by two decades the dome cars that were hailed as an innovative addition to luxury trains after World War II. Special Collections Division, University of Washington Libraries, UW 1662.*

and California. During the previous year, Pickwick had amassed five thousand miles of route stretching south from Portland to Los Angeles and from there east to El Paso. In late 1928 the Pioneer-Yelloway System began operating the nation's first daily transcontinental bus schedules. When Lewis Freeman repeated his cross-country bus journey from New York to the West Coast that year, it required only five and a half days. By 1930 almost one-fifth of all intercity commercial travel in the United States was by bus.

When Washington Motor Coach inaugurated service between Spokane and Seattle via Snoqualmie Pass in April 1930, the trip took eleven and one-half hours. A little over two years later the company introduced Conductorettes on its cross-state buses. These were apparently the first women employed in such capacity on any common-carrier motor bus in the United States. Their responsibilities for passenger comfort were similar to those of the first stewardesses only recently hired by United Air Lines.[11]

## Friendly Skies?

LIKE EARLY AUTOMOBILES AND THE first primitive trucks and buses, the airplane as serious competitor was beyond the comprehension of most railroad executives. If someone were to claim today that snowmobiles posed a competitive threat to long-distance passenger trains, railroaders would greet the idea with no less contempt than they once reserved for predictions that commercial aviation would become a serious competitor, and for some of the same reasons. Most early airplanes could hold no more passengers than the average snowmobile does today and were subject to some of the same limitations imposed by weather conditions.

The Pacific Northwest's first passenger-carrying

airlines date from the mid-1920s. They were exceedingly small operations often consisting of little more than one or two open-cockpit planes that carried a passenger in addition to the mail. In 1928 the West Coast Air Transport Company began offering two round trips daily between Portland and Seattle, with an intermediate stop in Tacoma. Its eight-passenger, trimotor Bach airplanes were called air yachts because they featured enclosed cabins, card tables, a lavatory, and upholstered seats. "Each plane will carry a pilot and a mechanic, who will also be a trained pilot."[12] The one-way fare between Seattle and Portland was twelve dollars, and flying time was seventy-five minutes. Until better aircraft and navigation aids became available, no airline dared to fly passengers across the "wild Cascades." One carrier, Mamer Air Transport, operated three weekly flights in 1930 between St. Paul and Spokane; Seattle-bound passengers were required to transfer to Great Northern Railway cars at Spokane in order to complete their trip.

*The interior of a Spokane Airways plane in 1928 featured wicker seats to lighten the load. Eastern Washington State Historical Society, L87-1.37919-28.*

*"In those 'early days' of commercial aviation, passengers went through the inconvenience and formality of working themselves into 'monkey suits' before they climbed into the open cockpits of the 'speedy' 90-mile-an-hour planes then adopted for transport use. If mail, baggage or express was carried, it was piled in the lap of the passenger, or he was obliged to literally sit upon it when it was crowded in around his seat.*

*"Goggles protected the passenger's eyes, but there was nothing at all to protect his face and ears, and often his hands, from the biting effects of rushing air, damp clouds, wind, rain, snow and hail. When the plane landed at the end of its journey, the passenger's face was beet red from the torture he had suffered. His ears were deafened from the roar of the plane's motor and the swish of passing wind. An attendant helped him to wipe away the smudge of oil that flicked back upon his face."*

—Ray Conway, "Oregon Takes to the Air," *Oregon Motorist* (May 1934)

Another airline pioneer was the Boeing Company of Seattle, which in 1927 secured a federal contract to fly between San Francisco and Chicago carrying mail and two persons per plane. In 1931, Boeing Air Transport along with Varney Air Lines, National Air Transport, and Pacific Air Transport combined under the name United Air Lines. By 1934 the company scheduled fourteen arrivals and departures a day from Portland's Swan Island airport, and boosters could now claim that "Broadway of Portland is now only 21 hours from Broadway of New York, while Southern California may be reached by air without the loss of daytime business hours."

Revolving light beacons spaced ten miles apart lit the way, assisted by radio beams. Even with such improvements, few people in the mid-1930s could have imagined that by the mid-1950s more Americans would travel by air than by rail.[13]

## The New Competitive Era

ONE ADDITIONAL THREAT TO railroad hegemony in the Pacific Northwest was the Panama Canal, built for $463 million and maintained by the federal government. James J. Hill boasted early in the century that his railroads would be able to reduce freight rates so low that lily pads would grow on the unused waterway. Indeed, during the first few years after it opened in 1914, the Panama Canal had little impact on transcontinental rail freight traffic. As late as 1921 only 15 percent of the canal's traffic traveled from one coast to the other, but within the next two years the canal handled 52 percent of all coast-to-coast traffic. Now the transcontinental railroads protested that the canal profited at their expense because the Interstate Commerce Commission kept rail rates to the Pacific Coast artificially high and uncompetitive.[14]

Data for selected transcontinental tonnage compiled by the Interstate Commerce Commission revealed that, during the six months from June through November 1923, 156,000 tons of iron and steel traveled by rail while another 779,000 tons went via the Panama Canal; for paper, the amount was slightly less than 15,000 tons by rail and 25,000 by ship. Every 50,000 tons of freight diverted to the Panama Canal cost western railroads an estimated million dollars in revenues. By the late 1920s fully 20 percent of the lumber manufactured in the United States—and almost half the production of the Pacific Nothwest—traveled to market by ship through the Panama Canal. The new waterway

became one of several serious problems facing western railroads as they entered a new era of heightened competition combined with nationwide depression.[15]

In the Pacific Northwest, trucks, automobiles, all-weather highways, and gasoline-powered tractors and other implements noticeably altered daily life during the decade after 1917 by ending the isolation of the region's farms, ranches, and lumber camps. Many former harvest hands and lumber workers abandoned the life of the hobo, got married, and took their families with them to the job in their own automobiles. The transportation revolution of the 1920s changed the face of the city by encouraging urban dwellers to move to suburban neighborhoods. Motorized transportation encouraged rural school consolidations and extended the influence of regional trading centers at the expense of smaller villages, even as railroads began slowly receding from public consciousness as engines of regional development and social change. In short, the opening decade of the new age of competition transformed the Pacific Northwest as much as the first railway age did during the 1880s and 1890s.

*In sparsely settled territory where all the traffic ever available justified a railroad in running but two trains a day, one could scarcely expect a man to lose a whole day making a 12-mile round trip by train, when he could make it in his car in an hour or two.*—Railway Age *(Oct. 10, 1927)*

# An Industry in Trouble

**B**EFORE AMERICAN RAILROADS could experience the full impact of new competition, the nation's entry into World War I confronted the industry with a series of distracting problems. The year 1917 began with a severe freight car shortage that worsened after the United States declared war in April. Making matters intolerable were antiquated yards and tracks on some eastern railroads that became hopelessly clogged with freight. As a result, numerous mills were forced to close, perishable articles spoiled, and coal failed to reach power plants. Cars loaded with war materials piled up outside East Coast ports with no place to go, while western railroads desperately sought empty cars to ship lumber, apples, potatoes, and other commodities vital to the Allies. Railroads tried to coordinate their efforts, but the car problem only grew worse. As the volume of traffic surged to unprecedented highs, the shortage reached 164,000 cars in May. After that it fell slightly, only to climb again later in the year.

November's shortage of 150,000 freight cars was one reason why President Woodrow Wilson by proclamation took over operation of the railroads on December 28, 1917, for the duration of the war.[1] Creation of the United States Railroad Administration was a controversial step, as was Wilson's choice of William Gibbs McAdoo to head it. Two years after entering Wilson's cabinet as secretary of the treasury, McAdoo had married the president's youngest daughter. He was, however, no stranger to railroading. He had earlier been involved in financing and constructing the Hudson & Manhattan Railroad tunnels beneath the Hudson River to link New York City and New Jersey.[2]

As director general of the United States Railroad Administration, McAdoo curtailed unnecessary civilian travel by discontinuing a number of passenger trains, eliminating amenities on others, and requiring that limited trains handle local traffic. Despite consolidation, curtailment, and abandonment, railroads actually handled 8 percent more passenger traffic in 1918 than they had a year earlier and were able to reduce significantly their freight car shortage. The United States Railroad Administration also introduced many new forms of standardization, including a generic series of locomotives and freight cars and a basic eight-hour day for all railroad workers.

Wilson's take-over marked the culmination of growing federal involvement in the railroad industry that began with creation of the Interstate Commerce Commission three decades earlier. Nothing, however, in various congressional enactments since

**256**

*Members of the Idaho militia enjoy lunch en route by train during World War I. Idaho Historical Society 284-35.*

1887 had required federal or state regulators to set railroad rates high enough to support an adequate level of service. Many in the industry believed that the infamous car shortage of 1917 was really a product of poorly conceived regulatory measures that weakened railroads financially and left them short of funds needed to upgrade track and equipment. Railroad leaders were angry and fearful of either permanent government ownership or inadequate compensation if the lines were returned to private hands.

Government operation included steam railroads as well as their coastwise transportation subsidiaries. Federal authorities thus acquired railroad-owned steamships that served the Pacific Northwest, notably the Great Northern Pacific Steamship Company, which was jointly owned by Hill-allied companies.

Since its beginning in 1915, the operation had been more a matter of ego than profit, and Great Northern Pacific officials gladly terminated the money-losing service in September 1917 when federal officials purchased the steamships *Northern Pacific* and *Great Northern* for service as troop carriers.[3]

Among the directives from federal overseers was one in October 1918 notifying telegraphers on the Northern Pacific Railway that their vacations with pay were to be abolished the following January 1, and in lieu thereof an additional two cents an hour would be included in their pay scale. But before the change took place, the war ended in mid-November. Railroaders hardly had time to celebrate the return of peace because an influenza epidemic wreaked havoc both in the shops and along the right-of-way. The Great Northern was so hard hit that in October

GREAT NORTHERN PACIFIC S.S. CO.

Twin Palaces of the Pacific

car repairers had to be sent out as firemen to keep passengers trains running. The lack of a healthy crew delayed freight trains on several occasions.[4]

When Uncle Sam returned individual railroads to their owners on March 1, 1920, having lost about a billion dollars during the previous two years of operation, all was not well in the industry. The Transportation Act of 1920 formally ended federal control but subjected railroads to stringent new regulations even as largely unregulated competitors took aim at the freight-and-passenger business. At the same time railroads grappled with the rising cost of materials, taxes, and labor. Half a decade of worker unrest culminated when shop craft unions walked out on July 1, 1922, and although labor lost the strike, the conflict was one more in a succession of blows that since 1917 left the railroad industry dazed and confused. In addition to labor unrest,

wartime inflation by 1920 had pushed the cost of living 70 percent higher than in 1913.

The dizzying upward spiral was followed by an equally disorienting decline that began in 1921 and dropped the price of wheat from nearly $2.06 a bushel in 1919 to $.84 in 1921 and brought many rural areas to the brink of ruin. Although prosperity later returned to enrich the lives of urban dwellers, who fondly recalled the 1920s as the Jazz Age or Prosperity Decade, the pall of hard times never really lifted from timber towns and farm settlements across the Pacific Northwest. The 1921 agricultural depression and the increasing flow of commodities through the Panama Canal dealt the region's railroads a severe blow. As a consequence, they seemed to suffer more than railroads in any other part of the country. The principal lines of the Pacific Northwest earned 35 percent less in 1924 than they had in 1916.

*The Spokane, Portland & Seattle Railway in mid-1916 operated the California Steamer Express between Portland and Flavel (107 miles) to connect with the Great Northern Pacific Steamship Company's "Twin Palaces of the Pacific." A passenger who left Portland at 9:30 a.m. any Tuesday, Thursday, or Saturday would arrive in San Francisco at 3:30 the following afternoon. The total distance from Portland to San Francisco's Pier 11 was 665 miles. The round-trip fare including meals and berth was $32. On the Southern Pacific, the quickest train between Portland and San Francisco was the extra-fare Shasta Limited, which took twenty-seven hours to make the same trip. That was only three hours less than by train and coastal steamship. Oregon Historical Society, 76722, no. 1177.*

During the first half of the 1920s, American railroads continued to live with the uncertainty of whether the industry would be nationalized. As late as the election of 1924, Senator William La Follette of Wisconsin campaigned for president on a platform that advocated government ownership of railways. His defeat appeared finally to bury the issue. For the remainder of the decade the most troubling problem for American railroads was their alarming loss of passenger traffic.

## The Passenger Traffic Problem

**P**RESIDENT SAMUEL M. FELTON OF the Chicago Great Western shared a stunning revelation with the Nebraska Bankers Association in 1916 when he noted that the combined capacity of the 2,445,644 automobiles then registered in the United States was more than three times that of the nation's railway passenger cars. He claimed that in Nebraska alone there were 81,000 automobiles for which railways had paid $2.6 million in taxes to build road. Although Felton was an astute observer of the American railroad industry—he had been a friend of Edward H. Harriman and was widely esteemed as a "doctor of sick railroads"—his intimations of trouble ahead were not fully appreciated until the highway-building boom of the 1920s.[5]

After reaching a historic high in 1920, when railroads carried nearly 1.3 billion revenue passengers, their ridership slipped noticeably with each passing year. During the decade, the population of the United States increased by 13.5 percent, but railroad passenger traffic decreased dramatically, especially on lines west of the Mississippi River. In that part of the country, travel by rail declined 40 percent from

*Passengers relax in the observation car of a Spokane, Portland & Seattle train in 1930. Oregon Historical Society, 67996, LOC/ORIG: 0332-P-127.*

1920 to 1929, compared to 32 percent in the South and only 18 percent in the East. By 1929 American railroads hauled fewer passengers than they had in any year since 1909. The decline would have been even more severe had it not been for increased train travel to Florida during the land boom there in mid-decade.[6]

Throughout the 1920s, railroad passenger operations as a whole remained profitable, but only barely so. An excellent measure of the financial health of any railroad was the "operating ratio" that compared expenses to income. Any figure above seventy warned of poor financial health, and any above one hundred signaled a loss. By 1929 the operating ratio for railroad passenger service was some twenty-three points higher than for freight and would soon top the dreaded hundred mark. Without freight income, most steam railroads would have collapsed, as many electric interurban lines did during the 1920s.

Railroad executives were unprepared for what happened to their passenger business in the aftermath of World War I. During the first half of the 1920s, some passenger departments seemed almost too stunned to fight back in any meaningful way. Some of the largest railroads knew little about marketing passenger service apart from encouraging tourism; passenger officers prior to 1920 tended to devote their time to perfecting methods of handling a constantly growing load of traffic. "So certain had the railways become that the passenger business was their rightful heritage, that they accepted it as a matter of course."[7] The prevailing assumption was that as prosperity increased the wages of laborers it also increased their ability to travel by train. Railroad passenger traffic fell sharply with the panic of 1893, but it did not decrease even one year between 1899 and 1920.

During the decade prior to June 30, 1915, ridership in the United States increased 48 percent. Union Pacific passenger revenues increased 290 percent from 1898 to 1910, but then they began to level off. By the eve of American entry into World War I, there were signs that the passenger business as a whole was no longer growing, but troop movements and general business prosperity masked that trend until after 1920. Since that date, "its decline has been one of the remarkable phenomena in the entire field of transportation."[8]

At first the decline seemed only temporary. When statistics indicated an upturn during the last four months of 1925, many in the industry eagerly concluded that "passenger revenues have touched bottom and are now definitely on the increase. The expectation appears to be well founded that passenger revenues hereafter will show increases, although possibly not so large as prior to five years ago."[9]

Indeed, railroad passenger traffic continued to increase through May 1926, but then it fell off sharply again and continued down for the rest of the decade. Industry publications carried numerous articles on the problem, but no one offered a comprehensive solution. *Railway Age* complained bitterly in 1928 that railway passenger service is "probably the most unprofitable large-scale business conducted in the United States."[10]

One realistic response to the slump occurred on April 1, 1925, when the Union Pacific, Northern Pacific, and Great Northern railroads received permission from the Interstate Commerce Commission to pool local and through passenger trains between Seattle and Portland to cut costs. The Northern Pacific owned and maintained the tracks from Vancouver to Tacoma and granted the Great Northern and Union Pacific running rights. This arrangement, however logical, was not repeated elsewhere in the Pacific Northwest or in most other parts of the United States.

A far more common but less realistic response was to assert, despite all evidence to the contrary, that motor bus travel was only a fad. As soon as the novelty of riding on rubber wore off, customers would return to the ever-reliable passenger trains. And even when it became clear that railroads had lost a large portion of their short-haul customers, many railroaders remained supremely confident of retaining long-distance passengers.

The industry took a measure of comfort from the fact that, even while automobiles made inroads into their coach business, ridership in sleeper and parlor cars actually increased. Airplanes were certainly no threat in either area, or so it seemed in the 1920s. Many within the railroad industry continued to repeat this confident refrain with minor variations even as late as the 1940s, although as early as 1929 it had become obvious that the bus was a formidable long-haul competitor and that commercial aviation was persistently pecking away at the luxury business too.

The real culprit in declining passenger-train revenues was the private automobile. During the 1920s the most dramatic loss of revenues occurred on local, not long-haul, passenger trains most vulnerable to automobile competition. It was on numerous branch lines that extended into sparsely settled areas and earned only marginal returns that railroads of the Pacific Northwest first lost the battle with new modes of competition.

## Branch-line Blues; or, Travail by Train

ALTHOUGH THE ENTIRE UNION Pacific system in 1930 served only thirty-six communities of ten thousand people or more, it emphasized passenger service between metropolitan centers, as did every other large railroad in the United States. That was where most passengers and revenues were, yet the practice created a headache for both railroads and local-train riders: "One of the most serious shortcomings is the glaring disproportion between the amount of attention given and money devoted to providing through passenger service and local passenger service."[11]

On a typical branch line (as well as on the region's few short-line railroads), passenger service was limited to no more than a single train a day each way, and none on Sunday. Travel by local train was also very slow. Passengers on Oregon's Sumpter Valley Railway in 1910 needed four hours to complete the sixty-two-mile journey from Baker to Austin. No wonder locals referred to the circuitous railroad as the stump dodger. In many cases, travel by train from one town or village to another, even one nearby, could be a complicated matter; and branch lines were typically cursed with the worst rolling stock in the industry.

There had been a trade-off, however. Passenger trains provided residents of remote parts of the Pacific Northwest a regularity and dependability in transportation that they had never known before. But by the 1920s that alone was not enough. "The rural steam railroad in many instances is an anachronism in communities of homes equipped with steam heating plants, radios, modern plumbing conveniences and telephones, the owners of which have their own automobiles. It is 1875 set down in the midst of 1925."[12] Trains, moreover, carried people along designated routes—about 250,000 miles of rail—at specified times; automobiles could drive off the beaten track or to another town or city at any hour of the day or night.

By the mid-1920s, life in isolated towns and villages no longer centered on the arrival and departure of the train or stagecoach. A majority of commercial travelers, or salesmen, abandoned the passenger train for the automobile, especially in sparsely populated territory served by only one or two trains a day. Some companies purchased automobiles to make their salesmen more efficient. Railroads responded with statistics showing that it cost more to own a car than to travel by train, but

even when rail fares were as low as two cents per mile, most people still preferred the convenience of traveling in their own vehicles. "I can take my motor car and my family of four and drive [to the old family farm] now in six hours (225 miles) in greater comfort and at less cost than I can go alone by railroad, and I am free from the annoyance of petty bureaucrats. Most of the people of the United States are similarly freed. They will not go back to the old railroad transportation methods."[13]

Small-town railroad stations in the 1920s began to show the impact of the automobile. As passenger trains became less frequent or ceased running altogether, the stove in the waiting room went cold, paint faded on the outside, and the usual crowd of people ceased to gather there. It was not uncommon for passenger stations less than two decades old to be boarded up or converted to other uses. Many were simply torn down. The railroad station was once a community portal to the outside world; the highway and the gas station increasingly assumed that function in the 1920s.

Railroads might have been eager to rid themselves of the burden of local passenger trains but for the widespread belief that when they abandoned such service "they lost a most valuable part of contact with the people in the smaller towns, who, after all, are the foundation of our economic structure." In fact, no scientific proof existed to confirm any meaningful connection between railway freight and passenger business, although the industry believed that passenger trains generated goodwill that translated into freight profits.[14]

Even before the threat of automobile competition, railroad executives had wrestled with the problem of how best to maintain some type of low-cost branch-line passenger service. During the interurban craze early in the century, Northern Pacific executives toyed briefly with the idea of electrifying their line between Walla Walla and Pasco. But installation of electric wire and equipment was too expensive.

The Northern Pacific and many other railroads found a more cost-effective solution in railway cars that operated under their own power—"interurbans without wires."

The Union Pacific took the lead in developing such a vehicle, one it could substitute for lightly patronized and money-losing conventional steam-powered passenger trains. In 1904 Edward H. Harriman commissioned William R. McKeen, Jr., his superintendent of motive power and machinery in Omaha, to do something about the high-cost, low-patronage business of carrying branch-line passengers. McKeen's self-propelled railcar, which made its debut in 1905, was the first in a series of gasoline vehicles that transmitted power mechanically to the driving wheels. The demonstration so impressed Harriman that in 1908 he set McKeen up in business, with Harriman railroads serving as his primary customers.

In all, McKeen's company built 152 cars between 1905 and 1920, when it was dissolved. At various times, self-propelled cars accommodated passengers on the Oregon-Washington Railroad & Navigation Company, North Coast Railroad, Oregon Short Line, and numerous other carriers large and small. Well into the 1930s, McKeen cars clanked along country tracks to serve towns and villages as varied as Burns and Joseph, Oregon, Walla Walla and Yakima, Washington, and Moscow and Malad, Idaho.

Although the design of individual models varied as the years went by, the typical McKeen car had space for seventy passengers, baggage, and express. When the cars were introduced in 1909 on a run from Dayton to Walla Walla and Wallula, local residents called them Torpedo cars. With their porthole windows and streamlined profile, McKeen cars did have a vaguely nautical appearance.

McKeen was not the only builder of railcars. Among his many competitors were General Electric and Brill, and a common name applied to all their

products was doodlebug. The Chicago, Milwaukee & Puget Sound put two 77-passenger General Electric gas-electric cars into service in 1913—one between Everett and Monroe and another between Seattle and Enumclaw via Cedar Falls. The Milwaukee Road, which had an unusually high proportion of branch-line to main-line service, early substituted self-propelled cars for many steam-powered locals or formed mixed trains to integrate passenger and freight service, but this expedient only drove away most remaining passengers. By 1923 the Great Northern had gas-electric-powered passenger trains on thirty-two runs. The Northern Pacific was also a big user of such equipment by the late 1920s.[15]

The absence of cinders and the ability to make road-crossing stops was a big advantage for self-propelled vehicles in local service. They could also be used to compete with parallel electric interurban lines. In theory only two or three employees were required to operate a railcar instead of the usual four or five on steam-powered passenger trains, but laws in many states and union work rules prohibited any reduction in crew size. Nonethless, self-propelled cars reduced the cost of local passenger service even though their purchase price offset any savings in operation and they seldom regained lost business.

Another way for railroads to address the problem of declining local and branch-line patronage was to replace local trains with buses on parallel highways. In 1924 the Spokane, Portland & Seattle Railway became the nation's first steam railroad to enter the bus business: it made tickets interchangeable on its buses and trains between Portland, Astoria, and Seaside. As Union Pacific officials grew increasingly alarmed at the rapidly declining number of passengers on some of its branch lines, they too turned to buses. In August 1925, the Oregon-Washington Railroad & Navigation subsidiary substituted

DEPOT AT ROCKAWAY BEACH ORE.

a twenty-one-passenger White bus for local trains between Walla Walla and Pendleton as part of an experiment to determine its practicality for use on other parts of the Union Pacific system. At this time the railroad's involvement in highway transportation was limited to operating tour buses in the Zion National Park area.

The Walla Walla to Pendleton train incurred a net loss of $3,707 for the last four months of 1924; during the corresponding months in 1925, the bus showed a net profit of $4,174. So successful was the trial in the Walla Walla Valley that by mid-1927 the newly established Union Pacific Stages company was running buses from Walla Walla to Yakima and to Pendleton and Portland.[16]

Ten railroads in the United States operated 300 buses in 1925. Just four years later, seventy-eight railroads used 2,389 motor coaches. By the late 1920s it was obvious that bus subsidiaries could save railroads millions of dollars by taking the place of local trains that cost four to five times as much to operate. Huge bus systems providing service under railroad auspices developed in all parts of the nation, the Union Pacific becoming a leader in this movement. By 1931 the railroad had amassed a far-flung network of more than ten thousand miles of bus routes that enabled it to trim numerous money-losing passenger trains. Under a variety of corporate titles, Union Pacific buses made travel possible from Portland to Chicago in five days and four nights. The Southern Pacific operated buses from Portland to San Francisco by 1928. None of the other major steam railroads of the Pacific Northwest immediately followed suit, although the Great Northern developed an extensive network of bus lines in Minnesota.[17]

The pioneer phase of the intercity bus industry ended by 1930, when Greyhound Lines (Motor Transit) emerged as the dominant carrier. This holding company, formed in the mid-1920s and initially dominated by railroads, absorbed many bus subsidiaries, including Pickwick and the Union Pacific's Interstate Transit. During the 1930s the early-day connections between railroads and the intercity bus industry grew more tenuous, yet some unusual forms of rail and highway coordination continued in the Pacific Northwest for many more years.[18]

The Northern Pacific Transport Company began coordinated bus-truck-train operations alongside Northern Pacific tracks in Montana in early 1932. Highway transportation replaced mixed trains and less-than-carload freight service on many Northern Pacific lines. Train-bus coordination in the 1930s also took the form of several "detours," or alternate routes, offered to railroad passengers. The Southern Pacific operated a Redwood Empire tour through northern California and southern Oregon, and the Union Pacific a Utah Parks and Boulder Dam alternative. When the spectacular Going-to-the-Sun Highway opened in 1933, it allowed the Great Northern to advertise a scenic detour by bus or private automobile through Glacier National Park.

## A New Look in Long-Haul Passenger Service

**D**URING THE LAST HALF OF THE 1920s, railroads sought to maintain the popularity of long-haul passenger service by refurbishing their luxury limiteds. The unlikely pacesetter in the Pacific Northwest was the Great Northern Railway. For years it had seemed to outside observers that James J. Hill and his successors were mainly interested in hauling freight while allowing most passenger traffic to gravitate to the Northern Pacific. The latter offered more scenery; the Great Northern had lower grades. From 1905 to 1924, the Great Northern's premier passenger train had been the Oriental Limited, a solid if uninspired performer.[19]

Then, on June 1, 1924, the Great Northern inaugurated a new Oriental Limited that featured passenger cars noted for quietness and easy-riding qualities and a special smoking lounge for women in the observation car. All sleepers for the 1924 Oriental Limited were from Pullman, ending the Great Northern tradition of owning and operating its own sleeping cars. The train featured a gray-green interior color scheme. "Telegraphic news bulletins and stock market reports are flashed during the day to the New Oriental Limited and posted in a conspicuous place in the car, keeping passengers in touch with the outside world."[20]

Following discovery of oil along its main line in Shelby, Montana, the Great Northern purchased twenty-eight new oil-fired "Mountain"-type steam locomotives to give the Oriental Limited and other premier trains plenty of power for steady running along the sixteen hundred miles between Williston, North Dakota, and Seattle, thereby eliminating the need for helper engines on mountain grades. The Great Northern bragged that this represented the "longest cinderless mileage on any railroad in the Northwest." In mid-1926 the Great Northern inaugurated sixty-three-hour service from Chicago to Seattle, the same travel time that California-bound passengers had enjoyed for several years.[21]

The best the Northern Pacific could do until 1926 was to add steel-sheathed wooden cars to the consist of its North Coast Limited. The Southern Pacific added spaces for passengers to park their cars at its stations, and its Cascade Limited introduced intra-train phones in 1927 to enable passengers to call the dining car steward for meal reservations. The Milwaukee Road installed floodlights on the Olympian to allow passengers in observation cars to view passing scenery at night. The Olympian in 1927 also became one of the first trains to feature roller bearings: "No jolts, no jerks, no jars, while starts and stops are scarcely perceptible."[22] But compared to the Great Northern's stunning new Oriental

**Oriental Limited**

A "Woman's Train"

A manicurist—a maid, valet, hairdresser, or barber ready to serve you. Surely you never lack for accustomed personal service when you travel on the Oriental Limited.

A. J. DICKINSON
*Passenger Traffic Manager*
St. Paul, Minn.

*A Dependable Railway*

**Sixty Miles of Glacier National Park from Car Window**

Limited, such changes were merely cosmetic.

On June 10, 1929, the Great Northern increased the competitive stakes once again when its Empire Builder went into service to honor James J. Hill and call attention to the railroad's newly opened Cascade Tunnel. The Empire Builder consisted of eight new sets of cars costing a total of more than four million dollars. Among its amenities were a barbershop and men's bath, and showers and tubs for women. A sun-parlor observation car replaced the open platform, much to the disappointment of some travelers. Completion of the Cascade Tunnel enabled the Great Northern to reduce the Empire Builder's

bearings and added radios to observation cars. Its Pullman sleeping cars had ten sections, one drawing room, and one compartment; its passengers "will sleep on box-spring beds thirteen inches deep, in the lower berths." The railroad emphasized that "insomnia will find no friend in North Coast Limited equipment." The North Coast Limited also had maid and valet service, a barbershop, a soda fountain, and cardroom. "Milady may have a manicure in the boudoir, or enjoy a refeshing shower bath."[23]

It was during the latter half of the 1920s that American railroads finally took a long-overdue look at the venerable day coach. For years, coach passengers had complained of dirty, overcrowded cars in which they were herded like sheep, while Pullman passengers were treated with the utmost courtesy. The Baltimore & Ohio Railroad pioneered individual-seat coaches in 1926. By the end of the decade, some railroads had replaced their hard, bench-type seats with reclining ones that featured rubber cushions and springs for added comfort on overnight runs. Some coaches even had smoking rooms, full-size lavatories, and porters.

The Southern Pacific established a deluxe coach train on a weekly basis from Portland to San Francisco in 1927. By midyear the service became triweekly, with reduced rates. In late 1928 the Union Pacific introduced a new type of coach that had double bucket-type seats, diffused lighting, and soft blue upholstery. *Green plush* became a byword for old-fashioned, scratchy, and generally uncomfortable seats.[24]

In 1928 American railroads for the first time employed outside experts in interior decoration to design furnishings and fittings for their passenger cars. The result was the introduction of bright, comfortable, and even luxurious equipment for both coach and Pullman passengers. This was quite a cheerful departure from the dark mahogany interiors so typical during the late nineteenth century, and the railroads used new interior designs to emphasize

running time between Chicago and the West Coast to little more than sixty-one hours, ten hours faster than the company's best travel time on the run immediately after World War I. The Oriental Limited remained on a slower schedule and took the place of the old Glacier Park Limited. The Empire Builder together with the Oriental Limited gave the Great Northern two premier trains between St. Paul and Seattle for the first time.

The Milwaukee Road responded immediately with a new Olympian, and the Northern Pacific followed in May 1930 with a new edition of the North Coast Limited, again with the latest styling and equipment. The Northern Pacific equipped the only all-Pullman train between Chicago and the North Pacific coast with smooth-running roller

*At the Southern Pacific's Brooklyn Yard in Portland in 1930, major repairs to the railroad's numerous steam locomotives were undertaken. Oregon Historical Society 64177, file 891-B-1.*

individuality in their passenger service after the enforced conformity of government operations during World War I. The ornateness of Victorian-era car interiors was, in any case, now widely regarded as the epitome of bad taste.

Ironically, credit for improvements in design and service, admitted *Railway Age*, must go to motor buses: "There is nothing particularly inviting about even the cleanest, newest day coach of what is now standard design. There is something definitely inviting, however, about a parlor motor coach with its individual cushioned chairs and luxurious appointments."[25] The seats of Spokane, Portland & Seattle's buses, for example, were upholstered in genuine brown-grained leather. Private automobiles

also played a part in the transformation of railway coaches, because their owners came to equate seats with cushions and comfort.

Regardless of the source of inspiration, railroads initially regarded the results of their heightened attention to long-distance passenger service with satisfaction. "The increased patronage of long distance trains, particularly the Oriental Limited, has more than offset the loss in local passenger traffic," the Great Northern emphasized in its 1925 report to stockholders. Yet notwithstanding heavy travel on long-distance passenger trains, the railroad still experienced a decrease of 6.5 percent in total revenue in 1926 over the previous year, and that was at a time when many national conventions were held in the Far West. The average number of miles that the Great Northern carried revenue passengers increased each year, from 92 in 1923 to 133 in 1926, reflecting the growing use of automobiles for short hauls. Premier trains like the Oriental Limited and Empire Builder continued to be popular, but real losses came in local service. In 1930, the start of the depression decade, Great Northern passenger revenues slipped 20 percent lower than in 1929.[26]

## Sins of the Fathers

EARLY IN THE 1920S, RAILROADS complained about excessive government regulation in the face of competition from largely unregulated motor carriers using publicly funded highways. Railroads, for instance, could not discontinue money-losing passenger trains without permission from government regulators, but trucks and buses could drop or initiate service in many states virtually overnight. They were unregulated by the federal government until 1935. The injustice seemed clear enough, but it was difficult for most Americans to feel sorry for the once almighty railroad industry. A writer in the *Atlantic Monthly* probably spoke for many people when he observed in 1925 that the nation's railroads were showing "many signs of decaying old age. There has been no substantial improvement in railroad equipment or management in twenty years or more."[27]

"The railroads of many years ago did things which don't look well in print. They were manipulated for the private gain of the officers and to help their especial friends over the line," asserted a member of the Indiana Railroad Commission, reiterating another widely held conviction. Other Americans were tired of hearing the "continued calamity howl of the railroads." Hostility was not as strong as it had been in the late nineteenth century, but "railroads are not yet popular."[28]

At a time of increasing competition, railroads found themselves trapped in a web of petty and contradictory regulations kept in place by hostile public opinion. One state would solemnly mandate a cuspidor between every two seats of a passenger car, while another outlawed cuspidors as vulgar and unsanitary; one would require screens on the windows of passenger coaches, while others forbade them. States occasionally set the size of train crews and even established maximum passenger fares.[29]

In short, what regulatory measures like the Transportation Act of 1920 did best was to visit the sins of the fathers on the children but without considering how radically circumstances had changed. Ironically, railroad regulation became most stringent at a time when governments at all levels gave unprecedented aid to the railroads' competitors by subsidizing construction of public highways, municipal airports, and, most notably, the Panama Canal.

By the end of World War I, the age of railroad monopoly was over, and automobiles, trucks, and buses had come to stay. The new forms of transportation had no overcapitalization to contend with, generally employed low-cost nonunion labor, and had few if any overpaid executives. Railroads, by contrast, had trouble raising money they desperately needed to modernize their plants and equipment. Ironically, the one bright spot in an otherwise gloomy picure was that automobile manufacturing and highway construction in the mid-1920s swelled railroad freight revenues. Ralph Budd, president of the Great Northern Railway, went so far as to claim at a meeting of the American Society of Civil Engineers in 1926 that the automobile industry's importance was "so great, taken as a whole, that the railways gain much more from the freight traffic it gives them, than they lost from the freight and passenger business it takes away."[30]

Budd could take further satisfaction from the fact that in 1923 the fruit crop that the railroad carried

*Fruit from orchards that surrounded Milton, Oregon, traveled to markets in refrigerator cars in the early twentieth century. Blocks of ice kept car interiors cool; mechanical refrigeration became common after World War II. University of Oregon, Angelus 1578.*

from the Wenatchee district was the largest on record, amounting to some twenty thousand carloads. The Great Northern also reported increases in the amount of wheat and potatoes shipped to market. But it was too true that competitors could take away almost any commodity that railroads considered their exclusive traffic. By 1932 the commodities being hauled in considerable amounts by trucks included fruits, vegetables, grain, coal, automobiles, tires, cement, sand, gravel, canned goods, livestock, and lumber.[31]

The Great Northern was a rich railroad that faced

increased freight and passenger competition during the 1920s without suffering any undue financial strain. That was not true for the Milwaukee Road, battered by declining passenger revenues and a series of self-inflicted financial wounds dating from its decision to build west to the Pacific and then to electrify mountainous portions of its track. Anticipated savings from electrification never offset the enormous expense of installation; neither was there hope of recovering millions of dollars' worth of freight lost annually through the Panama Canal, competition that Milwaukee road executives had not foreseen when they authorized the Pacific Coast extension.

As a result of the accumulated weight of these troubles, the company failed to pay a dividend on its common stock in 1918 for the first time since 1892. In 1921 and 1922, it leased two lines that enabled it to reach from Chicago into the coalfields of southern Indiana, but these proved so ramshackle and debt-encumbered that they only added to the company's intolerable financial burden. In the West, the traffic boom anticipated in the early twentieth century never materialized. In 1923 and 1924, the traffic handled on the Rocky Mountain and Missoula divisions was about the same as that in 1915; the Coast Division had less traffic than in 1915.

The combination of bad judgment and unforeseen competition caused common stock that sold for as much as two hundred dollars a share in 1905 to drop to less than four dollars a share when the railroad slipped into bankruptcy on March 18, 1925. Critics, including the Interstate Commerce Commission, contended that construction of the Pacific Coast extension was the chief cause of bankruptcy and blamed Albert Earling for this debacle.

Earling was in reality a very cautious executive and would not have built a line to the Pacific had it not made sense in the context of the time. In 1905 it would have been impossible for anyone to foresee the grievous blow the Panama Canal would deal transcontinental railroad traffic or to anticipate that in 1912 the Pacific Northwest would enter a five-year economic slump. Equally unseen during the first decade of the twentieth century was the competitive impact of automobiles, trucks, and buses in the 1920s. Still, no one could explain away the fact that some directors of the company knew little about its financial affairs, or that some, like John D. Ryan of Montana Power and Anaconda Copper, were guilty of conflict of interest by selling the railroad copper wire and electricity for its Pacific Coast extension.[32]

The 1920s were not kind to Pacific Northwest railroads, although except for the general malaise that beset the Milwaukee Road, their financial woes remained largely confined to declining passenger revenues. None of the carriers had yet grappled seriously with growing highway competition for the freight traffic that formed the bulk of their revenues. Only during the frightening days of the Great Depression did the venerable industry realize how much changing times demanded a truly radical response. Then, as in the 1920s, the passenger-train dilemma occupied center stage as American railroads formulated a response to new and unsettling forms of competition.

*The man in the street does not know anything about high-pressure boilers, feedwater heaters, roller bearings, etc., and above all, he does not care. He only sees the locomotive as a steam locomotive and, if locomotive Model 1936 looks to him like locomotive Model 1916 he refuses to be impressed.*
—Otto Kuhler, *"Appeal Design in Railroad Equipment,"* Railway Age
*(Nov. 30, 1935)*

# Response: The Streamliner Era

THE UNION PACIFIC'S CITY OF Portland was among the first of a new breed of passenger trains: the streamliners. Introduced in the mid-1930s, streamliners captured the attention of a nation infatuated with speed and glamour. Three or four years earlier these trains would have been unimaginable even in a railroader's wildest dreams, but the Great Depression forced the industry to adopt a host of innovations designed to lure passengers back to the trains.

Railroad executives in the early 1930s desperately sought a miracle train, one that was not only fast, economical, and mechanically reliable, but also attractive enough to recapture passengers lost to competing modes of transportation. During the decade and a half following World War I, ridership on western railroads declined by more than 70 percent. Improvements in automobiles and highways and the innovative equipment adopted by pioneer bus lines heightened popular dissatisfaction with train travel. The Portland *Oregonian* complained that "pounding over rail joints, eating smoke and dust, and digging cinders out of eyes became common in fact, story, and song." The public believed that railroads treated people callously and that passenger equipment was not up to date. One popular but overcynical view held that the Pullman Company was so tradition-bound that the only real improvement in its sleeping cars during the years 1915 to 1935 was the addition of a slot for used razor blades in the men's washroom.[1]

The Union Pacific's new train was an obvious attempt to improve the industry's tarnished image. Following tests in a wind tunnel at the University of Michigan, a scientifically designed prototype took shape in the shops of the Pullman Car and Manufacturing Company. The resulting M-10000 was a three-car articulated train of startling design: the lightweight aluminum-alloy cars narrowed slightly from bottom to top, the tail end was rounded, the front featured a raised cab atop a massive grill. The train must have reminded some observers of a yellow-streaked sea monster slithering along the track.

With considerable fanfare the Union Pacific introduced the M-10000 in February 1934. After a twelve-week promotional tour of the United States, it settled into regular service as the City of Salina, linking that community with Topeka and Kansas City. Operation of the M-10000 suggested several improvements that builders subsequently incorporated into the M-10001, the City of Portland.

For two days before the City of Portland entered regular service on June 6, 1935, the Union Pacific

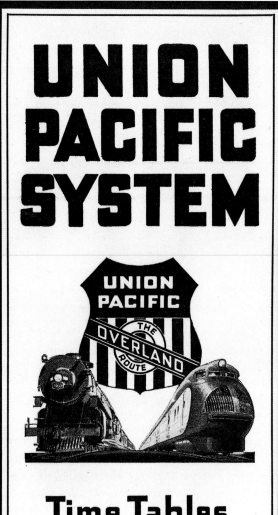

# UNION PACIFIC SYSTEM

**UNION PACIFIC**

THE OVERLAND ROUTE

# Time Tables

Union Pacific Railroad Co.

Oregon Short Line R. R. Co.

Oregon-Washington R. R. & Nav. Co.

Los Angeles & Salt Lake R. R. Co.

St. Joseph and Grand Island Ry. Co.

proudly displayed its streamliner at the Portland Union Station. Approximately fifteen thousand people came to view the future of rail travel. They noticed that the seven-car articulated train retained the distinctive appearance of its predecessor but had a more powerful diesel engine and three sleeping cars, the first used on any American streamliner. Christened the Abraham Lincoln, the Oregon Trail, and the Overland Trail, the sleepers featured four extra-long beds for tall people (like the Union Pacific's youthful chairman, W. Averell Harriman), fold-down washbasins in lower berths, and three individual dressing rooms for men and two for women. Ahead of the sleepers was a dining-lounge car, and behind them was a fifty-four-passenger reserved-seat coach with a buffet fitted into the train's contoured tail. The coach was quite an improvement over chair cars used on conventional trains. It featured reclining seats, footrests, indirect lighting, and fold-down trays that enabled passengers to eat at their seats.

The inaugural ceremony on June 6 was a gala occasion. The Rose Festival queen, Irene Hegeberg, christened the train after appropriate remarks by Mayor Joseph K. Carson and Governor Charles H. Martin. W. Averell Harriman, tanned and smiling, was widely acclaimed as the father of the new streamliner. Portland swelled with civic pride as it contemplated its advantage over West Coast competitors, especially its arch-rival, Seattle, which would not be served by streamlined trains for at least another decade.

Departing Portland at precisely the scheduled time of 3:15 p.m., the streamliner cruised through the Columbia Gorge and across the dry country of eastern Oregon. Afternoon temperatures hovered around the century mark, but the train's 118 passengers enjoyed a comfortable seventy-two degrees. Motorists along the way stopped to gawk at the "yellow cannonball" or "yellow bullet," as journalists variously described the new train. Whole communi-

*The Union Pacific Railroad advertised its new streamliner on the cover of a public timetable issued in July 1935. Courtesy William S. Greever.*

*This is obviously a publicity photograph of one of the Union Pacific's new streamliners, but specific information is lacking. The location is probably Pendleton, Oregon, and those are Umatilla Indians handing up the salmon. The Union Pacific painted the sides and nose of the streamliner canary yellow and the top and bottom a golden brown—colors chosen to provide maximum visibility day or night. The streamliner was in some ways a high-powered, lightweight descendant of the old McKeen car that the railroad first produced in 1905. Union Pacific Museum.*

ties turned out to watch it pass. A crowd of Pocatello citizens accompanied by a brass band greeted the City of Portland at 6:40 a.m. Passengers who had once dreaded crossing the deserts of Idaho and Wyoming in non-air-conditioned, uncomfortable coaches now found it a pleasure. Mile after mile the train sailed effortlessly toward Chicago, sometimes attaining speeds of better than 105 miles per hour.

Just east of Omaha, the City of Portland switched to the tracks of the Chicago & North Western Railway—part-owner of the streamliner—for the final leg of its journey. At the advertised hour of 9:30 a.m., the train eased to a stop in Chicago's North Western station. Mayor Edward J. Kelly and the Chicago & North Western's president, Fred W. Sargent, were there to meet it. Traveling 2,272 miles between Portland and Chicago in thirty-nine and three-quarters hours (eighteen hours less than

formerly required), the City of Portland claimed briefly the title of the world's fastest, regularly scheduled long-distance passenger train. Everyone was apparently pleased except the dining car cook, who complained that the high speed created a suction that kept snuffing out his oil-fired stove.

The City of Portland settled quickly into a routine of eight "sailings" a month each way. Four years later a streamliner of more conservative design, a ten-car train that the Union Pacific had used for a time on Chicago to California runs, replaced the original articulated City of Portland, which was retired. The City of Portland had no streamlined competitors between Chicago and Pacific Northwest cities for another decade. The financially strapped Milwaukee Road inaugurated a high-speed stream-lined train, the Hiawatha, between Chicago and Minneapolis in 1937, but no railroad—not the Milwaukee, the Great Northern, the Northern Pacific, or the Southern Pacific—introduced another on any Pacific Northwest run until 1947.[2]

During the 1930s the Union Pacific remained unchallenged as the most innovative railroad to serve the far Northwest. In addition to operating its City of Portland and other streamlined trains from Chicago to Denver, San Francisco, and Los Angeles, the railroad lowered passenger rates, rebuilt and redecorated coaches, and added air conditioning to numerous cars. In a speech to the New York Lions Club in late 1936, W. Averell Harriman explained why the Union Pacific was committed to passenger service during the depression years that most railroad leaders found so discouraging. He believed that railroads need not fear competition from motor trucks; only a small percentage of freight traffic would go to them. But railroads had suffered huge passenger losses as a result of highway competition. Although passenger service was a by-product of the railroad's main business—carrying freight— Harriman emphasized that in passenger service public opinion of the railroad was at stake.[3]

## End of the Line

FOR THE REGION'S ELECTRIC interurban lines, far more than public opinion was at stake when they lost passenger business. Because so few of them hauled significant amounts of freight, they felt the full impact of the motor age at least a decade earlier than most steam railroads did. The hard-pressed electric interurbans lacked money to modernize their equipment. By the mid-1920s it was obvious that the public would no longer board interurban cars for a short ride, nor would it travel on them for longer than a few hours. "The average man who rides around in his 1929 model motor car is reluctant to transfer his 'pampered anatomy' from the comfortable seat of his attractive looking automobile to an uncomfortable seat in a 1910 model trolley car."[4] Advantage slipped to the family automobile or to the bus that stopped near the front gate.

Some trolley and interurban lines survived into the 1940s. The Utah-Idaho Central Railroad served one of the least populated areas of the United States until its abandonment in 1947. In the final years more than 80 percent of its passenger revenues came from children, most of them transported under contract with local school boards. The majority of the region's electric lines succumbed to competition from private automobiles during the 1920s and 1930s.

Some went the way of the Washington Water Power interurban line from Spokane to Medical Lake and Cheney. Its demise in 1922 marked the first major interurban abandonment in the Pacific Northwest. Even more spectacular was the collapse of the Puget Sound Electric Railway, which ceased running in 1928 following several years of operating losses. This subsidiary of Puget Sound Power and Light Company had faced competition from the beginning from steamboats on Puget Sound and parallel steam railroad lines from the day it opened in 1902, but it

was completion of a paved highway from Seattle to Tacoma in the early 1920s that contributed most to the interurban's demise. Likewise, completion of a hard-surface highway between Portland and Salem caused ridership on the Oregon Electric Railway to plummet. The drop grew more noticeable when pavement was extended farther south to Eugene.

Fear of unsafe bridges on its line along Puget Sound caused Pacific Northwest Traction to end passenger service between Mount Vernon and Bellingham in late 1928. Two years later its highway subsidiary merged into the North Coast Lines to bring all Stone & Webster bus and trolley companies in Washington under one banner. The last trip on the company's Everett-Seattle interurban occurred in February 1939. Service on the Puget Sound interurbans was entirely abandoned and their tracks were removed. Several other interurban lines of the Northwest terminated passenger service but continued to haul freight. Among these were the Oregon Electric, which ran its last regular passenger train along the Willamette Valley in 1933, and the Walla Walla Valley Railway, which eliminated passenger service in 1926.

After the Spokane & Inland Empire Railroad sank into bankruptcy in 1919, it was divided into the Spokane & Eastern Railway and Power Company and the Inland Empire Railroad. In 1927 the Great Northern reacquired the two halves for $1.25 million and reunited them to serve as a feeder line, the Spokane, Coeur d'Alene & Palouse Railway, to gain access to lumber mills of northern Idaho and grain elevators of the Palouse country.

The interurban ended passenger service on its Palouse lines in 1939 and to Coeur d'Alene the following year. Its health remained so precarious that F. R. Newman advised F. J. Gavin of the parent Great Northern in 1940 that since interurban revenues depended upon dwindling lumber traffic at Coeur d'Alene, Gibbs, and Potlatch the railroad should be "kept in fair shape, but with no undue

*An interurban train pauses at the Oregon Electric Depot in Albany, Oregon; a city streetcar waits at the left. In 1917, when interurban railways of the United States still reported a net income of $17 million, companies in the Pacific Coast states recorded a deficit. It was the only region to do so, and that was obviously an ominous sign. The years 1920–24 showed a sharp drop in interurban revenues and profits. Oregon Historical Society 13601, file 891-C-7.*

expenditures" made for maintenance or improvements. "In my judgment, the prospects for this line are not exceptionally bright." The net book value of the road was $1.4 million; the Great Northern's investment in it was $3.1 million.[5]

By the 1960s all that remained of the region's interurban lines were portions of the Great Northern's old Spokane, Coeur d'Alene & Palouse Railway (159 miles); the Northern Pacific's Walla Walla Valley Railway (14 miles); the Union Pacific's Yakima Valley Transportation Company (21 miles); and the Spokane, Portland & Seattle's Oregon Electric Railway (154 miles) and its United Railways subsidiary (20 miles). Of all these interurban fragments, only the Yakima Valley Transportation Company was still powered by electricity.

Thirty years later, only the Oregon Electric Railway survived as a feeder for the Burlington

Northern. The Walla Walla Valley Railway and the Yakima Valley Transportation Company were abandoned completely in the mid-1980s; most remaining sections of the old Spokane, Coeur d'Alene & Palouse were abandoned piecemeal in the 1970s and 1980s.

The common fate of the region's electric interurban lines was the subject of a letter from former Spokane & Inland Empire president J. P. Graves to the Olmsted Brothers in the mid-1930s. In response to a question about the value of interurban stock they received as partial payment for landscaping the grounds of the Bozanta Tavern at Hayden Lake earlier in the century, Graves apologized, "I am sorry to say that we were large losers in this company as well as others, but that seems to have been the history of electric rail corporations." The historian Albro Martin aptly described the interurban interlude as "one of the last edifying chapters in the history of American transportation and finance."[6]

## Depression Daze

**T**HE GREAT DEPRESSION THAT DID so much to destroy the region's remaining interurban passenger service also dealt a severe blow to the region as a whole, especially to the agriculture, mining, and timber industries that formed its economic foundation. Hard times together with inroads by new modes of competition left steam railroads with less freight to haul and fewer passengers to carry. Truck registration rose spectacularly during the 1920s, and the trucking industry continued to expand even during the worst depression years. Many an unemployed driver managed to buy a truck on credit and establish a fly-by-night hauling business. Like bus operators, truckers were aided by concrete and asphalt right-of-ways that extended into all parts of the United

States. Trucks hauled every imaginable commodity, from Washington apples to Idaho potatoes, although it was the railroads' less-than-carload shipments that proved especially vulnerable to competition.

In the skies overhead, competition grew more intense. By the early 1930s three coast-to-coast airlines—American, Transcontinental and Western (TWA), and United—had been organized with backing from Wall Street holding companies. In a single landmark year, 1936, more than a million airline tickets were sold, and Douglas Aircraft Company introduced the DC-3, the popular all-metal plane that was the first to make a profit carrying passengers without benefit of mail subsidies.

During the depression decade even the strongest railroads suffered. Great Northern officials reluctantly shaved the annual dividend on common stock from five dollars to four dollars a share in 1931. For a weak carrier like the Milwaukee Road, however, economic depression meant not only trimming costs but descending again into bankruptcy. The company had emerged from bankruptcy on January 14, 1928, as the Chicago, Milwaukee, St. Paul & Pacific Railroad, but after two relatively prosperous years, hard times returned. In 1932 alone, its passenger-train revenues declined by 28 percent. A parallel drop in freight revenues forced the Milwaukee Road into its second bankruptcy on June 29, 1935.

During the years of the Great Depression, the Milwaukee Road also suffered the worst accident in its history: in the early-morning hours of June 19, 1938, near Saugus, Montana, the Olympian running late at high speed plunged through the Custer Creek bridge weakened only minutes earlier by a freak cloudburst. The wreck happened so fast that the engineer was still in his seat, hand on the throttle, when rescuers found him pinned there in death. Momentum carried the first five cars of the Olympian across to the west bank, but two railroad-owned tourist sleepers careened into the twenty-four-foot floodwaters of the normally dry creek. Forty-one passengers and six employees perished, and seventy-five people were injured. Critics claimed that the financially ailing railroad had skimped on track maintenance, but extensive investigation never sustained that allegation.

American railroads had hoped that their faltering passenger business would stabilize by 1929, but hard times only made a bad trend worse. From May 1926 to June 1933, a span of seven years, there were only two months (nonconsecutive) in which passenger-miles were greater than those recorded a year earlier. Many in the industry still talked wistfully about a rebirth of passenger service, as they had since 1920, but mostly they seemed to wring their hands in despair. "The condition of the passenger business of the railroads is nothing short of appalling. Since 1920 there has been a reduction of more than 70 percent in their passenger revenues, and the decline is continuing."[7] Passenger traffic reached a low point in March 1933 during the national banking moratorium.

The Great Depression forced railroads to tackle the problem of declining ridership anew. One way was to cut costs: from 1930 to 1935, railroads across America reduced expenditures for upkeep of passenger stations and office buildings by a hundred million dollars. During the hard times many railroads lost interest in direct operation of motor coaches. Several of them—notably the Burlington, Santa Fe, Missouri Pacific, and Rio Grande—placed their bus subsidiaries under the umbrella of the National Trailways, a voluntary association of independent bus lines created in March 1936. The nation's intercity bus industry had grown so fast that by 1937 it could brag that, with little more than 5 percent of the combined plant and equipment investment of the steam railroads, electric railroads, and airlines, it carried 29 percent of the total passengers hauled by its competitors.

Despite their financial difficulties, railroads also sought to improve their equipment in hopes of

luring back passengers. When the Union Pacific decided to air-condition its premier passenger trains, the Great Northern was unhappy about having to spend the money but, for competitive reasons, was forced to do likewise. In 1935 it advertised the Empire Builder as the "first completely air conditioned transcontinental train throughout the Northwest." Real innovations, however, came with the introduction of the entirely new streamlined passenger trains.

*During the early depression years, the Milwaukee Road briefly rerouted its Columbian across Iowa in an unsuccessful attempt to generate more passenger business. Courtesy William S. Greever.*

*Design of the Union Pacific's new City of Portland still revealed the lingering influence of the original M-10000 streamliner. Union Pacific Museum.*

## Streamliner Era

THE DECADE OF THE 1930S SAW streamlined locomotives, buses, automobiles, ferry boats, and even vacuum cleaners. Among the most notable proponents of streamlining was Otto Kuhler, who emigrated from Germany to the United States in 1923. Employed first as a painter and then as an industrial designer, Kuhler cared not about economy but about aesthetics. He believed that the average American judged how modern a product was by its appearance, and by that standard the passenger train was not very modern. Kuhler insisted that streamlining made railroad passenger trains look up to date and fashionable, and that gave them sales appeal.[8]

That was what railroad executives sought in the mid-1930s when they introduced streamlined passenger trains that featured air-conditioned cars and clean-burning internal-combustion locomotives. It was widely believed in the industry that streamliners added prestige and advertising value to the railroads.

One result of this thinking was spectacular new trains like the Union Pacific's City of Salina and City of Portland, which were among the first in the nation. The Chicago, Burlington, and Quincy's Pioneer Zephyr appeared only two months after the Union Pacific's M-10000 and actually beat the City of Salina into regular revenue service. In any case, the Union Pacific and the Burlington together ushered in the age of the streamliner.

The nation witnessed a steady parade of new trains. No fewer than fourteen streamliners of various configurations operated on ten different railroads by the end of 1935. Companies like the Milwaukee Road added streamlined shrouds to their steam locomotives. Only Pearl Harbor and the coming of World War II brought a temporary halt to the debut of new streamliners. When the first postwar trains appeared in 1947, streamlined diesel locomotives and lightweight cars had become standard equipment.

The Union Pacific's desire for innovation during the 1930s was not limited to streamliners. The

railroad also introduced the Challenger, an exclusively coach and tourist-sleeper train, demonstrating that economy travel could be made both attractive and profitable. The Challenger entered service between Omaha (later Chicago) and Los Angeles in August 1935 and was upgraded with modern equipment the following year. Among its innovations were two coaches reserved solely for women (one for women traveling with small children), free pillows, air conditioning throughout, and attendants who were graduate nurses from hospitals in Omaha, Salt Lake City, and Los Angeles. "If the mother wishes, the stewardess will prepare the baby's formula or take care of children while mother visits the diner."[9] On the Challenger the railroad eliminated the calling of stations during sleeping hours and provided low-cost meals: breakfast for twenty-five cents, lunch for thirty cents, and dinner for thirty-five cents.

Several other railroads followed suit with deluxe coach trains of their own, and not just in the West. To serve the highly competitive New York to Chicago market, all-coach streamliners appeared on the New York Central as the Pacemaker and on the Pennsylvania as the Trail Blazer in 1939. There was even the Gulf, Mobile & Northern's Rebel streamliner, which operated between New Orleans and St. Louis to pioneer a new standard of coach and sleeper luxury in the Deep South.

## Tourism: Auto versus Rail

AT THE SAME TIME THAT THE Union Pacific introduced streamlined trains to win back riders, it also took a new look at tourism to fill half-empty coaches and sleeping cars during the lean years of the depression. Like railroad passenger cars, western tourism changed noticeably during the first three decades of the twentieth century. Personally conducted tours from Chicago on the Union Pacific and Chicago & North Western lines dated from 1900. The two railroads originally emphasized California as a tourist destination but added Yellowstone Park and the North Pacific region in 1905. The joint tour department handled a total of 954 groups in 1917 and 5,600 in 1928, many of them by special trains. In 1900 most tour patrons came from the Chicago area, but by 1928 almost half of them were from the East Coast, and some were from as far away as Germany and England. In the latter year the favorite destinations were Yellowstone, Rocky Mountain, Zion, Grand Canyon, and Yosemite national parks, the Canadian Rockies, and Alaska. By then, however, emphasis had clearly shifted to a low-cost market to compete with automobile tourists.[10]

Automobiles were admitted to Mount Rainier National Park for the first time in 1908, Crater Lake in 1911, Glacier in 1912, and Yellowstone in 1915. Wonderland would never be the same. When in 1927 railway travel to national parks increased by 5 percent, auto travel grew by 9 percent. The noticeable switch from vacation travel by boat or passenger train to private automobile increasingly worried railroad executives.[11]

*Three Forks, Montana, and the Gallatin Gateway were the Milwaukee Road's entrance to Yellowstone National Park. A total of 5,313 people entered the park by this route when it opened in 1926. Some 75 percent of the tourists—called "Gallagaters"— came from Chicago and points east. The following year the railroad opened the magnificent Gallatin Gateway Inn to serve its tourist clientele. Milwaukee Road Collection, Milwaukee Public Library.*

Private Vehicles Entering National Parks

|  | 1916 | 1917 | 1918 | 1919 | 1920 | 1921 | 1922 |
|---|---|---|---|---|---|---|---|
| Yellowstone | 3,445 | 5,703 | 4,734 | 10,737 | 13,586 | 15,736 | 18,252 |
| Mt. Rainier | 3,070 | 5,894 | 7,602 | 10,434 | 10,814 | 12,271 | 17,149 |
| Crater Lake | 2,649 | 2,756 | 3,106 | 4,637 | 5,158 | 7,892 | 9,429 |
| Glacier | 902 | 1,121 | 1,065 | 1,607 | 2,009 | 2,614 | 2,416 |

SOURCE: *Report of Director of National Park Service, for Travel Season, 1922* (Washington, D.C.: Government Printing Office, 1922).

*Railway Age* speculated that an increasing number of people of modest income took vacation trips by automobile because they felt uncomfortable traveling

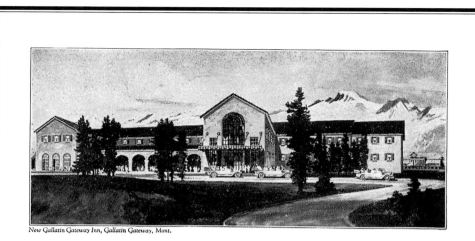

by railway Pullman cars and being confronted with the custom of having to give tips. "They would much prefer to sidestep this fearful and wonderful experience and knock around in their own cars, living in tourist camps, where they need not put on any sort of front and can behave naturally." One observer believed the "up-to-date motor camp to be the finest melting pot of our democracy."[12]

Budget-conscious tourists felt out of place in any resort where guests were expected to change their clothes three times a day, which was typical for some posh hotels. The formality of a railroad outing was captured by these words: "Provision will be made at Yellowstone station for the care of ladies' hats, and for cleaning and pressing clothing while passengers are en route through the Park. A nominal charge is made for the service."[13] Moreover, a two-week trip to Montana was beyond the means of most families, if railroad fares and hotel bills had to be paid for four or five people; traveling by car and camping out at night greatly reduced such expenses.

Auto vs. Rail Passengers in Yellowstone

| Year | West Entrance | | | North Entrance | |
|------|------|-----------|--------|------|--------|
| | UP | Milwaukee | Car | Rail | Car |
| 1930 | 10,271 | 1,637 | 71,565 | 9,209 | 36,930 |
| 1933 | 2,146 | 328 | 26,932 | 2,955 | 43,380 |
| 1935 | 6,566 | 986 | 94,008 | 6,346 | 43,856 |

SOURCE: Southwestern Passenger Association. 1935. Copy in Great Northern Papers, Box 19C92F, Minnesota Historical Society.

Western railroads had for years encouraged travel, especially in the summer, to vacation centers in the Pacific Northwest by advertising their scenic beauty or recreational attractions, but a new development urged western winter travel during the 1930s: the ski resort. Prior to its appearance, winter was a time of diminished tourist revenues.[14]

*Yellowstone's automobile campers, some of whom are seen here in 1923, became increasingly numerous as the decade progressed. Doubtless many Pullman travelers would have felt uncomfortable living in tourist camps, although the vogue changed from train trips to motor trips in scenic parts of the West. Library of Congress, 11600 LC-USZ62.*

During the depression years, W. Averell Harriman and the Union Pacific Railroad undertook to develop a world-class ski resort in the western United States to provide a destination that might enhance the railroad's lagging passenger revenues. The company hired Count Felix Schaffgotsch, an Austrian ski enthusiast, to search for the prime location. After visiting numerous western sites—Lake Tahoe, Jackson Hole, and Alta near Salt Lake City—all of which he dismissed as too high, too windy, or too remote, Schaffgotsch finally located an ideal place on the slopes above the old Idaho mining town of Ketchum. It had powder snow, spectacular vistas, and all-weather access from the Union Pacific main line at Shoshone. It was named Sun Valley, and Harriman later described it as the most beautiful site he had ever seen.

Upon Schaffgotsch's recommendation, the Union Pacific purchased a 3,888-acre ranch for $39,000. Soon a resort rivaling the best in Europe took shape. A massive 220-room lodge was constructed. Because of the company's fear of fires, builders used a good deal of dense concrete, but so cleverly did they etch and stain it to resemble wood that few guests realized the difference. The hotel housed 250 guests and featured a dance floor, beauty parlor, barbershop, elegant dining room, and a branch of Saks Fifth Avenue. The key was to get the "right people" to come to a resort designed to be St. Moritz in the Idaho outback. The lodge opened on December 31, 1936, although the first snow did not fall until more than a week later. Operating on the slopes outside were the West's first modern ski lifts, which came from Union Pacific shops in Omaha. The idea originated with a device used to load bananas onto ships in South America.

For less affluent guests, the Union Pacific built the Challenger Inn, named after its luxury tourist-class trains. For the opening on December 21, 1937, one of the new streamliners dashed from New York City to Ketchum bringing seventeen cars of vaca-

tioners including Harriman. After a flurry of activity, the railroad's chairman quietly slipped away and returned home to New York City on United Air Lines.

Just as Union Pacific streamliners were at the forefront of a new development in transportation, Sun Valley launched a new form of tourism. The resort was a progenitor of other winter sports facilities in the West. The Milwaukee Road's response was the Snoqualmie Ski Bowl, which opened on January 9, 1938, at the crest of the Cascade Range about sixty miles east of Seattle. It featured a ski tow, lodge, and lights for night use. This ski facility was designed to develop railroad passenger traffic from Seattle and Tacoma, where an estimated ninety-five thousand ski enthusiasts lived. The Milwaukee Road discovered that 35 percent of the passengers on its ski specials from Seattle and Tacoma had never been aboard a train before. The Snoqualmie Ski Bowl operated until 1949 when fire destroyed the lodge.[15]

## Slow Trains to Yesterday

WITH ALL THE EMPHASIS IN the 1930s on speed and glamour, it was easy to overlook the continued decline in popularity of local passenger trains, even on some of the region's largest steam railroads. The same Great Northern timetables that advertised the many amenities of the latest Empire Builder advised that "service between Marcus and Republic is by mixed train and schedules are so irregular that connection at Marcus with No. 256 northbound and with No. 255 southbound is not guaranteed." Certain local freight trains would carry male passengers but not women and children.[16]

On short-line railroads the situation was little better. Archie Robertson in his classic study of bucolic branch-line locals, *Slow Train to Yesterday*,

In isolated coal towns like Franklin, Washington, the passenger train was the sole link to the rest of the world; but such scenes had become rare by the early 1940s. Museum of History and Industry, 16056.

Slow Trains to Yesterday, June 1943:
The Short-line Railroads

| Railroad | Route (distance in miles) |
| --- | --- |
| *Idaho* | |
| Nez Perce & Idaho | Nez Perce to Craigmont (13) |
| Washington, Idaho & Montana | Lairds to Purdue (50) |
| *Montana* | |
| Montana, Wyoming & Southern | Bridger to Bear Creek (20) |
| Montana Western | Valier to Conrad (20) |
| Butte, Anaconda & Pacific | Butte to Anaconda (25) |
| *Oregon* | |
| Condon, Kinzua & Southern | Condon to Kinzua (24) |
| Valley & Siletz | Independence to Valsetz (40) |
| *Washington* | |
| Pacific Coast | Seattle to Black Diamond (30) |

SOURCE: Archie Robertson, *Slow Train to Yesterday* (Boston: Houghton Mifflin, 1945), 180–84 *et passim*.

recorded that by June 1943 only a few short-lines in the Pacific Northwest continued to offer passenger service.[17]

When gross passenger receipts on the Union Pacific increased 66 percent for 1934, the first year of its new streamliners, and another 36 percent the following year, Harriman hailed streamlining as a revolution and believed that the public once again perceived railroad managers as progressive. In fact, as laudatory as the aggressive approach to passenger service was, nothing short of fuel rationing and the 35-mile-per-hour speed limits imposed on motorists during World War II could arrest the downward trend in railroad passenger travel, and they did so only temporarily.[18]

It might be worth recalling that the same issue of the *Oregonian* that recited the breathtaking schedule of the City of Portland in 1935 contained an advertisement for United Air Lines, noting that its planes flew from Portland to all eastern cities "overnight."[19] The time was approaching when many Americans would regard even the fastest railroad streamliner as a slow train to yesterday.

*For many people—and I sympathize with them—one of the least-bearable wartime deprivations was the loss of their mobility. We are a wheeled people; it seems to me sometimes that I must have been born with a steering wheel in my hands, and I realize now that to lose the use of a car is practically equivalent to losing the use of my legs.—Wallace Stegner,* The Sound of Mountain Water *(1980)*

# Strange New World: War and a Troubled Peace

**D**ESPITE THE IMPRESSIVE PARADE of 143 streamlined trains on twenty-nine different railroads by 1942, it took the onset of World War II to boost passenger-train ridership to all-time highs. Revenue passenger-miles on American railroads climbed from a low of 16.3 million in 1933 to 87.8 million in 1944, about twice that of the previous high-water mark in 1920. The wartime increase in freight tonnage was equally staggering, and crews worked around the clock to keep traffic moving and to prevent car shortages. Once again the region's railroads occupied a prominent place in everyday life.

Many Pacific Northwesterners would recall the war years as a time of phenomenal population shifts and economic growth. Between 1940 and 1944, Seattle increased in population from 368,302 to approximately 530,000 people (650,000 in the greater metropolitan area). The city doubled its number of manufacturing employees between 1940 and 1942, many of them arriving from Idaho and Montana to build airplanes for Boeing. Both in aircraft plants and on railroads across America, an increasing number of workers were women. "Business women, housewives, clubwomen, coeds—a real army of women is joining forces with S.P. today to keep the war trains running."[1]

Oregon's population growth during the 1940s nearly equaled its increase for the entire nineteenth century. In Portland, where the sprawling Kaiser shipyards employed nearly 70 percent of the city's labor force, job seekers arrived from ranches in Idaho and Montana—even from as far away as New York on special Kaiser trains. Five such trains left New York City on a single weekend in late 1942 carrying five thousand workers. Kaiser charged a fare of seventy-five dollars to be deducted from subsequent paychecks.

High wages in shipyards and aircraft factories created an unreal situation for people who had only recently endured a decade of depression. Yet even as the standard of living rose, consumer goods and services became increasingly high priced, rationed, or unavailable. During the war, meat, milk, and clothing were all in short supply; when gasoline and tire rationing restricted automobile use in mid-1942, streetcars and buses labored under enormous passenger loads. Overcrowded passenger trains discouraged vacation travel or even short pleasure trips. Routine chores became challenges; shoppers either stood in long check-out lines or went without. People coped with shortages in a variety of ways, returning to horses and other forms of nonmotorized transport in the case of Idaho fish and game officials,

forgoing vacations, substituting honey for sugar in recipes. Because of gasoline rationing in late 1942, Sun Valley converted from a resort to a navy convalescent center.[2]

When the war ended in August 1945, harried railroad executives still faced the prospect of having to move crushing loads of freight and passengers in the months immediately ahead, but they also had reason to congratulate themselves. With half as many passenger cars as they had during World War I, they still had hauled twice as many people. Their skills in moving passengers and freight had staved off the dreaded prospect of government control. They were patriots.

*Arsenal of democracy: Boeing produced numerous B-17 bombers in its Seattle-area plants during World War II. Library of Congress, 15760, LC-USZ62-59739.*

# ...compliments of Milwaukee Road *"white coal"*

ALLIED bombers are raining ruin on the strongholds of the Axis, wrecking war production centers, transportation facilities, docks and warehouses. Do you realize that the fuel The Milwaukee Road is conserving by using "White Coal" may be helping to deal those crushing blows?

This "White Coal" is electricity from mountain water power, used for years to move Milwaukee Road trains across the Rockies, Bitter Roots and Cascades.

How fortunate that this electrification was functioning with proved efficiency when war came! It conserves many millions of gallons of oil that help provide America's ever-growing air armadas with needed flying power!

What's more, Milwaukee Road "White Coal" makes it unnecessary to tie up precious railway equipment in hauling fuel to our mountain divisions. This means more freight cars available to help ease the national transportation situation.

With a vast network of lines stretching across the continent from the dynamic midwest to the vital ocean ports of the Pacific northwest, The Milwaukee Road is handling a traffic volume these war days that was never approached before.

Heavy service, of course, is exacting its toll of all railroad equipment. But modernized operating methods—plus the active co-operation of shippers and essential travelers—enable The Milwaukee Road's 35,000 loyal, alert employees to do their full share for Victory.

CHICAGO
MILWAUKEE
ST. PAUL
AND
PACIFIC

## THE MILWAUKEE ROAD

ELECTRIFIED OVER THE ROCKIES
TO THE SEA

THE MILWAUKEE MAGAZINE

*The Milwaukee Road published this image of terrified Nazis in 1943 to dramatize how hydroelectric power or "white coal" conserved oil and helped to win the war. Milwaukee Road Collection, Milwaukee Public Library.*

## Is This Trip Necessary?

THE GOOD NEWS FOR AMERICAN railroads was that passenger service operated in the black in 1942 for the first time since 1929. Only in 1920 had more Americans traveled by train than in 1942, and the following year railroads hauled even more passengers. During the 1944 Christmas season, ridership was higher than ever in railroad history.

The typical American soldier made eight moves by train from induction to embarkation; he made only three in World War I. All of these moves were accomplished with fewer passenger cars than at any time in the previous forty years. Only one-seventh of the nation's wartime fleet of 37,940 passenger cars were built from 1934 to 1944, while half were more than twenty-five years old. With the exception of 1,900 boxcarlike triple-deck troop sleepers, 400 troop kitchen cars, and 200 hospital cars, no new passenger cars were constructed until the war ended. Many an antiquated wooden car destined for scrap returned to active duty.

The volume of military traffic—of people traveling on furlough and under orders—was so great that civilians were exhorted to "give your seat to a serviceman." Better yet, avoid all unnecessary trips. During the summer of 1943, railroads eliminated resort trains in order to release equipment desperately needed elsewhere, sold seats in lounge and club cars, and slowed their passenger trains between Midwest and Pacific Coast points to accommodate a swelling volume of mail and express. For years travelers had avoided upper berths, but now the army assigned two men to lower berths and one to the upper, filling all available sleeper accommodations.

Colonel J. Monroe Johnson, director of the Office of Defense Transportation, emphasized that "any unessential traveler who gets caught in the invasion traffic will have only himself to blame if he is indefinitely stranded, or finds his Pullman reservations summarily canceled, or finds passenger schedules temporarily disrupted and intercity buses completely swamped."[3] There was talk of rationing passenger-train travel.

Passenger traffic grew especially heavy on railroads serving the West Coast as the United States stepped up war in the Pacific. Overall, train travel in the far Northwest climbed 286 percent from May 1940 to May 1943. During the first eight months of 1944, the Northern Pacific experienced a 40 percent increase in passengers over the same period a year earlier. The Great Northern reported that its passenger revenue reached an all-time high in 1945.[4]

Behind all the impressive statistics, however, lurked a reality only partially grasped in 1944 or 1945. The war hurt American railroads, particularly their passenger service, far more than it helped them. Railroad executives gave generously to the war effort, in some cases literally cannibalizing their track and equipment. A 2,400-pound bronze bison head mounted on the east end of the Union Pacific bridge over the Missouri River at Omaha had welcomed travelers to the West since 1888, but it was taken down and melted into copper and other metals for shell casings. The Union Pacific's first streamliner, the acclaimed M-10000, was reduced to scrap metal in 1942 to provide much-needed aluminum for the war effort. These two patriotic gestures were symbolic of what happened to railroad property during World War II.

Other streamliners of prewar vintage were pressed into service as strictly utilitarian vehicles carrying huge volumes of passengers. With maintenance limited chiefly to repairs to running gear, even progressive roads like the Union Pacific suffered overuse and abuse of passenger equipment. The Southern Pacific now served three times as many dining car meals as it had before the war. Dining cars were so packed that Union Pacific and Southern Pacific lines inaugurated the practice of serving

civilian travelers only two meals a day, breakfast and dinner, and they removed items like pancakes and poached eggs from the menu to save preparation time. Because of rationing, the Southern Pacific permitted only one cup of coffee at breakfast and none at dinner, and it used its public timetables to urge dining car patrons: "Please don't dally."[5]

*"We're rationed, too," the Great Northern explained to passengers in one of its World War II–era public timetables. Civilian passengers experienced an added but necessary inconvenience in 1945 when the Office of Defense Transportation prohibited railroads from operating Pullman sleepers on any run of 450 miles or less. In this way it withdrew 895 sleepers*

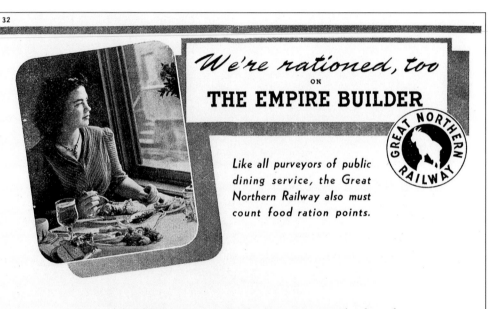

32

*We're rationed, too*
ON
THE EMPIRE BUILDER

GREAT NORTHERN RAILWAY

Like all purveyors of public dining service, the Great Northern Railway also must count food ration points.

And, in addition to conserving food, we must consider the welfare of dining car personnel these days. Stewards, chefs and waiters never have worked harder. They must have rest.

Toward maintaining, under these circumstances, the traditional high standards of Great Northern dining service, only two meals are now served daily on the EMPIRE BUILDER.

Breakfast is served from 6:30 A. M. until noon. Dinner at 4:30 P. M. and continuing until all are served.

★ ★ ★ ★ ★ ★ ★ ★ ★ ★ ★ ★ ★ ★ ★ ★ ★ ★ ★ ★ ★ ★ ★ ★

*for military use to aid in the redeployment of troops to the Pacific. Idaho State Historical Society.*

*T*he Northern Pacific used this advertisement in 1943 to dramatize its role handling the wheat crop of the northern tier states. Courtesy William S. Greever.*

Skilled help became scarce because so many of the railroads' best cooks and waiters were called to military duty. The Union Pacific pressed lounge cars into service as diners; the Southern Pacific operated 135 dining cars but was still short 50 cars to meet its food service needs. The Southern Pacific apologized to passengers in mid-1942 for the slipping quality of its dining car service, noting that its cooks and waiters were doing their best but often had to work double shifts. "Sometimes there isn't

as much spring in your step when you're tired."[6]

Little things had large effects. The military's use of Freon gas in mosquito sprays for the tropics, for example, meant that none was available for coolant aboard passenger trains. Without air conditioning and with windows permanently sealed shut, the interior of streamlined passenger cars became unbearably hot and stuffy in warm weather.[7]

Another casualty of war was the decade-long effort to lure more travelers onto the nation's premier passenger trains. From 1926 to 1942, American railroads had spent $456 million on capital improvements for their passenger fleet. From 1932 to 1942 they had installed 2,503 new cars and rebuilt another 13,627. But now the Northern Pacific advised, "Don't Plan a Trip This Christmas." The Southern Pacific advertised throughout its sprawling West Coast domain: "Next Time—Don't Take the Train," and by late 1943 it had spent $75,000 on advertising designed to *discourage* passenger travel. Along its tracks it erected billboards warning, "Don't travel unless you have to: Our locomotives and cars are needed more by Uncle Sam and his men." The Southern Pacific emphasized that "if gasoline rationing causes many more people to travel by train, we may have to hang out the 'Standing Room Only' sign." Intended to shame civilians out of unnecessary travel was the slogan "How's Your Conscience Today?"[8]

Because of gasoline and rubber rationing imposed in 1942, travelers ignored the warnings and flocked back to passenger trains in unprecedented numbers. Long lines, congested terminals, and interminable waits for crowded trains became the stuff of nightmares. Once on a train, a traveler often found standing room only; people crowded the aisles and overflowed into rest rooms, vestibules, and even overhead luggage racks. Car cleaners did their best, but their task was hopeless when eight hundred people crammed aboard a train designed for five hundred.

From the perspective of 1930s efforts to lure Americans back to passenger trains, travel conditions during World War II were a public relations disaster. Many people would later describe their experience aboard a passenger train in wartime as horrible. Some travelers remembered only the crowded trains, antiquated equipment, lack of courtesy on the part of harried railway employees, dirty washrooms on trains and in stations, messy coaches, and unsatisfactory dining car prices and service.[9]

A few railroad executives may have worried about what effect the experience would have on postwar travel by train, but most were simply too busy keeping things running to have time to take the long-range view. Nonetheless, *Railway Age* broached the subject when it wondered aloud, "What will the enforced train-riders of today, many of whom would probably never have boarded a train except for the war, think of railway passenger service?" The influential journal answered its own question by asserting that discomforts of wartime train travel would have little effect in the postwar era.[10]

Some travel experts predicted that, even with increased postwar competition from buses and planes, an expanding population of tourists would increase the market for passenger trains. Edward G. Budd envisioned a postwar market so huge that between New York and Pittsburgh alone railroads would need to add ten coach trains each way. Budd, one of the nation's leading railway car manufacturers, naturally had a vested interest in such rosy predictions, but statistics seemed to bear out the most optimistic projections.

A *Railway Age* item in 1943 calculated that in 1920 an inhabitant of the United States traveled an average distance of five hundred miles per year. By 1929 that figure had climbed to over two thousand miles per person, and there was reason to believe it would continue to climb in the postwar years ahead. In anticipation of a peacetime boom in travel, railroads lined up to order new streamliners.[11]

## After the War

THE FIRST OF THE POSTWAR streamliners was the Pere Marquette that went into service between Detroit and Grand Rapids, Michigan, on August 10, 1946. Even more impressive was the new Empire Builder that the Great Northern inaugurated between Chicago and Seattle and Portland on February 23, 1947. Designers adopted a Glacier Park motif and effectively combined plastics and new light metals to give its interior vibrancy; the train's exterior color scheme was a striking juxtaposition of olive green and deep orange. The first of a postwar generation of transcontinental streamliners, the Empire Builder's five sets of twelve-car trains represented an investment of $7 million. In anticipation of increased patronage, the Great Northern had ordered the equipment from Pullman-Standard on November 4, 1943, to be built when materials became available.

To compete with the Empire Builder, the Milwaukee Road raced to build a streamliner of its own, continuing a long-standing tradition by constructing most cars for the new train in its own shops. Meanwhile, the railroad upgraded its main line west from Minneapolis to achieve higher speeds; it improved the signaling system, eased the curves, and added heavier rails. In some places the improvements permitted speeds as high as seventy-nine miles an hour, enabling the Milwaukee Road to match the Empire Builder's time of forty-five hours between Chicago and Seattle.

The new Olympian Hiawatha that made its debut on June 29, 1947, included a "Touralux" sleeper for economy-minded travelers and a car for the exclusive use of women and children. Although it was almost a year before the Olympian Hiawatha consisted of all streamlined cars, the Milwaukee Road nonetheless advertised its postwar lineup of deluxe passenger trains in 297 daily newspapers, 527 weekly newspapers, 54 national magazines and on 26 radio stations. At the head of the Olympian Hiawatha were impressive new chrome-faced Fairbanks-Morse diesels, and at the rear was a Skytop lounge car designed to assure passengers unprecedented visibility. The existing Olympian became the new Columbian.[12]

During the first two years after the war, the Union Pacific spent some $20 million on new passenger cars and diesel passenger locomotives. The City of Portland went into service on a daily basis on February 14, 1947, offering a forty-two-hour schedule from Chicago to Portland. The railroad also added stewardesses to the City of Portland and other luxury trains that year. The Northern Pacific, citing the need for economy and safety, initially bowed out of the postwar speed-and-equipment

derby, then reconsidered. In November 1946 the railroad's board of directors authorized $9.8 million to purchase six diesel locomotive sets and seventy-eight lightweight passenger cars for the streamlined North Coast Limited, which entered service on September 20, 1948, although it remained on a slow and uncompetitive schedule until late 1952.

In early 1947 the Southern Pacific advertised that "space is now available on most S.P. trains." Two years later, on July 10, 1949, the railroad introduced its beautiful new Shasta Daylight and placed "The Luxury Train That Everyone Can Afford" on a record-breaking 15½-hour daytime schedule between Portland and Oakland. The railroad streamlined the Cascade on the same route on August 13, 1950.[13]

In many ways the Empire Builder, like the Olym-

pian Hiawatha, the North Coast Limited, and the Shasta Daylight, represented refinements of prewar technology, such as improved air conditioning and modified color schemes and interior design. But the General Motors Train of Tomorrow caught the public fancy with a series of innovations that appeared truly new. When unveiled to the public in late May 1947, it drew crowds—much as the first streamliners had in the 1930s. During its tour of the United States, a curious public marveled at "Astra-Dome" cars and numerous other refinements.

When the Great Northern introduced its new Mid-Century Empire Builder in 1951 and put the 1947 equipment into service as the Western Star, it was the first time any railroad had offered double-daily streamliner service between Chicago and the Pacific Northwest. The carrier's passenger revenues increased 22 percent over the previous year in what was the first reversal of a decline since 1945.[14]

Why had the Great Northern invested nearly $21 million in modern passenger equipment when it served so sparsely populated a region? The answer was a familiar one: John M. Budd, president of the railroad, asserted that the new passenger trains definitely attracted freight business, improved the railroad's public image in its service region, and attracted sufficient revenue to meet direct out-of-pocket expenses. In fact, the railroad believed that but for the Empire Builder the loss in passenger revenues since 1945 would have been even greater. Added Budd, "If you stop 100 people on the street and strike up a conversation about railways, I'll bet my last nickel that 99 of them will be able to talk only about passenger service."[15]

Not all improvements were confined to long-distance trains. On June 18, 1950, the Great Northern introduced two new five-car Internationals between Seattle and Vancouver, British Columbia. There was still an obvious gap between Seattle and Portland, where there had never been streamliner service

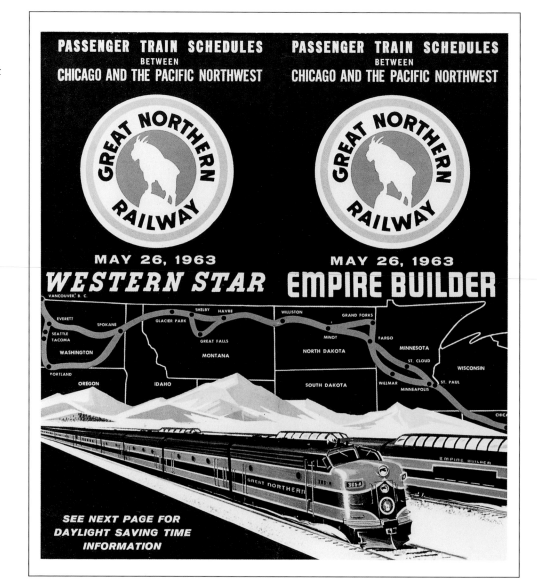

except for a short time late in World War II, when hand-me-down Union Pacific equipment from one of its early City of Los Angeles trains provided a connection for the City of Portland. This train was known unofficially as the City of Seattle. In February 1950, the Oregon journalist Richard Neuberger denounced nonstreamliner service between the region's two largest cities as the "musty filling in a streamlined sandwich."[16] As if in response

*In 1963 the Great Northern Railway advertised its Chicago–Pacific Northwest passenger trains on the cover of its public timetable. Author's collection.*

to the criticism, the Union Pacific supplied new equipment in midyear.

New trains ordered during the excitement of the wartime crush continued to be delivered until 1950, and not all innovation was confined to western railroads. The Pennsylvania Railroad announced that its streamlined all-coach Jeffersonian between New York and St. Louis would feature a game-and-reading room and newsreel theater. Television on trains arrived briefly in 1948 when the second game of the World Series was received on the Baltimore & Ohio's Marylander.[17]

But clearly by 1949 the railroad industry's wartime enthusiasm for recapturing lost passenger business was waning. For all their efforts, including expenditure of vast sums of money for advertising and new equipment, railroads realized that rising labor costs and high price tags for streamliners made the break-even point for passenger trains in the late 1940s almost double that in 1939. In other words, either a hundred passengers were needed where fifty had previously supplied sufficient revenue to break even, or fifty passengers had to ride twice as far.[18]

Even with new streamliners, passengers during the first five years after the war did not always find train travel pleasant. When the war ended, the Union Pacific pointedly reminded its employees to heed passenger complaints about callous attitudes dating from the wartime crush. P. J. Lynch, the railroad's vice-president for operations, was forced to send employees a notice in 1949 titled "Coach Passengers Are People." He noted that coach patrons constituted 70 percent of the Union Pacific's passenger business, and he reminded service workers that the coach traveler "keeps you in your job and me in my job." "Don't look upon a coach passenger as a poor or cheap person," and don't treat him like a "country cousin."

Lynch compiled and distributed a two-page summary of complaints that had reached his office from disgruntled travelers. A typical one was: "It looks to me as though the company spent hundreds of thousands of dollars for modern coaches—and then you are cancelling all that by letting a lot of autocratic, fossilized, cranky, domineering conductors to treat the public you've coaxed onto your trains like emigrants of 1890." Another rider complained, "We went to Sun Valley by coach—a miserable trip. No one to help us with luggage, conductor anything but cooperative. We hate the Union Pacific forever and ever."[19]

A general feeling among passengers during the first five years after the war was that too many railroad employees lacked courtesy. During the same time, as the industry knew only too well, airlines leaned over backwards to impress their passengers with courteous treatment—a practice derived from the days when airlines served free hot meals as a psychological sedative for travelers fearful of flying.[20]

Passenger Fatalities per Billion Passenger-Miles

| Year | Railroads | Domestic Airlines |
|------|-----------|-------------------|
| 1939 | 1.41 | 11.92 |
| 1946 | 1.78 | 12.36 |
| 1947 | 1.63 | 31.52 |
| 1951 | 4.33 | 12.97 |
| 1953 | 1.58 | 5.61 |
| 1954 | .78 | .92 |

SOURCE: *Railway Age*, 136 (May 16, 1955): 62.

## A Crucial Decade

A STUDY GROUP FOR THE Association of American Railroads publicly predicted in mid-1946 that passenger-miles would drop from fifty billion in 1945 (down from eighty-eight billion the year before) to thirty-five billion in 1950 but declined to speculate about what might happen during subsequent years. In fact, the Korean War that began in late June 1950 caused passenger traffic to climb briefly. Almost one-eighth of the total passenger revenues of American railroads for the last half of 1950 came from armed forces traffic created by the new conflict. In general, though, the long-term trend in passenger traffic was both downward and discouraging.[21]

For ten years, from 1947 to 1957, American railroads were locked in a struggle they could not win. In later years, critics accused them of trying to get out of the passenger business, but that certainly was not true during the postwar decade when American railroads invested millions of dollars to invigorate passenger service. To encourage ridership and trim expenses, railroads of the Pacific Northwest resorted to a standard formula. Several times during the years after the war, they introduced still newer passenger cars, offered still more amenities, lowered rates, and cut remaining local and branch-line service.

The sparse population of the Pacific Northwest presented a real problem with respect to secondary or branch-line passenger improvements. Most railroads felt that such service was unnecessary because the public had largely abandoned it anyway. Thus, the pruning of local trains that began in the 1920s continued into the 1950s and 1960s with such a vengeance that soon even the largest carriers had only a handful of locals left.

Where branch-line service could not be eliminated, several companies substituted rail diesel cars (RDC), as the Northern Pacific did in 1955 for regular trains between Spokane and Lewiston, Idaho. The Budd Company, which introduced the diesel-powered cars in 1949, merged the technology of the old doodlebug with streamlining techniques it had pioneered. Available in various configurations, the RDC had more usable space than the old-time self-propelled railcar and was its mechanical superior. Labor costs, however, were a big reason why the RDC failed to provide a truly economical alternative

to the bus. States with so-called full-crew laws, such as Oregon and Washington, affected operation of RDC cars. The RDC required only an engineer and conductor for successful operation, although some states mandated a brakeman, fireman, and flagman in addition.[22]

One of the most promising new developments in long-distance passenger trains was the dome car. After a tentative beginning on the Burlington in the late 1940s, it came into its own in the mid-1950s. "The handful of 'dome' passenger cars in service on American railroads can no longer be brushed off as fads." Dome cars were widely believed to increase passenger business. Every western transcontinental railroad had several of them in operation by 1955. The Northern Pacific added domes to its North Coast Limited in 1954 and to the "Traveller's Rest" lounge car the following year; the Great Northern added full-length domes to its Empire Builder a year later, as did the Milwaukee Road's Olympian Hiawatha. The dome dining cars that the Union Pacific introduced on its City of Portland in 1956 were a striking variation and the only equipment of its kind in the United States.[23]

Yet another innovation was the economy sleeper that Pullman and Budd introduced to solve the problem of sparsely occupied coach and sleeper facilities. "Slumbercoaches" appeared on the Burlington's Denver Zephyr in the fall of 1955 and the North Coast Limited in 1959. In the mid-1950s, American railroads also experimented with several entirely new types of trains. Among these were "Train X," one-third lighter than conventional trains, the "Talgo Train," a Spanish design, and the General Motors "Aerotrain," an ultralightweight contender using coaches that resembled buses, which for a time showed the most promise. The Union Pacific tried out the Aerotrain in 1956–57, running it between Los Angeles and Las Vegas as the City of Las Vegas. The railroad industry awaited public response with an air of expectancy, but this

*The camera of Richard Steinheimer recorded Union Pacific train no. 19 west of Wallula Junction, Washington, in July 1965. Known as the Spokane (local railfans dubbed it the City of Hinkle), it linked Spokane and the Union Pacific main line at Hinkle, Oregon. Almost all branch-line passenger service in the Pacific Northwest was gone by then, although this train lasted until the coming of Amtrak in early 1971. The only other survivors of this class of service were the Oregon Trunk's local to Bend and the Great Northern's to Great Falls. DeGolyer Library, Richard Steinheimer, Ag82.233.*

**The North Coast Limited's "History Book on Wheels"**

*"The Lewis and Clark Traveller's Rest buffet-lounge car is a veritable 'history book on wheels.' Traveller's Rest was the name given by the famed explorers to the favorite camp site in western Montana, near Missoula. Colorful wall murals depict scenes and show the route of Lewis and Clark's journey from St. Louis to the Pacific and return. Color reproductions of the famous Peale portraits of Lewis and Clark and reproductions of documents pertaining to the expedition also adorn the walls. Included in the historical exhibit is a reproduction of a Harper's Ferry flintlock rifle carried by members of the expedition and a peace pipe symbolic of the explorers' success in establishing friendly relations with the Indians. You'll find this method of studying history most palatable."*

*—Train Service Guide Vista-Dome North Coast Limited ([St. Paul: North Pacific Railway, 1966]), b*

time neither new equipment nor new trains brought back many passengers for the long term.[24]

A combination of developments, some of which could scarcely have been anticipated in 1945, derailed industry hopes for reversing the trend away from passenger trains that been so noticeable since the 1920s. Foremost among these was the passenger train's old nemesis, the private automobile. Ironically, the American people returned to their automobiles in the 1940s just as railroads introduced their expensive, new streamlined trains.

When gasoline rationing ended, Americans withdrew money from their bulging savings accounts, cashed in their war bonds and stamps, and took to the road in record numbers. The number of visitors to Mount Rainier in 1946 broke all previous records. The buying power created by enforced

saving during the war years promoted a frenzy in dealer showrooms when the first new cars became available in 1946. The baby boom further encouraged family travel by private automobile, as did suburban living, which made the downtown railroad station an anachronism.

Still another blow to rail hopes for a passenger-train revival was the federal Highway Act of 1956 with its vision of forty-one thousand miles of limited-access highway by 1972. As each new section of superhighway opened, automobiles and intercity buses became even more competitive with passenger trains. In fact, as early as 1957, express buses took only fifteen minutes longer than the fastest trains between Seattle and Portland, and between Seattle and Spokane the bus was actually forty-five minutes faster than the Empire Builder and almost two hours faster than the North Coast Limited. In the late 1950s Continental Trailways even revived an old idea by offering through buses between Seattle and Los Angeles that featured deluxe service. Total intercity bus traffic in the United States (in terms of

*The Great Northern continued to offer passengers a variety of sleeping accommodations on its Empire Builder in the 1960s. Author's collection.*

## Your choice of Pullman comforts!

Whether you are watching your budget or in a mood to splurge a bit, one of the seven selections in Pullman comfort available on the famous Empire Builder will likely match both your purse and your pleasure.

On your next trip enjoy the privacy and relaxation that only Pullman travel can provide.

**UPPER AND LOWER BERTH**
**Economy comfort.** A limited number of upper and lower berth sections available. Foam rubber mattresses. Modern washrooms.

**DUPLEX-ROOMETTE**
**Perfect privacy.** Ideal for business travel. Sitting room by day, private bedroom by night. Individual washroom facilities, heat and air controls.

**ROOMETTE**
**Home on wheels.** Spacious comfort for the single traveler. Plenty of room to move about, change clothes, wash in privacy. Bed pulls down from wall.

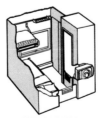

**DOUBLE BEDROOM**
**Roomy, relaxing.** Perfect for vacationing couple or single traveler. Sofa by day makes into bed; second berth pulls down. Private washroom.

**COMPARTMENT**
**Luxury living.** Superb accommodations for one or two. Sofa seat plus chair. Washroom facilities. Weather controls.

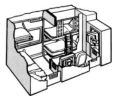

**COMPARTMENT-BEDROOM SUITE**
**Grand style.** Nothing finer for family or group. Spacious living room by day, two full bedrooms by night. Ample room to relax, entertain.

*The Northern Pacific featured stewardess service on its modern North Coast Limited. Author's collection.*

passenger-miles) exceeded the volume of rail passenger business for the first time in 1962.[25]

Truly radical departures in long-distance travel occurred in the air. The war that did so much to cannibalize railroad passenger equipment and degrade service promoted several technological breakthroughs beneficial to commercial aviation. Although the war curtailed civilian air travel, military needs spurred development of radar and improved engines, aircraft designs, and navigational aids.

Aircraft manufacturing, which before 1940 was something of a cottage industry, mushroomed into big business. Seemingly overnight, the Boeing company became one of the largest employers in Washington, turning out record numbers of B-17 and B-29 bombers from its plants in the Seattle area. Even before the war ended, plane builders revealed prototypes of commercial aircraft that would dominate the skies in the 1940s and 1950s. New Douglas DC-4s entered commercial service as early as October 1945. Four months later the pressurized Lockheed Constellations reduced travel time from coast to coast to just over ten hours. Boeing developed the 377 Stratocruiser for Pan American out of its design for the B-29 Superfortress bomber at the end of the war. The plane set a new standard of luxury by seating sixty and including even a honeymoon suite in the tail. Northwest Airlines, which became the nation's fourth transcontinental carrier in 1945, used Stratocruisers on coast-to-coast routes.

Travel by air surpassed that by Pullman in 1951 and threatened even that by railway coach. The railroad industry had anticipated that airlines might cut into their first-class business, but air coach was something new. By 1950 air coach had been conducted on an experimental basis for about eighteen months and was battering railroad passenger revenues. Air coach took away hundreds of thousands of dollars that otherwise would have gone to the railroads. In 1957 airlines surpassed railroads to become America's leading common carrier in terms of revenue passenger-miles. At that time Northwest Orient Airlines offered through air coach service between New York City and Seattle for ninety-nine dollars. Jet air travel, introduced the following year, dealt yet another blow to railroad passenger service.[26]

Finally, there was the nationwide recession of 1957–58 when railroad traffic and revenues dwindled and employment in the industry shrank to the lowest level yet in the twentieth century. By February

Leading Carriers of Passengers
(in passenger-miles)

| Rank | 1946 | 1950 | 1955 |
|------|------|------|------|
| 1 | Pennsylvania RR | Pennsylvania RR | American Airlines |
| 2 | New York Central | New York Central | United Airlines |
| 3 | Santa Fe RR | Santa Fe RR | Eastern Airlines |
| 4 | Southern Pacific | American Airlines | Pennsylvania RR |
| 5 | Union Pacific | Southern Pacific | New York Central |

SOURCE: *Railway Age*, 140 (May 21, 1956): 94.

1958, 45 of 114 of the nation's largest and best-capitalized (Class 1) railroads operated in the red and failed to make enough money even to cover the interest on their debts. The passenger deficit climbed to an alarming $723 million a year and represented an intolerable burden. Just about the only bright spot in all the gloom was a surge in piggyback freight service.

During the recession of 1958, not only passenger trains but entire railroads were at risk. Some were in worse financial shape than they had been at the depths of the Great Depression. Industry giants like the Pennsylvania and the New York Central railroads struggled to remain solvent. The 1950s would prove to be one of the most traumatic decades in the history of American railroads.[27]

*Train routes are revealing. No one goes to any trouble to tidy up the landscape for train travelers. Railroads run through our collective backyards.*
—George F. Scheer III, Booked on the Morning Train *(1991)*

# A Changing Signature

**A**N EXCELLENT PLACE TO VISUAL-ize one railroad's changing signature across the Pacific Northwest is in Nebraska, at the Union Pacific's Harriman Dispatching Center near downtown Omaha. Located in a refurbished freight warehouse where E. H. Harriman and other investors bought the railroad in 1897, the fifty-million-dollar futuristic complex allows dispatchers to move more than seven hundred trains a day across twenty-three thousand miles of Union Pacific track in eighteen states. On two screens, each the length of a football field, are a myriad of color-coded symbols that reveal the location of signals, switches, tracks, and trains. Fiber optics and computer technology permit dispatchers in Omaha to talk to train crews in Oregon or line switches in Idaho. It is noteworthy that the massive schematic diagram of the Union Pacific system is not painted but is only projected on the screen. This method allows for quick and simple addition and deletion of lines and reflects the fact that the signature of the Union Pacific, and every other major railroad serving the Pacific Northwest, changed as radically during the years from 1958 to 1990 as at any time in the twentieth century.

That was true not just for the map of their tracks but also for the corporations themselves. After the

Union Pacific Railroad's energetic young chairman Michael H. Walsh came to the company in 1986, he streamlined the corporate bureaucracy and promoted new technology like the Harriman Dispatching Center to trim costs. Changes in union work rules to permit three-person crews to operate a freight train, and innovations such as double-stacked containers on flat cars in trains often a mile in length enable the Union Pacific to compete successfully with truckers for long-haul cargoes. As of 1988 the Union Pacific and other railroads of the United States still moved 37 percent of the nation's intercity freight—more than any other mode of transportation including pipelines, trucks, and inland waterways—although that portion was considerably less than the almost 75 percent that moved by rail in 1929. Without railroad freight service, the region's economy would still grind to a halt, yet in the public consciousness, railroads continue to recede from view as they have since the beginning of the age of competition, with the exception of the World War II years. Major events affecting railroads went unnoticed by most Pacific Northwesterners.

## The Big Three

**A** PROCESS OF CONSOLIDATION and pruning whereby strong railroads grew stronger and weak ones withered and died redrew the railroad map of the Pacific Northwest after 1970. The shake-out left just three big railroads—the Burlington Northern, the Southern Pacific, and the Union Pacific—and a series of local and regional carriers, most of which did not exist prior to 1980. The first of the region's megamergers occurred on March 3, 1970, when the Great Northern, Northern Pacific, and Chicago, Burlington & Quincy combined to form the Burlington Northern Railroad. The Spokane, Portland

& Seattle Railway became part of the new company a few months later. Representing the culmination of James J. Hill's long-deferred dream, the Burlington Northern had its share of start-up troubles as it integrated its sprawling system (24,398 miles), but they were minor compared to those of the combined New York Central and Pennsylvania railroads, or Penn Central, which ended in bankruptcy in 1970. That was the worst business failure in American history to that time. Meanwhile, the Burlington Northern grew even larger with acquisition of the St. Louis–San Francisco Railway in 1980, forming a system that sprawled diagonally across the United

*Even in the midst of war, the automobile remained at the center of American family life. Russell Lee recorded this picnic in Klamath Falls, Oregon, in 1942. Library of Congress, 11604, F34 73243.*

States from Vancouver, British Columbia, to Pensacola, Florida.

During the 1980s the Union Pacific grew by acquiring three major railroads: the Western Pacific (1982) gave it access to central California and the San Francisco Bay area, the Missouri Pacific System (1982) allowed expansion into the Southwest, and the Missouri-Kansas-Texas Railroad (1988) provided a shortcut from Kansas City to Texas. Unlike the Burlington Northern, which coined a new title for its merged railroads, the Union Pacific retained the most venerable name in American railroad history.

Of the remaining big three railroads serving the Pacific Northwest, the Southern Pacific initially seemed least affected by line changes. Nonetheless, it too abandoned some branches. It was taken over by Rio Grande Industries, but a weak economy in its West Coast service area in the 1980s threatened for a time to transform the once mighty Southern Pacific into the new sick man of Pacific Northwest railroads, a designation that had formerly applied to the Chicago, Milwaukee, St. Paul & Pacific, one familiar name conspicuously missing from the redrawn map of the Pacific Northwest's trunk-line railroads in the late 1980s.

For years the Milwaukee Road had been the weakest of the northern transcontinentals. Continuing financial malaise caused it to shrivel and finally fade into history. The company's third and final bankruptcy occurred on December 19, 1977, following three years of heavy losses. Its troubles multiplied after 1970 and creation of the Burlington Northern. The giant new competitor proved a fatal blow, despite the Milwaukee Road's acquisition of trackage rights in 1973 that extended its service from Louisville, Kentucky, to Portland, Oregon. The Milwaukee, however, was never able to capitalize on this arrangement by developing long-haul traffic to and from the Pacific Coast.

But intensified competition was not the only cause of the railroad's troubles. Critics blamed Milwaukee Road management, which they charged had become provincial and ingrown compared to that of its competitors, the Chicago & North Western and the Burlington Northern, and slow to respond to changing circumstances or to the liabilities of too many miles of marginal railway line. In an interview in 1988, the retired Milwaukee Road president Curtiss E. Crippen added, "I think the Milwaukee, traditionally and as a normal pattern, never had the revenues it needed to do a good job of maintaining and operating the railroad."[1]

Studies showed that although the Milwaukee was the nation's fifteenth largest railroad in terms of revenues in 1958, 96 percent of its traffic could be handled by competing lines. Bankruptcy was perhaps inevitable and probably would have come earlier had the railroad not tapped the resources of its land company. Everything on the Milwaukee Road west of Miles City, Montana, was amputated on March 1, 1980. Track was simply pulled up in many places; other portions of the line were parceled out to the existing carriers or became new short-line railroads. On January 1, 1986, having abandoned more than seven thousand miles of track, the Milwaukee Road officially merged into the Soo Line.

## New Regional and Local Railroads

EVEN AS THE MILWAUKEE ROAD disappeared from the map, parts of its track lived on in the likes of the St. Maries River Railroad (formed in 1980), which the Potlatch Corporation operated from St. Maries to Bovill, Idaho, and the Pend Oreille Valley Railroad that in 1979 began operating the sixty-two-mile route between Newport and Metaline Falls, Washington. There was also the Seattle & North Coast Railroad that ran along the Olympic Peninsula from Port Townsend to Port Angeles serving a variety of

*A Milwaukee Road fast freight from Chicago to Seattle, Tacoma, and Portland was photographed under the wires east of Alberton, Montana. The Milwaukee Road ceased electric operation in 1974 because the once state-of-the-art system had become obsolete. Even finding spare parts was difficult and expensive. Leading the quartet of diesels in this picture was one of the Milwaukee's most modern electric locomotives, a Little Joe, so named because it was part of a lot of twenty General Electric engines destined for the railways of Joseph Stalin's Soviet Union until the cold war intervened. The Milwaukee Road acquired twelve Little Joes. Montana Historical Society.*

*Approaching the end of an era is a Northern Pacific locomotive photographed in Livingston, Montana, on September 2, 1956. The final generation of steam freight power on the Northern Pacific were these massive Challenger-type articulated locomotives first delivered to the railroad twenty years earlier. DeGolyer Library, Jim Ehernberger, Ag82.232.26300 B.*

forest- and wood-products concerns. Connected to Seattle via a barge on Puget Sound, this forty-five-mile line did not survive.

The Burlington Northern spun off several lines during the 1980s to form new regional carriers. From Billings, Montana, west to Seattle, much of the historic Northern Pacific main line was parceled out to new carriers like the 994-mile-long Montana Rail Link between Huntley, Montana (just east of Billings), and Sandpoint, Idaho, in 1987, and the 353-mile-long Washington Central Railroad, which a year earlier took over service from Kennewick to Cle Elum and other points. The old Northern Pacific line across Stampede Pass went unused for several years.[2]

Railroads like the Montana Rail Link were a direct result of the Staggers (Railroad Deregulation) Act of 1980, which gave unprecedented freedom to

railroads to abandon unprofitable branch lines or to spin them off as regional and local carriers. From 1980 to 1987, 173 such railroads were established across the United States, and as of 1987, all but four were still operating. Regional and local railroads had the advantage of a lower wage structure and flexible work rules. Most operated their trains with a crew of two who worked a full eight-hour day.

## A Changing Signature

AS DRAMATIC AS SUCH CHANGES were during the 1980s, large-scale abandonment of railway line actually came comparatively late to the states of the Pacific Northwest. Even after the Milwaukee's second bankruptcy in the mid-1930s, there was little

trimming of steam railway lines in the region. Despite growing competition from highway carriers, the primary cause of rail abandonment across the United States between 1920 and 1940 was depletion of natural resources, and the two western states hardest hit were Colorado and Nevada, both of which were affected by slumps in metal mining.

It was not until the 1980s that railroads (apart from electric interurbans and logging lines) abandoned lengthy sections of track in the Pacific Northwest. Besides the Milwaukee Road pulling up tracks, the Burlington Northern and the Union Pacific—as they acquired new railroads or spun off track to form regional carriers—also abandoned lightly used lines in an effort to improve the efficiency of their systems. Union Pacific tracks, for example, were removed along a seventy-two-mile-long section of right-of-way from Shoshone to Ketchum, Idaho, in 1987. The roadbed from Bellevue to Ketchum became a bike-and-jogging path. The Wood River branch had opened in May 1883, and over the years it carried ore, sheep, and finally skiers to Sun Valley. Three times a year the Union Pacific ran a special ski train from Los Angeles to Ketchum with reservations required a year ahead of time. Regular passenger service ended in the mid-1960s when the Union Pacific sold its ski resort to the Janss Corporation.[3]

Abandonment of track was even more dramatic in the Palouse country. During a span of seventeen years, from 1970 to 1987, the 825 miles of track that once crisscrossed the region's landscape was reduced by 285 miles, or 35 percent. Such abandonments together with changes in union work rules nearly depopulated towns like Avery, Idaho, and Malden, Washington, which were once almost wholly dependent on railroads. In Wishram, Washington, and Huntington, Oregon, yards that had been busy around the clock now stood nearly empty and the towns themselves struggled to survive. Numerous local agencies closed in rural areas of the Pacific Northwest, and new service centers opened in distant cities where customers could reach railroads via toll-free numbers.

Even the physical appearance of trains changed. Although diesel locomotives antedated World War II, they did not turn up on American railroads in large numbers until after 1946. In 1941 there were 41,911 steam locomotives and only 1,517 diesels; twenty years later there were 30,123 diesels and a mere 210 steam locomotives in service. The Union Pacific purchased its last steam locomotive in 1944. Known as engine 844 (later 8444), it sped main line passenger trains across Nebraska and Wyoming until the mid-1950s and then saw occasional duty until the end of the decade hauling grain during the harvest season. By the early 1970s, steam locomotives had become such a historical curiosity that the Union Pacific placed locomotive 8444 at the center of its exhibit at Spokane's Expo '74, and it still attracts large and admiring crowds whenever it makes an appearance at the head of special passenger trains.

Diesels represented a revolutionary advance in transportation technology: they required less maintenance and were more efficient than steam locomotives and hence less costly to operate. Diesels required no stops for water and could run five hundred or six hundred miles without refueling, compared to only a hundred miles or so for steam engines. In addition, they decreased and then eliminated the need for firemen. Diesels not only reduced the size of the work force, but also rendered many a small railroad town obsolete because there was no need to stop to service the engines. Admittedly diesels were far less picturesque than steam engines, but railroads struggling to survive the troubles of the 1950s had to put financial considerations first. For that reason it is not surprising that the first major railroad in the Pacific Northwest to completely dieselize was the hard-pressed Milwaukee Road.[4]

*One of Southern Pacific's new diesel locomotives crests the Cascade Range east of Eugene on February 19, 1956. The 1950s and 1960s were difficult years for railroads burdened by increasing competition, regulation, and antiquated work rules. Technologies like diesel locomotives brought greater efficiency to railroad operations even as competitors gained additional advantages. Oregon Historical Society 84228, file 891-B-2.*

By the late 1950s, steam locomotives were an uncommon sight on railroads in the Pacific Northwest, and by the end of the 1980s, so were cabooses. Gone too were the once familiar slat-sided stockcars that hauled bawling herds of cattle to market. As late as 1969, American railroads still had more than fifteen thousand stockcars in service, but by the early 1980s they had become a rarity. Much of what freight trains now carry consists of new automobiles, merchandise in double-stacked containers, and bulky commodities like lumber, grain, and coal, much of it traveling in single-purpose unit trains. An increasing volume of the railroads' transcontinental freight might once have gone by way of the

Panama Canal. It takes from thirteen to seventeen days to move freight from Tokyo to New York by ship and rail compared with twenty-three to thirty-one days on the all-water route.[5]

In 1966 railroad freight traffic in the United States (in ton-miles) was roughly twice what it had been in 1916, but it had dropped from 77 percent to less than 43 percent of the total intercity freight movement. Competitors included river and canal barges, pipelines, and especially intercity trucks. Railroads battled back with unit trains of grain and coal, so that by 1980 an estimated 60 percent of all grain in the United States went by rail. Until the 1960s, grain was typically hauled by boxcar; now it traveled in covered hopper cars.[6]

Perhaps the most dramatic development of recent times was the increased amount of coal hauled by western railroads. As late as the 1950s the coal industry was declining or stagnant. The Northern Pacific liquidated its mining operations at Roslyn, Washington, and Colstrip, Montana, in 1956 when coal was not competitive with oil at three dollars a barrel. Then came a series of sharp price increases for oil, and Colstrip made a remarkable comeback. When the first dedicated coal train left Colstrip for an electric-generating plant in Minnesota in 1969, it signified a new era. In October 1973, the Arab-Israeli war sent the price of oil up to thirteen dollars a barrel and further spurred coal production in Montana and Wyoming. As a result of the energy boom of the 1970s and 1980s, both the Union Pacific and the Burlington Northern laid hundreds of miles of new track across Wyoming.[7]

Across the Pacific Northwest, welded rails and concrete ties gave even the right-of-way a new look. Heavier freight loads meant that track had to be redesigned to carry more weight at the expense of express-train speeds. One way to do this was to flatten the elevation of the outer rail on curves, although this forced passenger trains to operate at slower speeds.

## To Be Discontinued

PERHAPS THE SINGLE MOST DRAmatic change to occur on American railroads in recent decades was the almost complete disappearance of intercity passenger trains. During the recession of 1958, people in the railroad industry talked wistfully of a crash program to save the passenger train. They recalled how a quarter of a century earlier, western railroads had introduced lightweight, diesel-powered streamliners and slashed fares to generate business during the Great Depression. But no miracle train appeared after 1958.[8]

With the exception of the four war years—1942 to 1945—the ratio of passenger-train revenues to expenses had indicated a loss every year since 1930, although no one could say with confidence just how much money that entailed. Beginning January 1,

*The camera of Russell Lee captured workmen loading bulk wheat into a barge at Port Kelley, Washington, on the Columbia River in July 1941. The waterway made a spectacular comeback as a competitor to railroads in the 1970s when a series of federal dams created a water highway from Lewiston, Idaho, to the sea. Much of western Montana's grain crop traveled by truck to Lewiston and from there by water to markets in the Far East. Library of Congress 15761, LC-USF3439847.*

*A Burlington Northern freight hauls the twin commodities of grain and lumber north along a branch line through Washington's Palouse country to Spokane in the summer of 1985. Photo by author.*

1936, the Interstate Commerce Commission required railroads to separate their passenger and freight revenues according to an accounting formula that made industry executives increasingly aware of just how little passenger service contributed to total corporate income. The Milwaukee Road reported in 1938 that freight accounted for eighty-three cents of every income dollar, and passenger service for a mere eight cents.[9]

The Interstate Commerce Commission (ICC) formula, however, obscured as much as it clarified. It was designed to make sure that passenger revenues not only met direct costs but also covered part of a railroad's general overhead expenses, such as the cost of shops or management, although there was little likelihood that salaries of top executives added to the expense of carrying passengers. Passenger service on all but a handful of lines was a by-product of carrying freight, yet the ICC formula

saddled it with expenses that would drop only slightly even if all passenger trains were eliminated.

Because of apparent flaws in the accounting formula, some railroad executives remained certain that streamliners more than covered their direct costs of operation. The Santa Fe, for instance, recorded a passenger deficit of $23 million in 1948 and $30 million in 1949 under the ICC formula, but when its managers considered only direct costs, they concluded that their passenger trains actually showed a profit of $23 million for 1948 and $26 million for 1949. They had sufficient faith in their own calculations to justify modernizing long-distance trains like the popular El Capitan. Even if passenger service lost money, railroad executives remained convined that streamliners had prestige value and that an El Capitan, Empire Builder, or Olympian Hiawatha was justified because it generated additional freight as well as passenger revenues.

Some people went so far as to argue that passenger-train deficits were actually nothing more than an accounting problem. They blasted the so-called deficit based on the Interstate Commerce Commission's formula as "largely illusory and unreal." There were others, however, who believed that the formula missed the mark on the low, not the high, side. Yet in 1957 when the passenger-train deficit climbed to $723 million according to the formula, it was hard to argue that such losses were illusory. American railroads were now spending $161.86 for every $100 of passenger revenue grossed. No wonder many railroad executives after that year considered passenger service an intolerable financial millstone, especially during the 1958 recession.

In response to the railroad industry's crisis, Congress passed the Transportation Act of 1958, one section of which allowed railroads to appeal to the Interstate Commerce Commission when state authorities were unwilling or unreasonably slow in responding to petitions to reduce passenger service being operated at a loss within the state. Prior to passage of the measure, the federal government had no authority over discontinuance of intrastate passenger trains. That was a matter for state regulators.

State utility commissioners or other authorities were subjected to enormous political and labor pressures to prevent discontinuance of the last passenger train on a line. Despite this, the state of Washington had generally granted railroads permission to discontinue unprofitable passenger trains, a total of twenty-one between 1952 and 1956, but North Dakota had done just the opposite, jealously guarding its right to preserve the last local on any major branch line in the state even when it ran nearly empty.

Only one month after passage of the Transportation Act of 1958, the Interstate Commerce Commission published a special report by its examiner Howard Hosmer. He predicted that in another decade the railroad passenger coach "may take its place in the transportation museum along with the stage coach, the side-wheeler, and the steam locomotive." He emphatically denied that the passenger service deficit was a bookkeeping phantom. The problem "is real and serious," he warned, and it would impair the ability of railroads to transport freight efficiently. He blamed the deficit on the "tremendous inflation in railroad operating costs" since World War II—caused in part by government promotion of highway and air transportation.[10]

Hosmer's prediction of the demise of intercity passenger-train service in the United States by 1970 was remarkably close to the mark. During the decade after 1958, the Interstate Commerce Commission approved elimination of nearly a thousand passenger trains, even though the process remained long and tedious. Federal regulators permitted discontinuance of a steady parade of passenger trains across the Pacific Northwest, yet they sometimes denied a petition, as they did the Southern Pacific's request to terminate service between Portland and Oakland. Still other trains ceased under state provisions.[11]

A sharp decline in passenger ridership forced the Milwaukee Road to file notice with the Interstate Commerce Commission on December 6, 1960, that it desired to drop all service west of Minneapolis under a provision of the 1958 law, citing competition from highways and commercial aviation as the reason. The railroad revealed that for the year ending in October 1959 passenger expenses west of Minneapolis were $4.23 a mile and income was $2.51.

Public hearings held in early 1961 revealed the full dimension of the featherbedding problem. An employee workday was typically based on the distance a passenger train could travel in 1919 at an average speed of twenty miles per hour, although a streamliner averaged forty miles per hour and was powered by a diesel locomotive that required no stoking by a fireman. This arachaic practice together with full-crew laws in some states meant that the

Olympian Hiawatha between Minneapolis and Tacoma required twenty-six different engine crews and twenty-one different train crews. That translated into twenty-one conductors, fifty-five trainmen, twenty-six engineers, twenty-seven firemen, plus a varying number of stewards, waiters, cooks, and porters.[12]

The Interstate Commerce Commission was sympathetic to the Milwaukee Road's plight because the Olympian Hiawatha was an unprofitable train sapping the strength of a weak railroad. A fifty-year tradition ended on May 22, 1961, when the Olympian Hiawatha ceased running on the western seven hundred miles beyond Butte (actually Deer Lodge, a division point, where the train was serviced and turned around). The Milwaukee Road estimated that discontinuing the westernmost route of the Olympian Hiawatha saved $1.7 million a year. Following further petitions, the train was cut back to Aberdeen, South Dakota, in early 1964, and finally eliminated altogether in 1969. Federal regulators had been reluctant to terminate service in South Dakota where it was the sole passenger train running east and west across the state.[13]

For the Milwaukee Road's three former competitors in the Pacific Northwest, the Seattle world's fair and elimination of the 10 percent federal transportation tax in 1962 boosted passenger service revenues—3.5 percent over 1961 for the Union Pacific, 11.4 for the Northern Pacific, and 16.1 for the Great Northern. These were the highest passenger service revenues recorded for the Northern Pacific since 1929, with the exception of the war years, and during that summer the Great Northern often operated a second section of its Western Star.[14]

It was, however, only a temporary increase, because in 1963 Union Pacific passenger revenues slipped 9.4 percent, and those of both the Great Northern and Northern Pacific dropped more than 17 percent. Making the decline all the more discouraging was that, during the same year, promotion

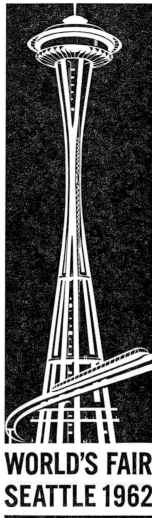

**PLAN NEXT SUMMER'S VACATION**

to include Seattle's great

**CENTURY 21**

**SPACE AGE WORLD'S FAIR**

The Fair will be open April 21 through October 21, 1962 and will attract thousands of visitors from all parts of the world.

Be sure to include this "look into the future" in your vacation plans for next summer. Ask any Northern Pacific representative or your favorite travel agency for routing, schedules, fares and other travel information.

NP offices are located in most principal cities (see back cover of this folder), or address

**G. W. Rodine
Passenger Traffic Manager**

**NORTHERN PACIFIC RAILWAY**
St. Paul 1, Minn.

by four passenger-minded western lines—the Santa Fe, Union Pacific, Northern Pacific, and Great Northern—had accounted for over half the total advertising expenditure by all American railroads.[15]

By 1964 the railroad share of intercity passenger service in the United States by common carrier was down to 20 percent, while that of airlines climbed to 53 percent, the first time the figure topped 50 percent. The 4,600-mile-long St. Louis–San Francisco became the longest freight-only railroad in the United States in 1967. At this time even railroads that had been loyal supporters of the passenger train gave up hope.

Contributing to their gloomy outlook was a decision by the Post Office Department in the mid-1960s to divert mail from railroads to highway and air carriers. Introduction of the Zip Code system further accelerated abandonment of railway post office cars. So much mail was removed from passenger trains that the railroads' annual mail revenues dropped by eighty million dollars during a five-year period. When the Post Office removed its cars from nearly all Santa Fe trains in the fall of 1967, that company responded with a proposal to discontinue passenger service except for its top three streamliners.

The *Saturday Review* in a 1969 article titled "Ten Best Rail Rides in the U.S." commended the Empire Builder, North Coast Limited, and City of Portland. Louis W. Menk, head of the Northern Pacific, admitted that he would like to discontinue the North Coast Limited but emphasized that "it is our intention to continue this crack train on a daily schedule, to continue upgrading the service and maintaining the fine tradition of excellence it had earned." That was despite the train's annual loss of $2.6 million. The Union Pacific was committed to maintaining excellent trains between key cities and a minimum of anything else. The railroad reduced the once popular Portland Rose to a mixed freight operating out of a modest building on the north edge of the Kansas City stockyards and similarly downgraded the Spokane to a single coach between its namesake city and Hinkle, Oregon, where no connection was made.[16]

An era ended on December 31, 1968, when Pullman ceased to operate sleeping cars and turned that responsibility and about a thousand leased cars over to individual railroads. The move was a long time coming. From 1947 until the end of service, all newly built Pullman cars were owned by the individual railroads and leased to Pullman for operation. Dining cars, one of the other amenities of rail travel, had long been regarded as "loss leaders," and now they disappeared from many trains. Following the Seattle world's fair of 1962, the Southern Pacific announced that "automat cars" with vending machines would replace diners on trains between Portland and San Francisco.

Things got so bad on the Penn Central that thirty-five passengers on its once deluxe Spirit of St. Louis in 1969 sat down in front of the train and refused to budge until repairs could be made to the train's single coach. The car was without lighting, air conditioning, or drinking water despite hundred-degree weather outside. Such horror stories prominently featured in daily newspapers raised questions about whether the American passenger train was a victim of suicide or murder. Senator George Smathers of Florida pondered aloud during discussion of the abortive Passenger Train Act of 1960: "It's sort of a question which comes first, the chicken or the egg, and we are not quite certain whether some of the passenger loss results from bad service or whether the passenger loss then results in the deterioration of cars and so on."[17]

The evidence is mixed, but one thing is clear, the federal government must take primary responsibility for the death of the passenger train. During the crucial years from World War II to 1978, the national government gave $103 billion in subsidies to highway users, $31 billion to air, and only $6 billion to rail. Between 1946 and 1956, Class I railroads and the Pullman Company installed 5,858 new passenger cars at an investment of $652 million.[18]

The Southern Pacific was much maligned for the

*The stark cover design of Amtrak's first timetable seemed to symbolize the bare-bones nature of its passenger service. Author's collection.*

declining quality of its passenger service during the 1960s, but during the previous decade the railroad had spent $35.5 million to update passenger equipment, not including locomotives. "It's just a change in the American way of life," explained the Southern Pacific president Donald J. Russell. "You can't make people do what they don't want to."[19] Whereas passenger trains had once introduced new technologies that reshaped society, they now were the victims of profound social and technological change.

## Amtrak

FROM 1958 UNTIL THE CREATION OF Amtrak in 1971, the nation's passenger trains seemed destined for extinction. By 1970 the number of intercity passenger trains in the United States had dropped from a pre–World War II high of approximately twenty thousand per day to fewer than four hundred. Long-distance passenger trains probably would have disappeared exactly as Howard Hosmer predicted back in 1958 but for creation of the National Railroad Passenger Corporation. Popularly known as Amtrak (from *American travel by track*), the federally supported agency started life with $40 million in direct government grants, $100 million in government-guaranteed loans, and another $200 million from railroads buying into the system. Most American railroads—with the conspicuous exceptions of the Denver & Rio Grande Western, the Chicago, Rock Island & Pacific, and the Southern—turned their passenger operations over to Amtrak.[20]

The twenty railroads that bought into Amtrak paid fees over a three-year period equivalent to 50 percent of each carrier's 1969 passenger service deficit. For the Burlington Northern that was $33 million, and for the Union Pacific it was $19 million. Of Amtrak's original 1,190 cars, 441 came from the

Nationwide Schedules of Intercity Passenger Service

Effective May 1, 1971

National Railroad Passenger Corporation
955 L'Enfant Plaza
Washington, D.C. 20024

Santa Fe, 196 from the Burlington Northern, 120 from the Union Pacific, and 80 from the Southern Pacific. The only nonwestern railroad to contribute a substantial number of passenger cars was Seaboard Coastline. When Amtrak began at 12:01 a.m., May 1, 1971, it preserved fewer than two hundred daily trains on a nationwide passenger network that in a single day shrank from 43,000 miles to 16,000. Amtrak hauled an average of 45,000 passengers a day, or approximately .5 percent of all intercity travelers in the United States.[21]

The number of lines with passenger-train service in the Pacific Northwest shrank to two. Amtrak preserved the Empire Builder between Seattle, St. Paul, and Chicago on the old Great Northern route across Montana and inaugurated a new train, the Coast Starlight, to offer triweekly service from Seattle, Portland, and Oakland to Los Angeles (and

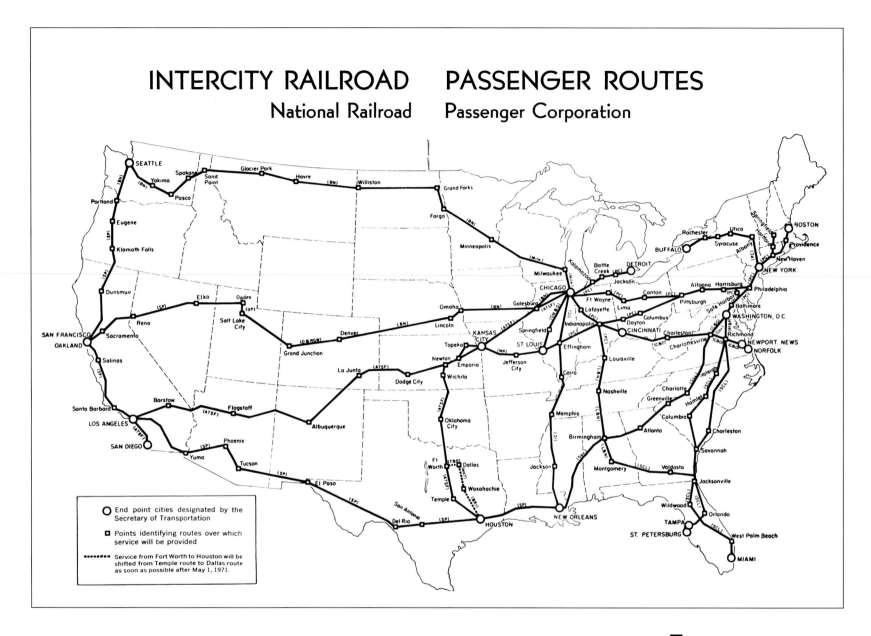

# INTERCITY RAILROAD     PASSENGER ROUTES
## National Railroad     Passenger Corporation

O End point cities designated by the
  Secretary of Transportation

□ Points identifying routes over which
  service will be provided

•••••• Service from Fort Worth to Houston will be
  shifted from Temple route to Dallas route
  as soon as possible after May 1, 1971.

even through to San Diego for a few months), service that had no historic precedent. Dropped were the Union Pacific's City of Portland and the Northern Pacific's venerable North Coast Limited.

Subsequently restored to the Amtrak system were the Pacific Internationals between Seattle and Vancouver, British Columbia (from July 1972 through September 1981), the North Coast Hiawatha from Minneapolis to Spokane along the old Northern Pacific route (from June 1971 until October 1979), and the Pioneer across southern Idaho to link Salt Lake City and Portland (in June 1977). In 1981 Amtrak established an Empire Builder connection to Portland along the scenic Columbia River route of the old Spokane, Portland & Seattle Railway. For more than a year beginning in October 1980, Amtrak

*The initial map of Amtrak's passenger service shows only two routes serving the Pacific Northwest. Author's collection.*

operated four Willamette Valley trains between Portland and Eugene under funding agreement with the state of Oregon. This was part of a failed attempt to offer frequent service in the heavily populated corridor between Seattle, Portland, and Eugene.[22]

The diversity of equipment in Amtrak's early years gradually gave way to uniformity as old cars were refurbished and new ones built. In October 1979, double-deck "Superline" cars appeared on the Empire Builder, the first long-distance train to receive them. Even before such equipment was added to the Coast Starlight, heavy ridership had already made it an outstanding success. One of Amtrak's biggest problems was that across most of the United States it operated on tracks of the freight-carrying railroads, which meant lower speeds for passenger trains and occasionally a less direct route between major population centers. Its coach fares, moreover, were often higher than economy fares on airlines, and the price of sleeper accommodations made them an expensive luxury.

No national railroad or passenger system anywhere in the world makes money, something ignored by critics who noted that the federal subsidy for Amtrak had reached $578 million in 1978, or about $2 for every $1 taken in. A round of federal budget cutting wiped out the North Coast Hiawatha, although a nationwide gasoline shortage in 1979 brought some short-term benefits to Amtrak, and the Union Passenger Terminal in Los Angeles enjoyed some of the best business in its history. Ironically, in the battle with automobile and airline competitors during the 1970s and 1980s, bus lines fared no better than railroads in retaining passengers. Greyhound did the same thing that railroads had once done by pruning unprofitable routes, and it also absorbed its onetime rival, Continental Trailways. But when faced with a prolonged strike, the beleaguered carrier declared bankruptcy in the spring of 1990.

## Competition and a Changing Signature

WITH THE NATION'S INTERCITY bus industry suffering from airline and automobile competition much as railroad passenger service had suffered from bus and automobile competition in the 1920s and 1930s, events seem to have come nearly full circle in recent years. In fact, if one theme dominated the history of Pacific Northwest railroads during much of the twentieth century it was the changing nature of competition and the industry's response to it. No decade since 1920 failed to witness a dramatic development either in new modes and levels of competition or in the amount of federal or state involvement with various competitors.

Percentage Distribution of Intercity Passenger Traffic in the United States

| Year | Automobile | Train | Airline | Other |
|------|-----------|-------|---------|-------|
| 1926 | 71 | 22 | <0.1 | 7.0 |
| 1937 | 85 | 10 | 0.2 | 5.0 |
| 1944 | 54 | 31 | 2.2 | 12.8 |
| 1954 | 89 | 5 | 3.1 | 2.9 |
| 1990 | 82 | 1 | 12.0 | 5.0 |

Over the years, competition had taken such forms as the increased use of private automobiles during the 1920s, air coach and interstate highways during the 1950s, and jumbo jets and commuter airlines during the 1970s and 1980s. There were also related developments in growing government regulation, and then, starting with the airline industry in the late 1970s, dramatic deregulation of American transportation. In response to nearly a century of change, railroads adopted new technology— perhaps the most important being streamlined

*Aerial view of Spokane's industrial heart in the late 1930s. In 1974 Spokane hosted an international exposition that brought dramatic changes to its downtown area by spurring conversion of an unsightly 3,800-acre complex of warehouses and railroad tracks into park-and-recreation facilities along the Spokane River. The theme of the fair, "Progress without Pollution," was in tune with the region's growing environmental consciousness. Eastern Washington State Historical Society, 6472.*

passenger trains, diesel locomotives, and computerized dispatching systems—and these in turn had an impact on work rules and jobs. There was the creation of mega-railroads through merger, and then the shrinkage of systems through formation of regional carriers. If anything, the changes demanded by competition only accelerated in recent decades.

Competition likewise redefined the relationship between railroads and Pacific Northwest history. During the first two railway ages, until 1917, railroads and regional development formed two sides of the same coin. During the era of competition, that relationship grew far less obvious to most people, although railroads still played a vital role in hauling the region's commodities to market, and they remained among its largest landholders. There is still abundant evidence of the railroad industry's historic role in shaping the modern Pacific Northwest, if one knows where to look. The signature in steel forged in the late nineteenth century remains in place, in some cases only in the form of enduring patterns of trade, travel, settlement, and ways of perceiving the region's character.

*It is the same everywhere, from the Mississippi to the Pacific. Men seem to live in the future rather than in the present: not that they fail to work while it is called to-day, but that they see the country not merely as it is, but as it will be, twenty, fifty, a hundred years hence, when the seedlings shall have grown to forest trees.*
—James Bryce, The American Commonwealth *(1893)*

# Epilogue: Pacific Northwest Railroads in Perspective

THERE ARE MANY REASONS WHY the railroad signature across the Pacific Northwest is less visible today than it was even a generation ago. The most basic one became clear to me in 1982 when I flew from Seattle to San Francisco and returned home by train a few days later. Juxtaposing the two modes of transportation made me realize as never before that commercial aviation has become an integral part of contemporary consumer society, while railroads serve the important but far less visible producer economy. At the entrance to airports in Seattle and San Francisco, billboards beckoned me to vacation in Mazatlan or Acapulco or Honolulu. In-flight magazines and an accompanying airline catalog encouraged me to purchase electronic gadgets I had never realized I needed. In the terminal a steady parade of smartly dressed travelers sought to impress with the latest fashions from Brooks Brothers, Gucci, and Calvin Klein.

A person traveling on Amtrak's Coast Starlight is certainly not isolated from consumer society. But I was overwhelmed at the contrast between the somewhat contrived ambience pervading a commercial flight and the genuine ugliness of industrial neighborhoods that suffused my train trip. Coming into any community of consequence between Oak-

land and Seattle, we threaded our way through an unsightly maze of warehouses, wholesale distributors, parts shops, and storage depots. It struck me then that what I was really seeing aboard the Coast Starlight was California and the Pacific Northwest in their dirty but functional overalls. Here was the production side of America that many people today seldom know unless the closure of a mine or steel plant makes the evening news. From the train I also saw productive farmland and ranchland close at hand, while from the air the same areas formed a checkered tablecloth spread out thirty thousand feet below me.

Our national system of interstate highways has done much the same thing to isolate Americans from the production side of the national economy. Instead of being able to sample sun-ripened tomatoes or sip fresh cherry cider at a farmer's roadside stand, we are confined to the concrete and asphalt by endless miles of fence wire. Even at the interchanges we experience the consuming side of America in the fast-food outlets and service stations that appear to have been stamped from the same cookie cutter. John Steinbeck expressed it well in *Travels with Charley* (1961) when he prophesied—tongue in cheek, perhaps—that, when the expressways were completed, "it will be possible to drive from New

*Recorders of the railroad signature in steel: members of the press corps huddle with their bulky movie and view cameras before the Cle Elum, Washington, substation of the Milwaukee Road. They were there to commemorate the activities staged to celebrate electrification of the Milwaukee Road's line across the Cascade Range. Washington State Historical Society, Curtis 39297.*

York to California without seeing a thing."[1]

Numerous freight trains still thunder along the main lines of the Pacific Northwest, and Amtrak maintains a tradition of long-distance passenger-train service, but like the production side of the economy, the influence of railroads on the Pacific Northwest tends to remain at the back edge of public consciousness. To be sure, railroads had their most immediate impact on everyday life through the once ubiquitous passenger trains. When they discontinued those trains in response to changing social trends, railroads receded from direct contact with the public. Only when there is a nationwide rail strike, or a freight train accident severe enough to make the evening news, or a special celebration involving one of the remaining active steam locomotives do most people (apart from buffs) notice the railroads.

In addition, even the railroads' physical signature written in track across the region is shorter and less visible than it once was. The network of tracks in the four Northwest states in 1986 was 11,959 miles long, having declined more than one-quarter from

its peak of 17,216 miles in 1933, and that total does not reflect the formerly numerous logging and electric interurban railroads. The disappearance of the twin ribbons of steel has been especially noticeable in the region's mining, timber, and agricultural counties. Here, ironically, railroad signatures of another sort have become progressively more visible in some places where there never were any tracks, primarily in the forests of the Pacific Northwest. Railroad land grants dating from the 1860s have created contention between industry and environmentalists. Plum Creek Timber Company, the logging arm of Burlington Resources (the heir to the old Northern Pacific land grant), was criticized by environmentalists for its forest management practices and by organized labor for exporting raw logs to Asia.[2]

Railroads probably left their longest and yet most subtle impact on Pacific Northwest life as a result of their century-long effort to advertise the region to prospective tourists and settlers. In this way railroads served not merely as carriers of passengers and freight but also as transmitters of visual information. The journalist Ray Stannard Baker grasped this fact shortly after 1900 when he naively suggested to a railroad agent that his company might be interested in development. "Why," responded the official, "the West is purely a railroad enterprise. We started it in our publicity department." The remark contained more than the usual grain of truth, thought Baker, who added that "the West was inevitable but the railroad was the instrument of its fate."[3]

During the past century, tens of thousands, perhaps even millions of people scanned railroad brochures and broadsides that portrayed life in the Pacific Northwest essentially in terms of an advertiser's idealized civilization. Boosters sought to inspire newcomers to find personal success and happiness in the larger-than-lifesize natural landscape of the Pacific Northwest, to be inspired to fashion a "new empire" for themselves and their children. The future of the region could be whatever people of perception and ambition willed it to be. The railroad vision for the region was essentially optimistic and unencumbered by history (unlike that of the South) except to glorify the feats of explorers like Lewis and Clark, who were presented as preparing the way for the latter-day empire builders.

Even today the average resident of the Pacific Northwest appears inclined to define the region's character in terms of its natural setting rather than its history or economic activities or culture. The Pacific Northwest is a region where human landscapes are often "prettified" to make them appealing to tourists. Along the Oregon coast an abandoned sawmill becomes a storage facility for yachts and other pleasure craft of the affluent, while in other locations industrial facilities become shopping centers and malls catering to bargain-conscious consumers. The Pacific Northwest is still a major producer of raw materials, but in future years it will become more than ever a consumer-oriented region with a growing service economy and booming tourist trade. Ideas and images created by railroad promoters a century ago to sell the Pacific Northwest will become perhaps even more important in determining how residents perceive the character of their changing region.

*Finis. This spectacular wreck occurred as a result of a snowslide that destroyed a portion of the Northern Pacific's "S"-bridge on the line that crossed the Bitterroot Mountains between Wallace, Idaho, and Missoula, Montana, on February 10, 1903. Special Collections and Archives, University of Idaho Library, Barnard-Stockbridge Collection, 8-X254.*

# Notes

## Preface

1. John R. Stilgoe, *Metropolitan Corridor: Railroads and the American Scene* (New Haven: Yale University Press, 1983).

2. Lucius Beebe and Charles Clegg, *The Age of Steam: A Classic Album of American Railroading* (New York: Rinehart & Co., [1957]).

3. James W. Scott with Colin R. Vasquez, John G. Newman, and Bruce C. Sarjeant, *Washington: A Centennial Atlas* (Bellingham: Center for Pacific Northwest Studies, Western Washington University, 1989), 90.

## Introduction: Railroad Time and Space in the New Northwest

1. Dorothy M. Johnson, "Flour Famine in Alder Gulch, 1864," *Montana, the Magazine of Western History* 7 (January 1957): 18–27.

2. Ian R. Bartky, "Running on Time," *Railroad History* No. 159 (Autumn 1988): 18–38.

3. C. S. Stebbins, "Standard Time," *Union Pacific Magazine* 1 (May 1922): 9.

4. As quoted in Stewart H. Holbrook, *The Story of American Railroads* (New York: Crown Publishers, 1947), 354–59.

5. John H. White, *The Great Yellow Fleet: A History of American Railroad Refrigerator Cars* (San Marino, Calif.: Golden West Books, 1986).

6. Harold H. Baetjer, *A Book That Gathers No Dust* ([Washington, D.C.: Association of American Railroads, ca. 1950]).

7. *The Official Guide of the Railways and Steam Navigation Lines of the United States, Porto Rico, Canada, Mexico and Cuba* (New York: National Railway Publication Co., June 1916); *First Annual Report of the Statistics of Railways in the United States to the Interstate Commerce Commission for the Year Ending June 30, 1888* (Washington, D.C.: Government Printing Office, 1889).

8. The popular name Milwaukee Road did not come into widespread use until the mid-1920s, but as a matter of convenience it will be used throughout *Railroad Signatures across the Pacific Northwest* to designate the Chicago, Milwaukee & St. Paul Railway. In earlier years the carrier was often called the St. Paul Road.

9. *Automobile* 33 (Dec. 30, 1915): 1.

10. Stewart H. Holbrook, *Far Corner: A Personal View of the Pacific Northwest* (New York: Macmillan Co., 1952), 245; Kramer A. Adams, *Logging Railroads of the West* (Seattle: Superior Publishing Co., 1961).

## Portages by Rail

1. James F. Shepherd, "The Development of Wheat Production in the Pacific Northwest," *Agricultural History* 49 (1975): 258–71.

2. W. W. Baker, *Forty Years a Pioneer: Business Life of Dorsey Syng Baker, 1848–1888* (Seattle: Lowman & Hanford Co., 1934); Alfred McVey and Iris Meyers, eds., *Doctor Baker's Railroad: The Walla Walla & Columbia River Railroad* (Walla Walla: Walla Walla City-County Bicentennial Committee, [1975]).

3. William F. Willingham, "Engineering the Cascades Canal and Locks, 1876–1896," *Oregon Historical Quarterly* 88 (1987): 231.

NO 14 DEPOT AT DALLAS ORE

*When the depot was a center of community life: Dallas, Oregon, was a busy junction of two Southern Pacific branches serving the west side of the Willamette Valley. Oregon Historical Society, 11179.*

4. Frank B. Gill, "Oregon's First Railway: The Oregon Portage Railroad and the Cascades of the Columbia River," *Oregon Historical Quarterly* 25 (1924): 171–235.

5. E. Kimbark MacColl and Harry H. Stein, "The Economic Power of Portland's Early Merchants, 1851–1861," *Oregon Historical Quarterly* 89 (1988): 150. See also Dorothy O. Johansen, "Capitalism on the Far Western Frontier: The Oregon Steam Navigation Company," Ph.D. diss. (University of Washington, 1941).

6. Idaho is not a Shoshone word that means Gem of the Mountains as is commonly thought. See Carlos A. Schwantes, *In Mountain Shadows: A History of Idaho* (Lincoln: University of Nebraska Press, 1991), 59.

7. The Oregon Steam Navigation Company built the steamboat *Shoshone* on the banks of the middle Snake River in southern Idaho and later risked losing it on a dangerous one-way voyage to Lewiston in 1870. No steamboat ever made the journey upriver through Hells Canyon.

8. Donald Jackson, *Voyages of the Steamboat Yellow Stone* (New York: Ticknor & Fields, 1985); William E. Lass, *A History of Steamboating on the Upper Missouri* (Lincoln: University of Nebraska Press, 1962); Kenneth M. Hammer, "River and Rail: Competition in the Upper-Missouri Basin," in *Railroads in the West*, ed. Don L. Hofsommer (Manhattan, Kans.: Sunflower University Press, 1978), 41–51.

9. Lewiston *Morning Tribune*, Nov. 19, 1939.

10. F. E. Smith, "Evolution of Traveling Comforts," *Union Pacific Magazine* 1 (August 1922): 5.

11. Quoted in Eugene V. Smalley, *History of the Northern Pacific Railroad* (New York: G. P. Putnam's Sons, 1883), 65.

12. Quoted in Smalley, *History of the Northern Pacific*, 89.

13. W. Milnor Roberts, *Special Report of a Reconnoissance of the Route for the Northern Pacific Railroad between Lake Superior and Puget Sound* (Philadelphia: Jay Cooke & Co., [1869]).

14. Smalley, *History of the Northern Pacific*, 173.

15. Elmo Richardson, *BLM's Billion-Dollar Checkerboard: Managing the O&C Lands* (Santa Cruz, Calif.: Forest History Society, 1980).

16. The history of the Oregon & California Railroad land grant is very complex. Among the stipulations of Congress was that land be sold to actual settlers only in lots of 160 acres. The railroad ignored this clause by selling over half the grants in units of more than 2,000 acres each. After lengthy investigation, the federal government forced the Southern Pacific to return 2.9 million unsold acres in 1916.

## Henry Villard and the Empire of the Columbia

1. Two additional transcontinenal lines were completed in Canada after this time: the Grand Trunk Pacific Railway (1914) and Canadian Northern Railway (1915).

2. Henry Villard, *Memoirs of Henry Villard*, 2 vols. (Boston: Houghton Mifflin & Co., 1904), II:311.

3. Villard, *Memoirs*, II:311.

4. Portland *Oregonian*, Sept. 9, 1883.

5. *Oregonian*, Sept. 9, 1883.

6. Fearful of being bypassed by the Northern Pacific, hundreds of Puget Sound residents contributed money and labor to build the Seattle & Walla Walla Railroad. Later, under the name Columbia & Puget Sound, the railroad tapped important coal deposits in the Cascade foothills east of Seattle but never crossed the range. The parent Oregon Improvement Company defaulted in 1893 and was reorganized as the Pacific Coast Company.

7. James F. Rustling, *Across America: or, The Great West and the Pacific Coast* (New York: Sheldon & Co., 1875), 265.

8. As quoted in Julius Grodinsky, *Transcontinental Railway Strategy, 1869–1893: A Study of Businessmen* (Philadelphia: University of Pennsylvania Press, 1962), 206.

9. Charles Francis Adams, Jr., as quoted in Julius Grodinsky, *Jay Gould: His Business Career, 1867–1892* (Philadelphia: University of Pennsylvania Press, 1957), 159.

10. The Utah Northern Railroad was reorganized as the Utah & Northern Railroad in 1878 and its contemplated route through southeastern Idaho reoriented. Before the railroad converted to standard gauge in 1887, some observers claimed that it was the longest narrow-gauge line in the world.

11. James L. Onderdonk, *Idaho: Facts and Statistics Concerning Its Mining, Farming, Stock Raising, Lumbering and Other Resources and Industries* (San Francisco: A. L. Bancroft, 1885), 143.

12. The best account of building the line across the Cascades to Tacoma is in Murray Morgan's *Puget's Sound: A Narrative History of Early Tacoma and the Southern Sound* (Seattle: University of Washington Press, 1979), 195–211.

13. Thomas W. Riddle, "Populism in the Palouse: Old Ideals and New Realities," *Pacific Northwest Quarterly* 65 (1974): 97–109.

14. The Union Pacific was probably right about the power behind the Hunt system. The Washington & Columbia River Railway, as it was formally known after a foreclosure sale in 1892, was absorbed by the Northern Pacific in 1907.

15. *Railway Age* 17 (Aug. 12, 1892): 275; *The Oregonian's Handbook of the Pacific Northwest* (Portland: Lewis & Dryden, 1894), 47.

16. The Central Pacific became part of the Southern Pacific in the mid-1880s.

17. James J. Hill to George, Lord Mount Stephen, June 15, 1904, James J. Hill Papers, James Jerome Hill Reference Library, St. Paul, Minn.

## Shapers of a New Northwest

1. Robert Strahorn, "Ninety Years of Boyhood" (1942), 243. This typescript is located in the Terteling Library, College of Idaho, Caldwell, and is available also on microfilm from the Idaho State Historical Society in Boise.

2. Strahorn, "Ninety Years of Boyhood," 43.

3. Strahorn, "Ninety Years of Boyhood," 246–47.

4. Carrie Adell Strahorn, *Fifteen Thousand Miles by Stage*, 2 vols. (1911; rpt. Lincoln: University of Nebraska Press, 1988), II:45.

5. Strahorn, "Ninety Years of Boyhood," 253; Oliver Knight, "Robert E. Strahorn, Propagandist for the West," *Pacific Northwest Quarterly* 59 (1968): 33–45.

6. Strahorn, "Ninety Years of Boyhood," 280, and *To the Rockies and Beyond, or, a Summer on the Union Pacific Railroad and Branches* (Chicago: Belford, Clarke, and Co., 1881), 124–25. A readily available example of Strahorn's work is his *Resources and Attractions of Idaho Territory* (1881), reprint, with an Introduction by Judith Austin (Moscow: University of Idaho Press, 1990).

7. Edward S. Salomon, "Message to the Third Biennial Session of the Legislative Assembly, October 2, 1871," *Messages of the Governors of the Territory of Washington to the Legislative Assembly, 1854–1889*, ed. Charles M. Gates (Seattle: University of Washington Press, 1940), 167.

8. Arthur J. Brown, "The Promotion of Immigration to Washington, 1854–1909," *Pacific Northwest Quarterly* 36 (1945): 3–17; Seattle *Daily Press*, Feb. 4, 1888.

9. *Fertile Logged-off Lands of Latah County, Idaho* (Potlatch, Idaho: Potlatch Lumber Co., n.d), 1; Richard White, "Poor Men on Poor Lands: The Back-to-the-Land Movement of the Early Twentieth Century," *Pacific Historical Review* 49 (1980): 105–31; Emma Adams, *To and Fro, Up and Down in Southern California, Oregon and Washington, with Sketches in Arizona, New Mexico and British Columbia* (Cincinnati: Cranston & Stowe, 1888), 375.

10. No systematic effort has ever been made to identify and catalog all forms of railroad ephemera devoted to the Pacific Northwest.

11. James B. Hedges, *Henry Villard and the Railways of the Northwest* (New Haven: Yale University Press, 1930), 127–28.

12. Eugene V. Smalley, *History of the Northern Pacific Railroad* (New York: G. P. Putnam's Sons, 1883).

13. Edward Hungerford, "Railroad Advertising," *Railway Gazette* 58 (May 14, 1915): 1012.

14. Patrick Gass, *Gass's Journal of the Lewis and Clark Expedition* (1811; rpt. Chicago: A. C. McClurg, 1904), 142, 145.

15. Washington Irving, *Astoria; or, Anecdotes of an Enterprize beyond the Rocky Mountains* (1836; rpt. Boston: Twayne Publishers, 1976), 207.

16. *The Expeditions of John Charles Frémont* (1845), reprint, edited by Donald Jackson and Mary Lee Spence (Urbana: University of Illinois Press, 1970), I:520.

17. Lawrence Dodd, ed., *Narcissa Prentiss Whitman, My Journal, 1836* (Fairfield, Wash.: Ye Galleon Press, 1982), 18–20.

18. Robert Athearn, *Union Pacific Country* (Chicago: Rand McNally, 1971), 321.

19. *Inaugural Address of Governor Sylvester Pennoyer to the Legislative Assembly of the State of Oregon* (Salem: Frank C. Baker, 1887), 16.

20. Henry Villard, *The Early History of Transportation in Oregon* (Eugene: University of Oregon, 1944), 49; *West Shore*, May 1884, p. 60. The *West Shore*, first published in August 1874, was "devoted to the development of the Great West." During the years from the end of the nineteenth century until World War I, other promotional journals of this genre included the *Pacific Monthly* in Portland and the *Up-to-the-Times Magazine* in Walla Walla. The latter billed itself as an illustrated monthly of city and rural life in the intermountain Northwest.

21. Northern Pacific Railroad, *Report of the President*, 1882, p. 35.

22. Northern Pacific Railroad, *Report of the Board of Directors*, 1884, p. 39.

23. *Many Acres Open to Settlers: Along the Pacific Coast Extension of the Chicago, Milwaukee & St. Paul* ([Chicago:

*Epitomizing the first railway age was construction activity on James J. Hill's St. Paul, Minneapolis & Manitoba Railway as it extended across the plains of eastern Montana Territory in 1887. Montana Historical Society.*

*P*ortland erected a commemorative arch at First and Salmon streets to welcome Henry Villard and the Northern Pacific Railroad in September 1883. "In its social life, Portland has none of that crudity, which is the result of the hasty throwing together of incongruous elements and which is so often found in the active and rapidly growing cities of the West," bragged the Oregon State Board of Immigration. Oregon Historical Society, 891-D-Z.

Chicago, Milwaukee & St. Paul Railway, ca. 1907]), 2. This pamphlet was a reprint of an article that originally appeared in the Chicago *Record-Herald*, Dec. 1, 1907. John Foster Carr, "The Great Northwest," *Outlook* 86 (1907): 363–77.

24. *Montana* ([Chicago: Chicago, Milwaukee & St. Paul Railway, 1910]), 3; Randall R. Howard, "Following the Colonist," *Pacific Monthly* 23 (1910): 530.

25. [Rinaldo M. Hall], *The Pacific Northwest, Embracing Oregon, Washington, Idaho* (Portland: Oregon Railroad & Navigation Co., 1904), 3.

26. Helena *Record*, May 5, 1911.

27. *Inaugural Address of Governor Sylvester Pennoyer*, 15.

28. *Wealth and Resources of Oregon and Washington* (Portland: Union Pacific Railway, 1889), 1.

29. Frances Fuller Victor, *Atlantis Arisen; or, Talks of a Tourist about Oregon and Washington* (Philadelphia: J. B. Lippincott, 1891), 351–52.

30. Strahorn, "Ninety Years of Boyhood," 260.

31. Strahorn, "Ninety Years of Boyhood," 265–66, 360.

32. Villard, *The Early History of Transportation in Oregon*, 50.

33. Ray Stannard Baker, "Destiny and the Western Railroad," *Century Magazine* 75 (1908): 894.

## Traveling Too Fast: Adjustments to Railroad Power

1. Daniel Maxwell, "1885: The Railroad and Yakima City," unpublished manuscript in the author's possession. Maxwell's essay uses Northern Pacific records at the Minnesota Historical Society, St. Paul, and Washington Territory newspapers.

2. Frederick Jackson Turner, "The West and American Ideals," in Frederick Jackson Turner, *The Frontier in American History* (1920; rpt. Huntington, N.Y.: Robert E. Krieger Publishing Co., 1976), 299.

3. Alexander C. McGregor, "The Economic Impact of the Mullan Road on Walla Walla, 1860–1883," *Pacific Northwest Quarterly* 65 (1974): 118–29.

4. Ray Stannard Baker, "Destiny and the Western Railroad," *Century Magazine* 75 (1908): 893.

5. James J. Hill to C. H. Coster, Oct. 10, 1898, James J. Hill Papers, James Jerome Hill Reference Library, St. Paul, Minn.

6. For the Spokane rate controversy see Charles Edward Russell, "The Heart of the Railroad Problem," *Hampton's Magazine* 22 (1909): 592–604; Glenn Chesney

Quiett, *They Built the West: An Epic of Rails and Cities* (1934; rpt. New York: Cooper Square Publishers, 1965), 496–541.

7. Thomas R. Cox, *Mills and Markets: A History of the Pacific Coast Lumber Industry to 1900* (Seattle: University of Washington Press, 1974).

8. Frances Fuller Victor, *Atlantis Arisen; or, Talks of a Tourist about Oregon and Washington* (Philadelphia: J. B. Lippincott, 1891), 380.

9. Hill to Gaspard Farrer, Feb. 3, 1896, James J. Hill Papers, James Jerome Hill Reference Library.

10. Hill to Jacob H. Schiff, June 13, 1901, James J. Hill Papers, James Jerome Hill Reference Library.

11. *Solidarity*, May 1, 1915, p. 2.

12. On itinerant labor see Carlos A. Schwantes, "Images of the Wageworkers' Frontier," *Montana, the Magazine of Western History* 38 (Autumn 1988): 38–49.

13. E. Keogh, "Characteristics of the Hobo," *Railway Age Gazette* 52 (June 21, 1912): 1566.

14. Hill to H. D. Hurley, July 26, 1899, James J. Hill Papers, James Jerome Hill Reference Library.

15. W. Thomas White, "Protest Movements on the Northern Tier: The Pullman Boycott of 1894 and the 1922 Shopmen's Strike," in *Centennial West: Essays on the Northern Tier States*, ed. William L. Lang (Seattle: University of Washington Press, 1991), 194–226.

16. Ezra Meeker, *The Busy Life of Eighty-five Years of Ezra Meeker* (Seattle: Ezra Meeker, 1916), and *Seventy Years of Progress in Washington* (Seattle: Ezra Meeker, 1921), 319.

## The Railway Landscape

1. Hamlin Garland, "Western Landscapes," *Atlantic Monthly* 72 (1893): 808.

2. *6,000 Miles Through Wonderland* ([St. Paul: Northern Pacific Railroad, 1893]).

3. *Oregon, Washington, Idaho and Their Resources* (Portland: Oregon Railroad & Navigation Co. and Southern Pacific Co., [1904]), 71.

4. *The Fertile and Beautiful Palouse Country in Eastern Washington and Northern Idaho* (St. Paul: Northwest Magazine, 1889).

5. *The Great Northwest: A Guide-Book and Itinerary for the Use of Tourists and Travelers over the Lines of the Northern Pacific Railroad* (St. Paul: Northern News Co., 1888), 334.

6. Great Northern Railway, *Annual Report for 1928*, p. 7.

7. A. L. Eidemiller to Asahel Curtis, Aug. 3, 1929, Asahel Curtis MSS, Pacific Northwest Collection, University of Washington Libraries, Seattle.

8. Oregon Railroad & Navigation Company, *Public Timetable*, October 1900, 30.

9. *Rocky Mountain Vacations* ([St. Paul]: Northern Pacific Railway, [ca. 1910]), 7.

## New Beginnings for a New Century

1. Ray Stannard Baker, "Destiny and the Western Railroad," *Century Magazine* 75 (1908): 892.

2. Virgil G. Bogue, "Stampede Pass, Cascade Range, Washington," *Bulletin of the American Geographical Society* 27 (1895): 239–55.

3. Louis W. Hill to G. S. Wilson, July 18, 1923, Louis W. Hill Papers, James Jerome Hill Reference Library, St. Paul, Minn.

4. George R. Stewart, *Names on the Land: A Historical Account of Place-Naming in the United States* (New York: Random House, 1945), 323–25.

5. Hill County, Montana, is one exception.

6. G. Thomas Edwards and Carlos A. Schwantes, eds., *Experiences in a Promised Land: Essays in Pacific Northwest History* (Seattle: University of Washington Press, 1986), 153.

7. Ray Stannard Baker, "The Great Northwest," *Century Magazine* 65 (1903): 653.

8. Carlos A. Schwantes, *The Pacific Northwest: An Interpretive History* (Lincoln: University of Nebraska Press, 1989), 216–19.

9. James J. Hill to D. C. Shepard, March 7, 1906, James J. Hill Papers, James Jerome Hill Reference Library.

10. George Kennan, *E. H. Harriman: A Biography*, 2 vols. (Boston: Houghton Mifflin, 1922), I:139–43.

11. Carl Snyder, *American Railways as Investments* (New York: Moody Corporation, 1907), 335.

12. Hill quoted in John F. Stevens, *An Engineer's Recollections* (New York: McGraw-Hill, 1936), 32.

13. Stewart Holbrook, *The Story of American Railroads* (New York: Crown Publishers, 1947), 186.

14. Hill to J. P. Morgan & Co., Nov. 8, 1898, James J. Hill Papers, James Jerome Hill Reference Library.

15. St. Paul *Daily Dispatch*, June 2, 1912.

16. New York *Sun*, Aug. 10, 1912.

17. Frank H. Spearman, *The Strategy of Great Railroads* (New York: Charles Scribner's Sons, 1904), 84–87.

18. Hill to Gaspard Farrer, July 22, 1904, James J. Hill Papers, James Jerome Hill Reference Library; Robert Strahorn, "Ninety Years of Boyhood" (1942), 394, Terteling Library, College of Idaho, Caldwell.

19. Leonard J. Arrington, *David Eccles: Pioneer Western Industrialist* (Logan: Utah State University, 1975).

20. See John Fahey, *Inland Empire: D. C. Corbin and Spokane* (Seattle: University of Washington Press, 1965).

21. *Idaho Statesman* quoted in Anaconda *Standard*, Aug. 23, 1911.

22. *Upper Washington County Promotional League* (n.p., n.d.). The Pacific & Idaho Northern went into receivership in 1915 and was acquired by the Oregon Short Line, subsidiary of the Union Pacific, in 1936. The Gilmore & Pittsburgh Railroad operated only from 1909 to 1940.

23. Hill to George F. Baker, Aug. 11, 1910, and to Charles Steele, May 26, 1911, both in James J. Hill Papers, James Jerome Hill Reference Library.

## Fiefdoms and Baronies: Harriman and Hill Redraw the Railroad Map

1. Walter Woehlke, "The Inland Emperors," *Sunset* 27 (1911): 486.

2. Robert Strahorn, "Ninety Years of Boyhood" (1942), 387–88, Terteling Library, College of Idaho, Caldwell.

3. James A. Ward, *Railroads and the Character of America, 1820–1887* (Knoxville: University of Tennessee Press, 1986).

4. *Oregonian* quoted in Lute Pease, "The Story of the North Bank Road," *Pacific Monthly* 21 (1909): 1–14.

5. James J. Hill to Jacob Schiff, Jan. 22, 1900, James J. Hill Papers, James Jerome Hill Reference Library, St. Paul, Minn.

6. M. M. Mattison, "Rail Transportation in Washington," *Pacific Monthly* 19 (1908): 459.

7. Albro Martin, *James J. Hill and the Opening of the Northwest* (New York: Oxford University Press, 1976); Hill to George F. Baker, Aug. 11, 1910, James J. Hill Papers, James Jerome Hill Reference Library.

8. John F. Stevens, *An Engineer's Recollections* (New York: McGraw-Hill, 1936), 61; Hill to Charles Steele, May 26, 1911, James J. Hill Papers, James Jerome Hill Reference Library.

9. Salt Lake City *Herald-Republican*, April 27, 1910. Whether the story was true or not, Hill had the clippings in his file.

10. H. Roger Grant, "Seeking the Pacific: The Chicago

*Tracks of the Utah & Northern Railroad bridged the Snake River at Idaho Falls in this 1889 photograph. Idaho State Historical Society, 72-139.16.*

and North Western's Plans to Reach the West Coast," *Pacific Northwest Quarterly* 81 (1990): 67–73.

11. Seattle *Times*, Nov. 11, 1908.

12. Conversely, the Union Pacific also had large holdings of Northern Pacific and Great Northern securities, but it had no representatives on their boards.

13. Chicago, Milwaukee & St. Paul Railway, *Annual Report for 1913*, p. 12.

14. Milwaukee Road passenger trains served Great Falls until service was discontinued in 1955.

15. Carl Snyder, *American Railways as Investments* (New York: Moody Corporation, 1907), 223.

16. St. Paul *Daily Dispatch*, April 13, 1909. Just the next year L. W. Hill accused the Union Pacific of trying to block the Great Northern from Oregon. He built "spite" lines into southern British Columbia in response to severe competition from the Canadian Pacific. St. Paul *Pioneer Press*, June 9, 1910.

17. St. Paul *Daily Dispatch*, June 6, 1912.

18. Woehlke, "The Inland Emperors," 485–86.

19. Strahorn, "Ninety Years of Boyhood," 457.

20. Strahorn, "Ninety Years of Boyhood," 455.

21. As quoted in Great Northern Railway, *Annual Report for 1912*, p. 24.

## The Promise of Electric Motive Power

1. Bob Carter, "Trip to Salem on the Oregon Electric Railway," *Bonville's Western Monthly* 4 (1909): 216–18.

2. F. Lewis Clark to Howard Elliott, June 25, 1912, Northern Pacific Presidents Subject File 207, Minnesota Historical Society.

3. Spokane *Spokesman-Review*, Aug. 2, 1909.

4. Jonathan Dembo, "Disasters, Natural and Otherwise: The Wellington Slide," paper delivered at the Pacific Northwest History Conference, April 18, 1980.

5. *How Science Aids the Traveler* ([Chicago]: Chicago, Milwaukee & St. Paul, 1924), 6.

## Twentieth-Century Empire Builders

1. Bend *Bulletin*, Oct. 11, 1911.

2. Bend *Bulletin*, Oct. 11, 1911.

3. Bend *Bulletin*, Oct. 11, 1911.

4. C. R. Gray to L. W. Hill and Howard Elliott, May 15, 1911, Elliott to Gray, May 28, 1911, both in Northern Pacific Presidents Subject File 207, Minnesota Historical Society.

5. Elliott to J. N. Hill, Jan. 11, 1912, Northern Pacific Presidents Subject File 207, Minnesota Historical Society.

6. Emma Adams, *To and Fro, Up and Down in Southern California, Oregon and Washington, with Sketches in Arizona, New Mexico and British Columbia* (Cincinnati: Cranston & Stowe, 1888), 375.

7. Julian Ralph, *Our Great West: A Study of the Present Condition and Future Possibilities of the New Communities and Capitals of the United States* (New York: Harper & Brothers, 1893), 308–309.

8. Rudyard Kipling, *From Sea to Sea and Other Sketches*, 2 vols. in 1 (Garden City, N.Y.: Doubleday, Page, 1925), II: 90–93; James Bryce, *The American Commonwealth*, 2 vols. (New York: Macmillan, 1911), II: 895–96.

9. *The Puget Sound Catechism; A Convenient Compendium of Useful Information Respecting the State of Washington, and Its Chief City, Seattle, for Intending Immigrants and Investors* (Seattle, 1881), 18.

10. *Free Land and Good Wages: Information in Regard to Columbia County, Oregon* (St. Helens, Oreg.: Oregon Mist, [1889]).

11. James L. Onderdonk, *Idaho: Facts and Statistics Concerning Its Mining, Farms, Stock Raising, Lumbering, and Other Resources and Industries* (San Francisco: A. L. Bancroft, 1885), 25. One of many examples of this tendency was William Reid, *Progress of the State of Oregon and the City of Portland, from 1870–1885* (Portland: Portland National Bank, 1885). Walter Woehlke, "The Inland Emperors," *Sunset* 27 (1911): 476.

12. *Photographs Tell the Truth: Pictures of the Great Northwest* (St. Paul: Great Northern Railway, [ca. 1900]).

13. Randall R. Howard, "Following the Colonists," *Pacific Monthly* 23 (1910): 520–21.

14. *Along the Chicago, Milwaukee & St. Paul Railway in the Dakotas and Montana* (Chicago: Poole Bros., [ca. 1908]); *General Information about Montana* (St. Paul: Great Northern Railway, 1900).

15. Stewart H. Holbrook, *Far Corner: A Personal View of the Pacific Northwest* (New York: Macmillan, 1952), 4.

16. Great Northern Railway, *Public Timetable* (ca. 1901), 35.

17. Tom D. Kilton, "The American Railroad as Publisher, Bookseller, and Librarian," *Journal of Library History, Philosophy, and Comparative Librarianship* 17 (Winter 1982): 39–64.

18. As quoted in *Electric Railway Journal* 32 (Oct. 15, 1908): 1087

19. James H. Hawley, *History of Idaho: Gem of the*

*Mountains*, Vol. 1 (Chicago: S. J. Clark, 1920), 292–93.

20. *General Information about Montana*, 11.

21. *Rocky Mountain Vacations* (St. Paul: Northern Pacific Railroad, [ca. 1910]); *The Missoula and Blackfoot Valleys, Montana* ([Chicago: Chicago, Milwaukee & St. Paul Railway, 1914]), 6.

22. Will H. Parry, "Why an Alaska-Yukon-Pacific Exposition?" *Pacific Monthly* 19 (1908): 417; R. S. Jones, "What the Visitor Sees at the Seattle Fair," *American Review of Reviews* 40 (1909): 65–68.

23. "Address delivered by Mr. James J. Hill at the Opening of the Alaska-Yukon-Pacific Exposition" (June 1, 1909), James J. Hill Papers, James Jerome Hill Reference Library.

24. *The Account of a Trip along the Pacific Coast Extension of the Chicago, Milwaukee & St. Paul Railway* (Chicago: Chicago, Milwaukee & St. Paul Railway, [1909]), 2.

25. "The Pacific Northwest Advertising Campaign, 1923," copy in Northern Pacific Papers, 10-B-11-5, Minnesota Historical Society.

26. Roy V. Scott, *Railroad Development Programs in the Twentieth Century* (Ames: Iowa State University Press, 1985).

27. "The Pacific Northwest Advertising Campaign, 1923."

28. "The Pacific Northwest Advertising Campaign, 1923." The Milwaukee Road's passenger timetable for May–June 1932 said of the West, "The *highest* mountains . . . crested with perpetual snow. The *deepest* canyons . . . tinted with Nature's most vivid hues. The *largest* ocean. The *biggest* trees that grow."

29. *The Land of Opportunity Now: The Great Pacific Northwest* ([St. Paul]: Chicago, Burlington & Quincy Railroad, Northern Pacific Railway, Great Northern Railway, 1923), 5–6.

30. *The Great Pacific Northwest and Alaska* (Omaha: Union Pacific System, [ca. 1920]), 2; Dorothy O. Johansen and Charles M. Gates, *Empire of the Columbia: A History of the Pacific Northwest* (New York: Harper & Brothers, 1957).

31. *The Story of the Monad* (n.p., n.d.), 2.

32. New York *Sun*, Aug. 10, 1913 (clipping).

33. *The Musselshell Country, Montana* ([Chicago: Chicago, Milwaukee & St. Paul Railway, ca. 1911]).

34. J. J. Hill, "Development of the Northwest," address before the Chicago Commercial Association (Oct. 6, 1906), James J. Hill Papers, James Jerome Hill Reference Library.

35. K. Ross Toole, *Twentieth-Century Montana: A State of Extremes* (Norman: University of Oklahoma Press, 1972), 80.

## Selling the Great Northwest

1. Paul C. Johnson, ed., *The Early "Sunset" Magazine, 1898–1928* (San Francisco: California Historical Society, 1974). *Sunset* was published under the Southern Pacific aegis from 1898 until 1914 and was originally designed to advertise the West to easterners.

2. W. B. Wells, unpublished autobiographical sketch (n.d.), 74, William Bittle Wells Papers, Box 18, University of Oregon Special Collections, Eugene.

3. "Community Publicity, Oregon-Washington Railroad & Navigation Company and Southern Pacific Company (Lines in Oregon), Report for the Fiscal Year Ending June 30, 1911," William Bittle Wells Papers, Box 19, University of Oregon Special Collections.

4. Jan Cohn, *Creating America: George Horace Lorimer and the "Saturday Evening Post"* (Pittsburgh: University of Pittsburgh Press, 1989).

5. William Bittle Wells to Thomas Vaughan, Nov. 11, 1957, Wells MSS 894, Oregon Historical Society, Portland.

6. "Community Publicity . . . for the Fiscal Year Ending June 30, 1911," William Bittle Wells Papers, Box 19, University of Oregon Special Collections. The Atchison, Topeka & Santa Fe Railway employed or purchased the work of numerous artists beginning in the early 1890s. They painted scenes that could be used in Santa Fe advertising, and these commissions eventually resulted in a priceless collection numbering more than 600 images: Sandra D'Emilio and Suzan Campbell, *Visions and Visionaries: The Art and Artists of the Santa Fe Railway* (Salt Lake City: Peregrine Smith Books, 1991).

7. "Community Publicity . . . for the Fiscal Year Ending June 30, 1911," William Bittle Wells Papers, Box 19, University of Oregon Special Collections.

8. Wm. McMurray to Wells, Aug. 31, 1911, Box 19, and William Bittle Wells, "Autobiographical Outline," Box 7, both in William Bittle Wells Papers, University of Oregon Special Collections.

9. Wells's diaries providing details of his life before 1900 are at the Oregon Historical Society, Portland.

10. W. B. Wells, *Pacific Northwest Literature* (n.p., n.d.), William Bittle Wells Papers, Box 2, University of Oregon Special Collections. By literature Wells means the promotional brochures he is responsible for issuing.

11. Wells, "Autobiographical Outline," William Bittle Wells Papers, Box 7, University of Oregon Special Collections.

## Wonderlands: Railroad Tourism

1. C. E. Flagg as quoted in Hiram T. French, *History of Idaho*, 3 vols. (Chicago: Lewis Publishing Co., 1914), I: 527.

2. As quoted in *Wilderness Kingdom: Indian Life in the Rocky Mountains: 1840–1847: The Journals and Paintings of Nicholas Point, S.J.*, trans. Joseph P. Donnelly (New York: Holt, Rinehart and Winston, 1967), 181.

3. *Inter-Mountain Resorts* (Salt Lake City: Passenger Depart., Union Pacific Railway, [ca. 1886]).

4. *World's Pictorial Line* (Omaha: Union Pacific Railway, 1893).

5. *Health and Pleasure along the Line of the Oregon Railroad and Navigation Company* (Portland: Oregon Railroad & Navigation Co., 1903).

6. *Rocky Mountain Horseman*, July 23, 1885, as quoted in Marilyn McMillan, "'An Eldorado of Ease and Elegance': Taking the Waters at White Sulphur Springs, 1866–1904," *Montana, the Magazine of Western History* 35 (Spring 1985): 37.

7. *Western Resorts for Health and Pleasure Reached via the Union Pacific Railway* (Omaha: Union Pacific Railway, 1888), 60; Rinaldo M. Hall, *Restful Recreation Resorts* (Portland: Oregon Railroad & Navigation Co., 1905).

8. *Western Resorts for Health and Pleasure*, 75.

9. *World's Pictorial Line*.

10. *North Pacific Coast Resorts* (St. Paul: Northern Pacific Railroad, 1909).

11. Great Northern Railway, *Public Timetable* (ca. 1901), 36.

12. John K. Campbell, "Trapping and Hunting in the Cascades," *Washington Magazine* 2 (1890): 250–53.

13. Olin D. Wheeler, *Wonderland '97: A Story of the Northwest* (St. Paul: Northern Pacific Railway, 1897), 61. Each Wonderland booklet was then available for the cost of a six-cent postage stamp; the going cost in antique stores is now from $75 to $300 dollars apiece.

14. *Pacific Northwest: The Wonderland* (Chicago: Chicago, Milwaukee & St. Paul Railway, 1924); Edward F. Colborn, *Where Gush the Geysers* ([Salt Lake City?]: Oregon Short Line, 1910).

15. Arthur D. Martinson, *Wilderness above the Sound: The Story of Mount Rainier National Park* (Flagstaff, Ariz.: Northland Press, 1986). The best source of information on railroads and the national parks is Alfred Runte, *Trains of Discovery: Western Railroads and the National Parks*, rev. ed. (Niwot, Colo.: Roberts Rinehart, 1990).

16. Michael G. Schene, "The Crown of the Continent: Private Enterprise and Public Interest in the Early Development of Glacier National Park, 1910–17," *Forest and Conservation History* 34 (April 1990): 69–75.

17. St. Paul *Daily News*, Aug. 27, 1912.

18. Quoted in James H. Hawley, *History of Idaho: Gem of the Mountains*, Vol. 1 (Chicago: S. J. Clarke, 1920): 814.

19. *Railway Age Gazette* 53 (Oct. 11, 1912): 682. A *See America First Magazine* began publication in Tacoma, Washington, in 1912 and within two years claimed a circulation of 10,000.

20. Robert S. Lynd and Helen Merrell Lynd, *Middletown: A Study of Modern American Culture* (New York: Harcourt, Brace & World, 1929), 261–62; Oregon Railroad & Navigation Co., *Public Timetable* (October 1900), 1.

21. *Oregon and Washington Sights and Scenes via the Union Pacific* (Omaha: Union Pacific Railroad, 1892), 19. The inn ceased to function commercially in the 1920s.

22. *Bonneville on the Columbia River* (Portland: Oregon-Washington Railroad & Navigation Co., [1912]).

23. C. W. Parker, "Amusement Parks," *Electric Traction* 13 (April 1917): 255.

24. Parker, "Amusement Parks," 255.

25. *Electric Traction* 14 (April 1918): 188; Frederick Thompson, "Amusing the Million," *Everybody's Magazine* 16 (1908): 386. For electric parks see John F. Kasson, *Amusing the Million: Coney Island at the Turn of the Century* (New York: Hill & Wang, 1978).

26. *Electric Traction* 20 (April 1924): 18.

27. *Electric Railway Journal* 33 (Jan. 30, 1909): 364–66; Spokane, Portland & Seattle Railway, *Public Timetable* (June 17, 1916), 14.

28. *Electric Railway Journal* 32 (Oct. 15, 1908): 1086–87.

## The Golden Age of Passenger-Train Travel

1. Philip Curtiss, "Elegy for the Branch-Line Railroad," *Harper's Monthly Magazine* 169 (1934): 505–508.

2. Don Marquis, "My Memories of the Old-Fashioned Drummer," *American Magazine* 107 (February 1929): 20–21, 152–54.

3. Barney & Smith built standard sleepers for the 1911 Olympian; Pullman operated the tourist sleepers and dining cars.

4. *Railway Age* 83 (July 23, 1927): 133–35; 129 (Oct. 28, 1950): 164.

5. Jack Santino, *Miles of Smiles, Years of Struggle: Stories of Black Pullman Porters* (Urbana: University of Illinois Press, 1989); Silas Bent, "On Riding in a Pullman," *Outlook* 149 (1928): 343.

6. H. I. Phillips, "The Book of Etiquette for Railroad Travelers," *Colliers* 76 (October 1924): 10, 38.

7. New York *Herald-Tribune* quoted in *Railway Age* 91 (Nov. 28, 1931): 841.

8. *Railway Age* 129 (Oct. 28, 1950): 104–105.

9. *Pacific Northwest: The Wonderland* ([Chicago: Chicago, Milwaukee & St. Paul Railway, ca. 1925]), 6.

10. Olin D. Wheeler, *Wonderland 1904* (St. Paul: Northern Pacific Railway, 1904).

11. *Railway Age* 76 (April 5, 1924): 888.

12. *Railway Age* 81 (Oct. 30, 1926): 854; *Southern Pacific Bulletin* 15 (November 1926): 7–8.

13. Great Northern Railway, *Public Timetable* (ca. 1901), 34.

14. *Great Northern Semaphore* 5 (January 1928): 2–5.

15. Keith L. Bryant, "Urban Railroad Station Architecture in the Pacific Northwest," in *Railroads in the West*, ed. Don L. Hofsommer (Manhattan, Kans.: Sunflower University Press, 1978), 15.

16. Seattle *Post-Intelligencer*, May 10, 1906. On Union Station see Walter Willard, "Evolution of the Passenger Station: Story of the Model Terminal in Seattle," *Sunset* 29 (July 1912): 105–107.

17. C. F. J. Galloway, *The Call of the West: Letters from British Columbia* (London: T. Fisher Unwin, 1916), 23.

18. R. S. Williams, "The Motor Bus as an Adjunct to the Railroad," *Railway Age* 75 (Dec. 29, 1923): 1199.

19. Edmond S. Meany, *Origin of Washington Geographic Names* (Seattle: University of Washington Press, 1923), 11.

20. *The Pacific Northwest Official ABC Railway and Marine Guide* (Portland: Bushong & Co., April 1905); *Koch and Oakley's Railway and Navigation Guide* (Seattle: Koch and Oakley Publishing Co., January 1891), 4; *Lewis and Dryden's Railway Guide: Official Organ of All Transportation Lines in the Northwest* (Portland: Lewis and Dryden, 1889).

21. Frank P. Donivan, *The Railroad in Literature* (Boston: Railway and Locomotive Historical Society, 1940); Thomas W. Jackson, *On a Slow Train through Arkansaw* (1903), reprint, edited by W. K. McNeil (Lexington: University of Kentucky Press, 1985).

22. *Rules and Regulations: Operating Department, Washington & Columbia River Railway Company* (Jan. 1, 1903).

23. *Railway Age Gazette* 61 (Aug. 11, 1916): 219.

24. *Railway Age Gazette* 48 (Feb. 25, 1910): 419; *Railway Age* 94 (June 3, 1933): 807.

25. *Koch and Oakley's Railway and Navigation Guide*, 30.

26. *Railway Age* 129 (Oct. 28, 1950): 104.

27. Oregon Railroad & Navigation Co., *Public Timetable* (October 1900), 30.

## New Competition

1. For a detailed study of the jitney craze, see Carlos A. Schwantes, "The West Adapts the Automobile: Technology, Unemployment, and the Jitney Phenomenon of 1914–1917," *Western Historical Quarterly* 16 (1985): 307–26. All quotations in this section are from that essay.

2. W. M. Tyler, "Topeka, Kansas, to Portland, Oregon, in 1914," *Oregon Motorist and Good Road Advocate* 1 (March 1918): 11–15.

3. *Railway Age Gazette* 61 (Dec. 1, 1916): 997.

4. *Good Roads* 40 (November 1910): 410; Bruce E. Seely, "Railroads, Good Roads, and Motor Vehicles: Managing Technological Change," *Railroad History* No. 155 (Autumn 1986): 34–63.

5. John C. Long, "Motor Transportation over Radial Frontier," *Journal of Land and Public Utility Economics* 2 (January 1926): 114.

6. *Railway Age* 69 (Aug. 6, 1920): 214–15.

7. *Electric Railway Journal* 67 (May 1, 1926): 749.

8. *Public Roads* 4 (November 1921): 22.

9. Lewis R. Freeman, "From Chicago to Los Angeles on Common Carrier Lines," *Bus Transportation* 5 (June 1926): 302.

10. *Christian Science Monitor* as quoted in *Literary Digest* 94 (Aug. 27, 1927): 71–72.

11. *Bus Transportation* 12 (August 1933): 337; Francis Vivian Drake, "Air Stewardess," *Atlantic Monthly* 151 (1933): 185–93.

12. *Pacific Airport News* 1 (February 1928): 24, and (March–April 1928): 12.

13. Ray Conway, "Oregon Takes to the Air," *Oregon Motorist* 14 (May 1934): 10; Paul T. David, "Federal Regulation of Airplane Common Carriers," *Journal of Land and Public Utility Economics* 6 (November 1930): 359–71; J. C. Furnas, "Mr. Milquetoast in the Sky: The Airlines' Campaign to Make America Air-Minded," *Scribner's Magazine* 104 (September 1938): 7–11, 60–61.

14. J.G. Woodworth, *The Panama Canal* (St. Paul: Northern Pacific Railway, [ca. 1924]); Franklin Snow, "The Railways and the Panama Canal," *North American Review* 224 (March 1927): 29–40.

15. Eliot Grinnell Mears, *Maritime Trade of Western United States* (Stanford: Stanford University Press, [ca. 1932]), 138.

## An Industry in Trouble

1. The Army Appropriations Act of August 29, 1916, gave the president power to run the nation's railroads during a war. Congress affirmed federal control on March 21, 1918.

2. Walker D. Hines succeeded McAdoo as director general in January 1919. See Walker D. Hines, *War History of American Railroads* (New Haven: Yale University Press, 1928).

3. The *Great Northern* returned to Pacific Coast waters in 1922 after being acquired by the expanding Admiral Lines and renamed the *H.F. Alexander*. The liner saw wartime service as a troop ship once more and would be prominent at Omaha Beach on June 6, 1944.

4. United States Railroad Administration, Director General of Railroads, "Northern Pacific Railroad" (n.d.), 24, and Office of the Director General of Railroads, Oct. 8, 1919, "Office Memorandum No. 52," copies of both documents in Great Northern Papers, Presidents Office File 23-267, Minnesota Historical Society, St. Paul.

5. *Railway Age Gazette* 61 (Dec. 1, 1916): 997.

6. *Railway Age* 82 (Jan. 22, 1927): 277–78; 87 (Dec. 7, 1929): 1317.

7. *Railway Age Gazette* 51 (Aug. 25, 1911): 361.

8. *Railway Age* 78 (March 14, 1925): 729.

9. *Railway Age* 80 (Feb. 13, 1926): 416.

10. *Railway Age* 85 (Nov. 3, 1928): 863.

11. *Railway Age Gazette* 54 (Jan. 31, 1913): 195.

12. *Bus Transportation* 4 (January 1925): 27.

13. *Railway Age* 94 (June 3, 1933): 807. A good case study of this class of service is Donovan L. Hofsommer, "Working on the (Branch Line) Railroad," *Railroad History* No. 137 (Autumn 1977): 80–93.

14. *Railway Age* 103 (July 17, 1937): 71.

15. Great Northern Railway, *Annual Report for 1933*, p. 7.

16. *Railway Age* 91 (Aug. 22, 1931): 296–98.

17. *Air Transportation* 4 (Oct. 13, 1928): 1, 8 (July 6, 1929): 45; *Official Aviation Guide*, October 1931. The Union Pacific briefly considered entering the airline business, just as it had so successfully entered the field of bus transportation.

18. John T. Flynn, "Riding on Rubber," *Colliers* 87 (April 18, 1931): 18–19.

19. Carl Snyder, *American Railways as Investments* (New York: Moody Corporation, 1907), 532.

20. Great Northern Railway, *Annual Report for 1923*, p. 3; *The New Oriental Limited* ([St. Paul: Great Northern Railway, ca. 1929]).

21. Great Northern Railway, *Annual Report for 1923*, p. 3, and *Annual Report for 1928*, p. 7.

22. Chicago, Milwaukee, St. Paul & Pacific Railroad, *Public Timetable*, June 1929.

23. *New North Coast Limiteds* ([St. Paul: Northern Pacific Railway, ca. 1930]).

24. America's first all-coach deluxe train was the Central Railroad of New Jersey's Blue Comet. From February 21, 1929, until September 27, 1941, it offered twice-daily service from New York City (Jersey City) to Atlantic City. *Railway Age* 86 (March 2, 1929): 529–31.

25. *Railway Age* 81 (Nov. 20, 1926): 967.

26. Great Northern Railway, *Annual Report for 1925*, p. 8, *Annual Report for 1926*, p. 8, and *Annual Report for 1930*, p. 7.

27. *Railway Age* 93 (Dec. 3, 1932): 812; George W. Anderson, "Roads—Motor and Rail," *Atlantic Monthly* 135 (1925): 393–404.

28. *Railway Age Gazette* 58 (Jan. 15, 1915): 102; A.M. Schoyer, "The Reason for the Unpopularity of Railroads," ibid., 57 (Dec. 4, 1914): 1053–54; P. Harvey Middleton, *Railways and Public Opinion: Eleven Decades* (Chicago: Railway Business Association, 1941); "Need of Reconciliation between Railroads and the Public," *Engineering Magazine* 43 (May 1912): 222–26.

29. E.D. Sewall, "The Railways and the Public," *Milwaukee Railway System Employees' Magazine* 3 (June 1915): 10–13.

30. *Great Northern Semaphore* 3 (May 1926): 6.

31. Great Northern Railway, *Annual Report for 1923*, p. 3.

32. ICC Case 17021, 131 ICC, "Investigation of the Chicago, Milwaukee & St. Paul Railway Company" (reprint).

## Response: The Streamliner Era

1. For a list of changes made to Pullman cars from 1858

to 1930, see *Railway Age* 88 (May 19, 1930): 1195–97.

2. Information on the introduction of the City of Portland is from Carlos A. Schwantes, "Riding on the City of Portland," *Oregon Historical Quarterly* 85 (1984): 194–208.

3. *Railway Age* 101 (Nov. 14, 1936): 732.

4. *Electric Railway Journal* 72 (Sept. 19, 1928): 585.

5. F. R. Newman to F. J. Gavin, Presidents Office File, 17-c-11-5B, Minnesota Historical Society, St. Paul.

6. J. P. Graves to Olmsted Brothers, June 18, 1936, Olmsted Papers, copy in Idaho State Historical Society, Boise; Albro Martin, *Railroads Triumphant: The Growth, Rejection, and Rebirth of a Vital American Force* (New York: Oxford University Press, 1992), 109.

7. *Railway Age* 94 (April 8, 1933): 501.

8. Otto Kuhler, "Appeal Design in Railroad Equipment," *Railway Age* 99 (Nov. 30, 1935): 712–16.

9. *A Picture Story of Train Travel Today via the Progressive Union Pacific Railroad* (Chicago: Poole Brothers, 1937), 3.

10. *Railway Age* 85 (Dec. 29, 1928): 1309.

11. *Railway Age* 83 (Oct. 29, 1927): 842.

12. Frank E. Brimmer, "Vacationing on Wheels," *American Magazine* 102 (July 1926): 56–57, 172–76.

13. Edward F. Colborn, *Where Gush the Geysers* ([?]: Oregon Short Line, 1910).

14. *Railway Age* 102 (Jan. 23, 1937): 177.

15. *Railway Age* 104 (March 26, 1938): 572.

16. Great Northern Railway, *Public Timetable* (Summer 1938), 6.

17. Archie Robertson, *Slow Train to Yesterday: A Last Glance at the Local* (Boston: Houghton Mifflin, 1945).

18. *Railway Age* 101 (Nov. 14, 1936): 732.

19. Portland *Oregonian*, June 6, 1935.

## Strange New World: War and a Troubled Peace

1. *Why It Pays to Get a War Job with S. P.* ([n. p.], Oct. 1, 1943), 6.

2. For a summary history of the Pacific Northwest in World War II, see Carlos A. Schwantes, ed., *The Pacific Northwest in World War II* (Manhattan, Kans.: Sunflower University Press, 1986).

3. *Railway Age* 116 (May 6, 1944): 858.

4. Great Northern Railway, *Annual Report for 1945*, p. 7.

5. Southern Pacific, *Public Timetable*, Nov. 22, 1942.

6. Southern Pacific, *Condensed Public Timetable*, July 26, 1942.

7. *Railway Age* 117 (Nov. 4, 1944): 695.

8. *Railway Age* 114 (April 24, 1943): 816.

9. *Railway Progress* 1 (May 1947): 4.

10. *Railway Age* 115 (Oct. 23, 1943): 631–32.

11. *Railway Age* 114 (Feb. 13, 1943): 359.

12. Chicago, Milwaukee, St. Paul & Pacific Railway, *Annual Report for 1947*, p. 13.

13. Southern Pacific, *Public Timetable*, Jan. 12, 1947; *Railway Age* 129 (Sept. 23, 1950): 26–29.

14. Great Northern Railway, *Annual Report for 1951*, p. 6. Winning names among employees were the Evergreen and the Eight-Stater, but the railroad chose Western Star.

15. *Railway Age* 134 (June 1, 1953): 64.

16. *Railway Progress* 3 (February 1950): 28.

17. *Modern Railroads* 3 (May 1948): 51; 3 (November 1948): 40.

18. *Railway Age* 124 (Jan. 10, 1948): 119; 125 (Nov. 20, 1948): 934.

19. "Coach Passengers Are People," Union Pacific Records, Nebraska Historical Society, Lincoln; *Railway Age* 121 (Aug. 24, 1946): 343.

20. *Railway Age* 117 (Nov. 18, 1944): 754.

21. *Railway Age* 120 (June 1, 1946): 1114; 130 (May 21, 1951): 94.

22. ICC Finance Docket No. 23820, p. 489; John F. Stover, *The Life and Decline of the American Railroad* (New York: Oxford University Press, 1970), 217.

23. *Railway Progress* 10 (May 1956): 8–9.

24. *Railway Progress* 9 (October 1955): 31–36.

25. *Russell's Official National Motor Coach Guide*, Jan. 8, 1957; *The Official Guide of the Railways and Steam Navigation Lines of the United States, Puerto Rico, Canada, Mexico and Cuba* (New York: National Railway Publication Co., January 1957). In 1971 Greyhound had three through buses each way between Chicago and Seattle that roughly paralleled the old Northern Pacific line. They took approximately 51 hours. Between Seattle and Portland there were 21 buses each way taking approximately 3 hours. From Portland to San Francisco, an express bus required approximately 13 hours.

26. *Railway Progress* 4 (August 1950): 33; *Official Airline Guide*, January 1957.

27. *Senate Subcommittee Hearings on the "Deteriorating Railroad Situation"* (Washington, D.C.: Association of American Railroads, 1958); Robert Bendiner, "The Railroads from Overlord to Underdog," *Reporter* 19 (Aug. 7, 1958): 19–24.

## A Changing Signature

1. Curtiss E. Crippen interview with Jim Scribbins, recorded in *Milwaukee Railroader* 19 (December 1989): 40.

2. Kenneth G. Johnsen, "Semaphores and Seahawks: The Washington Central," *Railfan and Railroad* 109 (September 1987): 46–51.

3. *Wood River Journal* (Hailey, Idaho), July 27, 1987.

4. The best summary of the transition from steam to diesel is Maury Klein, "The Diesel Revolution," *American Heritage of Invention and Technology* 6 (Winter 1991): 16–22. See also Maury Klein, "Replacement Technology: The Diesel as a Case Study," *Railroad History* No. 162 (Spring 1990): 109–20.

5. New York *Times*, Jan. 13, 1992.

6. John H. White, Jr., "Changing Trains," *American Heritage of Invention and Technology* 7 (Spring/Summer 1991): 34–41; on the disappearing caboose see *Trains* 50 (August 1990), an entire issue devoted to the subject.

7. Fred W. Frailey, "Powder River Country," *Trains* 50 (November 1989): 40–63.

8. *Modern Railroads* 13 (March 1958): 96.

9. "Passengers: Profit or Loss?" *Fortune* 30 (August 1944): 160–64, 256–65. Pioneering investigations into the problem include Julius H. Parmelee, "The Separation of Railway Costs between Freight and Passengers," *Quarterly Journal of Economics* 20 (1920): 346–62; and William J. Cunningham, "The Separation of Railroad Operating Expenses between Freight and Passenger Services," *Quarterly Journal of Economics* 17 (1917): 209–40.

10. Hosmer quoted in *Railway Age* 145 (Sept. 22, 1958): 9; George W. Hilton, *The Transportation Act of 1958: A Decade of Experience* (Bloomington: Indiana University Press, 1969); Michael Conant, *Railroad Mergers and Abandonments* (Berkeley: University of California Press, 1964); Dwight R. Ladd, *Cost Data for the Management of Railroad Passenger Service* (Boston: Harvard University, Graduate School of Business Administration, Division of Research, 1957).

11. David P. Morgan, "Who Shot the Passenger Train?" *Trains* 19 (April 1959): 43. Under ICC accounting rules the railroads serving the Pacific Northwest had the following passenger deficit in 1957: Milwaukee Road, $24.2 million; Union Pacific, $43.6 million; Northern Pacific, $17.5 million; Great Northern, $26.1 million; and Southern Pacific, $47.3 million. John Stover, *The Life and Decline of the American Railroad* (New York: Oxford University Press, 1970), 192.

12. George Hilton, *Transportation Act of 1958*, p. 110; *Milwaukee Road Magazine* 58 (November-December 1960): 3; ICC Finance Docket No. 21391, p. 696, and No. 24855, p. 19. In 1967 William Quinn, then president of the Chicago, Burlington & Quincy, made a comparison between the California Zephyr and a Boeing 727 operating between Chicago and San Francisco: the Zephyr required a crew of 47, and the jet 6, with wages costing $2,228 and $391 respectively.

13. Chicago, Milwaukee, St. Paul & Pacific Railway, *Annual Report for 1961*, p. 9.

14. Great Northern Railway, *Annual Report for 1962*, p. 7.

15. Union Pacific Railroad, *Annual Report for 1962*, p. 6, and *Annual Report for 1963*, p. 6; Great Northern Railway, *Annual Report for 1962*, p. 7, and *Annual Report for 1963*, p. 7; Northern Pacific Railway, *Annual Report for 1962*, p. 4, and *Annual Report for 1963*, p. 6; *Railway Age* 156 (May 18, 1964): 20, and 158 (May 17, 1965): 34.

16. *Railroad Magazine* 86 (November 1969): 39.

17. *Railroad Magazine* 86 (November 1969): 31; *Proposed Passenger Train Act of 1960*, Hearing before the Surface Transportation Subcommittee of the Committee on Interstate and Foreign Commerce, United States Senate, 86th Cong., 2d Sess. (Washington, D.C.: Government Printing Office, 1960): 59.

18. Charles E. Hosmer, "Passenger Train Deficits," ICC No. 31954.

19. As quoted in Don L. Hofsommer, "SP and Passengers: The Bittersweet Love Affair," *Trains* 46 (July 1986): 46–53.

20. The idea of pooling intercity passenger-train service in the United States was not new. In 1930, A. L. Riordan proposed a "Railway Passenger Service" along the lines of the Railway Express Agency to take over all passenger trains in the nation, pick the best routes, and eliminate duplicate routes. *Railway Age* 89 (Dec. 27, 1930): 1379–80.

21. *Trains* 32 (July 1972): 3.

22. A convenient summary of Amtrak's first 20 years can be found in a special issue of *Trains* 51 (June 1991). See also *Passenger Train Journal* 22 (May 1991).

## Epilogue: Pacific Northwest Railroads in Perspective

1. John Steinbeck, *Travels with Charley: In Search of America* (New York: Viking Press, 1961), 81.

*In 1883 the Northern Pacific's new Pullman Palace Sleeping Cars reflected the fascination of Gilded Age America with highly ornamented interiors. DeGolyer Library, Southern Methodist University.*

2. Burlington Northern Incorporated's subsidiary Burlington Northern Railroad spun off its energy and natural resources holdings to its shareholders as Burlington Resources in 1988.

3. Ray Stannard Baker, "Destiny and the Western Railroad," *Century Magazine* 75 (April 1908): 892–94.

# Suggestions for Further Reading

*A wood-burning Northern Pacific locomotive hauls a train across Pack River trestle along the northern edge of Idaho's Lake Pend Oreille in mid-1883. An earthen causeway eventually replaced most of the trestle, which in the 1990s formed part of the main line of Montana Rail Link. Haynes Foundation Collection, Montana Historical Society, H-1116.*

The following bibliography seeks both to guide readers to my sources and to suggest where they might pursue further study of a specific subject. Although *Railroad Signatures across the Pacific Northwest* devotes little attention to railroads north of the international boundary, I do include a few citations for western Canada. Some sources are mentioned only in the Notes.

## Introduction: Railroad Time and Space in the New Northwest

Chandler, Alfred D., Jr., ed. *The Railroads: The Nation's First Big Business: Sources and Readings.* New York: Harcourt, Brace & World, 1965.

Cordz, Marian. "Bibliography of Railroads in the Pacific Northwest." *Washington Historical Quarterly* 12 (1921): 91–114. This is an especially valuable source of information on early government documents.

Cronon, William. *Nature's Metropolis: Chicago and the Great West.* New York: W. W. Norton, 1991.

Danly, Susan, and Leo Marx, eds. *The Railroad in American Art: Representations of Technological Change.* Cambridge, Mass.: MIT Press, 1988.

Fahl, Ronald H. "S. C. Lancaster and the Columbia River Highway: Engineer as Conservationist." *Oregon Historical Quarterly* 74 (1973): 100–44.

Fogel, Robert William. *Railroads and American Economic Growth: Essays in Econometric History.* Baltimore: Johns Hopkins Press, 1964.

Holbrook, Stewart H. *The Story of American Railroads.* New York: Crown Publishers, 1947.

Lyon, Peter. *To Hell in a Day Coach: An Exasperated Look at American Railroads.* Philadelphia: J. B. Lippincott Co., 1968.

Martin, Albro. *Railroads Triumphant: The Growth, Rejection, and Rebirth of a Vital American Force.* New York: Oxford University Press, 1992.

Mazlish, Bruce, ed. *The Railroad and the Space Program: An Exploration in Historical Analogy.* Cambridge, Mass.: MIT Press, 1965.

Mills, Randall V. "A History of Transportation in the Pacific Northwest." *Oregon Historical Quarterly* 47 (1946): 281–312.

Modelski, Andrew M. *Railroad Maps of the United States: A Selective Annotated Bibliography of Original Nineteenth-Century Maps in the Geography and Map Division of the Library of Congress.* Washington, D.C.: Library of Congress, 1975.

O'Malley, Michael. *Keeping Watch: A History of American Time.* New York: Viking Penguin, 1990.

Peterson, Robert L. "The Idea of the Railroads: Regional Economic Growth." *Oregon Historical Quarterly* 67 (1966): 101–103. Introduction to a special issue on the impact of transcontinental railroads.

Riegel, Robert Edgar. *The Story of Western Railroads: From 1852 through the Reign of the Giants.* New York: Macmillan Co., 1926.

Schivelbusch, Wolfgang. *The Railway Journey: Trains and Travel in the Nineteenth Century.* New York: Urizen Books, 1979.

Stilgoe, John R. *Metropolitan Corridor: Railroads and the American Scene.* New Haven: Yale University Press, 1983.

Stover, John F. *The Life and Decline of the American Railroad.* New York: Oxford University Press, 1970.

———. *American Railroads*. Chicago: University of Chicago Press, 1961.

Ward, James A. *Railroads and the Character of America, 1820–1887*. Knoxville: University of Tennessee Press, 1986.

White, W. Thomas, ed. *Great Northern Railway Company Papers* and *Northern Pacific Railway Company Papers* (Frederick, Md.: University Publications of America, 1984–85). This is an extremely useful microfilm collection of important railroad documents housed at the Minnesota Historical Society.

Williams, John Hoyt. *A Great and Shining Road: The Epic Story of the Transcontinental Railroad*. New York: Times Books, 1988.

## Portages by Rail

Athearn, Robert G. "Railroad to a Far-off Country: The Utah and Northern." *Montana, the Magazine of Western History* 18 (October 1968): 2–23.

Baker, W. W. "The Building of the Walla Walla & Columbia River Railroad." *Washington Historical Quarterly* 14 (1923): 3–13.

Beal, Merrill. "The Story of the Utah Northern Railroad, Part I." *Idaho Yesterdays* 1 (Spring 1957): 53–10.

———. "The Story of the Utah Northern Railroad, Part II." *Idaho Yesterdays* 1 (Summer 1957): 16–23.

Bolino, August C. "The Big Bend of the Northern Pacific." *Idaho Yesterdays* 3 (Summer 1959): 5–10.

Chasan, Daniel Jack. *The Water Link: A History of Puget Sound as a Resource*. Seattle: University of Washington Sea Grant Program, 1981.

Coelho, Philip R. P., and Katherine H. Daigle. "The Effects of Developments in Transportation on the Settlement of the Inland Empire." *Agricultural History* 56 (January 1982): 22–36.

Corning, Howard McKinley. *Willamette Landings: Ghost Towns of the River*. Portland: Oregon Historical Society, 1973.

Cotroneo, Ross R. "United States vs. Northern Pacific Railway Company: The Final Settlement of the Land Grant Case." *Pacific Northwest Quarterly* 71 (1980): 107–11.

Cox, Thomas R. *Mills and Markets: A History of the Pacific Coast Lumber Industry to 1900*. Seattle: University of Washington Press, 1974.

Edwards, G. Thomas. "Walla Walla: Gateway to the Pacific Northwest Interior." *Montana, the Magazine of Western History* 40 (Summer 1990): 28–43.

Ellis, David Maldwyn. "The Oregon and California Railroad Land Grant, 1866–1945." *Pacific Northwest Quarterly* 39 (1948): 253–83.

Frederick, J. V. *Ben Holladay, the Stagecoach King: A Chapter in the Development of Transcontinental Transportation*. Glendale, Calif.: A. H. Clark Co., 1940.

Freeman, Otis W. "Early Wagon Roads in the Inland Empire." *Pacific Northwest Quarterly* 45 (1954): 125–30.

Ganoe, John Tilson. "The History of the Oregon and California Railroad." *Oregon Historical Quarterly* 25 (1924): 236–83, 330–52.

Gill, Frank B. "Oregon's First Railway." *Oregon Historical Quarterly* 25 (1924): 171–233.

Greever, William S. "A Comparison of Railroad Land-Grant Policies." *Agricultural History* 25 (April 1951): 83–90.

Hilton, George W. *American Narrow Gauge Railroads*. Stanford: Stanford University Press, 1990.

Hult, Ruby El. *Steamboats in the Timber*. Caldwell, Idaho: Caxton Printers, 1953. Steamboating in northern Idaho.

Jackson, Donald. *Voyages of the Steamboat "Yellow Stone."* New York: Ticknor & Fields, 1985.

Jackson, W. Turrentine. "Federal Road Building Grants for Early Oregon." *Oregon Historical Quarterly* 50 (1949): 3–29.

———. "Portland, Wells Fargo Hub for the Pacific Northwest." *Oregon Historical Quarterly* 86 (1985): 229–67.

———. *Wells Fargo and Co. in Idaho Territory*. Boise: Idaho State Historical Society, 1984.

———. "Wells Fargo Stagecoaching in Montana: Into a New Territory." *Montana, the Magazine of Western History* 29 (January 1979): 40–53.

———. "Wells Fargo Stagecoaching in Montana: Trials and Triumphs." *Montana, the Magazine of Western History* 29 (April 1979): 38–53.

———. "Wells Fargo Stagecoaching in Montana: The Overland Mail Contract for 1868." *Montana, the Magazine of Western History* 29 (July 1979): 56–68.

———. "Wells Fargo Stagecoaching in Montana: Final Months." *Montana, the Magazine of Western History* 29 (October 1979): 52–66.

Johansen, Dorothy. "The Oregon Steam Navigation Company: An Example of Capitalism on the Frontier." *Pacific Historical Review* 10 (1941): 179–88.

Jones, Larry R. "Staging to the South Boise Mines." *Idaho Yesterdays* 29 (Summer 1985): 19–25.

Kline, M. S., and G. A. Bayless. *Ferryboats: A Legend on*

*Puget Sound.* Seattle: Bayless Books, 1983.

Lass, William E. *A History of Steamboating on the Upper Missouri River.* Lincoln: University of Nebraska Press, 1962.

———. "Steamboats on the Yellowstone." *Montana, the Magazine of Western History* 35 (Autumn 1985): 26–33.

Lewis, Sol H. "A History of Railroads in Washington." *Washington Historical Quarterly* 3 (1912): 186–97.

Lewty, Peter J. *To the Columbia Gateway: The Oregon Railway and the Northern Pacific, 1879–1884.* Pullman: Washington State University Press, 1987.

McDougall, N. A. "Indomitable John: The Story of John Hart Scranton and His Puget Sound Steamers." *Pacific Northwest Quarterly* 45 (1954): 73–84.

McGregor, Alexander C. "The Economic Impact of the Mullan Road on Walla Walla, 1860–1883." *Pacific Northwest Quarterly* 65 (1974): 118–29.

McIntosh, Clarence F. "The Chico and Red Bluff Route: Stage Lines from Southern Idaho to the Sacramento Valley, 1865–1867." *Idaho Yesterdays* 6 (Fall 1962): 12–15, 18–19.

Meinig, D. W. *The Great Columbia Plain: A Historical Geography, 1805–1910.* Seattle: University of Washington Press, 1968. Especially Chapter 9: "Strategy: Settlers and Railroads, 1870–90."

———. "Wheat Sacks Out to Sea." *Pacific Northwest Quarterly* 45 (1954): 13–18.

Meyer, Bette E. "The Pend Oreille Routes to Montana, 1866–1870." *Pacific Northwest Quarterly* 72 (1981): 76–83.

Mills, Randall V. *Railroads down the Valleys: Some Shortlines of the Oregon Country.* Palo Alto, Calif.: Pacific Books, 1950.

———. *Stern-Wheelers up Columbia: A Century of Steamboating in the Oregon Country.* 1947. Reprint. Lincoln: University of Nebraska Press, 1977.

Moore, Miles C. "A Pioneer Railroad Builder." *Oregon Historical Quarterly* 12 (1911): 171–89.

Murray, Keith A. "Building a Wagon Road through the Northern Cascade Mountains." *Pacific Northwest Quarterly* 56 (1965): 49–56.

Newell, Gordon, and Joe Williamson. *Pacific Coast Liners.* Seattle: Superior Publishing Co., 1959.

Oviatt, Alton B. "Pacific Coast Competition for the Gold Camp Trade of Montana." *Pacific Northwest Quarterly* 56 (1965): 168–76.

Perko, Richard, "A Forgotten Passage to Puget Sound: The Fort Steilacoom–Walla Walla Road." *Montana, the Magazine of Western History* 35 (Winter 1985): 38–47.

Richards, Kent D. *Isaac I. Stevens: Young Man in a Hurry.* Provo: Brigham Young University Press, 1979).

Rylatt, R. M. *Surveying the Canadian Pacific: Memoir of a Railroad Pioneer.* Salt Lake City: University of Utah Press, 1991.

Simon-Smolinski, Carol. *Journal 1862: Timothy Nolan's Account of His Riverboat and Overland Journey to the Salmon River Mines, Washington Territory.* Clarkston, Wash.: Northwest Historical Consultants, 1983. A fictional account solidly grounded in the history of the Clearwater rush.

———. *Clearwater Steam, Steel, and Spirit.* Clarkston, Wash.: Northwest Historical Consultants, 1984.

Smalley, Eugene V. "The Great Coeur d'Alene Stampede of 1884." *Idaho Yesterdays* 11 (Fall 1967): 2–10.

Smith, C. J. "Early Development of Railroads in the Pacific Northwest." *Washington Historical Quarterly* 13 (1922): 243–50.

Stewart, Earle K. "Steamboats on the Columbia: The Pioneer Period." *Oregon Historical Quarterly* 51 (1950): 20–42.

Stratton, David H. "Hells Canyon: The Missing Link in Pacific Northwest Regionalism." *Idaho Yesterdays* 28 (Fall 1984): 2–9.

Taylor, George Rogers. *The Transportation Revolution, 1815–1860.* New York: Holt, Rinehart and Winston, 1951.

Throckmorton, Arthur L. *Oregon Argonauts: Merchant Adventurers on the Western Frontier.* Portland: Oregon Historical Society, 1961. Discusses the relationship between the Idaho 1860s gold rushes and Portland's merchants.

Timmen, Fritz. *Blow for the Landing: A Hundred Years of Steam Navigation on the Waters of the West.* Caldwell, Idaho: Caxton Printers, 1973.

Weinstein, Robert A. *Grays Harbor, 1885–1913.* New York: Viking Press, 1978.

———. *Tall Ships on Puget Sound: The Marine Photographs of Wilhelm Hester.* Seattle: University of Washington Press, 1978.

Willingham, William F. "Engineering the Cascades Canal and Locks, 1876–1896." *Oregon Historical Quarterly* 88 (1987): 229–57.

Winther, Oscar Osburn. *The Old Oregon Country: A History of Frontier Trade, Transportation, and Travel.* 1950. Reprint. Lincoln: University of Nebraska Press, 1969.

Wright, E. W., ed. *Lewis and Dryden's Marine History of the Pacific Northwest.* Seattle: Superior Publishing Co., 1967.

## Henry Villard and the Empire of the Columbia

Athearn, Robert G. "The Firewagon Road." *Montana, the Magazine of Western History* 20 (April 1970): 2–19. This is a study of the relationship between western railroads and the military.

———. "The Oregon Short Line." *Idaho Yesterdays* 13 (Winter 1969–70): 2–18.

———. *Union Pacific Country*. Chicago: Rand McNally, 1971.

Austin, Ed, and Tom Dill. *The Southern Pacific in Oregon*. Edmonds, Wash.: Pacific Fast Mail, 1987.

Baker, Abner. "Economic Growth in Portland in the 1880s." *Oregon Historical Quarterly* 67 (1966): 105–23.

Beal, Merrill D. *The Utah and Northern Railroad: Narrow Gauge*. Pocatello: Idaho State University Press, 1980.

Belknap, George N. *Henry Villard and the University of Oregon*. Eugene: University of Oregon, 1976.

Best, Gerald M. *Ships and Narrow Gauge Rails: The Story of the Pacific Coast Company*. Berkeley, Calif.: Howell-North Books, 1981.

Bolino, August C. "The Big Bend of the Northern Pacific." *Idaho Yesterdays* 3 (Summer 1959): 5–10. Route selection across northern Idaho.

Boyd, William Harland. "The Holladay-Villard Transportation Empire in the Pacific Northwest, 1868–1893." *Pacific Historical Review* 15 (1946): 379–89.

Bryan, Enoch A. *Orient Meets Occident: The Advent of the Railways of the Pacific Northwest*. Pullman, Wash.: Students Book Corp., 1936.

Cameron, Walter A. "Building the Northern Pacific in 1881." *Montana, the Magazine of Western History* 33 (Summer 1983): 70–76.

Chadwick, Robert A. "Montana's Silver Mining Era: Great Boom and Great Bust." *Montana, the Magazine of Western History* 32 (Spring 1982): 16–31.

Combs, Barry B., ed. *Westward to Promontory: Building the Union Pacific across the Plains and Mountains, a Pictorial Documentary*. New York: Garland, 1969.

Davison, Stanley R., and Rex C. Myers, "Terminus Town: Founding Dillon." *Montana, the Magazine of Western History* 30 (October 1980): 16–29.

Edwards, G. Thomas. "'Terminus Disease': The Clark P. Crandall Description of Puget Sound in 1871." *Pacific Northwest Quarterly* 70 (1979): 163–77.

Fahey, John. *The Inland Empire: Unfolding Years, 1879–1929*. Seattle: University of Washington Press, 1986.

Note especially the chapter called "The Railroads: Beneficent, Malignant, Fickle."

Forsling, O. E. "Sheep to Cheyenne." *Idaho Yesterdays* 8 (Summer 1964): 26–32.

Fuchs, Thomas. "Henry Villard: A Citizen of Two Worlds." Ph.D. dissertation, University of Oregon, 1991.

Gittins, H. Leigh. *Pocatello Portrait: The Early Years, 1878 to 1928*. Moscow: University Press of Idaho, 1983.

Grinnell, George Bird. "Building the Northern Pacific." *Idaho Yesterdays* 16 (Winter 1972–73): 10–13. First-person account from 1882.

Hedges, James B. *Henry Villard and the Railways of the Northwest*. New Haven: Yale University Press, 1930.

Hidy, Ralph W., Muriel E. Hidy, and Roy V. Scott, with Don L. Hofsommer. *The Great Northern Railway: A History*. Boston: Harvard Business School Press, 1988.

Hofsommer, Don L., ed. *Railroads in the West*. Manhattan, Kans.: Sunflower University Press, 1978.

Klein, Maury. *Union Pacific: Birth of a Railroad, 1862–1893*. New York: Doubleday, 1987.

Lang, William L. "Corporate Point Men and the Creation of the Montana Central Railroad, 1882–87." *Great Plains Quarterly* 10 (1990): 152–66.

McKee, Bill, and Georgeen Klassen. *Trail of Iron: The CPR and the Birth of the West*. Vancouver, B.C.: Douglas & McIntyre, 1983.

Morgan, Murray. *Puget's Sound: A Narrative of Early Tacoma and the Southern Sound*. Seattle: University of Washington Press, 1979.

———. *Skid Road: An Informal Portrait of Seattle* (1951). Reprint. Seattle: University of Washington Press, 1982.

Nagel, Paul C. "A West That Failed: The Dream of Charles Francis Adams II." *Western Historical Quarterly* 18 (1987): 397–407.

Nesbit, Robert C. *"He Built Seattle": A Biography of Judge Thomas Burke*. Seattle: University of Washington Press, 1961. This book contains much useful material on railroads and early Seattle.

Nolan, Edward W. "'Not without Labor and Expense': The Villard–Northern Pacific Excursion, 1883." *Montana, the Magazine of Western History* 33 (Summer 1983): 2–11.

———. *Northern Pacific Views: The Railroad Photography of F. Jay Haynes, 1876–1905*. Helena: Montana Historical Society Press, 1983.

Quiett, Glenn Chesney. *They Built the West: An Epic of Rails and Cities*. 1934. Reprint. New York: Cooper Square Publishers, 1965.

Renz, Louis Tuck. *The History of the Northern Pacific*

*Railroad.* Fairfield, Wash.: Ye Galleon Press, 1980.

Seckinger, Katherine Villard, ed. "The Great Railroad Celebration, 1883: A Narrative by Francis Jackson Garrison." *Montana, the Magazine of Western History* 33 (Summer 1983): 12–23.

Smalley, Eugene V. *History of the Northern Pacific Railroad.* New York: G. P. Putnam's Sons, 1883.

Spence, Clark C. "The Boom of the Wood River Mines." *Idaho Yesterdays* 23 (Summer 1979): 4–12.

Villard, Henry. *The Early History of Transportation in Oregon.* Edited by Oswald Garrison Villard. Eugene: University of Oregon, 1944.

———. *Memoirs of Henry Villard.* 2 vols. Boston: Houghton Mifflin & Co., 1904.

Watts, Donald W. "Mr. Pegram's Bridges: Engineering Legacies in Idaho." *Journal of the West* 31 (January 1992), 79–87.

White, W. Thomas. "Commonwealth or Colony? Montana Railroads in the First Decade of Statehood." *Montana, the Magazine of Western History* 38 (Autumn 1988): 12–23.

———. "Paris Gibson, James J. Hill, and the 'New Minneapolis': The Great Falls Water Power and Townsite Company, 1882–1908." *Montana, the Magazine of Western History* 33 (Summer 1983): 60–69.

Winks, Robin W. *Frederick Billings: A Life.* New York: Oxford University Press, 1991.

Winther, Oscar Osburn. *The Transportation Frontier: Trans-Mississippi West, 1865–1890.* New York: Holt, Rinehart and Winston, 1964.

Wood, Charles R. *The Northern Pacific: Main Street of the Northwest.* Seattle: Superior Publishing Co., 1968.

Wrigley, Robert L., Jr. "Utah and Northern Railway Co.: A Brief History." *Oregon Historical Quarterly* 48 (1947): 245–53.

## Shapers of a New Northwest

Athearn, Robert G. *Westward the Briton.* New York: Charles Scribner's Sons, 1953.

Brown, Arthur J. "The Promotion of Emigration to Washington, 1854–1909." *Pacific Northwest Quarterly* 36 (1945): 3–17.

Clinch, Thomas A. "The Northern Pacific Railroad and Montana Mineral Lands." *Pacific Historical Review* 34 (1965): 323–35.

Cochran, John S. "Economic Importance of Early Transcontinental Railroads: Pacific Northwest." *Oregon Historical Quarterly* 71 (1970): 26–98.

Cotroneo, Ross R. "Western Land Marketing by the Northern Pacific Railway." *Pacific Historical Review* 37 (1968): 299–320.

Emmons, David M. *Garden in the Grasslands: Boomer Literature of the Central Great Plains.* Lincoln: University of Nebraska Press, 1971. This study suggests how scholars can profitably study regional booster literature.

Fields, Ronald. *Abby Williams Hill and the Lure of the West.* Tacoma: Washington State Historical Society, 1989. An examination of railroads and their promotional art in the Pacific Northwest.

Goetzmann, William H. *Looking at the Land of Promise: Pioneer Images of the Pacific Northwest.* Pullman: Washington State University Press, 1988.

Hart, E. J. *The Selling of Canada: The CPR and the Beginnings of Canadian Tourism.* Banff, Alta.: Altitude Publishing, 1983.

Hedges, James B. "Colonization Work of the Northern Pacific Railroads." *Mississippi Valley Historical Review* 13 (1926): 311–42.

———. "Promotion of Immigration to the Pacific Northwest by the Railroads." *Mississippi Valley Historical Review* 15 (1928): 132–203.

Hudson, John C. "Main Streets of the Yellowstone Valley." *Montana, the Magazine of Western History* 35 (Autumn 1985): 56–67.

———. "Railroads and Urbanization in the Northwestern States." In *Centennial West: Essays on the Northern Tier States.* Edited by William L. Lang, 169-93. Seattle: University of Washington Press, 1991.

Isch, Flora Mae Bellefleur. "The Importance of Railroads in the Development of Northwestern Montana." *Pacific Northwest Quarterly* 41 (1950): 19–29.

Knight, Oliver. "Robert E. Strahorn, Propagandist for the West." *Pacific Northwest Quarterly* 59 (1968): 33–45.

Kraig, Beth. "The Bellingham Bay Improvement Company: Boomers or Boosters?" *Pacific Northwest Quarterly* 80 (1989): 122–32.

Overton, Richard C. *Burlington West: A Colonization History of the Burlington Railroad.* Cambridge, Mass.: Harvard University Press, 1941.

Reps, John W. *Panoramas of Promise: Pacific Northwest Cities and Towns on Nineteenth-Century Lithographs.* Pullman: Washington State University Press, 1984.

Rhodes-Jones, Carolyn. "An Evolving View of the Landscape: Trappers, Tourists, and the Great Shoshone Falls." *Idaho Yesterdays* 23 (Summer 1979): 19–27.

Strahorn, Carrie Adell. *Fifteen Thousand Miles by Stage.*

1911. Reprint. Lincoln: University of Nebraska Press, 1988.

## Traveling Too Fast: Adjustments to Railroad Power

Arrington, Leonard J. "The Promise of Eagle Rock: Idaho Falls, Idaho, 1863–1980." *Rendezvous* 18 (Spring 1983): 2–17.

Bonney, Richard J. "The Pullman Strike of 1894: Pocatello Perspective." *Idaho Yesterdays* 24 (Fall 1980): 23–28.

Bruns, Roger A. *Knights of the Road: A Hobo History*. New York: Methuen, 1980.

Ducker, James H. *Men of the Steel Rails: Workers on the Atchison, Topeka & Santa Fe Railroad, 1869–1900*. Lincoln: University of Nebraska Press, 1983.

Gabler, Edwin. *The American Telegrapher: A Social History, 1860–1900*. New Brunswick, N.J.: Rutgers University Press, 1988.

Grant, H. Roger, ed. *Brownie the Boomer: The Life of Charles P. Brown, an American Railroader*. DeKalb: Northern Illinois University Press, 1991.

Laurie, Clayton D. "Civil Disorder and the Military in Rock Springs, Wyoming: The Army's Role in the 1885 Chinese Massacre." *Montana, the Magazine of Western History* 40 (Summer 1990): 44–76.

Leuthner, Stuart. *The Railroaders*. New York: Random House, 1983. An oral history of railroad workers.

Licht, Walter. *Working for the Railroad: The Organization of Work in the Nineteenth Century*. Princeton: Princeton University Press, 1983.

Mercier, Laurie. "'I Worked for the Railroad': Oral Histories of Montana Railroaders, 1910–1950." *Montana, the Magazine of Western History* 33 (Summer 1983): 35–59.

Monkkonen, Eric H., ed. *Walking to Work: Tramps in America, 1790–1935*. Lincoln: University of Nebraska Press, 1984.

Niemann, Linda. *Boomer: Railroad Memoirs*. Berkeley: University of California Press, 1990.

Riddle, Thomas W. "Populism in the Palouse: Old Ideals and New Realities." *Pacific Northwest Quarterly* 65 (1974): 97–109.

Schwantes, Carlos A. "Coxey's Montana Navy: A Protest against Unemployment on the Wageworkers' Frontier." *Pacific Northwest Quarterly* 73 (1982): 98–107.

———. "Law and Disorder: The Suppression of Coxey's Army in Idaho." *Idaho Yesterdays* 25 (Summer 1981): 10–15, 18–26.

Scott, Mary Katsilometes. "The Greek Community in Pocatello, 1890–1941." *Idaho Yesterdays* 28 (Fall 1984): 29–36.

Smart, Douglas. "Spokane's Battle for Freight Rates." *Pacific Northwest Quarterly* 45 (1954): 19–27.

Stromquist, Shelton. *A Generation of Boomers: The Pattern of Railroad Labor Conflict in Nineteenth-Century America*. Urbana: University of Illinois Press, 1987.

White, W. Thomas. "Boycott: The Pullman Strike in Montana." *Montana, the Magazine of Western History* 29 (October 1979): 2–13.

———. "Railroad Labor Protests, 1894–1917: From Community to Class in the Pacific Northwest." *Pacific Northwest Quarterly* 75 (1984): 13–21.

Wrigley, Robert L., Jr. "The Early History of Pocatello, Idaho." *Pacific Northwest Quarterly* 34 (1943): 353–65.

## New Beginnings for a New Century

Abbott, Carl. *The Great Extravaganza: Portland and the Lewis and Clark Exposition*. Portland: Oregon Historical Society, 1981.

Butler, W. Daniel. "The Camas Prairie Railroad and Its Larger Railroad Owners." *Idaho Yesterdays* 26 (Winter 1983): 2–8.

Corbin, D.C. "Recollections of a Pioneer Railroad Builder." *Washington Historical Quarterly* 1 (1907): 43–46.

Due, John F., and Giles French. *Rails to the Mid-Columbia Wheatlands: The Columbia Southern and Great Southern Railroads and the Development of Sherman and Wasco Counties, Oregon*. Washington, D.C.: University Press of America, 1979. A study of transportation and agriculture.

———, and Frances Juris. *Rails to the Ochoco Country: The City of Prineville Railway*. San Marino, Calif.: Golden West Books, 1968.

Fahey, John. *Inland Empire: D.C. Corbin and Spokane*. Seattle: University of Washington Press, 1965. A narrative history of railroad building in northern Idaho.

———. "Big Lumber in the Inland Empire: The Early Years, 1900–1930." *Pacific Northwest Quarterly* 76 (1985): 95–103.

Ficken, Robert E. *The Forested Land: A History of Lumbering in Western Washington*. Seattle: University of Washington Press, 1987.

Haines, Francis D., Jr. "The Jacksonville Cannonball: The History of the Rogue River Valley Railway, 1890–

1925." *Pacific Northwest Quarterly* 50 (1959): 144–55.

Hidy, Ralph W., Frank Ernest Hill, and Allan Nevins. *Timber and Men: The Weyerhaeuser Story.* New York: Macmillan Co., 1963.

Hofsommer, Don L. *The Southern Pacific, 1901–1985.* College Station: Texas A&M University Press, 1986.

Kennan, George. *E. H. Harriman: A Biography.* 2 vols. Boston: Houghton Mifflin Co., 1922.

Kensel, W. Hudson. "Inland Empire Mining and the Growth of Spokane, 1883–1905." *Pacific Northwest Quarterly* 60 (1969): 84–97.

———. "The Early Spokane Lumber Industry, 1871–1910." *Idaho Yesterdays* 12 (Spring 1968): 25–31.

Klein, Maury. *Union Pacific: The Rebirth, 1894–1969.* New York: Doubleday, 1989.

MacKay, Donald. *The Asian Dream: The Pacific Rim and Canada's National Railway.* Vancouver, B.C.: Douglas & McIntyre, 1986.

Martin, Albro. "Hill or Harriman—What Difference Did It Make to Spokane." In *Spokane and the Inland Empire: An Interior Pacific Northwest Anthology.* Edited by David H. Stratton, 109–21. Pullman: Washington State University Press, 1991.

Mercer, Lloyd J. *E. H. Harriman: Master Railroader.* Boston: Twayne Publishers, 1985.

Merrell, Bonnie Cheney. "W. T. Cheney: Photographer of Lima and the Oregon Short Line." *Montana, the Magazine of Western History* 32 (Winter 1987): 36–43. Views of Lima, Montana.

Myers, Rex C. "The Gilmore and Pittsburgh: Lemhi Valley's Railroad." *Idaho Yesterdays* 15 (Summer 1971): 18–23.

Riegger, Hal. *The Camas Prairie: Idaho's Railroad on Stilts.* Edmonds, Wash.: Pacific Fast Mail, 1986.

Rydell, Robert. "Visions of Empire: International Expositions in Portland and Seattle, 1905–1909." *Pacific Historical Review* 52 (1983): 37–66.

Tattersall, James N. "The Economic Development of the Pacific Northwest to 1920." Ph.D. dissertation, University of Washington, 1960.

Wood, Charles, and Dorothy Wood. *The Great Northern Railway: A Pictorial Study.* Edmonds, Wash.: Pacific Fast Mail, 1979.

Wood, John V. *Railroads through the Coeur d'Alenes.* Caldwell, Idaho: Caxton Printers, 1983.

## Fiefdoms and Baronies: Harriman and Hill Redraw the Railroad Map

Asay, Jeff. *Union Pacific Northwest: The Oregon-Washington Railroad & Navigation Company.* Edmonds, Wash.: Pacific Fast Mail, 1991.

Butler, W. Daniel. "The Nez Perce Railroad War." In *Railroads in the West*, edited by Don L. Hofsommer, 21–27. Manhattan, Kans.: Sunflower University Press, 1978.

Cotroneo, Ross R. "Snake River Railroad." *Pacific Northwest Quarterly* 56 (1965): 106–13.

DeNeffe, Frederick M. "The Mysterious Shoe-String Railroad," *Oregon Historical Quarterly* 57 (1956): 205–28. Building the Eugene–to–Coos Bay line.

Derlieth, August. *The Milwaukee Road: Its First Hundred Years.* New York: Creative Age Press, 1948.

Gaertner, John T. *North Bank Road: The Spokane, Portland & Seattle Railway.* Pullman: Washington State University Press, 1990.

Grant, H. Roger. "Seeking the Pacific: The Chicago & North Western's Plans to Reach the West Coast." *Pacific Northwest Quarterly* 81 (1990): 67–73.

Hofsommer, Don L. "For Territorial Dominion in California and the Pacific Northwest: Edward H. Harriman and James J. Hill." *California History* 70 (Spring 1991): 30–45.

———. "Rivals for California: The Great Northern and Southern Pacific, 1905–1931." *Montana, the Magazine of Western History* 38 (Spring 1988): 58–67.

Jessett, Thomas E. "The Ilwaco Railroad." *Oregon Historical Quarterly* 58 (1957): 145–60.

Martin, Albro. *Enterprise Denied: Origins of the Decline of American Railroads, 1897–1917.* New York: Columbia University Press, 1971.

———. *James J. Hill and the Opening of the Northwest.* New York: Oxford University Press, 1976.

Mercer, Lloyd J. "Dissolution of the Union Pacific–Southern Pacific Merger." *Railroad History* No. 164 (Spring 1991): 53–63.

Morrell, James F., and Giles French. "Bubble Skinner." *Oregon Historical Quarterly* 69 (1968): 293–305. Deschutes Canyon "railroad war" of 1909.

Schwantes, Carlos A. "The Milwaukee Road's Pacific Extension: 1909–1929: The Photographs of Asahel Curtis." *Pacific Northwest Quarterly* 72 (1981): 30–40.

Twohy, John Roger. *Ten Spikes to the Rail: Twohy Brothers—Early-Day Northwestern Railroad Builders.* Jenner, Calif.: Goat Rock Publications, 1983.

Wood, Charles R. *Lines West: A Pictorial History of the Great Northern Railway Operations and Motive Power from 1887 to 1967.* Seattle: Superior Publishing Co., 1967.

Wood, Charles, and Dorothy Wood. *The Milwaukee Road West.* Burbank, Calif.: Superior Publishing Co., 1972.

———. *Spokane, Portland and Seattle Railway.* Burbank, Calif.: Superior Publishing Co., 1974.

## The Promise of Electric Motive Power

Engeman, Richard H. "Electric Streetcars in Seattle: The Lawton Gowey Photograph Collection." *Pacific Northwest Quarterly* 77 (1986): 59–67.

Hilton, George W., and John F. Due. *The Electric Interurban Railways in America.* Stanford, Calif.: Stanford University Press, 1960.

Holley, Noel T. *The Milwaukee Electrics.* Hicksville, N.Y.: N. J. International, 1987.

Johnsen, Kenneth G. *Apple Country Interurban: A History of the Yakima Valley Transportation Company and Yakima Valley Interurban Trolley Lines.* San Marino, Calif.: Golden West Books, 1979.

Labbe, John T. *Fares, Please! Those Portland Trolley Years.* Caldwell, Idaho: Caxton Printers, 1980.

Middleton, William D. *The Interurban Era.* Milwaukee: Kalmbach Publishing, 1961.

———. *The Time of the Trolley: The Street Railway from Horsecar to Light Rail.* San Marino, Calif.: Golden West Books, 1987.

———. *When the Steam Railroads Electrified.* Milwaukee: Kalmbach Publishing, 1974.

Mills, Randall V. "Early Electric Interurbans in Oregon." *Oregon Historical Quarterly* 44 (1943): 82–104, 386–410.

———. "Recent History of Oregon's Electric Interurbans." *Oregon Historical Quarterly* 46 (1945): 112–39.

Mutschler, Chas. V. "Rails to the Urban Frontier." *Journal of the West* 31 (January 1992), 36–42.

———, Clyde L. Parent, and Wilmer H. Siegert. *Spokane's Street Railways: An Illustrated History.* Spokane: Inland Empire Railway Historical Society, 1987.

Myers, Rex. "Trolleys of the Treasure State." *Montana, the Magazine of Western History* 22 (April 1972): 34–47.

*Puget Sound Electric Railway.* Interurbans Special No. 23. Los Angeles: [Ira L. Swett], 1960.

Steinheimer, Richard. *The Electric Way across the Mountains: Stories of the Milwaukee Road Electrification.* Tiburon, Calif.: Carbarn Press, 1980.

Turbeville, Daniel E. *The Electric Railway Era in Northwest Washington, 1890–1930.* Bellingham: Center for Pacific Northwest Studies, Western Washington University, 1978.

Wing, Warren. *To Seattle by Trolley: The Story of the Seattle-Everett Interurban and the "Trolley That Went to Sea."* Edmonds, Wash.: Pacific Fast Mail, 1988.

## Twentieth-Century Empire Builders

Abbott, Carl. "'To Arouse Interest in the Outdoors': The Literary Career of Enos Mills." *Montana, the Magazine of Western History* 39 (April 1981): 2–15.

Casner, Nicholas. "'Two-Gun Limbert': The Man from the Sawtooths." *Idaho Yesterdays* 32 (Spring 1988): 2–11.

Cotroneo, Ross R. "Selling Land on the Montana Plains, 1905–1915: Northern Pacific Railway's Land-Grant Sales Policies." *Montana, the Magazine of Western History* 37 (Spring 1987): 40–49.

Edwards, G. Thomas. "'The Early Morning of Yakima's Day of Greatness': The Yakima County Agricultural Boom of 1905–1911." *Pacific Northwest Quarterly* 73 (1982): 78–89.

———. "Irrigation in Eastern Washington, 1906–1911: The Promotional Photographs of Asahel Curtis." *Pacific Northwest Quarterly* 72 (1981): 112–20.

Greever, William S. "Railway Development in the Southwest." *New Mexico Historical Quarterly* 32 (1957): 151–203. This article provides a valuable comparative perspective on Pacific Northwest developments.

Lovin, Hugh. "'New West' Dreams and Schemes: John H. Garrett and His Enterprises in Idaho and Montana." *Idaho Yesterdays* 34 (Spring 1990): 2–17.

Runte, Alfred. "Promoting the Golden West: Advertising and the Railroad." *California History* 70 (Spring 1991): 62–75.

Scott, Roy V. *Railroad Development Programs in the Twentieth Century.* Ames: Iowa State University Press, 1985.

White, W. Thomas. "Main Street on the Irrigation Frontier: Sub-Urban Community Building in the Yakima Valley, 1900–1910." *Pacific Northwest Quarterly* 77 (1986): 94–103.

## Wonderlands: Railroad Tourism

Belasco, Warren James. *Americans on the Road: From Autocamp to Motel, 1910–1945.* Cambridge, Mass.: MIT Press, 1979. See especially the early chapters on railroad tourism.

*C*onstruction of the Idaho &
Washington Northern Railroad
between Ione and Metaline Falls
around 1910. The Milwaukee
Road acquired the line a short time
later. Eastern Washington State
Historical Society, L84-277.

Buchholtz, Curtis. "William R. Logan and Glacier National Park." *Montana, the Magazine of Western History* 19 (July 1969): 2–17.

Cox, Thomas R. *The Park Builders: A History of State Parks in the Pacific Northwest.* Seattle: University of Washington Press, 1988.

Fifer, J. Valerie. *American Progress: The Growth of the Transport, Tourist, and Information Industries of the Nineteenth-Century West.* Chester, Conn.: Globe Pequot Press, 1988.

Hanson, Inez Stafford. "When the Train Reached Seaside . . ." *Oregon Historical Quarterly* 58 (1957): 127–44. Travel to Oregon beaches in the nineteenth century.

Hazard, Joseph T. "Winter Sports in the Western Mountains." *Pacific Northwest Quarterly* 44 (1953): 7–14.

Hyde, Anne Farrar. *An American Vision: Far Western Landscape and National Culture, 1820–1920.* New York: New York University Press, 1990.

Jakle, John A. *The Tourist: Travel in Twentieth-Century North America.* Lincoln: University of Nebraska Press, 1985.

McMillan, Marilyn. "'An Eldorado of Ease and Elegance': Taking the Waters at White Sulphur Springs, 1866–1904." *Montana, the Magazine of Western History* 35 (Spring 1985): 36–49.

Martinson, Arthur D. *Wilderness above the Sound: The Story of Mount Rainier National Park.* Flagstaff, Ariz.: Northland Press, 1986.

Nolan, Edward W., ed. "Summer at the Lakes: An Album of Frank Palmer's Photographs." *Idaho Yesterdays* 34 (Summer 1990): 16–20.

Pomeroy, Earl. *In Search of the Golden West: The Tourist in Western America.* New York: Alfred A. Knopf, 1957.

Reeves, Thomas C. "President Arthur in Yellowstone National Park." *Montana, the Magazine of Western History* 19 (July 1969): 18–29.

Renk, Nancy F. "Off to the Lakes: Vacationing in North Idaho during the Railroad Era, 1885–1917." *Idaho Yesterdays* 34 (Summer 1990): 2–15.

Runte, Alfred. "Burlington Northern and the Legacy of Mount Saint Helens." *Pacific Northwest Quarterly* 74 (1983): 116–23.

————. *Trains of Discovery: Western Railroads and the National Parks.* Rev. ed. Niwot, Colo.: Roberts Rinehart, 1990.

Wright, Donald T. "Recollections of Cloud Cap Inn." *Oregon Historical Quarterly* 77 (1976): 61–66.

## The Golden Age of Passenger-Train Travel

Beebe, Lucius, and Charles Clegg. *The Trains We Rode.* 2 vols. Berkeley, Calif.: Howell-North Books, 1965–66.

Dubin, Arthur D. *More Classic Trains.* Milwaukee: Kalmbach Publishing, 1974.

————. *Some Classic Trains.* Milwaukee: Kalmbach Publishing, 1964.

Ferguson, Ted. *Sentimental Journey: An Oral History of Train Travel in Canada.* Toronto: Doubleday Canada, 1985.

Grant, H. Roger, and Charles W. Bohi. *The Country Railroad Station in America.* Boulder, Colo.: Pruett Publishing Co., 1978.

Grant, H. Roger, ed. *We Took the Train.* Dekalb: Northern Illinois University Press, 1990.

Hollister, C. Will. *Dinner in the Diner: Great Railroad Recipes of All Time.* Corona del Mar, Calif.: Trans-Anglo Books, 1965.

Hult, Ruby El. *Northwest Disaster: Avalanche and Fire.* Portland: Binfords & Mort, 1960. Contains an account of the Wellington avalanche.

Jonasson, Jonas A. "They Rode the Train: Railroad Passenger Traffic and Regional Reaction." *Pacific Northwest Quarterly* 52 (1961): 41–49.

Kennedy, Ludovic, comp. *A Book of Railway Journeys.* New York: Rawson, Wade, 1989.

Kratville, William W. *Steam, Steel and Limiteds: A Definitive History of the Golden Age of America's Steam Powered Passenger Trains.* Omaha, Neb.: Kratville Publications, 1983.

Liddel, Ken. *I'll Take the Train.* Saskatoon, Sask.: Western Producer Prairie Books, 1977.

McDonald, Paul R. *Forty-one Years in the D. C. and H.* Cedar Falls, Iowa: Paul R. McDonald, 1983. Recollections of Jules Hansink of work in the Dining Car and Hotel Department of the Union Pacific Railroad.

McKenzie, William A. *Dining Car Line to the Pacific: An Illustrated History of the NP Railway's 'Famously Good' Food, with 150 Authentic Recipes.* St. Paul: Minnesota Historical Society Press, 1990.

Meeks, Carroll L. V. *The Railroad Station: An Architectural History.* New Haven: Yale University Press, 1956.

Runte, Alfred. "Promoting Wonderland: Western Railroads and the Evolution of National Park Advertising." *Journal of the West* 31 (January 1992): 43–48.

Scribbins, Jim. *The Hiawatha Story.* Milwaukee: Kalmbach Publications, 1970.

Whitaker, Rogers E. M., and Anthony Hiss. *All Aboard with E.M. Frimbo, World's Greatest Railroad Buff.* New York: Grossman, 1974.

White, John H., Jr. *The American Railroad Passenger Car.* Baltimore: Johns Hopkins University Press, 1978.

## New Competition

Berger, Michael L. *The Devil Wagon in God's Country: The Automobile and Social Change in Rural America, 1893–1929.* Hamden, Conn.: Archon Books, 1979.

Bottles, Scott L. *Los Angeles and the Automobile: The Making of the Modern City.* Berkeley: University of California Press, 1987.

Cole, Terrence M. "Ocean to Ocean by Model T: Henry Ford and the 1909 Transcontinental Auto Contest." *Journal of Sport History* 18 (1991): 224–40.

Dembo, Jonathan. "Dave Beck and the Transportation Revolution in the Pacific Northwest, 1917–41." In *Experiences in a Promised Land: Essays in Pacific Northwest History,* edited by G. Thomas Edwards and Carlos A. Schwantes, 339–52. Seattle: University of Washington Press, 1986.

Flink, James J. *America Adopts the Automobile, 1895–1910.* Cambridge, Mass.: MIT Press, 1970.

———. *The Automobile Age.* Cambridge, Mass.: MIT Press, 1988.

———. *The Car Culture.* Cambridge, Mass.: MIT Press, 1975.

Foster, Mark S. *From Streetcar to Superhighway: American City Planning and Urban Transportation, 1900–1940.* Philadelphia: Temple University Press, 1981.

Harris, Patrick. "The Exhibition Era of Early Aviation in Oregon, 1910–1915." *Oregon Historical Quarterly* 87 (1986): 245–76.

Horn, C. Lester. "Oregon's Columbia River Highway." *Oregon Historical Quarterly* 66 (1965): 249–71.

Lewis, David L., ed. *The Automobile and American Culture.* Special issue of *Michigan Quarterly Review* 19 (Fall 1980) / 20 (Winter 1981).

Manchester, Albert D. *Trails Begin Where Rails End: Early-day Motoring Adventures in the West and Southwest.* Glendale, Calif.: Trans-Anglo Books, 1987.

Mansfield, Harold. *Vision: A Saga of the Sky.* New York: Duell, Sloan and Pearce, 1956. A popular history of Boeing.

Meier, Albert E., and John P. Hoschek. *Over the Road: A History of Intercity Bus Transportation in the United States.* Upper Montclair, N.J.: Motor Bus Society, 1975.

Patton, Phil. *Open Road: A Celebration of the American Highway.* New York: Simon & Schuster, 1986.

Rae, John B. *The American Automobile: A Brief History.* Chicago: University of Chicago Press, 1965.

Schlisgall, Oscar. *The Greyhound Story: From Hibbing to Everywhere.* Chicago: J. G. Ferguson Publishing Co., 1985.

Sears, Stephen W. *The Automobile in America.* New York: American Heritage, 1977.

Seely, Bruce E. *Building the American Highway System: Engineers as Policy Makers.* Philadelphia: Temple University Press, 1987.

Solberg, Carl. *Conquest of the Skies: A History of Commercial Aviation in America.* Boston: Little, Brown, 1979.

Tweney, George H. "Air Transportation and the American West." *Montana, the Magazine of Western History* 19 (Autumn 1969): 68–77.

Wik, Reynold M. *Henry Ford and Grass-Roots America.* Ann Arbor: University of Michigan Press, 1972.

Wright, Kathryn Stephen. "Hobo Heresy: Three Women on an Unconventional Tour of the American West in 1922." *Montana, the Magazine of Western History* 39 (Summer 1989): 16–29.

## An Industry in Trouble

Barrett, Gwynn, and Leonard Arrington. "The 1921 Depression: Its Impact on Idaho." *Idaho Yesterdays* 15 (Summer 1971): 10–15.

Butler, W. Daniel. "Passenger Service on the Camas Prairie Railroad." *Idaho Yesterdays* 27 (Spring 1983): 31–40.

Cotroneo, Ross R. "The Great Northern Pacific Plan of 1927." *Pacific Northwest Quarterly* 54 (1963): 104–12.

Jones, David C. "The Strategy of Railway Abandonment: The Great Northern in Washington and British Columbia, 1917–1935." *Western Historical Quarterly* 11 (1980): 141–58.

Keilty, Edmund. *Doodlebug Country: The Rail Motorcar on the Class I Railroads of the United States.* Glendale, Calif.: Interurban Press, 1982.

———. *Interurbans without Wires: The Rail Motorcar in the United States.* Glendale, Calif.: Interurban Press, 1979.

———. *The Short Line Doodlebug: Galloping Geese and Other Railcritters.* Glendale, Calif.: Interurban Press, 1988.

Shaw, Douglas V. "Ralph Budd, the Great Northern Railway, and the Advent of the Motor Bus." *Railroad History* 166 (Spring 1992): 57–79.

White, W. Thomas. "Railroad Labor Relations in the Great War and After, 1917–1921." *Journal of the West* 25 (April 1986): 36–43.

## Response: The Streamliner Era

Bartlett, Richard A. "Those Infernal Machines in Yellowstone Park." *Montana, the Magazine of Western History* 20 (July 1970): 16–29. A study of the first automobiles in Yellowstone National Park.

Beebe, Lucius. *Mixed Train Daily: A Book of Short-Line Railroads.* Berkeley, Calif.: Howell-North, 1961.

Meinkle, Jeffrey L. *Twentieth Century Limited: Industrial Design in America, 1925–1939.* Philadelphia: Temple University Press, 1979.

Neuberger, Richard L. *Our Promised Land.* New York: Macmillan Co., 1938. A lively account of the Pacific Northwest during the 1930s.

Oppenheimer, Doug, and Jim Poore. *Sun Valley: A Biography.* Boise: Beatty Books, 1976.

Podas, Ralph S. "A Point in Time on the Milwaukee Road: The Custer Creek *Olympian* Tragedy, June 19, 1938." *Railroad History* 166 (Spring 1992): 34–56.

Ranks, Harold E., and William W. Kratville. *The Union Pacific Streamliners.* [Omaha]: Kratville Publications, 1974.

Reed, Robert C. *The Streamliner Era.* San Marino, Calif.: Golden West Books, 1975.

Robertson, Archie: *Slow Train to Yesterday: A Last Glance at the Local.* Boston: Houghton Mifflin, 1945.

## Strange New World: War and a Troubled Peace

Dorin, Patrick C. *Coach Trains and Travel.* Seattle: Superior Publishing Co., 1975.

———. *The Domeliners: A Pictorial History of the Penthouse Trains.* Seattle: Superior Publishing Co., 1973.

Duke, Donald, and Edmund Keilty. *RDC: The Budd Rail Diesel Car.* San Marino, Calif.: Golden West Books, 1990.

Itzkoff, Donald M. *Off the Track: The Decline of the Intercity Passenger Train in the United States.* Westport, Conn.: Greenwood Press, 1985.

Maiken, Peter T. *Night Trains: The Pullman System in the Golden Years of American Rail Travel.* Chicago: Lakme Press, 1989.

Nash, Gerald D. *The American West Transformed: The Impact of the Second World War.* Bloomington: Indiana University Press, 1985.

———. *World War II and the West: Reshaping the Economy.* Lincoln: University of Nebraska Press, 1990.

Schwantes, Carlos A., ed. *The Pacific Northwest in World War II.* Manhattan, Kans.: Sunflower University Press, 1986. A compilation of seven essays on the Second World War in the Pacific Northwest and Alaska.

## A Changing Signature

Evans, William B., and Robert L. Peterson. "Decision at Colstrip: The Northern Pacific Railway's Open-Pit Mining Operation." *Pacific Northwest Quarterly* 61 (1970): 129–36.

Hall, Fred R., and Mabel Park Hall. "Crescent Lake, Steam to Diesel, 1934–45." *Oregon Historical Quarterly* 84 (1983): 365–88; and 85 (1984): 75–83.

Hofsommer, Don L. "Hill's Dream Realized: The Burlington Northern's Eight-Decade Gestation." *Pacific Northwest Quarterly* 79 (1988): 138–46.

McCarter, Steve. *Guide to the Milwaukee Road in Montana.* Helena: Montana Historical Society Press, 1992.

Nelligan, Tom. *VIA Rail Canada: The First Five Years.* Park Forest, Ill.: PTJ Publishing, 1982.

Pindell, Terry. *Making Tracks: An American Rail Odyssey.* New York: Grove Weidenfeld, 1990.

*Rails across Canada: 150 Years of Passenger Train History.* Montreal: VIA Rail Canada, 1986.

Repp, T. O. *Main Streets of the Northwest: Rails from the Rockies to the Pacific.* Vol. 1. Glendale, Calif.: Trans-Anglo Books, 1989. Emphasizes contemporary Oregon, Idaho, and Montana.

Scheer, George F., III. *Booked on the Morning Train: A Journey through America.* Chapel Hill, N.C.: Algonquin Books, 1991. Like the Pindell book above, this is a contemporary account of travel on Amtrak.

Scribbins, Jim. *The Milwaukee Road Remembered: A Fresh Look at an Unconventional Railroad.* Waukesha, Wisc.: Kalmbach Books, 1990.

*The Southern Pacific and Railroad Passenger Service.* Chicago: National Association of Railroad Passengers, 1967.

Zimmermann, Karl. *Amtrak at Milepost 10.* Park Forest, Ill.: PTJ Publishing, 1981.

## Epilogue

Offering a hostile view of the 1864 Northern Pacific grant is *Transitions: Journal of the Inland Empire Public Lands Council.* Especially see its issue called "Train Wrecks, Abandoned Communities and Clearcuts" 5 (February 1992): 1–56.

# Index

*The rugged terrain of the Pacific Northwest challenged the skills of civil engineers. The Milwaukee Road used a traveling crane to bridge chasms like Clear Creek in northern Idaho's Bitterroot Mountains as it extended its mainline west to Puget Sound. Milwaukee Road Collection, Milwaukee Public Library.*

59

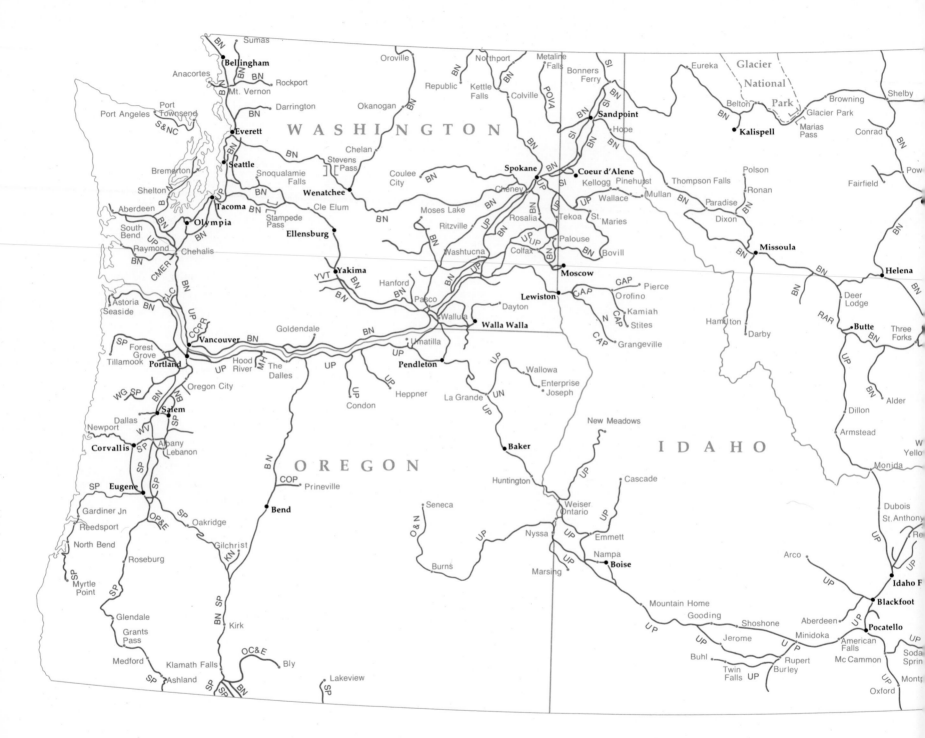

## Railroad Signatures

### Across the Pacific Northwest: ca. 1985

| | |
|---|---|
| Burlington Northern | BN |
| Camas Prairie | CAP |
| Central Montana | CM |
| Chelatchie Prairie | CCPR |
| Chicago and Northwestern | C&NW |
| City of Prineville | COP |
| Colorado and Wyoming | C&W |
| Columbia and Cowlitz | CLC |
| Curtis, Milburn and Eastern | CMER |
| Klamath Northern | KN |
| Mount Hood | MH |
| Oregon and Northwestern | O&N |
| Oregon, California and Eastern | OC&E |
| Oregon, Pacific and Eastern | OP&E |
| Pend Oreille Valley | POVA |
| Rarus | RAR |
| Seattle and North Coast | S&NC |
| Soo Line | SOO |
| Southern Pacific | SP |
| Spokane International | SI |
| St. Maries River | STMA |
| Union Pacific | UP |
| Willamette Valley | WV |
| Willamina and Grand Ronde | WG |
| Yakima Valley Transportation | YVT |

▲
N

0 ——————————— 100 miles